Documentation, libraries and archives: studies and research   6

Titles in the series *Unesco manuals for libraries:*

Titles in this series:

Standards for library service: an international survey

by F. N. Withers
Research associate:
the Polytechnic of North London School of Librarianship

The Unesco Press
Paris 1974

Published by the Unesco Press
7 Place de Fontenoy, 75700 Paris

Printed by Imprimerie des Presses Universitaires de France, Vendôme

ISBN 92–3–101177–4
French edition: 92–3–201177–8
Spanish edition: 92–3–301177–1

Preface

In recent years, it has become recognized that a country's documentation and library services, indispensable for all forms of economic, social and cultural development, should be considered as one co-ordinated information system and accordingly included in any national development plans. However, planning can only be carried out if the necessary statistical data and other information are available. Unesco therefore concluded a contract in 1968 with the International Federation of Library Associations (IFLA) for a survey of standards for library services currently recommended for libraries of all types in different countries. The work was entrusted to F. N. Withers, a research fellow at the Polytechnic of North London School of Librarianship (United Kingdom).

The survey was issued as a document in 1970 and was most favourably received.

It was therefore decided to revise and extend it to cover a wider selection of countries. A further contract was therefore concluded with IFLA in 1972 and Mr Withers agreed to undertake the revision.

As a former official of the Department of Education and Science in London, the author has had wide experience of servicing committees dealing with aspects of national planning of libraries, including library standards. Perhaps the most significant contribution he has made here is the work of summary and description, since it is the documents themselves and their backgrounds which are important.

After a general introduction to the subject of standards as applied to library service, there are chapters dealing with the position in national libraries, university and college libraries, special libraries, public libraries and school libraries.

The author also outlines standards for different kinds of libraries which could be applied generally, and more particularly to library services in developing countries.

This book should be of interest to all government and other officials dealing with information and library services, and institutions, organizations and individuals working in this field.

Contents

Foreword

Library standards are essential when planning library services and subsequently for evaluating them. This survey of recommended standards for library service in some twenty countries starts with national libraries, covers also libraries in universities and colleges, special libraries, public libraries, and concludes with school libraries. It illustrates how each is but one part of a wide spectrum of inter-dependent library provision, and brings out the common ground there is, not only in the standards for different countries for the same kind of library, but also in the standards for all types of library. This is because standards everywhere represent principles of good librarianship which cannot vary greatly from country to country.

Standards written in one country have often influenced the form and content of standards produced in others and standards prepared by the International Federation of Library Associations, influenced by existing national standards, have encouraged other countries to prepare similar statements. That library standards need constant revision because of rapid changes in conditions affecting them is apparent from the number of documents of recent date referred to in this survey and from the fact that so many earlier statements are under review.

In drawing up model sets of standards for the principal types of library for use in developing countries, it has been possible to produce a framework—much of which is common to all libraries—which gives guidance in general terms. But the framework does not include quantitative standards since these must vary according to local circumstances and must be worked out in individual countries or on a regional basis.

After a general introduction to the subject of standards as applied to library service, there are chapters dealing with the position in:

National libraries. This is brief as it concentrates on the aspects which up to now have received most attention—the role and functions of national libraries.

University and college libraries. It is not difficult to write about the desirable features of university and college libraries, but it is very difficult to write quantitative library standards for institutions concerned with large areas of advanced academic and research work. The chapter describes separately the standards documents concerned with establishments officially designated as universities or commonly recognized as of comparable status, and those referring to institutions which are not so regarded. The distinction is often only a reflection of the organization of higher education in the particular country, as not all the institutions in this second category work at lower academic levels than universities. The distinction is, however, convenient, as it brings out differences in levels of work which are reflected in levels of library provision.

Special libraries. These are treated next because they often form a bridge between other academic libraries and public libraries (in many countries increasingly performing a research function) in catering for the public in their official, professional or private capacities.

Public libraries. These are, judged quantitatively in terms of total expenditure, bookstocks, etc., the most important libraries, catering for the whole population, and in this area, where there is greater uniformity of needs and perhaps a greater opportunity to work on common lines, there is no shortage of standards documents. There are so many that a choice had to be made between being very selective or including most of those which had been discovered. The latter course was chosen, hoping that the most widely representative survey would enable readers to find examples from countries where conditions in many ways were comparable to their own.

School libraries. School libraries, though placed last, are certainly not the least important. These are exceptional institutions because of the need for the closest integration of the work of the library into the work of the school. There are signs of an increase in the number of standards documents in this field, due

no doubt to changes of the role and a greater importance of
school libraries in an ever-changing educational scene.
It is hoped that the general framework proposed in the final chapter
will be of some help to those who for library planning and evaluation
have to write statements of desirable standards for libraries in their
countries. Before they can attempt to write quantitative standards
they must have a clear idea of what purposes the library is intended to
serve and how it is both desirable and practicable to carry these out.

This survey has not been concerned with standards or standardization of library and documentation techniques, matters which
are important if the standards of library service achieved are to be
satisfactory and the library conducted efficiently and economically. This subject has been separately studied and reported on.[1]

Documents on standards are referred to here from some twenty
countries. The author is grateful to national libraries, government
departments and other agencies, State library inspectorates, to
library and other associations, as well as to publishers for permission to use and refer extensively to copyright documents.

Acknowledgements are gratefully given to the following bodies,
and to the individuals concerned, as well as to other organizations
submitting information which for a variety of reasons has not been
included in the survey.

Government organizations: The Lenin State Library in the U.S.S.R.;
the national libraries of Malaysia, Poland and Singapore, and
the Staatsbibliothek Preussicher Kulturbesitz, Berlin, as well
as ministries, government departments, directorates, inspectorates and methodological centres concerned with library work,
namely Australia (Department of Education, Canberra, and
State library boards); Belgium (Ministry of Education and
Culture, Public Libraries Department); Canada (Library Development Commission, British Columbia); Denmark (Ministry of
Culture, State Inspection of Public Libraries); France (Ministry
of National Education, Direction des Bibliothèques et de la
Lecture Publique); German Democratic Republic (Central
Institute for Librarianship and the Methodological Centre for
Academic and Research Libraries); Hungary (Centre for Library

1. Author's collective of the FID Hungarian National Committee, revised by
F. W. Torrington and F. L. Schick (IFLA), *International Standardisation of Library and
Documentation Techniques*, Paris, Unesco, March 1972 (ref. COM/WS/257, mimeo.,
limited distribution).

Science and Methodology); Netherlands (Ministry of Culture,
State Inspection of Public Libraries); Norway (Ministry of
Church and Education, State Library Inspectorate); Sweden
(National Board of Education, State Library Inspectorate);
United Kingdom (Department of Education and Science, Arts
and Libraries Branch).

Library and other associations: Australia (Library Association of
Australia and State library associations); Canada (Canadian
Library Association); Federal Republic of Germany (German
Library Association, Arbeitstelle für das Büchereiwesen); Japan
(Japan Library Association); Malaysia (Malaysian Library As-
sociation); Netherlands (Central Association of Public Libraries);
New Zealand (New Zealand Library Association); South
Africa (South African Library Association); United Kingdom
(Library Association, School Library Association); United States
(American Library Association, Special Libraries Association).

In respect of the United Kingdom acknowledgement is made
that Crown copyright material has been used and reproduced
with the permission of the Controller of Her Majesty's Stationery
Office. Similar acknowledgements are made to other governments and governmental organizations, to the various library
and other associations, and to the Ryerson Press, Toronto, which
allowed the use and reproduction of material published by them.
Thanks are also expressed to Otto Harrassowitz, Wiesbaden,
publishers of *Libraries in the Federal Republic of Germany,* and
Clive Bingley, London, publishers of *Australian Libraries, Canadian
Libraries, Libraries in France* and *South African Libraries,* and the
respective authors, and to Miss Madelaine de la Haye for permission to use material from an unpublished essay. Thanks are
also expressed to the publishers of *Library Trends,* Champaign,
Illinois, and the *Scandinavian Public Library Quarterly.*

In addition the author wishes to thank many who in their
official or private capacities have helped him in this work. In
certain cases, where language and other difficulties would have
proved insurmountable and left important countries unrepresented
in the survey, special documents were prepared in English, on
the basis of which sections of the book have been written. He
wishes to refer particularly to this help given in respect of the
U.S.S.R. by the Lenin State Library; the German Democratic
Republic by the Central Institute for Librarianship and the

Methodological Centre for Academic and Research Libraries of the Ministry of Culture; Hungary by the Centre for Library Science and Methodology of the National Szechenyi Library; and Japan by the Japan Library Association. For convenience the material about library standards in the Soviet Union has been included in the chapter on public libraries. The text refers principally to these libraries but makes reference to others.

Few references have been made to standards documents coming from Central or South America. There are many general documents concerned with national and regional planning of library services as part of over-all educational development, in which the subject of library standards is implicit, as well as the documents issued by the Organization of American States, based largely on standards produced in the United States for American libraries. But few items have been identified which could usefully be referred to in the survey as having been produced in the country or countries concerned with local conditions in mind.

Despite all the help received, which the author gratefully acknowledges, the responsibility for what has been written in the text must rest with him. In particular he must stress that the references to sets of standards or other standards material, especially to the summaries of already concise documents prepared with great care and precision, cannot do full justice to the documents themselves and must omit points regarded by their writers as significant. Anyone, therefore, wishing to make specific use of particular sets of standards or other publications in his work should refer to the original and complete text.

Finally the author wishes to thank Anthony Thompson, Andrea Polden and others for help with translation, and his wife, Margaret Withers, for her indispensable help in preparing the typescript for publication.

Introduction

At a time when everywhere in the world there is a desire to improve social institutions but a shortage of the means by which this can be done, there is need to know what requires to be provided collectively and how to provide it efficiently, as well as truly economically. This applies most particularly to educational and cultural institutions and equipment, since it is very largely on the efforts and achievements of individuals that the economic strength and resources which make social progress possible depend. Among the educational, cultural and social institutions which make an essential contribution to this end are libraries and information services of all kinds.

In an increasingly cost-conscious world, with more and more activities being provided, administered or in various ways supervised on a national (or greater than local) scale, the provision of library service is one of many management problems. Those responsible for deciding the issues raised—and they are not all likely to be librarians—should know the essential facts about the service, what roles it must play in society, and in a particular institution, and how best it can carry out its functions.

That the ideal in particular circumstances is unattainable at a given moment is not a reason for not stating it, but only for deciding what purposes are best served in the short run so as to make it possible for more to be done in the future. Having decided what roles are essential, those responsible must then consider what material and other resources are required, so that the functions are carried out efficiently.

The roles to be played and the means by which they are played are the essence of the 'standards for library service' described in this survey of documents and their background. Anything, whether it is labelled 'standards recommended for . . . libraries' or not, has been treated as relevant. Laws, decrees and regulations express in varying detail what it is intended should be done and what should be provided. Investigations and reports designed to make clear what needs to be done and how best to do it are *par excellence* standards documents. They bring out the essence of qualitative standards, which is how best to serve the ends in view, if only by pointing to present deficiencies and stating clearly how matters could be put right. Specific statements of desirable standards set out in conventional form, of which there are many examples discussed and described in this book, are a distillation of much hard fact and of very considerable thought and experience, drawing not only from current experience but on writings of a similar nature produced over many years.

The writer is not greatly concerned as to whether or the extent to which the documents use the term 'standards' or prefer the vaguer words 'guidelines', or 'goals', which, perhaps for strategic reasons, are found to be more acceptable. Nor is he concerned if the authors of documents were not particularly conscious that what they were writing was, in the sense employed here, 'library standards'.

What emerges from the mass of material surveyed is that the qualitative standards must come first, for without a clear understanding of what these are, no proper attempt can be made to express in quantitative terms what library materials, human resources, accommodation and equipment, and above all funds, are necessary.

It cannot be said, for example, how many library staff should be provided unless it is appreciated what the staff are there to do, not only in terms of the actual operations they perform but of the amounts of intelligence, skill and time they are able to apply to the work. Nor can it be said what minimum library materials are required without knowledge of what is available, what is likely to be useful, and how they are likely to be used.

The qualitative standards revealed in these documents show a great deal of uniformity. This is not unexpected since there is by now a large core of good library practice recognized and applied all over the world, to which past and present standards literature has contributed much. Where qualitative standards vary most, and why standards need to be frequently revised, is where, as they surely must, they reach out into the future and point the ways in which libraries are bound to go.

This is particularly relevant at the present time, with increasing rates of book and periodical production, when increasing attention is having to be given to the use of non-book materials in libraries, and with great changes in library technology. All of these will significantly change the pattern of library service in the future.

The difficulties in arriving at quantitative standards are great but they must be faced. This is because a principal use of standards is to indicate to those responsible for determining administrative arrangements into which libraries must fit, and for making available the necessary financial and other resources, what needs to be provided. If adequate guidance cannot be given, the standards are of restricted value and other, more arbitrary, means have to be defined for the purpose of allocating resources.

The problems involved in working out quantitative standards cannot in any event be ignored. They have to be faced every time a new library is built or an existing library extended or reorganized, and the present is probably the greatest period of library building ever known. Moreover, when new libraries are built or extended, and in existing libraries, it is necessary continually to evaluate the service in relation to its accepted roles and functions, to see what is being achieved and how this could be done better, and to justify continued demands for ever-increasing funds. For both planning and evaluation purposes standards are essential.

Every senior librarian has sources from which he draws his knowledge when he has to plan a library or library service, to run it, and to evaluate it. These sources are the standards material of the present and past, which he finds relevant to his situation, the current experiences of others—their new library buildings, their new methods—and above all his own experience and judgement.

But this is not enough, especially where formal guidance from an authoritative source, government or profession is lacking, or if existing, is not complete or not up to date. Moreover, this kind of information is not only necessary for librarians but for legislators, administrators, financial controllers, planners and others involved in considering the wider implications.

There is evidence in this survey of increasing numbers of standards documents being produced and of existing documents being updated. But there is clearly a lack of guidance in many countries on a national scale as to what is expected of the various kinds of library services. There is also evidence of a good deal of activity in the name of national planning of educational and cultural services, which may well result in specific allocations of resources to library and information services, without there having been the necessary investigations into their needs. This may be inevitable when allocations of resources have to be arbitrarily made. But this does not do away with the need on the part of those directly connected with the library services to define, in association with those responsible for educational, cultural and other services affected by library service, what requires to be provided, and to work out the available ways of achieving progress in coming years.

This need applies as much to many countries which are economically well developed, but where their library services are underdeveloped, as it does to what are commonly called developing countries. There is evidence of action directed towards library development in both groups of countries. In this survey the writer has, for example, been able to describe documents relating to desirable standards for library service recently produced in Malaysia and Singapore. He is aware also of the discussions on the subject of library standards at a recent annual conference of Spanish librarians[1] and of the production of draft standards for the various types of library in Iran, which are awaiting formal approval. Standards for different types of libraries are also being prepared in Yugoslavia and Romania. The next national conference of the Mexican Library Association will be on standards for library services in Mexico. It is hoped that the evidence presented in this survey will encourage those who have not so far attempted to formalize their library desiderata to attempt to set them down, in whatever form suits their circumstances best, as a contribution to the national planning of wider education and social facilities.

Although the chapters in this book follow the conventional

---

1. Congreso Nacional de Bibliotecas, Congreso Nacional de Archivos, Pamplona, *Ponencias, Comunicaciones y Cronica*, Madrid, Associación Nacional de Bibliotecarios, Archiveros y Arquelogos (ANABA), 1970.

   A valuable bibliography on the whole subject of standards for libraries is: Signe Otterson, 'A Bibliography on Standards for Evaluating Libraries', *College and Research Libraries*, March 1971. This contains 138 references.

pattern of treating the different types of libraries as separate institutions, this is not necessarily the way to proceed in all circumstances. The essential point is that the needs of the various sections of society for library services should be efficiently and economically satisfied. A library organization can serve, and often does serve, several roles. School libraries, particularly in rural areas, have often provided a public library service for children and also for adults. Combined school and public libraries are not uncommon and may be increasingly necessary, especially in the developing countries. A separate national library is perhaps unlikely to be established in every country, if existing arrangements, such as using the principal university library, are working satisfactorily. University and large city libraries have sometimes combined. A national library can also provide the public library and school library service. Such joint arrangements may be essential to ensure the best use of scarce bibliographical and other resources.

The work of writing standards now increasingly involves the librarians and also the audio-visual and other specialists. In the case of educational libraries—with the changing methods of instruction and learning—it increasingly involves the people most directly concerned with the teaching processes, the school, college and university teachers, as well as those responsible for financial and other aspects of administration in the institutions of which the libraries usually form a part. These are the local government organizations, local education authorities, the universities and the individual colleges and schools. Future standards writing is likely, more than in the past, to be a co-operative activity involving several, if not all, of these interests. This might make it more difficult to reach agreement about desirable levels of service but, once agreed, the outcome would probably command greater respect and have more general acceptance than have earlier recommendations.

Many of the qualitative standards, and even more of the quantitative standards, are affected by local conditions. While these conditions cannot be adequately described here, it has been considered useful to say something about them, in particular, about the organizational background into which the various libraries must fit. In many countries, including the United States, the Federal Republic of Germany, the U.S.S.R., and other socialist countries in Eastern Europe, it is relevant that standards for public libraries—and in some of the countries for other libraries—have been worked out in terms of 'systems' or 'networks' of libraries. This is usually because it is impossible to create large enough administrative areas locally, which would particularly suit public library organization. Even where suitable units are achieved, 'systems' in the less formal sense of co-operation between libraries are still necessary. Attempts have been made in this document, in as many cases as possible, to describe not only the standards but a little of the background to them. The recommended standards for university and college libraries are similarly affected by the size and the organization of the institutions of which they are part.

The standards, and the ways in which they are expressed and applied, also reflect the political and economic organization of countries, as the items concerning standards for library service in the U.S.S.R. and other socialist countries in Eastern Europe show. This applies particularly to the special libraries.

With the great expansion of library services, with all its implications, an increasing and deeper interest is being shown in many parts of the world in the subject of standards. Although the American Library Association, through its constituent bodies, has produced and revised library standards for different types of libraries over many years, it has only recently, in 1969, set up an over-all committee on standards. The committee has been given the task of 'assisting the ALA to improve and make consistent its procedures for developing and promulgating meaningful professional standards'. The statement of the committee's responsibilities declares that 'the development of standards should act as a powerful force for upgrading library services, resources and facilities'. As a further example, the work of the statutory Library Advisory Councils for England and Wales, established in 1965, has led to government-financed research projects on the location of library buildings, local library co-operation, the staffing of public libraries and the use of periodicals in public libraries. These studies will, *inter alia*, provide a sound basis for the revision of earlier standards documents. Research of this kind, which is being undertaken in the United States and elsewhere, will be a welcome addition to the battery of statistics and the indispensable 'wisdom of the seers' which has hitherto been the principal basis for establishing library standards.

National libraries

The literature on the subject of standards for national libraries, 'that comparatively modern product',[1] is mainly international in origin. It draws its data from the statutes and practices of existing national libraries and discusses the principles on which the work of national libraries should be based.

The discussion in international library circles, which goes back at least as far as the Symposium on National Libraries in Europe organized by Unesco in Vienna in 1958,[2] has tended to concentrate on the distinctive role and functions of national libraries. This may give the misleading impression that there has been little discussion of the other subjects which normally arise in a systematic consideration of library standards. This is true if one is thinking in terms of quantitative standards. In view of the great variety of institutions which the term 'national library' embraces and the different conditions prevailing in the individual countries affecting the working of these libraries, it is unlikely that the setting of quantitative standards, save in respect of certain aspects of national library buildings, will be attempted.[3] But consideration of the role and functions of national libraries necessarily involves consideration of questions such as the services which the libraries should provide; the materials which they should acquire and conserve,

---

1. Arundell Esdaile, *National Libraries of the World. Their History, Administration and Public Services*, London, 1934, 2nd ed. revised by F. J. Hill, London, Library Association, 1957.
2. *National Libraries: Their Problems and Prospects*, Symposium on National Libraries in Europe, Vienna, September 1958. Paris, Unesco, 1960 (Unesco Manuals for Libraries, No. 11).
3. A colloquy, organized by IFLA, on the building of national libraries, was held in Rome in September 1973.

how they should acquire them and what uses they should put them to; and the relation of national libraries to other libraries in the country, as well as elsewhere in the world. These subjects have certainly been included in the discussion of role and functions.

The conclusions and recommendations of the Vienna Symposium, which marked a turning point in the history of national libraries, show how widely a discussion on role and functions can range in this field, raising the whole question of national planning of library services. The conclusions and recommendations of this meeting are summarized below:

The national library should play a central role in co-ordinating the national library services and should itself provide the centre where full information is available on the national collections. Despite its responsibility regarding the acquisition of the total national production of printed material, it must be authorized to eliminate certain materials of an ephemeral nature. Parts of the national production stored elsewhere should be recorded in the national library. Micro-reproduction, particularly of newspapers, should not justify the destruction of the originals. The national library should also collect printed material concerning the country, wherever published, and be responsible for co-operation and co-ordination of efforts to secure all the foreign literature the country required. Legal deposit regulations should take account of non-commercial publications.

The national library had the responsibility of ensuring that a central inventory of manuscript collections was established and maintained. It should use guides, exhibitions, radio and television programmes, as well as catalogues, to make known its resources and functions.

The national library should co-ordinate the bibliographical activities of the country, establish sound bibliographical standards, propose methods for the proper training of bibliographers, and see that bibliographical work is performed by the most suitable agency and in a satisfactory manner.

It was the responsibility of national libraries to see to the production of current national bibliographies and, where required, of retrospective national bibliographies. It was also desirable that they should concern themselves with the production of special bibliographies.

The national library should have full and accurate knowledge of all sources of bibliographical information.

National libraries should play a constructive part in international bibliographical activities, and by means of bilateral agreements further the collection of bibliographical information on material relating to their respective countries.

In view of the archival functions of the national library with regard to its national literature, it should lend only duplicates of such literature.

Loans, whether domestic or international, should in general be made only to libraries.

There should be a national plan for acquisition of foreign materials, wherever one did not exist already. A general European plan should not be considered until national plans were more fully developed.

Since the Vienna meeting there have been further discussions at IFLA on the functions of national libraries in which Kenneth Humphreys played a prominent part. In a paper at the IFLA council meeting in Helsinki in 1965, he divided national library activities into three categories, fundamental, desirable and inessential.[1]

Classified as fundamental were the possession of the outstanding collection of the nation's literature and the fullest possible coverage of foreign literature; the possession of the most important collection of books received under legal deposit or under the terms of the copyright law; the publication of a national bibliography and to be the national bibliographical centre; and the publication of catalogues of material in the national library and in the country's libraries.

Duties which should, if possible, be assumed by a national agency were to act as a centre of inter-library lending and to initiate research into library techniques. Functions which could, if necessary, be undertaken by other agencies than national libraries were to be the centre for the country's international exchange service, for the distribution of duplicate material, for professional training in librarianship, for bibliographical and other assistance to libraries of all kinds, and the planning centre for the whole of the country's lending service.

1. K. W. Humphreys, 'The Role of the National Library: A Preliminary Statement', *Libri*, Vol. XIV, 1964, p. 356; also 'National Library Functions', *Unesco Bulletin for Libraries*, Vol. 20, No. 4, July–August 1966.

In the developing countries, national libraries and other important and often long-established libraries have played an important role in their country's library services and are likely to have greater responsibilities in the future. In different parts of the world regional meetings, organized by Unesco, have discussed the work and problems of national libraries or discussed the organization of library services as a whole.

A conference on the development of national libraries in Asia and the Pacific Area in Manila, in 1964,[1] came to the following conclusions:

The functions of a national library were largely defined by the social, cultural, economic and geographic conditions of the country in which it was located. The following functions, however, were appropriate: (a) to serve as a permanent depository for all publications issued in the country; (b) to acquire and store other types of material; (c) to provide bibliographical services; (d) to serve as a co-ordinating centre for co-operative activities; and (e) to provide services to the government.

Depending on circumstances, a national library might provide leadership among a nation's libraries, sometimes acting as the central organ of a national library service.

A national library should serve as a permanent depository for all publications issued in a country, and should enjoy the benefits of legal or copyright deposit free of all charges and inclusive of all materials both printed and audio-visual.

It should further acquire, preserve, and make available all library material concerning the home country wherever and whenever produced, and should have a comprehensive collection representative of all civilizations and providing a comprehensive subject coverage for purposes of research, study and inquiry.

It was preferable that national archives should be administered independently of, but in close co-operation with, the national library.

A national library had the responsibility of providing or co-ordinating the bibliographical services of a country. Its typical activities in this field concerned: (a) a current national bibliography, including all published materials, both printed and

1. 'Regional Seminar on the Development of National Libraries in Asia and the Pacific Area, Manila, Philippines, February, 1964', *Unesco Bulletin for Libraries*, Vol. 18, No. 4, July–August 1964.

audio-visual, and including a roman transliteration; (b) a retro-spective bibliography; (c) subject and selective bibliographies; (d) union catalogues facilitating inter-library co-operation; (e) making a contribution to national and international bib-liographical projects; and (f) periodicals indexing.

The national library must assume responsibility for initiating and promoting co-operation between itself and other libraries, nationally, regionally and internationally. A primary task was the planned acquisition of foreign literature based on a policy of national co-ordination on the lines of the Farmington Plan, the Scandia Plan and the programme of the Deutsche Forschungs-gemeinschaft.

Union catalogues were essential for identification of the national literature when it was dispersed in a variety of scattered libraries and private collections and to facilitate inter-library loans. The national library should serve as a clearing-house for the exchange of books and periodicals, including duplicates, and be respon-sible for co-ordinating national bibliographic activities. National libraries should promote knowledge about library resources through publications, assist library associations, provide photo-graphic and other technical services and establish and administer storage libraries.

A legislative reference service established as part of a national library could provide factual data, formulate arguments for or against a given proposition or arguments in support of pre-determined action and assistance in speech-writing both within and outside the legislature.

The meeting of experts on the national planning of library services in Latin America, organized by Unesco in Quito in 1966,[1] envis-aged, in the context of a library development plan for Ecuador, the following functions for the national library:

To rationalize the acquisition of printed matter, including period-icals, by the libraries covered by the plan.

To centralize the cataloguing and classification of printed matter and ensure the distribution of index cards or printed catalogues for certain types of libraries.

When its own organization and the development of the national

---

1. 'Meeting of Experts on the National Planning of Library Services in Latin America, Quito, 1966', *Unesco Bulletin for Libraries*, Vol. 20, No. 6, November–December 1966.

library plan rendered it advisable, to collaborate in extending and improving the services of school and public libraries.

To collect and ensure the conservation of the publications produced in the country, whether obtained in the form of legal deposit accessions or from other sources. To see that the legal deposit laws were complied with.

To provide national and foreign readers and research workers with an adequate and efficient information service by assembling the requisite general and reference works, preparing a union catalogue covering the stocks of all libraries in the country and compiling the national bibliography and other bibliographies necessary for the fulfilment of its task.

To organize the national and international exchange of publications.

To centralize inter-library loans in respect of foreign libraries.

A similar meeting on the national planning of library services in Asia, in Colombo in 1967, considered the term 'national library' did not 'imply a monumental storehouse of national treasures but an active organisation with dynamic leadership geared to a triple purpose: preserving the national culture; developing by all possible means systems and procedures which would make available the total library resources of the nation for the benefit of the whole national community; and establishing relations with libraries in other countries'.[1]

The meeting of this series in Kampala, in 1970, identified the functions of national libraries as: (a) to serve as the primary instrument for the achievement of co-ordinated library development; (b) to serve as a permanent depository for all publications issued in the country and to collect printed material concerning the country, wherever published; (c) to publish the national bibliography; and (d) to organize the national and international exchange of publications and information. The meeting recognized that in one country the functions of a national library might be shared between two other libraries.[2]

There are undoubtedly extensive writings on the functions and organization of individual national libraries in many countries,

1. *Unesco Meeting of Experts on the National Planning of Library Services in Asia, Colombo, Ceylon, 1967. Final Report*, Paris, Unesco, 1968 (mimeo).
2. Unesco, *Expert Meeting on National Planning of Documentation and Library Services in Africa. Kampala, Uganda, 1970. Final Report*, Paris, Unesco, 1971 (mimeo).

much of it of recent date, but the writer has been unable to inquire into these closely. He is naturally not unconscious of the developments in this field in his own country. These have arisen out of the consideration of the needs of university libraries by a committee of the University Grants Committee[1] (whose work is discussed in the chapter on university and college libraries, pages 67–71) which made important proposals about the future organization of national libraries in the United Kingdom, and from the need to provide new library accommodation for the library departments of the British Museum. Before proceeding with the new building the government called for a review by a further committee of the functions and organization of the British Museum Library, the National Central Library, the National Lending Library for Science and Technology and the Science Museum Library in providing national library facilities. This committee reported in 1969.[2] The outcome is the setting up of a new largely unified national library organization for the United Kingdom on principles described in a Government White Paper[3] and put into effect by legislation, the British Library Act, 1972.[4] The documents referred to above are all standards material of the first order. They merit the attention of those interested in the organization of national libraries, whether the libraries are regarded as the apex of a centralized national library service or merely the hub of a less formal, and possibly more flexible, system.

These extensive world-wide discussions, referred to in this chapter, about the role and functions of national libraries have established a number of principles and standards which can be clearly stated. An attempt has been made to set them down in the model sets of standards included in the final chapter.

1. University Grants Committee, *Report of Committee on Libraries*, London, HMSO, 1967.
2. United Kingdom, Department of Education and Science, *Report of the National Libraries Committee*, London, HMSO, 1969 (Cmnd. 4028).
3. *The British Library*, London, HMSO, January 1971 (Cmnd. 4572).
4. *British Library Act, 1972, Statutes*, Eliz. II, 1972, Chapter 54.

Libraries in universities and colleges

General

Desirable minimum standards for libraries in universities and other institutions of higher education form a more complex subject than in some other groups of library where the degree of homogeneity is more marked. In higher education the differences between institutions—and between their libraries—are very wide, both as to the range and the level of work which they undertake.

Only in a very general way can these libraries be treated as a single group. Rather they form a number of groups united by the common factor that they are all educating and training people beyond the school-leaving age appropriate to their circumstances and talents. The libraries are divided in many ways, but notably by the level of their work. From the viewpoint of standards of library provision the most divisive factor is the extent to which the establishments and their libraries undertake a serious research function.

The institutions of higher education and their libraries can be divided into several groups, not always of function but sometimes dictated by the organization of higher education in the particular country. It is convenient to follow the definitions proposed by Unesco for the international standardization of statistics, considering separately the desirable standards of service in universities, properly so called, and in libraries in institutions not forming part of universities.

It would be wrong to assume that all institutions and their libraries falling into the second category work at a lower academic level than those in the first. In practice most of them do so, because

29

of the far greater number and variety of institutions involved. But in some instances the distinction between university and non-university institutions may be little more than one of name and legal status, or source of financial support. Some examples which illustrate this point are the universities and the *grandes écoles* in France, the universities and certain *Hochschulen* in the Federal Republic of Germany, and the universities and polytechnics in England and Wales.

In the first category, the universities proper, there is great variation in the nature and extent of the libraries' collections, staff, buildings and equipment, as well as of the other facilities they offer. The institutions themselves range from universities or colleges of university status with very high, sometimes almost exclusive, loads of post-graduate (particularly doctoral and often post-doctoral) work and other research work, to those mainly concerned with preparing students for first degrees.

In the second category the range is also wide. Included are institutions so classified because they are not universities though their work is recognized as being of university level, and similar institutions of national status. The list contains the various levels of colleges of technology, colleges of commerce, colleges of art and of music, as well as colleges exclusively dealing with the education and training of teachers, liberal-arts colleges and, for more mature students, colleges concerned with the liberal education of adults are represented.

Both these main groups of higher education institutions have experienced quite phenomenal expansion in the last two decades. This expansion has been in the total number of institutions, in the numbers in the different categories of library and in the range and level of work in all the categories. Above all there has usually been a considerable increase in the numbers of persons each institution has to serve. Methods of instruction and learning have undergone great changes. This has been reflected in, and has been partly a reflection of, changes in the library and information services in the institutions. Technological changes in the libraries themselves have increased their potential usefulness to staff and students.

Much has been written of recent years about the organization of these institutions and their libraries. All over the world this sector has been one of the most rapidly expanding and nationally significant parts of a country's educational system. Governments now accept that the development of higher education institutions, with the parallel development of their libraries and other instructional media services as a high priority, must be an important part of their economic policies, designed to maintain and to improve the living standards of their people.

It was stated in the working papers for Unesco's Colombo Conference on the national planning of library services in Asia that 'bibliographic information is a source of national wealth'. Few governments and persons directly responsible for the provision of library facilities in these institutions will fail to appreciate this fact. The wide acceptance of this view has undoubtedly given an impetus to the discussion of standards of library provision in universities and other institutions of higher education in many countries, as it has in relation to other libraries.

The lack of homogeneity in this group and the many practical and methodological (as well as political) difficulties involved in the search for statements about desirable minimum standards of library service—particularly for standards which can be expressed quantitatively—have probably discouraged the setting out of formal statements of this kind in some countries.

The difficulties are well illustrated in the articles included in the October 1972 issue of *Library Trends*, devoted to standards for libraries, which describe the efforts made over many years to produce such standards in the United States and Canada and records recent experience in the United Kingdom and elsewhere.[1]

Documents have been published in many countries dealing in varying degrees with desirable standards of service, but the number widely known and easily accessible to any interested person are limited unless he has unusual linguistic capabilities or considerable resources for translation. The present writer refers here only to a

1. *Library Trends*, Vol. 21, No. 2, October 1972. The articles referred to are: Felix E. Hirsch (Issue Editor), 'Introduction: Why do we need Standards?'; David R. Watkins, 'Standards for University Libraries'; Helen M. Brown, 'College Library Standards'; James O. Wallace, 'Two Year College Library Standards'; Florence B. Murray, 'Canadian Library Standards'; K. W. Humphreys, 'Standards for Libraries in Great Britain'; Otto Löhmann, 'Efforts for International Standardisation in Libraries'.

Attention is drawn to many recent references to documents dealing with the planning of university and research libraries in the bibliography included in: Deutsche Bibliothekskonferenz, *Bibliotheksplan '73. Entwurf eines umfassenden Bibliotheksnetzes für die Bundesrepublik Deutschland*, Berlin, Deutscher Büchereiverband, Arbeitsstelle für das Büchereiwesen, 1973.

limited number of publications and other items of information on the subject which he has been able—or enabled—to understand. These are discussed, and described, in the sections which follow.

This is an area where a great deal of further work needs to be done, if only in reporting on studies recently made in respect of the planning and organization of university and research libraries and their relations with other libraries. In many of these studies the question of standards is raised. Information about such studies would be useful to persons in other countries faced with similar problems in this difficult field.

University libraries proper

GENERAL

Only three examples have been found, set out in the way familiar in standards for public and school libraries, with direct statements about objectives and functions and administrative, material, human and other requirements for a satisfactory library service in a university. These come from the United States and Canada, and from Mexico.

The second, and by far the larger, source of documents has been found in the more widely based reports on the planning and organization of libraries in universities and on their relation with other comparable libraries, including national libraries. These have been prepared officially for or by governments, or by professional and educational organizations.

A further source of information, which it has not been possible to study to any great extent, lies in the central directives on university and research library planning and administration in the U.S.S.R. and the other socialist countries in Eastern Europe. There, certain administrative arrangements and both qualitative and quantitative standards are commonly laid down by the central authority and followed with a high degree of uniformity. This is illustrated in the example from the German Democratic Republic.

A fourth category, which can in certain respects be compared with the third, consists of information about basic principles of university library organization and planning and, above all, of quantitative standards used by the central government in connexion with the building of new or additional library accommodation in countries where the government, because it bears the whole cost, exercises control over what is provided. Such information may not be made public in much detail, since the space requirements of each building have to be judged case by case. The writer is able to give some information about the current practice in France which, in view of that country's extensive university library building achievements in recent years, may be of interest in other countries.

The experiences in the United States of the Association of Research Libraries and Association of College and Research Libraries Joint Committee (ARL-ACRL) on University Library Standards, since 1968, in their attempts to establish an acceptable statement of general standards for university libraries, and of the American Library Association and other bodies in revising the 1959 standards for college libraries, illustrate the difficulties of trying to quantify minimum or any other levels of requirements. Similar discussions in the various reports of committees and planning groups (e.g. in the Federal Republic of Germany) appear to confirm the complexity of the problems involved.

Making due allowances for differences in functions, size and levels of work, very similar statements of standards have been written about university libraries and libraries in other institutions of higher education, when the desirable roles, structures, organization, services, materials, staffing and buildings are discussed in general terms. But the quantitative standards, particularly for book stocks and other materials and staffing, vary greatly, as would be expected. The statements of standards which have been considered in this survey are, however, in such different forms that they do not lend themselves to many useful quantitative comparisons.

It is of the utmost difficulty and complexity to state standards for book stocks and other materials (which to a large extent govern staffing and buildings), more particularly in institutions with a high proportion of advanced work. However, some figures quoted in the standards documents which have been discussed are of value, notably the figures for basic book stocks of 300,000 volumes, referred to in the Federal Republic of Germany's Wissenschaftsrat report, which satisfied 75 per cent of readers' needs, and the figure of 600,000 volumes, at which point the university was said to be able to stand on its own feet. Presumably it would then be in the region of the '90 per cent library' discussed in certain quarters.[1] Useful also are the Canadian figures of a minimum of 100,000 volumes and of 1,000 titles for the size of the periodical collections, and the model annual budgets put forward by the Standing Conference of National and University Libraries (SCONUL) to the British Parry Committee and those for a general university included in the Federal Republic of Germany document.

Also of interest and value is the concept referred to in the American, British, Canadian and Mexican publications, that a university library budget should be not less than a certain proportion of the total budget of the parent institution, recommended figures varying from 5 to 10 per cent. It should, however, be stressed that these figures refer to established universities and that in new universities the proportion would need to be very much larger for an appreciable number of years.

Kenneth Humphreys, in a paper on standards in university libraries, given at the IFLA General Council Meeting at Copenhagen in 1969, was pessimistic about the prospect of producing generally acceptable standards for libraries in universities.[2] Almost all the standards he had quoted, he said, had little or no validity outside the environment for which they had been invented. Probably outside the United States no country could contemplate building up every university library to a stock of 2 million volumes, or afford the expenditure on libraries recommended in a document issued by the ARL-ACRL joint committee. The 'standards' suggested in many countries for various aspects of their library's collections and budgeting requirements most likely represented the highest that were capable of being achieved in a reasonable period of time. Humphreys concluded that, while it might be possible to establish certain standards on the basis of time and motion studies, or acceptable building norms, it would not be possible to establish standards in other fields except on the basis of operational research and surveys of library services. This conclusion may not be acceptable to everyone, the older traditional methods of basing standards on good current practice still having their use and their supporters.

1. In the (United Kingdom) University Grants Committee, *Report of the Committee on Libraries (1967)*, p. 280–1, Annex to Appendix 9.
2. K. W. Humphreys, 'Standards in University Libraries', *Libri*, Vol. 20, 1970, p. 144–55.

The problems of finding standards for university libraries remains and is rooted both in an acceptable definition of institutional objectives and the resources available. Increasingly research is being undertaken into needs and the best methods of satisfying them and the outcome of this research will undoubtedly have a bearing on future standards.

A strong case can be made out for having statements of desirable or minimum university library standards, which are acceptable both to administrators who have to find the resources and to libraries who ask for them, despite the difficulties in establishing the criteria. The standards are necessary as a guide to the building of new, or additional, library provision. They are also required as a guide to the level of financial, material and human support necessary to ensure that the library—traditionally regarded as the heart of a university—will be able to fulfil its responsibilities to staff and students, both graduate and post-graduate, to other research workers and, in certain cases, to members of the general public.

CANADA

In contrast to the United States, where standards for college libraries and junior colleges have been in existence for many years, with standards for larger universities yet to be published, Canada began with standards for the large universities and only recently have steps been taken to produce standards for small universities and colleges. Two committees were set up by the Canadian Association of College and University Libraries, one to prepare standards for community colleges and technical institutes and the other for degree-granting colleges and smaller universities. When this text was being written, only one of these committees had finished its work, and the standards it recommended for Canadian community colleges were approved by the Canadian Library Association. These are referred to later in this chapter.

In 1961, the Canadian Library Association set up a committee to work on university library standards and college library standards and the functions of this committee were transferred in 1963 to a newly formed Canadian Association of College and University Libraries. Survey teams working for the committee visited universities and colleges and a report was issued in 1964.[1]

The committee decided to limit its investigations to those institutions defined as universities by the Canadian Universities Foundation, i.e. 'an institution of post-secondary education, training and research, which awards first and advanced degrees in two or more faculties', with the added requirement that they should have enrolments of over 1,000. In cases where standards might vary according to size of institution, the following subdivisions were used: Group I (enrolment of over 5,000); Group II (enrolment of between 1,500 and 5,000); and Group III (enrolment of less than 1,500, but not less than 1,000).

In all its general statements on objectives, the role and particular duties of the librarian and his relationship with the library committee, the general principles of library administration, communications, public services, etc., the report bears a close resemblance to the United States standards, but is written in much greater detail. It discussed the organization of different forms of departmental libraries and laid down a number of standards in general terms for these. It stressed the importance of the collection of library statistics in the evaluation of the work of the library and dealt with this subject in considerable detail. Some advice was given on the planning of new library buildings.

Other standards, where quantitative measurements predominate, which the committee recommended included the following:

Library staff

The committee considered the key to the situation to be the number of professional library staff. The supporting non-professional staff should be added in proportions varying according to the library department.

Professional librarians related to enrolment

A minimum ratio of 1 professional to 300 students was recommended. (Actual position report (1963/64): Group I, 325; Group II, 225; Group III, 315.)

1. Canadian Association of College and University Libraries, *Guide to Canadian University Library Standards*, Ottawa, 1964 (report of the University Library Standards Committee).

Professional librarians related to non-professional staff

Professional librarians should be at least 31 per cent of the whole staff. (Actual position report (1963/64): Group I, 29; Group II, 29; Group III, 35.)

Recommendations were made as to the proportions in different departments: administration 1 : 1; reference 2 : 1; departments giving both reference and circulation service 1 : 2; circulation, may be administered without professional staff; cataloguing 1 : 2; book orders 1 : 3.

Minimum professional staff

The smallest libraries in Group III (1,000–1,500 enrolments) should have not fewer than 5 professional staff as follows: chief librarian, 1; public services—reference and circulation, 2; technical services—processing departments, 2.

Span of management

A chief librarian could not effectively supervise more than 3–6 immediate subordinates. Therefore, in a large library system, he might delegate to assistant librarians with staff functions.

Within the library departments there should be at least 1 supervisor—who could be non-professional—to each 10 persons. Each service point with a group of staff should have a supervisor. When the departments became very large (i.e. 25–30 persons and over) it might be efficient to create 2 departments.

Financial standards of support

The report listed the significant factors to be taken into account in assessing the financial support needed, namely size and quality of book stocks, size of total student enrolment, extent and growth of graduate studies, rate of growth of the institution, amount of faculty research, extension projects and introduction of new courses. Of these the factor which most affected the budget from year to year was the student enrolment.

Two bases for stating and comparing financial support were

given: student *per capita* and library budget expressed as a percentage of university expenditure. The standard of financial support proposed by the committee was based on the expenditure of the third quarter of each university group for the preceding financial year.

The 'top averages'[1] for Group I based on 1963/64 figures were: full-time student *per capita* cost, $154.32; percentage of institutional expenditure, 5.63.

In the 1967 edition of the report additional tables were added, based on official statistics up to 1965/66 giving, *inter alia*, 'top averages' and averages for all institutions. Those in respect of the *per capita* expenditure and percentage of institutional expenditure showed the later position to have been that shown in Table 1.

Averages were given for different parts of the library budget by groups of universities (Table 2). Capital equipment was excluded. Any wide divergence would be justified only by an improved library service.

Advice was given on the expenditure of the book budget as to: (a) the basis of any allotments to teaching departments; (b) a substantial fund, approximately 50 per cent, for assignment by the librarian for special and general purposes (e.g. for gaps in the

TABLE 1

	Per capita (in dollars)		Percentage of institutional expenditure	
	'Top average'	Average	'Top average'	Average
Group I	177	152	6.5	5.9
Group II	212	163	10.5	8.7

TABLE 2

	Salaries (%)	Books and periodicals (%)	Binding (%)	Other (%)
Group I	56	34	3	7
Group II	50	42	3	5
Group III	46	43	4	7

1. 'Top average' is the mean of the upper half of the scores.

collection, reference works, expensive sets, works which cross subject lines, replacements and duplicates).

The periodicals budget: this should be a separate fund; the amount to be added annually would vary with the size of the institution but should not be less than $6,500 (1964 values).

The library collections

Book collections
The size of the book stock was an important indication of its value to staff and students but not the final criterion. A minimum total size was proposed, beyond which the standard was based on the number of books per student: (a) minimum—100,000 volumes (this was to be increased by 200 volumes per graduate student until the total is overtaken by the standard in (b)); (b) 75 volumes per full-time student.

The actual numbers of volumes per full-time student, averaged over three years were given as follows: Group I, 61; Group II, 67; Group III, 83; average of totals, 70. The standard of 75 volumes per student was the approximate average of the three groups in 1963. Advice was given on book selection.

Periodicals
A table, based on combined figures of United States and Canadian universities (excluding those with a total enrolment over 20,000 or with 50 per cent of the student population in graduate studies) was given as a guide to the average size of university periodical collections. This is a sliding scale from 1,000 titles for total student population of 1,000 to 7,250 titles for 13,000 students, with a median of 4,100 for 7,000 students.

Technical processes

A number of time and output standards in book ordering and cataloguing work were given.

Library planning—buildings

Some accepted standards related to the general points discussed were quoted: 25 ft² (2.3 m²) per undergraduate reader (reading table accommodation); 35 ft² (3.3 m²) per graduate reader and 75 ft² (7.0 m²) per faculty reader (accommodation in individual carrels or studies).

It was suggested that 25–40 per cent of total student enrolment should be taken as the number of seats to be provided for students. The maximum number should be requested within the limits set by finance and the site. A new and small institution would normally use the higher figure. Study halls in the library or other buildings, and study space in university residences, would reduce the percentage requested. As the total number of seats on the campus rose, a trend towards the lower percentage would be justified.

Using the space formula for reader accommodation as constant, 10 volumes per square foot for open-access stacks should be allowed with some interspersed reader accommodation and a spacing between ranges up to 5 ft (on centres). One should allow 12.5 volumes per square foot for stacks planned as book-storage areas with narrow aisles, spacing between ranges down to 4 ft 2 in (on centres).

Office areas 100 ft² (9.3 m²) per staff member in general office accommodation should be allowed; 125 ft² (11.6 m²) in processing departments; 150 ft² (14 m²) per senior staff member in a private office. These areas were minima; extra space should be allowed for special mechanical equipment.

In their *Brief to the Bladen Commission on the Financing of Higher Education*,[1] submitted in 1964, proposals made by the Canadian Association of College and University Libraries included: (a) 10 per cent of institutional operating budgets as a minimum for the operation and development of established libraries and 'considerably more' for the libraries of new institutions; (b) an initial book fund of $500,000 for books and a related amount for salaries during the first four years of library operation in a new institution; (c) special book funds to strengthen library holdings when specialists are appointed in new fields; (d) an average annual total of $50 million for the operating costs of Canadian academic libraries during the next decade; (e) the cost of library service to a graduate student should be reckoned at eight times the cost of service to an undergraduate.

Another Canadian document, issued in 1966, *Report to the*

1. Canadian Library Association, Canadian Association of College and University Libraries, *Forecast of the Cost of Academic Library Services in Canada, 1965–75. A Brief to the Bladen Committee, Ottawa, 1967*.

Committee on University Affairs and the Committee of Presidents of Prov-incially-assisted Universities of the Commission to Study the Development of Graduate Programmes in Ontario Universities,[1] known as the Spinks Report, referred to a problem of considerable importance in the standards field when it pointed to the impracticability of satisfying the needs of a large number of multi-purpose universities from comprehensive research libraries. This report has led to the establishment of a co-operative scheme—the Ontario Provincial University Library System—based on the library of the University of Toronto.

FRANCE

A description of the current situation in French universities, with particular reference to the position of university libraries, is given in the *Bulletin des Bibliothèques de France*.[2] This refers not only to the great influx of students, numbers having almost trebled between 1960 and 1970 (from 214,000 to 615,000), but also to the administrative changes dating from *Instructions du 20 Juin 1962*,[3] aimed at providing open access for students to the maximum amount of library material, and culminating in a Decree of 23 December 1970 introducing other changes as a consequence of major reforms in the organization of higher education.

The great increase in the number of students had led to the building of new and enlarged universities and new and enlarged library provision, particularly science libraries and medical libraries. From 1967 to 1971 nearly 45,000 m² of university library

1. Commission to Study the Development of Graduate Programmes in Ontario Universities, *Report to the Committee on University Affairs and the Committee of Presidents of Provincially-assisted Universities*, Toronto, 1966, p. 84.
2. Alban Daumas, 'Les Bibliothèques Universitaires', *Bulletin des Bibliothèques de France*, Vol. 18, No. 7, July 1973, p. 316–31. This article contains an appreciable amount of information of a 'standards' nature.
3. 'Instructions concernant les Nouvelles Sections et les Sections transférées des Bibliothèques des Universités (à l'Exclusion des Sections "Medicine"), 20 Juin 1962', *Bulletin des Bibliothèques de France*, Vol. 7, No. 8, August 1962, p. 401–10. A discussion of the principles of the 1962 library reforms can be found in: *University Libraries. Problems of Today and Tomorrow*, p. 32–9, Montreal, Association of Universities Entirely or Partly French-speaking, University of Montreal (account of a colloquy held in Geneva under the auspices of the University of Geneva, 27 September to 1 October 1965).

space had been put into use every year, about seven times more than ten years previously. Changes contemplated in teaching methods, such as many lecture courses being replaced by work in groups, on documents and with the help of books and periodicals, would have repercussions on the libraries.

In view of the scale of the university library building programmes undertaken by the Direction des Bibliothèques et de la Lecture Publique of the Ministry of National Education, requiring clear, albeit flexible, principles on which the buildings should be provided, the following note, supplied by the *direction*, on the library building standards adopted will be of interest and practical value.

Note on standards for university library buildings

The standard of 1.50 m² per student remains the average standard for university library buildings. Nevertheless, it has become apparent in practice that this standard must be modified according to the numbers of students and the subjects studied.

In fact a number of students below 1,500 requires a higher standard of about 2 m², which can be reduced to 1.20 m² when the number of students reaches about 10,000.

It has also been confirmed that the scientific subjects demanded less area than the literary and medical subjects.

The average standard is then 1.50 m². It makes it possible to determine the total floor area of the library. Various elements must be considered in the valuation of this total area: the level of studies and of research, the present or future size of the collections, their organization or not for open access, the size of the technical services (acquisitions, processing, etc.).

The space reserved for users is calculated on the basis of 1 seat for 10 students for the scientific subjects, 1 for 6 to 8 students for the literary, legal and medical subjects. One may therefore maintain 1 seat for 8 students as an average standard.

At the level of the first and second years, according to whether classification for open access is adopted in the reading rooms, the standard per seat varies from 2 m² to 3 m². In fact, in order to guard against thefts, the present tendency is to reserve only 2 m² per seat, and to form a lending stock with controlled access, where the works are kept which may be consulted by the students. This lending stock has a variable capacity, but it is reasonable to allot to it 200 m² for 20,000 volumes.

At the research level the area needed for a research worker is evaluated at 6 m². The number of research workers is calculated in relation to the number of students. Thus one arrives at a national average of 1 research worker's seat to 65 students.

As far as book stacks are concerned, the standard accepted is 60 m² per 10,000 volumes when the collections have open access.

The area allotted to technical services varies in proportion to the number of people employed in them, and to the amount of material. On average the area needed for each person can be estimated at 8 or 10 m².

GERMAN DEMOCRATIC REPUBLIC

What follows is based on material supplied by the Methodisches Zentrum für wissenschaftliche Bibliotheken beim Ministerium für Hoch- und Fachschulwesen, Berlin (Methodological Centre for Academic and Research Libraries).[1]

Standards for libraries of universities and colleges of university status

With a view to raising the efficiency of libraries in universities and colleges of university status, in the interest of socialist education, of academic studies and of the economy in the German Democratic Republic, a number of standards have been published in recent years. They deal with the functions, organization, methods and services of such libraries. The preparation of these standards was undertaken by the Ministry of Higher and Technical Education in association, in particular, with the Methodological Centre for Academic and Research Libraries (Methodisches Zentrum für wissenschaftliche Bibliotheken) and the Arbeitkreis der Hochschulbibliotheken (Working Group for Libraries in *Hochschulen*). Some of the standards are compulsory and others are recommendations.

The measures of standardization for university and college

---

1. The methodological centre is an organization of the Ministry of Higher Education of the German Democratic Republic. It is responsible for planning and research work and for methodological work for academic and research libraries.

libraries are based on the provisions of the Decree of 31 May 1968 on the functions of the library system in shaping the developed system of socialism in the German Democratic Republic, and on the regulations of the Council of Ministers on the extension of information and documentation in the field of the social sciences.

Functions and status

The institutions of the library system and scientific information and documentation of a university or comparable establishment are integrated and managed through a library which is directly subordinate to the rector.

The library system of a university or college of university status is an integrated institution which functions as the academic library of the establishment. For convenience it will be referred to as a university library. It is not only an institution of the establishment but part of the library system of the German Democratic Republic.

The university library collects, makes available and helps the reader to use literature in the relevant branches of learning for theoretical study and research, for information and documentation activities in its particular field of work, for the basic vocational education and training of students, and for advanced education and training.

In the solution of larger problems, the library plays an important part both inside and outside the area served. It contributes towards the enlargement of research stocks within the framework of the Sammelschwerpunktplan der wissenschaftlichen Bibliotheken der D.D.R. (Co-ordinated Acquisitions Scheme of Academic and Research Libraries of the German Democratic Republic).

The library institutions of universities and colleges form part of the State system for information and documentation and closely and formally co-operate with the corresponding central technical institutions and/or central and directing offices for information and documentation. The library institutions perform information and documentation work in the various disciplines to help the departments of the university or college achieve their aims in education and training as well as in research.

Administration

The university library is administered by a director who is an academically trained librarian who is expected to teach on library and information problems. The director administers the library on the principle of individual management and collective consultation. According to its size, up to three deputies and an academic secretary are required to assist him. He is the head of all library staff and in charge of all the library and information services of the university or college concerned. He is also a member of its academic council. The director is assisted by a library and information council, which he appoints, consisting of senior staff of the library and the heads of the library and information services in any department of the institution, as well as students' representatives.

These provisions are based upon Directive No. 22/69, issued by the Ministry for Higher and Technical Education on the position, functions and methods of librarianship and scientific information at universities and colleges, of 15 August 1969.[1]

Library services

Library materials

New standards have been worked out but are not yet authorized. While the old ones are based on marks per student, the new standards are based on volumes per thousand students. The materials necessary to meet the needs of the users of the libraries depend on the number of their main users, the students. The budget for the annual requirements can be calculated by a basic amount per student. The instability of book prices, however, makes it necessary to take the number of volumes per thousand students as a starting point for budget calculations.

Staff

New standards have been worked out but are not yet authorized. According to them the number of staff per thousand students will

---

1. 'Anweisung Nr. 22/1969 des Ministeriums für Hoch- und Fachschulwesen über die Stellung, Aufgaben und Arbeitsweise des Bibliothekswesens und der wissenschaftlichen Information an den Hochschulen vom 15. August 1969 [Regulation No. 22/1969 of the Ministry of Higher and Technical Education on the Position, Functions and Methods of the Library and Scientific Information Services at Universities and Colleges, of 15 August, 1969]', *Verfügungen und Mitteilungen des Ministeriums für Hoch- und Fachschulwesen*, No. 8/9, 1969, p. 2–4.

be higher than in the former ones, where, e.g. a staff of eighteen was provided for in a library serving 2,000 students, and of thirty for a library serving 5,000 students. In the new standards additional staff is provided for the information services which are being increasingly integrated into the work of the library.

Staff structure
In libraries of technical and economics *Hochschulen*, staff should be composed of 20 per cent scientifically trained librarians (university or college graduates); 45 per cent librarians (trained in library schools) without academic status; 35 per cent junior assistants (*Bibliotheksfacharbeiter*), technical and assistant personnel.

Special spheres of library administration

Acquisitions
In addition to the standard for the acquisitions budget of university and college libraries there are standardized methods for the establishment of principles by which a policy for acquisitions is arrived at. In regard to this the following points must be taken into account: (a) the functions of the library in relation to the State, the university or other institution concerned and the region; (b) the principles of selection—the disciplines represented at the individual establishments are required to be listed and differentiated according to five levels of collection; and (c) guidelines for acquisitions—these comprise directions for the technical and organizational aspects of stock acquisition.

Processing of newly acquired material
This standard deals separately with techniques used for university libraries and for college libraries. An introduction discussing the study and standardization of work in such libraries is followed by a description of the individual operations and the optimal organization, the time necessary for the work, staff requirements according to categories of personnel and a list of norms.[1]

1. *Der Geschäftsgang an Universitäts- und Hochschulbibliotheken* [Work Processes in University and College Libraries], 2., unveränd. Aufl., Berlin, Methodisches Zentrum für wissenschaftliche Bibliotheken beim Ministerium für Hoch- und Fachschulwesen, 1970, 99 p.

Reading rooms
This standard consists of recommended guidelines for the organization, building, and equipment of reading rooms.[1]

Calculation of the number of readers' places in reading rooms
For calculating the number of readers' places a mathematical
model has been worked out. This is based on the assessment and
appraisal of the factors influencing the readers' place requirements
(number of students, local situation of the library, quality of other
library facilities in the same town, structure of the university or
college, etc.). By this method no global fixing of a norm is necessary
and an individual calculation for any library is possible. In general
the calculations based on this model are showing a parabolical
dependence between the number of students and the required
number of places for readers.[2]

FEDERAL REPUBLIC OF GERMANY

The following account of the position of libraries in universities
and colleges of university status, with particular reference to the
question of standards of service is based on information contained
in *Libraries in the Federal Republic of Germany*,[3] which describes the
organization, recent history and current problems facing the universities and comparable institutions, on published and unpublished material on the *Empfehlungen des Wissenschaftsrats zum Ausbau
der wissenschaftlichen Einrichtungen, Teil II: Wissenschaftliche Bibliotheken*,[4] provided by Kenneth Garside, and on other documents.

1. *Lesesaalordnung. Material des Arbeitskreises der technischen und ökonomischen Hochschulbiblio-
theken vom Oktober 1968* [Reading Room Regulation. Material of the Working Group of
Colleges of Technology and of Economics, October 1968], Berlin, Methodisches
Zentrum für wissenschaftliche Bibliotheken beim Ministerium für Hoch- und Fachschulwesen (mimeo, for internal use).
2. Karl-Heinrich Bell, 'Mathematisches Modell zur Berechnung der notwendigen
Anzahl von Leserarbeitsplätzen in einer Universitäts- oder Hochschulbibliothek
[Mathematical Model for Calculating the Number of Readers' Seats in a University
or College Library]', *Zentralblatt für Bibliothekswesen*, Vol. 84, No. 7, 1970, p. 385-95.
3. G. von Busse and H. Ernestus, *Libraries in the Federal Republic of Germany*, rev. and enl.
English ed., Wiesbaden and London, Otto Harrassowitz and The Library Association,
1972.
4. *Empfehlungen des Wissenschaftsrats zum Ausbau der wissenschaftlichen Einrichtungen,
Teil II. Wissenschaftliche Bibliotheken* [Recommendations of the Council for Arts and

The recommendations of the Wissenschaftsrat, the most significant and comprehensive document existing about university libraries in the Federal Republic of Germany, was issued by this advisory council in 1964. The council was set up jointly by the Federal Government and the *Länder* in 1957 to formulate an over-all plan for the promotion of scholarship and research and to indicate priorities. Its first report in 1960 was concerned with the development of the universities and *technische Hochschulen*.[1] The second did for academic libraries what the first did for universities. This, like the British Parry Report, referred to later, and which was greatly influenced by it, was not primarily concerned with standards but in much of what it recommended for the future organization of university and other academic libraries important standards were in fact being laid down.

The committee which produced the report was convinced that major changes were necessary to enable existing libraries to meet demands on them by undergraduates and research workers and recommended a rationalization of library administration. The libraries had to keep pace with recent developments in research, particularly in the natural sciences and technology, which had led to a corresponding and vast increase throughout the world in learned and scientific literature. The libraries' efficiency depended on rational organization, large and well-selected book stocks, adequate and competent staffs, and adequate and well-planned accommodation.

On the question of organization the report discussed two major questions. The first was the position of the main library in the university. It recommended that in future the university library should be governed under the university statutes, which was rarely the case. (The university library is a State institution which has been set up within the university. The university librarian is appointed by the Minister of Culture, although with the approval of the rector and senate. His participation in library matters which concern the whole university is provided for in differing degrees

Science, Part II, Learned and Scientific Libraries], Tübingen, Mohr, 1964. The council's title is difficult to render in English. Garside refers to it as 'Council for Arts and Science', and von Busse and Ernestus as 'Science Council, covering also the Humanities and Social Sciences'. It has a distinguished membership, the representatives of the *Länder* being the Ministers of Culture or Ministers of Finance.
1. Described as colleges of advanced technology or technical universities.

in the universities' constitution. Requests for funds and additional staff are made by the librarian, through the rector to the ministry.)[1] The report recommended the appointment of a library committee under the rector, which should be responsible for acquisitions policy, co-ordination with departments, hours of opening and other matters concerning the use of the library, appointments of senior staff and finance. The university librarian should be kept informed of university affairs affecting the library, particularly finance.

The second and connected question concerned the issue of the relation of the central university libraries to the departmental and institute libraries. University library practice in the Federal Republic of Germany was characterized by the coexistence of a central general library and numbers of other libraries with reference collections in their own subject fields. These represented two independently administered systems within the same university, and their respective functions, it was recommended, must be clarified. The central library held the key position as a general library and lending library which also arranged inter-library loans. Departmental libraries attempted to be more comprehensive in their own fields than the central library but were not lending libraries.

The report did not consider that in existing universities the position could be bettered by incisive changes and recommended that the existing dichotomous system should be retained and improved by more appropriate relations between the two kinds of library and more equitable financial arrangements. The shortcomings of the main libraries had led to much criticism in departments and had been the excuse for increased autarchy. In the last decade departmental libraries had been receiving twice, and sometimes three or four times, as much money for purchase of library materials as the central library.

The report stated that all libraries in the university should form a single entity. There should be co-operation in acquisition, cataloguing, and use of both kinds of library. Departmental libraries should restrict themselves to their own specialized fields and lending should be allowed, if only at week-ends. Union catalogues of the holdings of all libraries within the university were necessary. An experiment should be undertaken in one university in carrying

1. G. von Busse and H. Ernestus, op. cit.

out all the technical processes for all libraries within the university.

A large information section should be set up to help users. Up-to-date author and subject catalogues were necessary and readers should have unrestricted access to them. Author catalogues throughout the university must be compiled according to the same rules.

Hours of opening should be extended. In term time, reading-rooms, catalogue halls, and information desks should be open for twelve to thirteen hours, Monday to Friday, if possible until 10 p.m., and for six hours on Saturday. When open there should be service from the stacks.

Senior staff should be available for book selection in particular subject fields and new publications should be made available as quickly as possible. The reader should have a book produced for him in a minimum time. Within a quarter of an hour should be normal practice. Staffing and building and equipment should be geared to this.

The report commented that open access to the book stacks was only practicable when these were arranged in classified order, which took up more space than one classified in *numerus currens*, but it was being tried in one of the new university libraries, at Frankfurt am Main.[1]

Library materials

On the subject of library materials it was said that many purchases of research literature were duplicated within the university. Only one copy of expensive items should be bought. A textbook collection should be set up in every main university library and sufficient copies of all textbooks available in the main library and departmental libraries. Students should still be expected to buy the books they needed most, but they should be able to consult the less important ones in the library. General cultural literature must also be provided for the students.

---

1. The main university libraries have traditionally been shelved in closed-access book stacks, from which there might be deliveries only once or twice a day. Since 1964, when the report was published, a degree of open access has been introduced, particularly in new universities.

Position of the new universities

The report discussed the position of new universities under various headings. It was for consideration whether they should follow the traditional pattern or a new one.

Organization of book provision

The opportunity to try out new methods of library service in new universities was welcomed and alternative forms of organization were listed in which certain points were common: (a) the need for a long-term acquisitions policy for both current and older materials, with a central acquisitions office assisted by an advisory committee of academic staff, as a useful instrument; (b) the need to maintain a union catalogue of all books and periodicals in all libraries in the university; (c) all libraries to admit all members of the university; (d) central ordering and administrative arrangements, including staffing; (e) the director of the university library to be effectively librarian of the university.

Scope and funds for development of new university libraries

New university libraries must have a comprehensive stock of literature available from the outset. Building up a library is one of the first tasks to be undertaken when a new university library is planned, and the library must be ready for use before teaching and research begin.

The holdings of periodicals must be built up quickly and systematically. A new library should have 5,000 titles, with sets of back volumes. It must also have the major reference works, source materials and basic textbooks.

Experience in the new universities at Mainz, Berlin and Saarbrucken had shown that a stock of 300,000 volumes was necessary before the point was reached when not more than 25 per cent of readers' needs had to be met from outside. A new library could only stand on its own feet when it contained 600,000 volumes. The basic stock of 300,000 volumes cost about DM.20 million.

The needs of technical university libraries must be measured by different standards from those applicable to university libraries. Scientific and technical literature became obsolete more quickly and sets of back volumes of periodicals need not be bought on such a large scale. For a technical university library a basic stock of 100,000 volumes was required at the outset, but since scientific and technical literature was more costly it would cost DM.8 million.

The funds necessary for building up the new library must be made available within the first few years. In addition, funds must be available for the purchase of current publications. Staff must be available to deal with this initial flow of acquisitions. The latest technical equipment must be available.

Library co-operation

Discussing library co-operation, the document said that the purchase of some foreign material might be organized with advantage on a co-operative basis. Union catalogues were essential and a bibliographical information office should be set up.

Inter-library lending was criticized for delays in meeting requests for books from other libraries. Requests must be met in the quickest possible way, even if this meant going outside the usual channels. Books costing less than DM.10 and still in print should be purchased by the library concerned and not borrowed from another library. Photocopies should be supplied of articles in periodicals, instead of lending the original volume.

Education and training

The report discussed training and professional matters. The proposed development of learned and scientific libraries depended on resources for the training of staff. More library schools were needed. Senior staff needed to have practical ability as well as wide academic interests.

Exchanges should be arranged for senior staff, who must keep up to date with their own academic subjects. Refresher courses were needed.

Requirements for materials and staff—model budgets

The report discussed specific requirements in terms of materials, staff and money for existing university libraries, providing some useful standards of a quantitative nature. It included two 'model budgets', one for a university library and another for a technical university library. The model budgets fell into two parts, acquisitions and staffing. The former was costed, in the latter only the number of different posts were given. Of these 'models' von Busse and Ernestus have said:

The estimates for acquisitions are based on the material that ought to be purchased. . . . The basis differs . . . from the ALA Standards for College libraries (1959) and for Junior College libraries (1960), according to which the college library should receive a fixed percentage of the total college budget. The number of students in a university is in Germany, quite apart from fluctuations, not a relevant consideration: library purchases, corresponding largely to the dual teaching and research functions of the university, cover not only students' books but research material—and upon that student numbers have no influence. Only for textbook collections are such numbers relevant. The policy of relating total library expenditure, for both acquisitions and staffing, to the total university budget is conceivable only in universities where the library system forms a unity: in the existing West German universities this is not the case.

The 'models' referred to the basic structure to be achieved and related only to what might be called 'normal' current requirements. The amounts referred only to the central libraries in universities. Institute and departmental libraries, administered independently of the central library, attracted further funds so the total university expenditure on libraries would be substantially higher. The 'models' applied only to conditions in the existing universities, and not to new universities.

The estimates for book purchases in the university model were as follows; those for the technical university are not quoted as they have been largely superseded by the restructuring of technical universities and the creation of additional faculties:

German and foreign periodicals (1,200 German titles; 1,500 basic foreign titles; 1,500 specialized foreign titles): DM.210,000.

Continuations and series: DM.105,000.

Monographs: DM.180,000.

Second-hand books and materials: DM.25,000.

Binding: DM.130,000.

This gives a total of DM.650,000. In addition an annual sum based on student numbers must be available for textbooks.

The 'model' budget was calculated on the following basis:

Funds for book purchases and binding

The calculation of the funds necessary for book purchases depended on the number of periodicals taken. The expenditure on periodicals represented a fairly constant proportion of the book fund. Experience both in the Federal Republic of Germany and abroad had shown that the expenditure on continuations and series worked out at 50 per cent of that on periodicals, and that the expenditure on books worked out at 75 per cent of that on periodicals.

Periodicals
Book production had increased by 5 to 6 per cent annually between 1957 and 1964. The total number of periodicals required by a university library had increased by 5 per cent annually, and the increase in the number of German and foreign periodicals required would be 40 per cent in technical university libraries over a period of eight years, and 35 per cent in general university libraries. Prices rose by 4 to 5 per cent annually, so that there must be an annual increase of 10 per cent in the book fund to allow for this necessary expansion of resources and to cover the increased costs.

Continuations and series
The allocation for continuations and series should be half that for periodicals.

Monographs
The relation between standing commitments in respect of periodicals, continuations and series, on the one hand, and the uncommitted funds available for the purchase of books on the other, was estimated at 7 : 4 in university libraries and 8 : 4 in technical university libraries.

Second-hand books
The need for funds for the purchase of second-hand books depended on how well the library was built up at the time when these books were current. University libraries must be in a position to buy important collections as such.

Binding
This would amount to at least 25 per cent of the book fund.

Textbooks
A sum equal to DM.4 per student should be spent annually on the collection of textbooks.

Expansion and increases in prices

The funds available to the library must keep pace with increases in book production and in book prices. There must be funds available for the filling of gaps in the library's resources and for the improvement of its bibliographical apparatus to increase its efficiency.

The cost figures were valid for 1965. An annual increment, corresponding to increases in production and in prices, has to be added. This has been assessed by the Wissenschaftsrat at 5 per cent for each type of increase, that is 10 per cent in all. This is now too low; von Busse and Ernestus refer to a figure of 15 per cent,[1] which may now be higher still. Despite this difficulty, the 'model' approach to the subject is valuable, the ratios are important, and the money estimates are no doubt meaningful for those familiar with the situation in the Federal Republic of Germany.

The 'model' staff estimates for a university library were: senior staff 14; professionally qualified assistants 36; unqualified assistants and clerks 36; attendants, etc. 24; bindery 5; photographic unit 4; total 75.

A 'model' allocation of duties was given, e.g. senior staff: director, heads of acquisitions, cataloguing and service to readers' departments; subject specialists. Other staff: administration (4 assistants—qualified and unqualified; 4 attendants); acquisitions (16 assistants); reading rooms (6 assistants; 3 attendants).

Developments since 1964

The recommendations made by the Wissenschaftsrat in 1964 have in certain respects been overtaken by events and since that date considerable efforts have been made to improve upon them. There have been a number of studies on a *Land* basis concerned with questions of rationalization and future planning of library provision in which both qualitative and quantitative standards are involved. Significant documents of this kind have been published, for example, in Baden-Württemberg[2] and North

1. G. von Busse and H. Ernestus, op. cit.
2. *Gesamtplan für das wissenschaftliche Bibliothekswesen.* Hrsg. von der Arbeitsgruppe Bibliotheksplan Baden-Württemberg. Bd. 1. *Empfehlungen,* Teil 1: *Universitäten,* Freiburg, Br. 1973, Universitätsbibliothek Freiburg (Over-all Plan for Academic Libraries, published by the Working Group for the Baden-Württemberg Libraries Plan. Vol. 1. *Recommendations.* Part 1: *Universities*).

Rhine-Westphalia.[1] In addition studies by individuals or groups into different problems have been undertaken such as those to which reference is made by von Busse and Ernestus.[2]

In the first category an official planning group on university libraries in North Rhine-Westphalia was set up to make recommendations for the establishment of libraries at the five new *Gesamthochschulen* (comprehensive universities) in Duisburg, Essen, Paderborn, Siegen and Wuppertal, which were formed by the amalgamation of existing institutions in each area. The planning group made its first proposals to the Minister of Culture of the *Land* in 1971 and early 1972, and in June published a *Zwischenbericht*, or interim report, to serve as a basis for further discussion.[3] The report discussed models and guidelines for the size of stock and the number of working places in the new institution. The following are examples.

Stock requirements

Each of the five libraries would have similar requirements as far as the basic book stock was concerned, but differing requirements for specialized material, depending on the subjects on which the institution concentrated and on the proportion of short- and long-course students. The basic literature in all five libraries is

1. Lohse Gerhart, *Das Bibliothekswesen an den Universitäten und den technischen Hochschulen des Landes Nordrhein-Westfalen. Bestandsaufname und Vorschlag zur Neuordnung. Gutachten erstellt im Auftrage des Kultusministers des Landes Nordrhein-Westfalen* [Libraries in the Universities and Technical *Hochschulen* in North Rhine-Westphalia. Present Position and Proposals for Future Development. Recommendations on behalf of the Minister of Culture for North Rhine-Westphalia], Wuppertal, 1970 (Strukturforderung im Bildungswesen des Landes Nordrhein-Westfalen, 12).

   Planungsgruppe Bibliothekswesen im Hochschulbereich Nordrhein-Westfalen beim Minister für Wissenschaft und Forschung des Landes Nordrhein-Westfalen [Planning Group for University Libraries in North Rhine-Westphalia on behalf of the Minister for Science and Research of North Rhine-Westphalia], *Empfehlungen für das Bibliothekswesen an den fünf Gesamthochschulen des Landes Nordrhein-Westfalen. Zwischenbericht* [Recommendations for the Libraries in the Five Comprehensive Universities of North Rhine-Westphalia. Interim Report], Dusseldorf, 1972.

   Planungsgruppe Bibliothekswesen im Hochschulbereich Nordrhein-Westfalen beim Minister für Wissenschaft und Forschung des Landes Nordrhein-Westfalen [Planning Group for University Libraries in North Rhine-Westphalia, on behalf of the Minister for Science and Research of North Rhine-Westphalia], *Allgemeine Zielvorstellungen für das Bibliothekswesen in den Gesamthochschulbereichen des Landes Nordrhein-Westfalen* [General Statement of Aims for Libraries in the Comprehensive Universities in North Rhine-Westphalia], Düsseldorf, 1973.
2. G. von Busse and H. Ernestus, op. cit., p. 188–90.
3. *Empfehlungen für das Bibliothekswesen. . .*, op. cit.

Table 3

Subject	Volumes per student	
	Long courses	Short courses
Humanities	100	30
Social sciences	40	20
Natural sciences	30	15
Engineering	20	10

broken down as follows: humanities, 250,000 volumes; social sciences, 100,000; natural sciences, 50,000; engineering, 40,000; general, 100,000. This gives a total of 540,000 volumes.

The specialized literature (calculated according to the number of students and volumes per student, differentiated by the different subjects, and long and short courses) is broken down in Table 3.

It was proposed that eventually each library should have approximately 800,000 volumes. The Wissenschaftsrat had recommended a minimum of 300,000 volumes, and therefore it was necessary that, in the first phase of planning (eight years to 1980), approximately 40 per cent of the ultimate total should be acquired at the rate of 40,000 a year.

Reading places

The group proposed that an over-all total of 12 reading places per 100 students (which they considered a low figure) should be provided, calculated on the following model.

	x places per 100 students	Places (staff) 10 per cent of x	Places in carrels, etc. 10 per cent of x
Total:	10	1	1

A notional breakdown of the total would be: humanities, 15 per cent; social sciences, 12 per cent; natural sciences, 8 per cent; engineering, 8 per cent; medicine, 8 per cent.

The *Allgemeine Zielvorstellungen* . . . (General statement of aims . . .), produced by the planning group in March 1973, set out more general recommendations for structural changes in the *Gesamthochschulen* (comprehensive universities) libraries in North

Rhine-Westphalia. To a certain extent these were alternatives to the proposals of the *Zwischenbericht* (Interim Report). The later recommendations referred to the relationship between the main library and the subject libraries in each university and underlined the recommendations of *Bibliotheksplan 1973* that each university library should be a part of the local and regional library network, undertake inter-library lending and take part in co-operative projects.

INDIA

In 1957 the Indian University Grants Commission appointed a committee, under the Chairmanship of Dr S. R. Ranganathan, to advise it about development of libraries and their organization. The committee organized a seminar, 'From Publisher to Reader: Work Flow in a University Library', in 1958, in preparation for which considerable data were collected from universities. The document containing the report, published in 1965, also contains the proceedings of the seminar.[1]

This report discussed many peculiarly Indian problems, in which historical and local circumstances inevitably played a considerable part. For example, in discussing library personnel, it was stated that, as many of the universities had been for a long time examining bodies without any teaching or research function, they had no libraries organized for service, even though they had acquired book collections of their own. These collections were left in charge of manual and clerical staff merely to keep them clean and listed. New universities with teaching functions had been established for about fifty years and their custom was to put an honorary librarian—usually a professor—over the clerical and manual staff. The first time a university had appointed a full-time professional librarian, with proper status and responsibility, was about forty years earlier. But this had only happened in about three of the older universities and four of the later ones. Most of the other universities were still under the pressure of the old tradition. Some universities still regarded the library as a section

1. University Grants Commission, *Report of the Library Committee, University and College Libraries*, New Delhi, 1965.

of general administration to be administered by the registrar of the university.

In discussing the current problems of Indian universities and making recommendations, many qualitative standards are discussed in this report. The following gives a number of examples.

Finance

The annual finance essential for a university library could be determined by a functional approach which took into account the number of faculties and the number and the nature of the departments of study and research in the library. A more realistic and equitable approach to the quantum of the annual finance necessary for a university library was based on the '*per capita* approach'. The report said that, in the pre-war period, world practice showed that the annual appropriation for the book fund of a university library corresponded to 15 rupees per student and 200 rupees per teacher or research fellow, and that the annual expenditure of all other kinds, including the cost of the administrative staff and reference staff for service, was roughly equal to the expenditure on books, periodicals and other reading material.

The committee recommended that, subject to local variation, the capacity of the university to spend and the amount at the disposal of the University Grants Commission for grants for reading and similar materials, 15 rupees *per capita* on the basis of students registered in the university and 200 rupees per teacher be given as grant to a university library for the time being and that the figures should be revised periodically in the light of changes in the cost of books and periodicals. In the case of a university not more than five years old, an additional grant of up to 300,000 rupees was recommended to build up the initial stock; this sum should be spent within three years.

Allocation of book funds, co-ordination of book selection, local co-ordination, regional co-ordination

Book funds should be equitably allocated to all disciplines. To avoid unnecessary duplication of periodicals and reference books, each university and college would need to formulate its own policy, in respect of which certain general principles were indicated, e.g. in connexion with retention in departments. Advice was given regarding duplication of advanced works and textbooks.

To obtain the benefit of the maximum number of learned periodicals, and reference books for the research workers, it was desirable to practice co-ordination on the basis of the whole locality or region. For some costly and occasionally used periodicals, the co-ordination might need to cover the whole country.

Inter-library loan

To make the most effective use of the total book fund of the several universities and colleges, the University Grants Committee should promote local, regional and national co-ordination of book selection, subscription to learned periodicals, and acquisition of back volumes of periodicals, among the several libraries; co-operation in the fullest use of the holdings in the several libraries through a scheme of inter-library loan; and production and continued maintenance of a union catalogue of learned periodicals, select treatises in foreign languages other than English and rare books of research value, in the field of social sciences and humanities, as was already done for the natural sciences.

The academic qualifications of the library staff—and their status and salaries—should be equal to those of the professors, readers, lecturers and tutors. Together the qualified staff should be familiar with the highways and byways of knowledge in every subject. They should divide the field of knowledge among themselves and practise specialization. Advice was given about qualifications and training and the desirable structure, gradings and salary scales for university library staff. The University Grants Commission was urged to subsidize the salaries of library staff, as it did of teaching and research staff, and to prevail upon the management of the universities to maintain library staff in accordance with the recommended formula. It was also recommended that the practice of appointing a person without the prescribed professional qualifications as honorary librarian should be abolished.

Quantitative standards were given for library staff, in respect of which it was claimed the administration of the universities needed to adopt a more informed attitude. A university library should provide staff for the following sections of work: books;

periodical publications; documentation; technical; reference; circulation; maintenance; administration.

It was recommended that staff, in addition to the librarian and deputy librarian, should be provided on the following basis:
Administrative section—minimum of 1 library accountant, 1 shorthand typist and 1 correspondence clerk.
Book section—1 person for every 6,000 volumes added yearly.
Periodical publications section—1 person for every 500 current periodicals taken.
Documentation section—1 person for every 1,000 entries prepared in a year.
Technical section—1 person for every 2,000 volumes added in a year.
Reference section—1 person for every 50 readers in a day (other than the users of the textbook collection).
Circulation section—1 person for every 1,500 hours for which 1 wicket gate of the library had to be kept open in a year.
Maintenance section—1 person for every 6,000 volumes added in a year, 1 person for every 500 volumes to be replaced in a day, and 1 person for every 100,000 volumes in the library.
Unskilled staff—1 cleaner for every 30,000 volumes in the library, 1 attendant for every 6,000 volumes added in a year, for every 500 current periodicals taken, and for each of the shifts in the circulation section, besides unskilled and semi-skilled workers normal to any institution.
A university library should be kept open on all days of the year.

Standards, prepared by a sectional committee on library buildings, fittings, and furniture of the Indian Standards Institution (of which Dr Ranganathan also became chairman) were recommended for library buildings and equipment.

Phased construction was recommended to allow for future expansion of the libraries.

MEXICO

The Asociación de Bibliotecarios de Instituciones de Enseñanza Superior y de Investigación—ABIESI—(Association of Librarians in Institutions of Higher Education and Research), through its Directive and Technical Council, prepared a statement *Standards*

for Library Service in Higher Teaching and Research Institutions,[1] which
was adopted by the Asociación Nacional de Universidades e Instituciones de Enseñanza Superior (National Association of Universities and Institutions of Higher Education) in 1968. In it it was
stated that ABIESI offered the standards to the authorities responsible for higher education in Mexico to help them in the creation,
development and maintenance of a service in line with the academic activities of the country. The association acknowledged that
it had used as a basis the standards for college libraries of the
Association of College and Research Libraries of the American
Library Association published in 1959.

The document followed closely the form and qualitative standards recommended by the American Library Association, but it
did not specify any minimum number of qualified librarians or
minimum numbers of volumes in the book stock, as the American
Library Association had done.

The association stated that, as the university strengthened itself
by improved teaching methods, encouraging study and the development of research, the demand for a satisfactory library service
would become evident. It referred to the deficiencies of Latin
American university libraries, noted by Unesco in connexion with
the Regional Seminar on the Development of University Libraries,
in Mendoza (Argentina), in 1962, and related them to the position
in Mexico. These deficiencies were also indicative of the current
conditions. Having in mind (a) the disadvantageous position of
Mexico compared with Latin American countries in regard to the
number of volumes per inhabitant in the libraries; (b) the acceler-
ation of economic and social development in Mexico, which was
endangered if graduates of its universities did not have up-to-date
information available; (c) the academic level of a university, which
was judged by the quality of its library services, and, taking into
account that it was the university authorities which could give the
necessary impulse for the development of the university libraries,
ABIESI presented the library standards, a summary of which is
given below.

1. Asociación de Bibliotecarios de Instituciones de Enseñanza Superior y de Investiga-
ción, *Normas para el Servicio Bibliotecario en Instituciones de Enseñanza Superior y de Investi-
gación. Adoptadas por la Asociación Nacional de Universidades e Instituciones de Enseñanza
Superior* [Standards for Library Service in Institutions of Higher Education and
Research. Adopted by the National Association of Universities and Institutions of
Higher Education], Mexico, ABIESI, 1968.

Functions of the library

The library was the centre of the most important activities in the academic life of the university where the most diverse types of study and research were conducted according to its resources and services. Its information sources should present a complete view of human culture, giving preference to those disciplines which formed part of the work of the institution. The library should be an extension of the teaching function. It should be strong to satisfy the needs of the whole academic community. It should awaken and stimulate habits of reading and research.

Structure and operation of library service

The library should be a separate department responsible to the rector, with its organization in accordance with the general structure of the university. The director of library services should be a full member of the university council, participating in its discussions. He should have complete freedom to direct the library, subject only to the rector for general policy. Where a library committee existed this could intervene in general policy matters but not in the administrative aspects thereof. The planning and application of the budget should be the responsibility of the director of library services. The administration and technical processes should be centralized. The collections should be concentrated in one building unless distances between different locations made this difficult. Where departmental libraries were necessary, they should be part of a nucleus serving the neighbouring schools of the university.

Budget

The minimum annual budget of the library should be 5 per cent of the university budget. When a new library was being set up this amount should be augmented by a special allocation, as also should special programmes. On the basis that maintenance costs and the purchase of equipment, as well as the cost of the construction or enlargement of library buildings, formed part of the general university budget, it was recommended that normal annual expenditure should be apportioned broadly as to 40 per cent for the acquisition and handling of library materials and 60 per cent for staff salaries.

Staff

The library service should be managed by professional librarians, who had undergone formal library training after obtaining at least a degree or its equivalent. Competent non-professional staff would also be required. The proportion between the two grades would vary according to the needs of each institution. The director of library services should select the professional and administrative staff. The qualified librarians should occupy the same professional level as the teaching staff of the institution and enjoy the same benefits. The salaries for non-professionals should be in accordance with training, skill and hours of work.

Library materials

While recognizing that in other countries a minimum of 130 volumes per student was recommended for libraries of small universities and that a library with less than 300,000 volumes was considered inadequate, it was important to realize that the adequate selection of the volumes and not the total number was the basis of a good library. Proposed numbers in the (Mexican) standards might appear to be too much reduced in the case of some universities, but the standards took into account the position in the whole of Mexico. Where new libraries were being built up, the provision of basic stocks required a large initial expenditure. The libraries which already had this stock would be able to plan an acquisitions policy and maintain it.

The library should include books, periodical publications and serials, pamphlets, official and special documents, maps, photo-reproductions and material relevant to the disciplines taught in the university. The library should acquire sufficient examples of textbooks considered sufficiently permanent and useful. The collections should also include works of a general cultural interest.

The basic general collection should be formed of ten current well-selected titles in each subject taught in the university. This would be a minimum which should be increased as soon as funds allowed or the needs of study and research required it.

A reference collection with a minimum of 500 different titles must be allowed for in the initial phase, including general and specialized encyclopaedias, dictionaries, bibliographies, annuals, statistical works, etc. A comprehensive list of subscriptions to periodical publications should be maintained. The number of subscriptions to basic periodical publications should be 15 to 20 titles per specialization or career taught in the university. The complete volumes of periodical publications, and also paperback volumes, should be bound.

The library should have a donations policy and the director of library services should have the right to retain or discard material at his discretion.

An exchange service should be maintained to fill gaps and to satisfy the needs of other libraries. The library should control the exchange of its own university's publications.

The library should acquire equipment and audio-visual material such as films, tapes, micro-films, records, to complement the teaching and research programmes.

An inventory of the book stock should be taken every two years.

Buildings, equipment and furniture

It was necessary to have a suitable library building, equidistant from the academic buildings. The building should be functional and should be convenient to the users. The dimensions and characteristics of the library building depended on the needs and resources of each university, but the following accommodation was recommended: space for reading and research sufficient to accommodate from 10 to 20 per cent of the student body, taking into account the probable growth during the next twenty to twenty-five years; cubicles for researchers and teachers; adequate space for lending services, corridors and staircases, space for exhibitions; space for administrative and technical activities, rest rooms and services; offices for directing staff; space for shelving, taking into consideration the probable growth in twenty years; space for audio-visual materials; space for cleaning services, toilets, loading and unloading of goods.

Advice was given on the planning of the library building, equipment and furniture.

Services

The principal objective of the library was to serve the university community. This required (a) uninterrupted hours of opening with a minimum of twelve hours daily from Monday to Friday and six hours on Saturday; (b) information and reference services; (c) internal and home lending service to the student body, academic and administrative staff; (d) access to the resources of the library, with restrictions when necessary; (e) instruction in, and advice to readers on, the use of the libraries; (f) cubicles for teachers and researchers; (g) inter-library loan and photo-reproduction of documents; (h) service (excluding home loans) open to university and research students not connected with the university; and (i) co-operative acquisition with other libraries.

Evaluation of services

Methods of evaluating the services of the library, in order to justify the claims made by the director of library services to the university council, were discussed. It was recommended that every five years there should be an analysis of the service to confirm policies adopted or correct deficiencies.

UNITED KINGDOM

The universities in the United Kingdom are institutions operating under royal charters. They are closely associated with the central government through the University Grants Committee, which provides them with the greater part of their income and meets the greater part of non-recurrent expenditure. This gives the University Grants Committee opportunities to influence policy on many matters, but each university is responsible for its own administration, including the extent, nature and organization of its library provision.

As in all other countries, the universities in the United Kingdom have gone through a period of massive expansion during the last twenty years. A number of new universities have been established from scratch or by the upgrading of existing, mainly technological, institutions. A review of the future pattern of full-time higher education was undertaken by a committee, the 'Robbins Committee', which reported in 1963. In the same year, the University Grants Committee set up a committee, the 'Parry Committee' whose task was

> . . . to consider the most effective and economical arrangements for meeting the needs of the universities . . . for books and periodicals, taking into account expanding staff and student population, the possible needs of other users, the growth of research, the rising cost of books and periodicals, and the increasing capital cost of library accommodation, to assess how far greater use might with advantage be made of shared facilities, both between the institutions themselves, and between them, outside systems and other institutions, and of modern methods of reproduction.

The committee report, published in 1967,[1] made comparisons between British universities and those of other countries. Of the United States, it said that, excluding the very large collections of Harvard (8 million volumes) and Yale (6 million volumes), there were twenty-three university libraries with over 1 million volumes. In the United Kingdom, excluding the Bodleian Library at Oxford and Cambridge University Library—which are deposit libraries—the largest university library had about 800,000 bound volumes and the smallest about 160,000, the average (excluding universities recently created) for all university libraries being about 350,000 volumes.

The report is an important document for universities. But, in the long term, it will perhaps be of even greater significance for having given the initial impetus to the creation of a new structure for the national libraries, providing a true apex to the library system of the country. The effect on university libraries of the absence of this apex was pointed out by the committee. While primarily concerned with discussing the organization of university libraries, their difficulties and deficiencies, pointing out ways in which the position might be improved, the committee wrote in effect a comprehensive standards document. It is a document, however, largely devoid of quantitative standards, but this is not, in the circumstances, a matter for criticism. The report should be read closely by those interested in the detail and considerations of space preclude an extensive summary of it. Notes follow on parts of the report which

1. University Grants Committee, *Report of the Committee on Libraries*, London, HMSO, 1967.

will illustrate how the committee treated some aspects of university library work out of which 'standards' could clearly be derived, as they also could out of other sections of the report.

The British system—general comments

British university libraries are organized and administered on lines more comparable to those in the United States and Canada than to continental Europe, where they are mostly administered by the State. In the United Kingdom the library is a recognized part of the university with which it is closely integrated. The British system made for a balanced development of the whole collection, while making use of the specialist knowledge of heads of departments and their colleagues. A balance should be preserved between the needs of undergraduate teaching and post-graduate research.

A factor affecting the comprehensiveness of university libraries was the need both to satisfy present users and to anticipate requirements. Comprehensiveness did not mean that the library should provide all the material required to follow up an investigation, but it should be able to set in motion the machinery to make the material available.

Functions of a university library

The University Grants Committee in 1921 had said:

The character and efficiency of a university may be gauged by its treatment of its central organ—the library. We regard the fullest provision for library maintenance as the primary and most vital need in the equipment of a university.

The increase in the number of students and the 'information explosion' had brought about changes in university libraries. They had increasingly to explore methods of making available to a research worker material that it could not itself purchase. The adoption of the tutorial method of teaching made an adequate stock for undergraduate use essential. Graduate studies were likely to become of increasing importance and would make considerable demands on library resources for monographs and periodicals and for bibliographical aids. The committee acknowledged the repository function of university libraries and the value of special collections of printed works and manuscripts.

While the British university libraries are primarily meant to serve the university's teaching and research interests, an increasing number of other people and organizations were being allowed to use them and this tendency was increasing, particularly in the libraries in the University of London.

Co-operation and inter-library loans

In estimating the efficiency of a university library, one could make the broad assertion that it should be able to meet all the needs of undergraduates from its own stock, and as many as possible of the needs of its research workers. With the increased number of academic people engaged in research and the mounting cost of books and periodicals, it had become necessary to explore all the means whereby a university library could co-operate with other libraries without impairing its own efficiency—indeed with a view to extending and improving its own services.

A distinction should be drawn between frequently and infrequently used material. In the absence of research into this and many other library problems, this distinction had to be approached pragmatically. The frequently used material should be held by the library which served the research worker, and the infrequently used material could be housed elsewhere, provided it was available for loan or in photocopies.

Some degree of co-ordination of the resources of university, special and public libraries in an area would be desirable. This was particularly true of a big city, where there might be two universities, some special libraries and a well-stocked public library. The grouping of libraries in an area was desirable for reasons other than the extension of coverage and the reduction of expenditure. It might be necessary to anticipate long-term problems of storage. Co-operation was considered in terms of study facilities, co-operation in acquisitions, communication, regular consultation and staff training. Separately discussed was (a) co-operation between libraries in institutions of higher education other than universities particularly the (then) future polytechnics and further education colleges and colleges of education; and (b) co-operation between university libraries.

The committee recommended that the entire resources of a geographical area should be regarded as a pool from which each individual library could draw. University libraries within an area should avoid unnecessary duplication of effort and should investigate the advantages of the forms of co-operation discussed. Public libraries should be able to make fully accessible their collections of material of value to academic research.

Inter-library lending was a legitimate and desirable aspect of a university library's activity, and should be closely integrated with all other aspects. It should be as efficient as possible, and should ensure that the publication required was delivered quickly.

Finance

Having discussed at length the nature of collections, the acquisition of library material, the co-operative acquisition of foreign material, the need for a reformed national library, university library accommodation, library services (including guidance on the use of the library), library techniques, and administration and staffing, the report dealt with the question of finance. There, for the first time, it touched on quantitative measures and, under the heading of 'A suitable standard', it gave support to the views of the Standing Conference on National and University Libraries (SCONUL) that the following criteria were among those which were important in determining the level of recurrent expenditure: the number of subjects and branches of subjects in which teaching and research were carried on; the depth of research in each subject and the range of interests among the teaching staff; the extent to which the topography necessitated the establishment of outlying subject libraries, which usually involved duplication; and special responsibilities, e.g. the existence of special collections, etc., and local responsibilities, such as to hospital authorities, agricultural research and colleges of education.

As an indication of the scale of operations the committee quoted SCONUL's model annual budget for books, journals, binding and sundries for an established library of 500,000 volumes in a university of 3,000 undergraduates, 1,000 research students and 500 teaching staff, totalling £98,055. SCONUL estimated also that the model staffing costs of a library for a university of this size and composition would be about £60,000. Details of how these estimates were arrived at are given in Appendix 8 of the report, and the techniques used by SCONUL were recognizably based on the work of the West German Wissenschaftsrat, discussed earlier in this chapter.

The committee considered SCONUL's estimates 'realistic estimates if facilities are to be provided here which are comparable to those which exist in other developed countries'. A university of the size described, the committee said, might have a total annual budget of about £3,350,000. Annual library expenditure of £200,000 (on the SCONUL model) would represent approximately 6 per cent of the total university expenditure. This, though a marked increase on the then average expenditure of 3.8 per cent, was not a large proportion in relation to the significance of the library within the university. The committee stated that the decision on the library budget must be made by each institution in the light of its own circumstances, and that central regulations would not be desirable nor practicable. It submitted the figures not as a firm recommendation but 'as an indication of the change in their scale of values which universities must accept if their libraries are to be adequately provided for'.[1]

The committee recommended the establishment by the University Grants Committee of a sub-committee on university libraries whose primary duty would be to keep under constant review the standards and the needs of British university libraries. Although there were good precedents for such a proposal, it was not favoured by the Committee of Vice-Chancellors and Principals which, while accepting the need for such a body, preferred to have it as a sub-committee of itself. Accordingly, this body has set up a libraries committee primarily to advise it on national issues concerning university library provision but also to act as a point of liaison with individual universities on such issues.[2] In the latter connexion the committee has collected and assessed university reactions to suggestions for improving the availability of thesis material and for inter-library collaboration and resource allocation to libraries. General conclusions reached by the committee have subsequently been circulated to universities by way of guidance.[3]

---

1. The money estimates suggested by SCONUL were appropriate in 1965, but would now be considerably higher.
2. See Thomas Parry, 'University Libraries and the Future', *Library Association Record*, Vol. 70, No. 9, September 1968.
3. No documents available. Based on letter from Secretary.

UNITED STATES OF AMERICA

No official statements of general standards applicable to all university libraries have been made by either of the associations of librarians concerned, the Association of Research Libraries, or the Association of College and Research Libraries. Since 1968 a joint committee of these two bodies has been considering whether it is possible to produce such a statement of standards or other criteria for libraries of academic institutions stressing advanced research which it is felt is required if the libraries are to play their proper part in the developing and expanding academic programme.

The joint committee made extensive inquiries using fifty leading university libraries in the United States and Canada, which supplied comprehensive statistical and other data. In a document dated June 1969, entitled *University Library Statistics*, certain norms, derived from this study, were listed under six headings: finances, resources, personnel, space, circulation and public service, and professional school libraries of law and medicine.[1]

While recognizing that what the document referred to as 'valid standards' could not be established without further research, on the basis of the statistics suitably adjusted for improvement and growth, it proposed that these norms should be looked upon as 'criteria for judging excellence in university libraries'. They should be regarded as minima, establishing levels from which libraries should build towards greater distinction. Examples of these 'criteria of excellence' which illustrate clearly that the universities and libraries referred to are very large are given here.[2]

Finance: total library budget, $3 million; library's percentage of university expenditure, 5.

Resources: Total number of volumes, 2 million; volumes added annually, 100,000; current periodicals to be received, 15,000.

Personnel: Number of professional staff, 90; percentage of professional staff, 35.

Public service: Hours open per week, 100.

The proposals made in this document, at the time of writing this, have not been formally adopted and published as recommen-

1. Robert B. Downs and John W. Heussman, *University Library Statistics*, Washington, D.C., Association of Research Libraries, 1969.
2. A more detailed statement of these norms is given in *Library Trends*, October 1972, p. 194–8.

dations by the Association of College and Research Libraries and its parent body, the American Library Association. The document is, however, on record and doubtless has some influence in circumstances when information about standards is relevant.

In default of formal acceptance of these criteria, the only current document officially approved by the Association of College and Research Libraries (ACRL) and the American Library Association (ALA) concerns standards for college libraries. The term 'college' is used in the United States to refer to colleges or universities granting bachelors' or bachelors' and masters' degrees, and these standards do not apply to junior colleges,[1] nor to libraries of academic institutions stressing advanced work (i.e. undertaking doctoral and post-doctoral programmes), discussed above.

Standards for college libraries have been produced on several occasions since 1929 by the ALA and its division, the ACRL. The currently valid standards for college libraries were produced in 1959 and they have been in the course of revision since 1968. Revised standards referred to as *Guidelines for College Libraries*[2] produced by an *ad hoc* committee of the ACRL's Committee on Standards and Accreditation were rejected in 1971 by the college section of the association, largely because of the absence from the document of qualitative standards.

In 1973, under a new chairman, the committee resumed the work of revising the 1959 standards.

The aim of the project will be to take account of the many significant changes in higher education since that date. The revised standards will be based upon careful definition of goals, explicit recognition of assumptions, comprehensive identification and searching evaluation of the relevance of the evidence to the goals, and clear formulation of criteria of judgment.[3]

The following is a summary of the 1959 *Standards for College Libraries*.[4] This has been described as:

... the first comprehensive guide for the evaluating of college libraries embodying ... the compelling factors in good college library administration [and as having had] widespread prestige and influence.[5]

1. Normally offering a two-year, non-degree, and commonly vocational, course.
2. Association of College and Research Libraries, Standards and Accreditation Committee, *American Library Association Guidelines for College Libraries*, draft, November 1970 (mimeo).
3. See *College and Research Library News*, No. 9, October 1973.
4. American Library Association, 'Standards for College Libraries', *College and Research Libraries*, Vol. 20, No. 4, July 1959.
5. Helen M. Brown, 'College Libraries', *Library Trends*, October 1972.

Functions of the college library

This statement is quoted in full.

The college library should be the most important intellectual resource of the academic community. Its services, given by a competent staff of adequate size, should be geared to implement the purposes of the college's general programme and to meet the specific educational objectives of the institution. Its collections should aim at presenting the heritage of Western and Eastern thought in all its richness, but should stress those particular areas which are central to the curriculum of the institution. No artificial barriers should separate the library from the classroom or the library staff from the teaching faculty. Beyond supporting the instructional programme to the fullest extent, the library should endeavour to meet the legitimate demands of all its patrons, from the senior professor engaged in advanced research to the freshman just entering upon the threshold of higher learning, to stimulate and encourage the student to develop the lifelong habit of good reading, and to play its proper role in the community and in the wider realm of scholarship beyond the campus.

The standards laid down in this document must always be interpreted in the light of the aims and needs of the institution of which the library is a part.

Structure and government

If there is a committee on the library, its duties and authority should be clearly defined. It should be concerned with general policy only, and the relationship of the librarian—who should be responsible for administrative and executive matters—should be stated. The librarian should be directly responsible to the president (the head of the university or college) and should rank with other chief administrative officers. He should work in particularly close relationship with the head of the academic programme and should be a member of the college planning group for the curriculum and of any other committee whose activities will vitally affect the future of library service.

As a rule there should be a library faculty committee, acting in an advisory capacity, to interpret the problems and policy of the library to the academic staff, and make suggestions for the improvement of library service. The librarian should be a regular member of the committee and may serve as its chairman. Where possible, a student committee on the library should be established.

The librarian should plan and administer the library budget. All materials purchased from library funds or otherwise acquired should be part of the library and under the control of the librarian.

The organization of the library should be logical and suitable. Lines of authority should be clearly drawn. The librarian should seek advice of members of his staff on important matters of policy and procedure. Channels of communication with the staff should be well defined.

Budget

The funds provided for the support of the library will, in large measure, determine the quality of the library resources and services. The library's holdings, the prevailing methods of instruction, the size of faculty and student body, the extent to which the college encourages and provides for individual study and the variety of graduate offerings, are factors which influence the budgetary needs of the library.

The library budget should be determined in relation to the total budget of the institution for educational and general purposes. The programme of library service outlined in the standards will normally require a minimum of 5 per cent of the total educational and general budget. The percentage must be higher if the library's holdings are seriously deficient, if there is a rapid expansion in student population or courses, or if the institution offers a wide range of studies at the master's level or programmes of individual study. Experience shows that a good college library usually spends twice as much (or more) for salaries as for books.

It should be considered a serious danger signal if the library budget sinks appreciably below the median ratio of library expenditures to total educational and general institutional expenditures for comparable institutions as indicated in the latest annual college library statistics.

Staff

The library should be operated by a broadly educated and highly qualified staff of professional librarians, under the direction of a chief librarian. The professional librarian is defined as one holding a graduate library degree.

Three professional librarians constitute the minimum for effective service—the chief librarian and librarians responsible for reader services and technical processes. As well as student enrolment, other factors determine the number of librarians needed, such as the type of organization within the library, the size and character of the collections, the teaching methods, hours of opening and arrangement of the building. At least one professional librarian should be on duty at all times when the library is open.

There should be an adequate non-professional staff. The ratio of professional to non-professional staff will vary according to the needs of institutions. Student assistants may be employed for certain tasks. As the size of the library increases, the ratio of non-professional to the professional staff should be larger. While it may be impossible to have uniform standards for library staff, attention is drawn to formulas in certain states (New York and California).

Professional librarians should have faculty status, with the salary and other benefits enjoyed by the teaching staff. They should undertake graduate work in suitable areas to improve their effectiveness and opportunity should be given for engaging in such studies. Library staff should take an active part in the instructional programme of the institution. This should include formal and informal instruction in the use of the library. They should advise faculty members on bibliographical matters, work on committees, prepare reading lists and reports on library facilities and services. They may also teach a course in a subject area.

Members of the library staff must be chosen with great care. The chief librarian must have skill in organization and his thinking and planning must be that of a teacher and scholar.

Library collections

Books and periodicals
The collection of books, periodicals, pamphlets, documents, newspapers, maps, microfilm, microcards, microprint and other materials must be constituted and organized to give effective strength and support to the educational programme of the institution. It should meet the full curricular needs of undergraduate students and be easily accessible to them. It should provide for the demands of graduate students in each field in which the institution offers a master's degree. It should provide material for use by members of the faculty to keep them abreast of the latest advances in modern scholarship and assist them in their professional growth. If special

programmes of independent study are carried on, provision must be made for them.

In addition to the materials related directly or indirectly to the curriculum, the collection should contain the standard works which represent the heritage of civilization. These should be supplemented by current books which will arouse the intellectual curiosity of students and satisfy their recreational reading needs.

There should be a strong and up-to-date reference collection of the most authoritative reference works and bibliographies in all major fields of knowledge, not restricted to the needs of the curriculum nor to publications in the English language.

Periodicals should be chosen to meet the needs of students for course reading, to provide for some of the research needs of advanced students and teaching staff, to keep the latter informed of developments in their fields and to afford thought-provoking general and recreational reading. Newspapers provided should cover national, regional and local levels and include leading papers from abroad. Various political points of view should be represented.

The right of the librarian to select materials representing all sides of controversial issues must be safeguarded.

Quality should not be sacrificed to unnecessary duplication of titles, but works of lasting or contemporary importance should be available in sufficient numbers.

Obsolete materials and worn-out volumes should be continuously weeded with the advice of the teaching staff. A gifts policy should be defined and gifts should normally be integrated with the regular collections.

If funds are allocated to departments, a substantial portion should be reserved for direct assignment by the librarian. This should be large enough for the purchase of reference works, general publications, expensive sets, books for recreational reading and works which cross departmental lines, as well as for correcting weaknesses in the library's collection.

Library holdings should be checked frequently against standard bibliographies, both general and subject. A high percentage of listed titles which are relevant to the work of the individual institution, should be included in the library collections.

The size of the library collections is largely determined by the extent and nature of the curriculum, the number and character of graduate programmes, the methods of instruction, the size of the undergraduate and graduate student body, both full-time and extension, and the need of the faculty for more advanced materials which cannot be met conveniently by the use of research libraries in the area.

Analysis of small college library statistics suggests that no library can be expected to give effective support to the instructional programme if it contains fewer than 50,000 carefully chosen volumes. A steady growth is essential but the rate of growth may slow down when the number of volumes reaches approximately 300,000.

A convenient measure which may serve as a guide is the following: As a minimum up to 600 students there should be 50,000 volumes. For every additional 200 students there should be a further 10,000 volumes. Part-time and extension students should be equated into full-time students for this purpose. Stronger institutions will demand considerably larger and richer collections.

The library's collection should be fully organized for use. The main catalogue of the library should serve as a union catalogue for all collections of the library whether housed in the main building or in college departments. Advice is given as to cataloguing and classification.

Audio-visual materials
These, including films, filmstrips, recordings and tapes, are an integral part of modern instruction and every college library must concern itself with them. The library should take the initiative in providing them, if there is no other responsible agency. If the library handles this material, it should have special budgetary provisions and extra staff. The programme must be both financially and operationally part of the whole of the library's function. It cannot succeed without adequate facilities for the use of equipment and materials.

The same high standard is required for the selection of films and recordings as for books.

Buildings

Successful library service requires an adequate building, centrally located and functionally designed. The type of building will depend on the character and aims of the institution (e.g. residential or day students) but it should always meet the general demands of efficient operation. New building plans should include provision for future expansion.

The size of the building will depend on the type and size of institution, the instructional methods, the character of the collections and the number of volumes.

The seating capacity should be based on anticipated growth over a twenty-year period. Accommodation for at least one-third of the student body will be essential. The changing concept of the role of the library in the academic community may lead to an upward revision of this figure.

Provision should be made for expansion of reading areas, and book space must be sufficient for the foreseeable future. Shelf space should be planned so that it allows for at least doubling of the collection. Adequate housing is required for materials other than books.

Well-planned areas are required for all services provided; e.g. circulation and reference, display, rooms for listening to recordings.

Adequate quarters are required for the technical processes of the library. Staff work rooms should comprise at least 125 ft^2 (11.6 m^2) of floor space per person. Persons holding administrative positions should have adequate private office space. A staff lounge with kitchen facilities is desirable.

There should be proper conditions for heat, light and air. These and decoration should be planned so that students and teaching staff are encouraged to study in a comfortable atmosphere. The proper control of humidity and heat should also be provided for books and material, especially the rare and valuable.

College libraries should be equipped with well-designed library furniture. A variety of types of seating should be available including tables, carrels, individual desks, and comfortable lounge chairs away from tables. The table space of 3 by 2 ft (90 × 60 cm) per reader is recommended for general library use.

The quality of the service and its evaluation

Advice is given how to evaluate the quality of the service given. Ways suggested include the continuous evaluation of the statistical records of the circulation department, surveys of what students are reading at a given time, studies of books not supplied, reference questions not answered, and the character of inter-library loans.

Such methods should be used with caution. Much depends on the teaching methods employed; therefore the teaching staff should be kept informed of new publications, and new acquisitions, and the librarian should work closely with them as they plan new courses. The effectiveness of the instruction given by the staff in the use of the library will be seen from the way the students avail themselves of the library's resources.

Inter-library co-operation

The librarian must consider the important benefits to be derived from pooling the resources of his library with those of other libraries in the same community, region, state and nation. In particular the college library should co-operate with other college, university, school and public library agencies in the community and neighbouring area for reference service to readers beyond the campus. The librarian should also investigate the possibility of co-operation with other libraries in the area, e.g. for the planned purchase of materials to avoid unnecessary duplication. But he should not seek to borrow from other libraries materials which are basic to the college programme.

Libraries of institutions not forming part of a university

GENERAL

Examples of standards for library service in these institutions are included from four countries, all English speaking. No doubt there are others, since among educational establishments this has been a vigorously growing sector in the last decade or more, and the library has been assuming an increasing importance.

As stated earlier the academic levels in these establishments can be very high. In the polytechnics in the United Kingdom graduate and post-graduate work is undertaken, as well as a great number of other courses. In the colleges of education for intending teachers degree and post-graduate courses are provided. In the technical colleges and institutes and similar establishments, there and in other countries, the level of work can be high and the range of work wide, courses being provided from craft to professional level, with also a great and growing variety of study of a general, cultural and academic nature.

The recommended standards for library service in the junior colleges in the United States, the community colleges in Canada and in technical institutes and teacher-training colleges in New Zealand are also discussed.

There is plenty of common ground where the qualitative standards are concerned but little in regard to other matters, such as book stock and finance. This is not surprising but there is a wide discrepancy between the 2–3 per cent of total expenditure for the cost of the libraries in technical colleges suggested in the United Kingdom, the 8 per cent suggested for community colleges in Canada and the even higher figures mentioned as being actually spent in some technical institutes in New Zealand.

CANADA

As an educational institution, the Canadian community colleges take various forms, including, as well as general post-secondary establishments operating under that title, junior colleges, colleges with religious affiliations offering the first one or two years of university, institutes of technology, colleges of applied arts and technology, and agricultural colleges. They provide another avenue to the university, as well as terminal—largely vocational—courses. The Canadian Association of College and University Libraries in 1970 set up a committee to formulate standards for these libraries. These standards were adopted by the Canadian Library Association in 1972 and issued under the title of *Standards Recommended for Community College Libraries*.[1] The following is an abridgement of this document.

Introduction

Recognizing the emergence of community colleges in Canada during the 1960s, the Canadian Association of College and

1. Canadian Association of College and University Libraries, *Standards Recommended for Community College Libraries*, Ottawa, Canadian Library Association, 1973.

University Libraries were concerned about the orderly development of libraries in these new institutions. The programmes and courses offered at Canadian community colleges differed from those offered in similar colleges in the United Kingdom and in the junior colleges of the United States. Therefore, library standards written for these two countries could not be directly translated but many of the standards modified and updated in the light of Canadian experience were incorporated.

The role of the library and its staff was brought out in the section on qualitative standards. The section on quantitative standards represented the minimum necessary to permit a library to fulfil its role in a college's educational effort. A goal of the college was to provide its community with special knowledge and skills and enable persons in that community to acquire a competence in finding things out for themselves. In this the role of the library was of primary importance.

Qualitative standards

Administration and organization
The final responsibility for the library belonged with the college's chief administrator and the governing board. The library was identified with the instruction process and was within the area of responsibility of the chief academic authority of the college. The professional library staff should be active members of all relevant curriculum planning committees. In multi-campus facilities library administration should be centralized, although it was necessary to provide adequate collections, staff, facilities and services at each campus. There should be a library committee representing all users, concerned also with policy relating to the community served by the college. Library administration should be based on library staff participation in policy, procedural and personnel decisions. There should be regular collecting and dissemination of information concerning the library.

Staff
Minimum qualifications for librarians, professional specialists and library assistants were specified. Librarians should be appointed on the same basis as teaching staff. The chief librarian should have demonstrated administrative abilities in addition to the minimum

academic qualifications. Each staff grouping should be assigned tasks appropriate to their education and training. Library technical and clerical staff should be responsible to a professional staff member. Continued professional development was both a responsibility and an obligation of professional staff. This included participation in college affairs and in professional associations. Students might be employed to supplement the technical and clerical staff but should not be considered as substitutes for an adequate full-time staff.

Collections
There should be a general statement of selection policy, frequently reviewed, and approved by the college's governing board. The collections might consist of any material, regardless of physical form, which would support the learning process. These materials should be carefully selected, systematically organized and attractively displayed. The needs of bilingual and multi-lingual communities should be reflected in the collections, together with materials encouraging informal education and cultural enrichment. The library staff faculty members and students should continually evaluate and upgrade the library's collections.

The reference stock should be as comprehensive and current as possible. Departmental collections of materials inhibited ready access to them and should be prohibited. Reserve book collections should not be considered as a substitute for an adequate number of copies in the main collections.

The selection, purchasing, etc., and disseminating of audio-visual materials should be administered in the library, together with their use in the library. Depending on local circumstances, the provision of other audio-visual services to the college community might be administered by the library. If provided by a separate agency within the college, adequate liaison with the library was essential.

Building
Library space should be planned and designed to meet the requirements of the individual colleges. The design of the building space should be the joint responsibility of the college administration, the librarian and the architect. The library should be centrally situated. Adequate space should allow for flexibility and variety for the use of materials by users with many needs. Spaces should be designed for such activities as discussion, listening, viewing,

typing and group/individual study. A variety of seating should be available: study carrels, group study places, informal seating, and seminar rooms. Adequate space should be provided for staff working areas, with consideration of proximity to essential equipment and materials.

Budget
The budget should be the responsibility of the chief librarian. Different kinds of financial support were needed: initial budgets for a new college library; special budgets for new courses; multi-campus operations, and continuing budgets for maintenance. The total library budget should be sufficient to provide for the optimum satisfaction of the library's users. The budget should include the cost of: books/audio-visual materials, promotional materials, salaries and wages, fringe benefits, travel, conference expenses, office expenses, etc. It should exclude buildings, janatorial, or other building services.

Public services
Hours of service should meet all reasonable demands and full services should be available when the library was open, except possibly for multi-campus colleges. Circulation services should provide an easily understood and consistent set of rules. The staff should provide formal and informal instruction in library use. The library should co-operate with all libraries and agencies to prevent unnecessary duplication of little-used material and services. All college libraries should participate with other libraries in international lending.

Technical processing services
The librarian should select the vendors for the purchase of library materials, for reasons of speed and economy. Whenever practicable college libraries should make use of a central agency for the acquisition, cataloguing, classifying and processing of library materials. Standards for the cataloguing and classification of library materials should meet the needs of its users and should conform to the accepted professional standards of the Anglo-American code. Catalogues should be designed for library users. The card catalogue was standard, but alternative forms should be explored for general and specialized use.

Quantitative standards

Collections
Colleges with special needs would require larger library collections than the minima.

To provide a basic collection for colleges with an enrolment of up to 1,000 full-time equivalent students, there should be a minimum of 40,000 bibliographic units (i.e. any print or non-print item, or group of items, requiring a separate and distinct catalogue entry). A basic collection should include at least 600 current periodical titles. In colleges with more than 1,000 full-time equivalent students, there should be an additional 5,000 bibliographical units for each additional 200 such students.

Seating
There should be independent study seating for 30 per cent of the student enrolment. Although the requirements would vary, the 'in-library' seating should not fall below 20 per cent of the full-time equivalent student enrolment.

Staff
Staff required depended on the size of the college, the number and types of programmes taught, the services offered to the college and community, the number of branch libraries maintained, the availability of centralized processing, formal agreements with other institutions for library services, hours of opening, etc. The following minima should be met: four professional librarians for colleges with up to 1,000 full-time equivalent students, and one professional librarian for each additional 300-500 students. There should be three library support staff for every professional librarian.

Budget
The budget during the establishment years of the college should enable the library to meet the minimum standards as quickly as possible. This amount should exceed the recommended percentage for continued operation, which was 8 per cent of the college's annual educational and general budget.

NEW ZEALAND

Standards for teachers' training-college libraries

The report of the commission on education in New Zealand, published in 1962, recommended that the provision of libraries for teachers' colleges be further examined, and the New Zealand Teachers' College Association asked the New Zealand Library Association to devise library standards for teachers' college libraries. A report entitled *Standards for Teachers' College Libraries* was issued in 1967.[1] The standards are currently being revised.

This described the role of the library, referring to the changes resulting from the extension of the training course from two to three years 'which will call for a much more imaginative and extensive use of the library'. The resources of the library should be mainly devoted to the subjects being taught in the college but should also include a comprehensive and up-to-date junior collection required for courses on children's books and for teaching practice. There should be available a collection of classroom texts covering the basic subjects in the curriculum. College libraries should provide some support for advanced reading by the staff in their own and related fields, and should also include a representative collection of good-quality recreational reading.

A college with 1,000 students, offering a three-year course, would require at least 50,000 carefully chosen volumes. Periodicals should be carefully chosen to support the college courses and to keep staff informed of developments in their subjects: 200 to 250 titles would seem to be a minimum to give a coverage for general college courses. Steady growth was essential; an annual growth rate of 4–5 per cent or 2,000 to 2,500 volumes was suggested. The stock should be as carefully weeded as selected. Audio-visual material, such as maps, classroom pictures, art prints, filmstrips, gramophone records, should be in sufficient quantity to meet student courses and teaching practice requirements. They should be centrally housed and administered.

Services provided by the library should include reading facili-

1. New Zealand Library Association, *Standards for Teachers' College Libraries*, Wellington, 1967.

ties, both reference and lending, reference and information services and formal instruction to students.

The role and responsibilities of the staff were described and minimum qualifications stated. Instruction of students to use the library skilfully was a co-operative activity in which both the teaching staff and the librarian play a part. Teaching the use of the library was part of the librarian's professional work. Staffing standards were suggested for a college of 1,000 students, namely a librarian and deputy librarian; two intermediate assistants; four library or clerical assistants. Criteria for professional, intermediate and clerical duties were indicated in an appendix.

The role and desirable characteristics of the library buildings were discussed and a number of standards stated. Reader accommodation was recommended at 20 per cent of the combined staff and student rolls, at 30 ft² (2.8 m²) staff and 25 ft² (2.3 m²) students. Space for books was estimated at 100 ft² (9.3 m²) for each 1,000 volumes. Space requirements were given for periodicals, visual-aid materials, staff room and other purposes, including a seminar room (300 ft² or 27.9 m²). A total working area of 13,800 ft² (1,280 m²) was suggested for a college of 1,000 students. (To compare this with other standards quoted an addition of the order of 25 per cent would need to be made for circulation, services, etc.)

Standards for libraries in technical institutes
The New Zealand Library Association published in 1973 *Standards for Libraries in Technical Institutes* described in the introduction as 'the new Institutes which will be at varying stages of development for yet some time to come'.[1] The institutes offer a wide range of instructional and vocational education varying from trade to professional level.

For a new institute with several fields of study amounting to 200,000 'weighted student hours' (WSH) it was suggested there should be a stock of 5,000 volumes to be achieved not later than three years after the establishment of the institute. For each succeeding 100,000 WSH there should be an increase of 1,500 books.

The number of periodical subscriptions should be related to weighted student hours. For a new institute with 200,000 WSH

1. New Zealand Library Association, *Standards for Libraries in Technical Institutes*, Wellington, 1973.

there should be a basic collection of forty periodicals and for each succeeding 100,000 WSH there should be an increase of sixteen journals.

Multi-media materials should be provided.

A growth rate of between 5 and 8 per cent in volumes would be appropriate once the basic stock had been achieved.

There should be adequate and continuing provision made to continue the full range of services provided by the library. The exact figure would vary according to the nature of the institution. In some institutions as high as 10–14 per cent of the institute's general expenses grant was being used for book stock, including periodicals, and higher figures would be necessary in developing institutions. As the size of grant varied from year to year and institution to institution, no fixed or minimum percentage could be recommended.

Staff numbers would depend on the work load, which in broad terms would vary with the teaching load. The smallest institute should have a minimum staff of three, if a full service, with long hours, was required. For an institute with an enrolment of 2.5 million WSH it was suggested that a staff of eleven would be required.

The ratio of professional to intermediate and clerical grades should normally be 40 : 60, professional : non-professional, as recommended by the United Kingdom Library Association.

Building and design standards were also included.

UNITED KINGDOM

In the United Kingdom the higher education establishments which are not universities, or parts of universities, are not without some guidance about the desirable provision for library service, either from the Department of Education and Science or from the Library Association. In this section reference will be made to the documents currently relevant.

Polytechnics

In the United Kingdom there have recently been established thirty institutions, called polytechnics, to exist side by side with universities and to undertake comparable but largely different work. These polytechnics have been formed out of a grouping of existing major technical colleges, colleges of commerce and colleges of art. Basically providing courses in science and various technologies, they are developing work in the humanities and social sciences.

The Library Association in 1968 issued recommended standards for the libraries in the new polytechnics in the form of a *Guide to Planning Requirements*.[1] The difficulties of creating standards for institutions which will not necessarily provide for similar ranges of disciplines, nor are necessarily housed on a single site, are noted but the document offers guidelines to the type of library materials needed and to the staffing, space and expenditure necessary.

It is proposed that the libraries should be developed as 'learning resource centres' containing books and periodicals covering in embryo the whole range of recorded knowledge and non-book material and facilities for their use. The library should play a central role in the educational programme as a major teaching instrument to stimulate intellectual curiosity and independent learning and to counteract the specialization inculcated by the teaching courses.

Additionally, the library had a positive role to play as an information communication centre. The implications of all these concepts have been described, e.g. use of the library must be associated jointly with lectures and practical work as principal media for teaching as well as learning.

In considering the requirements for stock and seating within the polytechnic library, in order to reflect the principles outlined, a number of factors had to be considered, e.g. the library must represent knowledge as a whole, although the majority of items added would be within the academic disciplines taught in the polytechnic; applied research and, in particular, project work in the final year of sandwich courses,[2] would call for a substantial provision of retrospective journal holdings in the library. Centralized technical services and the provision of specialized reading areas giving access to material associated with particular groups of disciplines were necessary. The library stock should include

1. The Library Association, 'Libraries in the New Polytechnics—A Guide to Planning Requirements', *Library Association Record*, Vol. 70, No. 9, September 1968.
2. Courses in which the students spend extended periods away from the polytechnic in practical training in industrial, commercial or other establishments.

tapes, records, films and microforms, with the necessary special equipment.

Quantitative standards proposed included the following:

Seating

A rough guide would be 1 : 4 for the scientific and technological disciplines; 1 : 3 for other disciplines; 1 : 10 for part-time students irrespective of discipline. Areas: 25 ft² (2.32 m²) per undergraduate; 35 ft² (3.26 m²) for post-graduate students, students of art, architecture and other similar disciplines.

Books and periodicals

A basic stock of 150,000 volumes and 3,000 periodical titles was required for a polytechnic with over 2,000 undergraduate students and offering a wide range of disciplines, including the humanities, and encouraging linguistic and regional studies in both commerce and technology. A minimum annual budget of £60,000, at 1967 prices, would be necessary for books and periodicals and £10,000 for other library recording material—tapes, records, films, etc.

For the book stock, 80 per cent should be in open access at 90 ft² (8.36 m²) per 1,000 volumes, and 20 per cent in limited access at 45 ft² (4.18 m²) per 1,000 volumes was proposed. For display of current periodicals, 1 ft² (90 cm²) per periodical was required.

Staff

A detailed guide to staffing requirements was provided. Number and kind of staff will vary with the work load. Responsibility for the reading areas should be in the hands of professional librarians with subject knowledge or experience. These librarians must be in close contact with the academic staff.

Accommodation

Guidance was given as to other space requirements, for library staff, lecture, seminar and tutorial rooms incorporated in the library suite, audio and visual equipment, etc.

The government's White Paper on polytechnics[1] indicated that these institutions needed to develop links with industry, colleges

---

1. Department of Education and Science, *A Plan for Polytechnics and Other Colleges*, London, HMSO, 1967 (Cmnd 3006, and Circular 8/66, 24 May 1966); Department of Education and Science, *Notes on Procedure for the Approval of Polytechnic Projects*, 1971.

and schools in their areas. The Library Association's document stated that the concentration and development of library resources in the polytechnics could make a significant regional contribution and help satisfy the information requirements of the professional community of the region. The need for inter-library co-operation and co-ordination was stressed, as also was the role the polytechnic libraries could play in helping industry and commerce, not only to consult recorded material but to obtain guidance in solving their problems.

Technical colleges

The Library Association in 1965 issued recommended standards of library provision in colleges of technology and other establishments of further education, a development of earlier documents first published in 1957. These standards were revised in 1971 by the association's Committee of the Colleges of Technology and Further Education Section and the latest document is *College Libraries: Recommended Standards of Library Provision in Colleges of Technology and Other Establishments of Further Education.*[1]

The standards were prefaced by a 'Policy Statement on College Libraries and Learning Resources' by the Council of the Library Association pointing out the large number (some 200) of college libraries which were actively engaged in organizing collections of audio-visual material, for which the library was the natural repository. Developments in educational technology and a change in emphasis from teaching to a variety of learning situations had led to the establishment of learning resource centres, which acted as a focal point for the storage, indexing and use of non-book media. The council recommended that learning resource areas should be a normal part of future college library provision, that those which were being developed apart from existing libraries should be associated with them and that college librarians and staff should be encouraged to attend relevant courses in the organization and exploitation of the media.

The new standards were called for by the increasing awareness

1. The Library Association, *College Libraries: Recommended Standards of Library Provision in Colleges of Technology and Other Establishments of Further Education,* 2nd ed., rev., London, The Library Association, 1971.

of the role of the library in the college, the exhortations of government departments in the United Kingdom concerned with education and science and of the Council for National Academic
Awards,[1] the growth of liberal studies and the widening of curricula.

Administration
The college library was a college service and must be an integral
part of the college. The professional staff must be members of
the academic staff of the college with a responsibility to the college
and to student users, and to one head, the principal. While
co-operation with other libraries was essential, subordination to
any outside authority would lead to the failure of the library to
function adequately and make it difficult for the librarian to
develop his true role within the college.

Standards of library use
Staff used the library for many purposes and they promoted its
use by example, precept and encouragement. The library's stock
should be sufficient to meet the main needs in all subjects taught
in the college, apart from the books which students should buy.
The college library service was a quality service, the personal
assistance received from the professional staff being of the greatest
value.

Services to users
These were discussed under headings: reading facilities—reference
and lending; guidance to users; courses in efficient library usage;
information services; co-operation with other library and information services; services to industry and commerce; index and
abstracting services; library publications; exhibitions and displays;
times of library service (normally 66 hours a week, except during
vacations when office hours would suffice).

Books and other library material
Stock planning policy. The main guiding principles for a stock
planning policy were (a) basic initial stock should be bought on
capital expenditure to meet all major requirements; (b) annual
additions should build up the library to meet all general demands

---

1. A national body responsible for accrediting courses and awarding degrees.

and to provide reasonably for the needs of all those engaged on project reports, theses and research; (c) stock which became dated or unreliable should be withdrawn or relegated to a historical collection; (d) adequate financial allowance should be made to cover advances in subject fields, wider coverage of existing subjects and provide for new courses.

Application of a stock planning policy
This was discussed in considerable detail under the headings: bibliographical aids; general reference books; standard works; liberal studies and general reading; periodicals; research material; pamphlets, reports and trade literature; illustrations and slides. Quantitative standards proposed in this section were: (a) periodicals—the number of current periodicals should range from around 100 for a small college to a minimum of 600 for a college with a substantial amount of advanced work. A college of art undertaking advanced work should take about 200 current periodicals, including the most important (especially European) journals; (b) illustrations and slides—these were indispensable in a college of art. A substantial collection was necessary—a minimum of 40,000 art and architecture slides and 20,000 general illustrations.

Basic initial stock on capital expenditure. The basic stock for a college without degree work should be not less than 10,000 book titles and for a larger college, with some degree work or specialized advanced courses, not less than 25,000 titles. Multiple copies of books, periodicals, pamphlets, audio-visual and other non-book material, and stock particularly for thesis and post-graduate work, were also required.

Annual additions to stock. These were supplementary to, and not a substitute for, the basic stock. They were required, for example, for new courses and new research topics; to fill gaps in subject coverage.

Stock revision. The policy should be to remove all superseded stock, permanently or by transfer to a reserve collection. Periodicals of an ephemeral nature should be discarded fairly quickly, the remainder being retained for about two to five years or to fit in with local or national schemes of co-operative storage. It was usually more economic to borrow older titles from a conserving library. For long runs microform would prove most satisfactory.

Trends of growth

Book stock growth was a steady natural process due to excess of additions over withdrawals. Research stock was a problem as it was virtually preserved indefinitely; in addition the bulk of research and abstract journals published doubled at least every fifteen years. Difficulties might be overcome by using microform and by local arrangements for sharing resources.

It was probable that large colleges would need to accommodate stocks of over 50,000 volumes. In colleges of art doing advanced work the figure would be 25,000 volumes. In addition thousands of pamphlets and much other non-book material would be required.

Library staffing

Staff numbers would depend on the work load which would vary with the college teaching load. A ratio of one member of library staff to every twenty teachers would be required, with normally a ratio of forty professional to sixty non-professional staff. Increases on the basic figure would result from the needs of separate libraries or extra service points, and particularly heavy demands made by certain types of user, e.g. research workers and advanced students.

The college librarian should be a chartered librarian[1] with wide library experience and some training in teaching. He should be directly responsible to the principal and be a member of the academic council and other college bodies. Professional library staff should also be chartered librarians competent to teach students how to use the library efficiently. There should also be sufficient non-professional staff.

Buildings

Guidance was given under the headings: (a) General—siting, concentration or dispersal of facilities; convenience of access; freedom from disturbance; planning for and methods of expansion. (b) Construction—functional planning; standards of finish; flexibility; noise control; lighting—natural and artificial; services. (c) Size—the library area was defined as laid down in the Department of Education and Science *Building Bulletin No. 5* and the

---

1. A chartered librarian is one who, having passed the requisite examinations and undergone the prescribed three years training under supervision in libraries, has been entered upon the register maintained by the professional body, the Library Association.

Scottish Education Department's *Further Education Building Code*, 1968. Student seating requirements should be on the basis of places to students, science and technology 1 : 5, pure science 1 : 4, other disciplines 1 : 3, with 25 ft² (2.32 m²) undergraduate and 35 ft² (3.25 m²) post-graduate. Also discussed were staff and research seating requirements; teaching accommodation; shelving capacities; other space requirements including specialist space (e.g. non-book media) and service space; cloakroom; display.

Total space requirements were estimated at 6,000 ft² (557 m²) for a small college and 18,000 ft² (1,672 m²) for a large college, but would be based on the Department of Education and Science's and Scottish Education Department's maximum student capacity figures in the two documents previously referred to.

Finance
Advice was given on capital funds and special grants and on the annual budget under the headings of annual expenditure on books, periodicals and other resource materials; annual periodicals expenditure; expenditure on other library material; other items of library expenditure.

Conclusions and recommendations
Measures which appeared necessary to ensure satisfactory standards of service in college libraries included (a) that college librarians should be members of bodies responsible for internal direction of general college affairs, (b) that college library expenditure should be 2 to 3 per cent of the total college expenditure, (c) that colleges took particular note of the guidance of the library advisory service and inspectors of the Department of Education and Science or the Scottish Education Department, (d) that annual reports and statistical information on the college library service should be supplied as required by the local education authority to the Department of Education and Science or the Scottish Education Department.

Concluding, the document stated that not all the recommendations could be applicable to every type of college and no standards could ever be final. Future developments would render some of the standards obsolete, but they were offered as applicable to the current and future foreseeable services necessary in the colleges.

The Department of Education and Science, the government department responsible for libraries, has issued a number of documents on library standards appropriate to technical colleges and similar establishments. The first, Circular 322 of 12 April 1957,[1] discussed the functions of the college library and gave advice about staff, accommodation, books and periodicals and equipment. This is by now in some ways out of date. The second, a building bulletin on new colleges of further education,[2] gave advice on libraries. The numerical standards quoted in the circular and bulletin have been largely superseded by more recent developments in which higher standards of buildings, derived from higher standards of service, have been indicated.

Such building standards were available in the *Notes on Procedure for the Approval of Further Education Projects (Other than Polytechnics)*.[3] The appropriate 'usable area' for such a college library was dependent on the number of students and on the level of courses, higher allowances being given for colleges where work at the advanced level was at least 30 per cent of the whole.

The allowances were as follows: (a) colleges with at least 30 per cent advanced work, 390 m² for the first 500 'full-time equivalent' students,[4] then 0.44 m² for each additional student; (b) colleges with less than 30 per cent advanced work, 300 m² for the first 500 'full-time equivalent' students, then 0.38 m² for each additional student.

These allowances were intended to permit the provision of readers' seats on a scale of one to every eight 'full-time equivalent' students, display and storage for books and periodicals, counter and catalogue areas, a librarian's office, a workroom, seminar and tutorial rooms and carrels for private study attached to the library suite, and, possibly, facilities for photocopying and a darkroom. For the remainder of the accommodation required, for circulation space, etc., a further allowance of 25 per cent of the usable area was made.

1. Ministry of Education, *Libraries in Technical Colleges* (Circular 322, 12 April 1957).
2. Ministry of Education, *New Colleges of Further Education*, 1959 (Building bulletin No. 5).
3. Department of Education and Science, *Notes on Procedure for the Approval of Further Education Projects (Other than Polytechnics)*, 1971.
4. 'Full-time equivalent' students were calculated on the basis of: full-time and sandwich course student = 1; block release = $\frac{1}{3}$; part-time = $\frac{2}{9}$; evenings only = nil.

Colleges of education

Colleges of education are normally concerned solely with the training of teachers through three-year non-degree, four-year Bachelor of Education, and one-year post-graduate courses. The Association of Teachers in Colleges of Education and Departments of Education and the Library Association jointly published in 1967 *College of Education Libraries: Recommended Standards for their Development.*[1]

This described the functions of this type of library and referred to the increased demands likely to be made on it by the development of the university degree courses in education.

The library must therefore be both a comprehensive general and academic library and a professional library for prospective teachers, where all aspects of education and children's interests, including textbooks, audio-visual aids and children's books are amply represented.

Library planning and organization were discussed and space standards proposed for staff and students seating, shelving and circulation space, work space and other requirements. Reading areas were suggested on the basis that at least 25 per cent of the staff and students might be in the library at the same time and an area of 25 ft² (2.32 m²) per reader. It was recommended that shelving for four-fifths of the library's book stock should be provided on the basis of 75 ft² (7 m²) per 1,000 volumes. The remainder should be in stack areas at 55 ft² (5.1 m²) per 1,000 volumes. The main college library should have a minimum of 20,000 volumes of currently effective stock, for loan and reference for the subjects taught and for other general needs. In addition, a school services section, comprising children's books and textbooks needed by students on school practice, must have a minimum of 7,500 volumes.

Experience, it was said, suggested that the rate of purchased additions required in a general college of 500 or more students was sixty books per student every ten years. In colleges of less than 500, a higher rate of at least seventy five books per student

---

1. Association of Teachers in Colleges of Education and Departments of Education and the Library Association, *College of Education Libraries: Recommended Standards for their Development*, London, 1967.

was needed to cover the same basic requirements. It was proposed that general colleges should aim at minimal book stocks in the main library and in the school services library within ten years (see Table 4).

It was recommended that the library should be in charge of a highly qualified graduate librarian. There should also be a deputy librarian and a sufficient non-professional staff. A minimum staffing scale, as seen in Table 5, was proposed.

Finally, the need was stressed to co-operate with other libraries, through the nation-wide system of inter-library lending, through

TABLE 4

No. of students in college	No. of volumes		
	Main library	School services library	Total
500	31,000	8,600	39,000
750	43,000	11,750	54,750
1,000	55,000	15,250	70,250

TABLE 5

Total number of students[1]	Total annual book fund[1] (in pounds sterling)	Professional staff	Non-professional staff
Up to 500	Up to 4,125	1 librarian, 1 assistant librarian	1
500–750	4,125–5,362	1 librarian, 1 assistant librarian	2
750–1,000	5,362–6,600	1 librarian, 2 assistant librarians	2
1,000–1,250	6,600–7,837	1 librarian, 1 deputy librarian, 2 assistant librarians	3
Over 1,250	Over 7,837	1 librarian, 1 deputy librarian, 2 assistant librarians	4

1. In the first and second columns apply whichever factor was higher.

local schemes and with the libraries of the institutes and schools of education in the universities.[1]

The Department of Education and Science, in communications to the colleges of education concerning the basis of grants paid to voluntary colleges and the design of college libraries, have indicated standards for these libraries which the government was able in current circumstances to support. These standards, while in certain respects lower than those proposed by the Association of Teachers in Colleges and Departments of Education and the Library Association, are broadly on similar lines.

A circular letter of 6 March 1968[2] included the following minimum book-stock targets to be reached over the next ten years, excluding provision for degree work and provision for out-posts: colleges with 500 or less students, 30,000 volumes; colleges with 750 students, 40,500 volumes; 1,000 students, 52,500 volumes; 1,250 students, 60,300 volumes; 1,500 students, 68,820 volumes.

A report of a committee on non-teaching staff in maintained colleges of education, issued by the department in 1968, gave advice on and recommended quantitative standards for staffing of libraries in these colleges.[3]

In small colleges of under 350 students, the practice of having the library under the control of a member of the teaching staff might, it said, have to continue, provided the library had a qualified librarian on the staff. With this exception the committee considered the college librarian should be a librarian and a graduate, that teaching qualifications and experience would also be ideal, and that a deputy librarian should be appointed in a college of about 1,000 students. The college librarian and deputy,

1. The institutes and schools of education are organizations whose primary objectives are the training of teachers, the development of educational research and the provision of advanced courses to teachers already practising in schools. Each institute has responsibility for these matters in its area and each (with one exception) is a department of a university. The area controlled by each institute is large and contains several thousand practising teachers, a number of colleges of education, and a university department of education (which provides a one-year post-graduate course for intending teachers). The Library Association in 1963 issued recommendations for libraries in institutes and schools of education. See: The Library Association, 'Libraries in Institutes and Schools of Education', *Library Association Record*, Vol. 65, No. 9, September 1963.
2. Department of Education and Science, *College Letter No. 2/68*, 6 March 1968 (ref. R34/65/01).
3. Department of Education and Science, *Second Report of the Committee on Non-teaching Staff in Maintained Colleges of Education*, 1968.

TABLE 6

No. of students in college	Librarians (equated with academic staff)	Assistant librarians (qualified but not equated with academic staff)	Clerks	Total
350–550	I	I	I	3
550–750	I	I	1–2	3–4
750–1,000	I	1–2	2–3	4–6
1,000–1,300	I	2–3[1]	2–3	5–7
Over 1,300	I	2–3[1]	3–4	6–8

1. One might be graded deputy librarian and equated with academic staff.

TABLE 7

No. of students	Recommended areas		No. of students	Recommended areas	
	ft²	m²		ft²	m²
100	1,150	100	700	7,590	710
200	2,300	210	800	8,510	800
300	3,450	320	900	9,430	880
400	4,600	430	1,000	10,350	960
500	5,750	530	1,100	11,210	1,040
600	6,675	620	1,200	12,070	1,120

Note: These areas are net. An addition of 25 per cent should be made for circulation, service, etc.

who would have tutoring functions, should be equated with the academic staff. Other qualified librarians of junior rank (not so equated) and non-professionals should be appointed as necessary on the scale as shown in Table 6.

On the design of libraries in colleges of education, the department in 1969 issued to colleges a study paper[1] and in procedural notes dated January 1969[2] indicated what areas, as seen from Table 7, would be approved for library (including book store) and private study space.

1. Department of Education and Science, *The Design of Libraries in Colleges of Education,* 1969.
2. Department of Education and Science, *Notes on Procedure for Approval of College of Education Building Projects,* January 1969.

UNITED STATES OF AMERICA

Junior colleges

The junior, or two-year, colleges have been defined as:

... any institution of higher education which offers less than a baccalaureate
degree and requires its students either to be high school graduates or beyond high
school age. Comprehensive community colleges, public and private junior colleges, and technical institutes are included.

The colleges have been described as a distinctly American contribution to higher education, whose role continued to be defined to
meet new demands placed on them. In such dynamic institutions,
as the institutional objectives of the institution change, standards
for learning resources have to be reviewed, and if necessary revised,
more frequently than for other types of academic institutions.
Quantitative standards prepared by librarians date from the early
1930s but present-day standards had their roots in the Standards
for Junior College Libraries published by the Association of College
and Research Libraries, American Library Association, in 1960.
    James O. Wallace, upon whose article much of the early part of
this section is based, has explained how these standards, which
raised controversial issues, constituted a professional landmark and
how they contributed to library development in two-year colleges.[1]
Gradually these standards became more obsolete, particularly
because of the need to accept the concept of the merging of library
and audio-visual services and of the development of State systems of
two-year colleges and other co-operative arrangements. It became
necessary in the late 1960s to revise the standards and this task was
undertaken by ALA through ACRL, jointly with representatives
of the American Association of Junior Colleges (AAJC). This led to
the issue of a new document, *A.A.J.C.–A.C.R.L. Guidelines for Two-
Year College Library Learning Resource Centers*, known as the 1971 joint
guidelines.
    The term 'guidelines' used in the title, was chosen to suggest a
level of performance for self evaluation, rather than 'standards', the
latter term now recognized by ALA as something measurable,

1. James O. Wallace, 'Two-year College Library Standards', *Library Trends*,
October 1972, p. 219.

enforceable and directly related to library goals. Unlike the 1960 standards, and like the rejected draft of the revised standards for college libraries, the new 'guidelines' did not contain quantitative recommendations on the grounds that research had not been available to support such figures.

But even before the new document was approved and published steps were being taken to revise it. A further document 'Guidelines for Two-Year College Learning Resources Programs' was thus written and approved during 1972 by ACRL–AAJC, with a third partner, the Association for Educational Communications and Technology.[1] Like its immediate predecessor, this document, summarized below, does not establish minimal, or accreditation, standards, but it provides qualitative recommendations based upon successful practice in leading institutions.

Guidelines for two-year college learning resources programmes, 1972

Introduction
A general section discussed the present and likely future role of two-year colleges. It referred to the parallel evolution of libraries away from their traditional function as repositories of books, and of audio-visual centres away from their traditional function as agencies showing films. Contemporary Learning Resources Programmes in two-year colleges were supportive of institution-wide efforts. Essential to the success of such programmes was the involvement of learning resources staff with teaching, and of administrative and other staff members in the design, implementation and evaluation of instructional and educational systems of the institution. Many aspects of traditional library and audio-visual services in the colleges and the integration of these services had not been studied adequately for long-range projection of needs. The guidelines might, however, serve as the foundations for research and experiment in organization, structures and services. The changing role of two-year colleges might well result in institutions quite different from those now in operation.

---

1. 'Guidelines for Two-Year College Learning Resources Programs', *College and Research Libraries News*, No. 11, December 1972, p. 305.

The role of the learning resources programme
Because of its direct relationship to the institutional and instructional objectives, the Learning Resources Programme had a fourfold role: (a) to provide leadership and assistance in the development of instructional systems which employed effective and efficient means of accomplishing those objectives; (b) to provide an organized and readily accessible collection of materials and supportive equipment needed to meet institutional, instructional, and individual needs of students and faculty; (c) to provide a staff qualified, concerned and involved in serving the needs of students, faculty and community; (d) to encourage innovation, learning, and community service by providing facilities and resources which would make them possible.

The student must be able to explore fields of knowledge which would enhance his potential and be relevant to him. This must include active participation in the classroom and the laboratory, self-directed study, and the use of individualized instructional resources. The design of the instructional system, utilizing a configuration of resources, was a joint responsibility of administrators, teaching faculty, and the learning resources staff.

Students' success in achieving instructional objectives was heavily dependent on access to materials. Both student and staff functioned at their best when learning resources programmes were adequately conceived, staffed and financed. Learning resources programmes expressed the educational philosophy of the institution.

A glossary defined terms used: two-year college; learning resources programme; learning resources unit; instructional development functions; instructional systems components; instructional product design; staff; professional staff; supportive staff; system(s) approach; materials.

The guidelines were given under the following six headings. Each criterion was stated affirmatively followed by an explanatory comment.

Objectives and purpose
Many of these have already been referred to in connexion with the introduction. An additional criterion was that learning resource programmes should have a statement of defined purposes and objectives, which should, among other things, state that the

programmes should co-operate in the development of area, regional, and state networks, consortia or systems.

Organization and administration

Responsibilities for all learning resources and services should be assigned to a central administrative unit, the chief administrator of which should report directly to the college's administrative officer responsible for the instructional programme. The professional staff members of the learning resources programme should participate in all areas of academic planning, through participation in college-wide committees. Advisory committees of faculty and students were essential for the evaluation and extension of services. Internal administration of a learning resources programme should be based on staff participation in policy, procedure and personal decisions. Statistics were required for internal analysis and planning, and should be collected in terms of the definitions and methods of reporting laid down in federal and professional publications.

Centralized administration was recommended in order to co-ordinate resources and services, to develop system approaches to needs and to utilize staff effectively. Materials should be located in the areas where learning took place. All collections of materials should be considered the resources of the whole college and not limited to use in separate departments.

Multi-campus two-year college districts should take advantage of opportunities for close co-operation, exchange of resources, and shared technical processes, while providing full resources and services for every campus.

Budget

Budget planning for the learning resources programmes should reflect the instructional materials needs. Purchases of materials were based on curricular requirements and other factors and should be made throughout the year and not yearly or half-yearly. Where possible they should be exempt from annual bidding requirements for learning materials, restricting purchases to one source of supply. Co-operative purchasing should be effected wherever possible.

Instructional system components

Staff. The chief administrator of the learning resources programme should be professionally knowledgeable in all types of materials and services and capable of management of instructional development functions. The number of professional and supporting staff would vary, depending on the size and programme of the institution, the hours operated, the physical facilities, the scope and nature of the services performed, and the number of specializations of professional and supporting staff. Student assistants should be employed to supplement the work of the supporting staff.

Professional staff members should have degrees and/or experience. They should have faculty status and benefits, and should undertake the obligations of such, advanced study, research, publication in learned journals, membership of professional organizations, etc.

Facilities. Planning of new or expanded facilities should involve the participation of the chief learning resources administrator and his staff with the architect and the administration. Advice from media and library specialists should be sought on technical requirements. Facilities should be located conveniently for use by students and teaching staff, close to the learning spaces or central to student traffic flow. The administration, acquisitions and cataloguing services should be in a central position.

Some students required programme learning equipment. Others learned best by use of isolated individual study areas. Proper arrangement and space for use of instructional equipment and materials should be provided for individualized instruction, browsing and media production. Physical facilities should be attractive, comfortable, and designed to encourage use by students.

Instructional equipment. Necessary instructional equipment should be available at the proper time and place to meet institutional and instructional objectives.

Materials. Materials should be selected, acquired, designed or produced on the basis of institutional and instructional objectives, developed by the faculty, students and administration in co-operation with learning resources. The materials should be properly organized and the necessary staff, facilities and equipment provided. Highly sophisticated systems for computer, video and audio access for retrieving, handling and displaying information might be necessary. Materials should be provided beyond curricular needs. These might arouse intellectual curiosity, help to develop critical thinking and cultural appreciation or stimulate use of the resources for continuing education and personal development.

The reference collection should include a wide selection of bibliographies, indexes, and standard reference books in all fields. Newspapers, representing various geographical, political, and social viewpoints, should be represented in the collection.

Services
Users had the right to expect facilities, materials and services available to meet demonstrated instruction needs; an atmosphere allowing sensitive and responsive attention to their requirements; professional staff readily available for interpretation of materials and services and for consultation on instructional development; suitable physical conditions; requests for services handled expeditiously; and acquisition, production and organization of materials to meet their instructional and personal needs.

Inter-agency co-operative activities
Co-operative activities with other institutions and agencies in the community, region, state and nation, were recommended in the areas of sharing of resources, through consortia, media co-operatives and loan arrangements. Where an undue burden was placed on a neighbouring institution, financial subsidy might be appropriate. The institution should also consider participating in co-operative projects, such as shared cataloguing and computer use, thus avoiding expense and wasteful duplication.

Special libraries

General

In an article, published in 1959, Leon Carnovsky said that the title 'Standards for Special Libraries—Possibilities and Limitations' involved a paradox. By their nature special libraries were unique. Not only was one kind different from another but special libraries in the same field of specialization differed widely from each other. He suggested that, in this field, the word 'standard' should be interpreted in the sense of supplying principles applicable to all special libraries, and therefore highly general, leaving it to the individual to apply it to his own situation.[1]

This was broadly the method adopted in the first authoritative statement of objectives ever produced. This was issued in 1964 by the Special Libraries Association, with members not only in the United States and Canada but also with some in Europe and Asia.

The preparation of standards for special libraries has received the attention of the Australian Library Association's Special Libraries Section since the early 1960s and the section was actively engaged in the production of a statement of standards between 1967 and 1969. These were approved and published in 1970. The sub-committee responsible acknowledged their debt to the work of the Special Libraries Association in the United States. They, however, went a little further than the Americans in the direction of quantitative standards, venturing a suggested breakdown of the items in an annual budget, salaries, library materials, etc.

1. Leon Carnovsky, 'Standards for Special Libraries: Possibilities and Limitations', *The Library Quarterly*, Vol. 29, No. 3, July 1959.

The writer agrees with those who have produced these two sets of standards about their usefulness in giving to senior management, in the words of the North American document, 'a clear guide to the elements which are present in a successful special library'. Indeed, the production in the United States and Canada of standards for other types of library containing little or no quantitative guidance (referred to in other chapters) indicates a widely held belief that in this form they have a useful part to play. He agrees also with those who feel that what are even more necessary are standards for the various types of special library. With greater identity of purpose, these would be more concrete and would lend themselves to more practical use, for example, for classes of industrial libraries (such as chemical libraries), planning and housing libraries, observatory and astronomical libraries, geography and map libraries.

If there is to be an increase in the number of sets of special library standards, it may be that general statements will be produced in countries where there are relatively few special libraries of different identifiable types, while in others, where there is a much more complex system of special libraries, separate standards for separate types of library will be produced. Alternatively standards for the main types of special library might be produced internationally.

The only example of standards prepared for a separate class of special library, which has been identified, is a set of standards for government libraries in Singapore. These were based largely on the American document but have also taken points from the Australian document. This is not an ideal example of standards for a particular type of special library, because each government department library necessarily deals with one or more distinct areas of work. Hence the difficulty in producing quantitative standards applicable to all government libraries remains, particularly for collections of materials. However, the Singapore document demonstrates how the American and Australian documents can be applied, if only in a general way, to a particular group of libraries.

A third general statement of special library standards identified is of particular interest as it comes from one of the socialist countries of Eastern Europe, the German Democratic Republic. In the German Democratic Republic, and doubtless in the other socialist countries, special libraries play a particularly important role, being more highly integrated into the total national library system than in non-socialist countries. The right to use these special libraries is understood to be less restricted in the latter countries. These standards differ radically from the American and Australian, since they are based on library laws and regulations in a highly centralized library administration. The libraries are also integrated among themselves functioning as networks of special libraries, supported by a system of central special libraries. In contrast to the other standards documents referred to, in the German Democratic Republic standards for library materials and space requirements are laid down and more detailed standards for staffing are prescribed.

Australia

The Library Association of Australia, in May 1970, approved a set of standards for special libraries produced by its Special Libraries Section. This is contained in 'Special Library Consensus Standards: A Compendium of Goals',[1] which owes a great deal to the published and unpublished work of the Special Libraries Association in America.

The standards proposed are not prescribed as minimum or maximum standards but are to be regarded as possible levels from which variations may be made for a number of reasons (of which examples are given) and as a guide to acceptable special library practice, to be adopted critically with due regard to special circumstances. The document presents first a number of statements of basic principles or general advice followed by a statement in more specific terms which it calls a standard. At the same time it refers to the total advice given as standards, a practice which will be followed in this summary.

OBJECTIVES

The objectives of the special library are threefold. It is a major source of information in the organization it serves. It acquires, organizes, maintains, utilizes and disseminates informational

1. 'Special Library Consensus Standards: A Compendium of Goals', *Australian Special Library News*, January 1970, p. 5–11.

material germane to the organization's activities. It serves all who have need of its services. A review, at least once a year, is recommended to see whether these objectives are being carried out.

ADMINISTRATION

The library should be a unit in the organization concerned and the librarian in charge responsible to a senior member of the staff, at least at the third most senior administrative level, who is knowledgeable in the subject disciplines of the collection.

STAFF

The quality of the staff is the most important single factor in providing an effective special library service. All professional staff must have acceptable professional library qualifications. The librarian in charge should have at least three years' professional experience in a special library, and should participate in management sessions concerned with library policy, in the selection of staff and salary determinations, and in relevant professional societies. At least one professional member of staff should be knowledgeable in the subject fields of the organization. Professional and non-professional duties are broadly defined and the minimum educational qualifications (four years' high school education) and technical skills are given.

The library should have at least one professional member of staff. Total staff should be sufficient to maintain an effective service. The proportion of professional to non-professional staff will depend on the number of professional staff, the size of the collection, the nature of the service and the number of records maintained. While the actual ratios will vary according to type of special library, in general there should be two professional to three non-professional staff and one library staff member to fifty persons served.

An important check on the adequacy of staff is by the examination of statistics. Statistics should be kept of all services and reports issued regularly. A statistical check on delays in achieving goals should be kept. A similar check on delays relating to the work of the library should be analysed regularly in terms of staff time required to keep the work up to date, and reports made regularly to management.

USERS

This section, which recognizes that the library must serve all sections of the organization and that the number of potential users within an organization will vary considerably, illustrates the difficulty of arriving at an estimate of this number. It defines a 'potential' user as a person eligible to use, and who might reasonably be expected to need access to, the information in the collection. In a private firm or government department a further qualification may be added: 'Information as required by a person in carrying out his work.' In the case of a library attached to a learned society, it is suggested that only 20 per cent of the 'potential' users, according to the definition, should be regarded as potential users. Users are discussed with reference to different types of library and employees or members, and libraries are advised to analyse the numbers of these potential users and to check against the numbers of registered or current users. It is recommended that the library should aim to serve 90 per cent of 'potential' users.

LIBRARY MATERIALS

The subject coverage of the special library's collection should be intensive and extensive enough to meet the current and anticipated requirements of the library's clientele. Special libraries are advised to define the major subject field (or fields) of their organization and to analyse: (a) the depth of subject approach required; (b) the years of publication most likely to be relevant; and (c) any other aspects relevant to their organization's particular needs. As a test of the adequacy of collections they are advised to select one or more representative bibliographies in the subject field of interest. They should hold 80–90 per cent of items in each bibliography within the subject field and pertinent to the needs of the organizations as defined, and 80 per cent of the items required by borrowers should be supplied from within the collection. Published subject indexes in the main and fringe subject fields should be part of the collection and the library should hold 90 per cent coverage of indexes in main subject fields and 50 per cent coverage in main fringe subject fields. A suitable collection of general reference books should be maintained and this should be revised annually. There should be at least an annual review of items for writing-off and for replacement. The collection should be centralized rather than scattered. The number of satellite collections should be checked annually and their continued separate existence considered.

SERVICES

The libraries should ensure effective use of their services by informing readers of resources, literature searching, compilation of bibliographies, abstracting and inter-library loans. If a title is borrowed frequently, the title should be acquired. The libraries should usually lend their material, with the possible exception of reference sources and other designated restricted items. It is suggested that an average of 20 to 30 items per annum should be used by each person served and that approximately 80 per cent of monograph holdings, depending on the age, size and type of the collection, should be lent each year.

PHYSICAL FACILITIES

The special library should be conveniently located for its users and provide for expansion. Its location should be central and space allowance should be at least in proportion 2 : 3 : 1 for the three major fields of activity in the order following: (a) library service functions; (b) storage (additional space will be required for collections with greater use of older materials and established collections with a high retention rate); (c) space for technical processes. Readers' tables and special purpose equipment should be provided, as required. These should be conveniently located for users and library staff, but placed outside the main traffic areas of the library.

BUDGET

The librarian in charge should be responsible for recommendations concerning the library budget, whether it is a separate budget or part of the budget of a larger unit. A budget showing proportions of expenditure is suggested, excluding overhead costs, capital expenditure and depreciation. In this salaries are given as 60 per cent; books, periodical subscriptions, etc., 25 per cent; binding and photocopying, 5 per cent; professional association expenses (including travel expenses and attendance at professional meetings), 2 per cent; and maintenance and minor equipment, 8 per cent. It is expected that the proportion of the library budget assigned to salaries will normally fall within the 60–79 per cent range, if overhead costs are excluded.

APPENDIX: STANDARD SPECIFICATIONS

In an appendix, standard specifications are given for stack and other shelf areas, and illumination.

The document contains a useful list of citations.

German Democratic Republic

What follows is based on material supplied by the Methodisches Zentrum für wissenschaftliche Bibliotheken beim Ministerium für Hoch- und Fachschulwesen, Berlin (Methodological Centre for Academic and Research Libraries).

STANDARDS FOR SERVICE IN SPECIAL LIBRARIES

The Methodological Centre for Academic and Research Libraries, in co-operation with a large number of special libraries of various disciplines and sizes, has published a set of standards for total stocks, annual accessions, staff requirements and structure, and requirements of space and equipment.[1] Separate standards have been worked out for special libraries in the fields of science and technology and of social sciences, though there is a great deal of common ground. These two types of special library have been subdivided into four categories on the basis of size. The document also

1. *Richtwerte für wissenschaftliche Fachbibliotheken* [Standards for Special Libraries], 2nd enl. ed., Berlin, Methodisches Zentrum für wissenschaftliche Bibliotheken beim Ministerium für Hoch- und Fachschulwesen, 1973, 41 p.

TABLE 8. Library materials

Category of library	Total stock[1] (volumes)	Annual accessions (volumes)	Periodicals—titles taken by special libraries	
			Science and technology	Social science
I	5,000–10,000	Up to 500	Up to 150	Up to 50
II	10,000–20,000	500–1,000	150–250	50–100
III	20,000–40,000	1,000–2,000	250–400	100–250
IV	40,000–100,000	2,000–5,000	400–800	250–500

1. The size of stock refers to active books and periodicals only. Historical or archival collections and little-used material are not included as their collection is the responsibility of the central special libraries.

TABLE 9. Staff

Category of library	Professional	Non-professional
I	1 librarian	—
II	1 librarian	1 junior assistant
III	1 librarian[1]	2 junior assistants
IV[2]	1 academically trained librarian[3]	4 junior assistants 1 technical assistant
	2 librarians	1 secretary[4]

1. In social science libraries the information work may justify a further qualified librarian.
2. In many social science libraries of this size a bibliographical information bureau should be established requiring additional staff as follows: 1–3 academically trained subject specialists, 1 junior library assistant and, possibly, 1 clerical assistant.
3. University degree in librarianship (4 years' study).
4. In social science libraries only, as technical libraries usually part of information centres.

deals with standards for libraries in technical colleges. In size these libraries approximate to the two lower categories of special library but the standards require modification, basing requirements on use by students, the pattern of which differs greatly from that in other types of special library.

Tables 8 and 9 summarize the quantitative standards laid down for special libraries in the two areas, science and technology and the social sciences.

EXPANDED SERVICES—ADDITIONAL STAFF

Acquisitions

If special technical literature is acquired, one additional junior assistant is needed in all sizes of library. If accessions exceed 2,000 volumes (up to Category III), one additional qualified librarian is required. If, in addition to alphabetical and subject catalogues, other catalogues are maintained, one additional junior assistant is required for all sizes of library.

Services

If normal advice is developed into an information service, one additional librarian is required. If the library is open exceptionally long hours, one additional librarian is required for every additional thirty hours a week.

The following are the space requirements for the various categories of library:

Workroom staff (and readers—categories I and II): Category I, 30 m²; Category II, 36 m²; Category III, 36 m²; Category 4, Chief Librarian 18 m², other staff 36 m².

Reading room (3.6 m² per place): Category I, 3 places in workroom (10.8 m²); Category II, 3 places in workroom (10.8 m²); Category III, 10 places (36 m²); Category IV, 30 places (108 m²).

Books: Category I, 10,000 volumes (open access), 100 m²; Category II, 20,000 volumes (open access), 200 m²; Category III, 40,000 volumes (open access), 400 m²; Category IV, 50,000 volumes (open access), 500 m²; for every further 10,000 volumes (closed access), 50 m².

Periodicals: Horizontal, 4 titles per shelf metre; vertical, 1.50 m height, 50 titles per metre; bound copies, 28 volumes per shelf metre.

Libraries in technical colleges (of non-university status)

Figures for total stock in such technical college libraries are based on a notional calculation of student numbers, one full-time student equalling three corresponding or evening students, as follows: for the first 600 students, up to 15 volumes per student; 600 to

1,000 students, up to 12 volumes per student; over 1,000 students, 10 volumes per student.

Stock size will be affected by the speciality of the college and by the existence of any large scientific general or special library to which the students have access. Basic textbooks and standard works for the students, on open access, are required; numbers of volumes required for this collection are based on 10 per cent of the potential student users.

The following classes of material should be available in the reading room, preferably on open access (except for little-used material): literature for basic study; general reference works; new acquisitions; periodicals; frequently used special literature; and current social science material. The number of reading places provided would depend on the number of students, particularly full-time students. Provision should be made for between 5 and 10 per cent of the total number of students likely to be in attendance. This figure would also be influenced by the existence of other libraries in the area.

Requirements for staff, space and equipment would be broadly those for the special libraries in Categories I and II. Longer than normal opening hours would affect staff numbers.

CENTRAL SPECIAL LIBRARIES

The continued development of the library system in the German Democratic Republic has necessitated the establishment in the most important economic and scientific fields of central special libraries and the Methodological Centre for Academic and Research Libraries, in co-operation with a working group of the Advisory Council for Library Affairs to the Minister of Culture, has prepared general regulations governing the organization and functions of central special libraries.[1]

1. 'Siebente Durchführungsbestimmung zur Bibliotheksverordnung—Aufgaben und Arbeitsweise Zentraler Fachbibliotheken—vom 5. Januar 1972 [Seventh Regulation on the Implementation of the Library Decree—Functions and Organization of Central Special Libraries]', *Gesetzblatt der Deutschen Demokratischen Republik*, Vol. II, No. 3, 1972, p. 26–7.
'Anweisung über das Rahmenstatut für die Zentralen Fachbibliotheken [Directions Concerning the General Regulations for Central Special Libraries]', *Verfügungen und Mitteilungen des Ministeriums für Kultur*, No. 2, 1972, p. 20–2.

The responsibilities of these libraries have been described in the document in the following terms:

> The central special library acts as the centre for the supply of materials and of methodological services to the special libraries in its special field throughout the G.D.R. It provides comprehensive library and bibliographical services in support of pure and applied science, education and further qualification, and for this purpose builds up stocks of relevant literature in its field. It provides reference services and bibliographical information, co-ordinates the activities of the special libraries with which it is concerned, gives methodological guidance and carries out specific scientific and other research work in the field of librarianship.

The regulations deal with the special questions of the building up and co-ordination of library holdings, with the principles of acquisition, and with their relation to user demands. They also govern the co-ordination of bibliographical services between the central special library and other special libraries and the functions of the central library in regard to library networks. Finally, they provide for the establishment of an advisory council to the Director of each central special library and determine the membership and duties of that body.

SPECIAL LIBRARY NETWORKS

Individual special libraries can cope with continually growing demands by intensifying their activities and raising their efficiency by the greatest possible utilization of their potential. This has required the establishment of networks of special libraries, their organization being made possible by the fact that all libraries are, in one way or another, State owned.

The Methodological Centre for Academic and Research Libraries, with the agreement of the Advisory Council on Library Affairs to the Minister of Culture, has prepared a draft model 'Functions and Structure of Special Library Networks'.[1] This defines the role of the networks as the co-ordination of the more effective special libraries working in the same field, i.e. those which are valuable not only to their own industrial concerns, institutes, etc., but to the library system as a whole.

---

1. *Aufgabe und Bildung von Fachnetzen* [Functions and Structure of Special Library Networks], Berlin, Deutscher Bibliotheksverband, 1971, 16 p.

The draft regulates the relations between the central special library and the member libraries of the network, and assigns particular tasks to the libraries, e.g. in building up holdings. It also deals with the important question of the relations between special libraries and information services, providing that the network of special libraries in a given field should coincide with the corresponding network of information centres.

After its authorization, the model will be published as a Regulation implementing the Library Decree of 31 May 1968.[1]

Singapore

An internal document prepared by the National Library of Singapore in 1970 entitled *Objectives and Standards for Government Libraries* is summarized below.[2] This was adapted from the standards for special libraries produced in 1964 by the Special Libraries Association (in the United States).

OBJECTIVES

The library was a major source of information in the department/ministry it served.[3] It acquired, organized, maintained, utilized and disseminated informational materials relevant to the activities of the department/ministry. It served those who had need of its services.

The objectives regarding whom to serve and the services to be provided should be clearly defined, preferably in writing. This policy must be reviewed periodically and revised in accordance with changes in the work of the department/ministry and advances in library and information technology.

1. 'Verordnung über die Aufgaben des Bibliothekssystems bei der Gestaltung des entwickelten gesellschaftlichen Systems des Sozialismus in der Deutschen Demokratischen Republik vom 31. Mai 1968 [Decree on the Functions of the Library System in Shaping the Developed Socialist System of the German Democratic Republic, of 31 May 1968]', *Gesetzblatt der Deutschen Demokratischen Republik*, Vol. II, No. 78, 1968, p. 565–71.
2. *Objectives and Standards for Government Libraries*, National Library of Singapore, 16 April 1970 (reference NL 91/70, mimeo).
3. Government libraries in Singapore may either be libraries of single departments or that of ministries which include several departments.

ADMINISTRATION

The library should be an administrative unit in the department/ ministry and the librarian responsible to a very senior member of the staff, knowledgeable in the subject disciplines of the collections.

STAFF

Professional staff should be librarians who could meet certain qualifications in education and experience. The librarian in charge was responsible for all administrative and professional duties in the library, which included administration, planning, evaluation and revision of systems and procedures, selection and organization of materials, reference and bibliographical services, supervision and in-service training of non-professional staff. The librarian in charge should participate in meetings concerned with library policy, in the selection of library staff, and in activities of relevant professional societies. Non-professional staff were responsible for the clerical tasks that supported the professional's work. There tasks were listed.

The number of library staff would depend on various factors likely to vary as between departments. There should be one professional librarian for a library whose collection exceeded 3,000 volumes, with an annual book budget of $10,000 or more, providing 60 per cent of items requested by staff, and serving at least thirty persons. The recommended ratio of non-professional to professional staff, which would, however, vary according to the type of library, was two to one.

COLLECTION

The collection should meet current needs and anticipate information requirements of users. It should include all basic, frequently used and potentially useful material in a variety of forms. The range was determined by the objectives of the department/ministry and the depth by nature of its work. Centralizing material in the library was preferable to separate office collections.

Acquisition policies—as to depth and extent of subject coverage, types of materials, gifts and exchanges—should be defined in relation to the library's objectives. Libraries in departments/ministries issuing publications might arrange the exchange of publications with other organizations. The librarian should be kept informed about activities and future plans of the department/ministry. His participation in planning sessions and discussions with subject specialists in the department/ministry were essential to a continuing acquisitions policy.

SERVICES

The library staff located library materials and provided reference services promptly on request. Reference services included literature searching, compiling bibliographies, abstracting, indexing. The library lent its materials with the possible exception of reference sources and other designated restricted items. Needed publications that were unavailable in the library of a department/ministry might be obtained from another library or institution. The resources of the National Library and other large libraries and research institutions in Singapore could be drawn upon through inter-library loans in accordance with the Inter-library Loan Code of the Library Association of Singapore and Library Association of Malaysia.

An effective system for maximum utilization of current periodical literature was an integral part of the library's programme. The library was responsible for informing its users of its resources. Various methods of achieving these ends were proposed.

PHYSICAL FACILITIES

The library's location should be conducive to the optimum use of resources and services. It should be central and free of noise. There should be provision for air-conditioning to ensure temperature and humidity control for the preservation of library material and adequate lighting for reading, study and reference work.

The initial choice of location must permit space expansion for at least five years. Anticipation of expansion would avoid need for frequent moving of equipment and materials, inherently difficult to move.

Space allocation must allow for library service functions, e.g. reference, reading and study, loans; storage, e.g. shelving and filing of the collections; and technical processes, e.g. acquisitions, cataloguing, etc.

BUDGET

The librarian should submit estimates for library expenditure for incorporation in the estimates of the department/ministry. Guidelines for the library budget to meet the standards described were: salaries, 60 per cent; books, periodicals, society membership for publications, 25 per cent; photo-copying, 3 per cent; professional association expenses, including travel, etc., expenses, 2 per cent; maintenance of library materials, 5 per cent; minor equipment, 5 per cent; total 100 per cent. Excluded were overhead costs. Depreciation was calculated at 10 per cent of capital.

United States of America and Canada

The Special Libraries Association, in the United States, published in December 1964, in *Special Libraries*, a document entitled *Objectives and Standards for Special Libraries*.[1] In preparation for this many members of the association completed questionnaires, on the basis of which *Profiles* of six of the many different kinds of special library were constructed and later published.[2] The work on the main document, which began in 1959, was undertaken by the association's Professional Standards Committee. Subsequently the document was reissued as a brochure entitled *Objectives for Special Libraries*, the few quantitative standards previously included

1. Special Libraries Association, 'Objectives and Standards for Special Libraries', New York, 1964, *Special Libraries*, Vol. 55, No. 10, 1964.
2. Special Libraries Association, 'Profiles of Special Libraries', *Special Libraries*, Vol. 57, Nos. 3, 4 and 5, 1966.

(which had referred only to some technical requirements for library premises) being omitted. A summary of this document follows:

PREFACE

The statement was not intended as a manual of operation, nor did it set out, except by inference, specific quantitative measures which gave automatic excellence. It was intended that senior organizational management should be given a clear guide to the elements present in a successful special library. The qualities to be sought were being presented in a context which would point the way to their attainment.

OBJECTIVES

The special library was a major source of information in the organization it served. It acquired, organized, maintained, utilized and disseminated materials germane to the organization's activities. It served all who had need of its services. The objectives of the library and its services should be clearly defined, preferably in writing, and reviewed and revised periodically.

STAFF

The quality of the special library's staff was the most important factor in the effectiveness of the library as an information centre for an organization. The responsibilities and qualifications of personnel competent to carry out the objectives and functions of the special library were set out.

The special library administrator was responsible for all administrative and professional functions of the library. These functions were listed under fourteen headings. He should hold a degree from a library school and have three years' experience in a special library, or he should be a subject specialist who had demonstrated his professional competence through at least three years of professional experience in a special library. A combination of formal subject training and education in librarianship was desirable. Other librarians similarly qualified should be employed as required, together with other specialists, such as literature searchers, translators, abstracters, indexers and information systems specialists.

Professional staff members had a continuing responsibility for furthering their education and should be encouraged to participate in professional societies concerned with their specialities.

The proportion of non-professional staff to professional staff depended on the number of professional staff, the size of the collection, the nature of the services and the quantity of the records maintained. The special library must have at least one professionally qualified librarian and one clerical worker and the recommended ratio of non-professional to professional was three to two. This was based on the findings of the association's Professional Standards Committee's unpublished 'Survey of Selected Libraries, 1964'.

COLLECTION

The special library's collection consisted of the information sources acquired, organized and administered for use by or on behalf of the library's clientele. The collection might include a variety of forms and types of materials (listed under thirty-eight headings) not all of which were appropriate to a particular type of special library. The range was determined by the objectives of the organization. The depth was governed by the nature of the organization's work. Centralizing materials in the library, rather than scattering them in office collections, was important in effecting the basic goal of general accessibility of all sources of information. The criterion of immediate availability of materials demanded major reliance upon the library's own resources. General reference works that supplemented the library's special collections broadened the scope of the library's information services.

The size of the collection depended upon the amount of material available relevant to the organization's special needs. Acquisition policies must be established, including policies for gifts and exchanges. The collection must be suitably organized and controlled. The nature of information sources in special libraries often required the creation of unique and special systems. In many cases a library must create its own indexing systems, and greater efficiency might be attained through the use of new tools such as electronic data-processing machines.

SERVICES

The service of a special library should be a dynamic one in which the staff anticipate needs. The library achieved its objective through reference and bibliographic services, flexible policies concerning loans and distribution of library materials, efficient dissemination of information and other activities that encouraged productive use of its resources. It should locate library materials and information promptly on request, provide reference services, including literature searching, compiling bibliographies, abstracting and indexing. It should lend its material, with the possible exception of reference sources and other specially restricted items. It should provide translations through a qualified staff member or a commercial translation service. Publications unavailable in the library or in the organization should be obtained from another library or institution. The staff should maintain information about sources of all types of material and for establishing a co-operative, reciprocal inter-library loan programme with other libraries of all types.

An effective system for maximum utilization of current periodical literature was an essential part of the special library's service programme. Consulting activities might be added responsibilities for the library staff. The library was responsible for informing its clientele of its total resources, and of new resources.

PHYSICAL RESOURCES

The special library needed adequate facilities in a physical environment conducive to optimum use of its collections and services. In planning a library there should be direct consultation between the special library administrator and the space planning group of the organization. The library administrator was responsible for giving precise and realistic statements of the physical requirements for collections, services and staff activities.

BUDGET

The initial analysis of the library's needs should come from the special library administrator, and the spending of the budget allocation rested upon his professional knowledge and judgement. This final budget was the joint responsibility of the library administrator and his immediate superior, who should agree on the desired scope and extent of the library's services and the estimated cost.

The greater part of the library budget should be allocated to professional and non-professional salaries and it was considered that the portion of the budget normally assigned to salaries would fall within the 60–79 per cent range, provided overheads were not charged to the library budget. Some variation in ratios must be expected for special libraries that received a large proportion of their materials without cost. The initial budget for a new library would require a considerably larger percentage of the whole for basic library materials and capital expenditures. The initiation of work in new subject areas would require increased expenditure on publications.

The *Profiles*—a very useful way of illustrating 'standards', particularly where it is difficult to generalize about quantitative requirements—were the result of consultations and visits to twenty-eight libraries and conferences, and correspondence with a further fifty librarians. In the preface to this second document, published in 1966, it was stated that while the 'profiles' represented composites of the specialized library collection, the space requirements had been calculated on the basis of recommended practices. It warned that comparisons of individual libraries with those in the *Profiles* should only be made in the light of individual library situations and that the descriptions used in the document must be used only as general guidelines. Services could be listed but depths and levels of service could only be implied. The preface also said that the Professional Standards Committee hoped especially that they would guide consultants, as organizations starting libraries wanted quantitative information. Even though the *Profiles* represented only a few of the many types of special libraries, the committee claimed that the guidelines would help all, giving as an example that, although six different libraries of varying sizes were represented, the percentage of the total budget allocated was about the same in all cases.

A typical 'profile' gave the background to the parent company organization and its library and discussed the role of the librarian and of his staff. It summarized the major library activities under: selection, acquisition and coverage of library materials; organization of the collections; reference and information services; special systems and procedures. Under the heading of 'Statistics', it gave information about the notional collection, equipment and library space. Budget ratios were broken down into salaries (professional and clerical); books, pamphlets, documents, etc., periodical subscriptions, society membership (for publications); binding, supplies, microform publications, photocopying expenses, etc; and professional association expenses and travelling.

Public libraries

General

Much more attention has been given to the production of standards for public library service than to standards for any other type of library. This subject has interested certain countries for a very long time—the United States as early as 1917—and it was given an impetus by the issue of the Unesco Public Library Manifesto of 1949 and by the activities of the International Federation of Library Associations over the past twenty-five years, of which the general statement of standards approved in Madrid in 1958 and the standards for public library buildings approved at Warsaw in 1959 are evidence. The Unesco Manifesto was revised in 1972 and the IFLA standards in 1973. The new texts will have benefited from the experience gained recently in the preparation of national standards.[1]

A high and increasing proportion of the standards have been initiated by governments, directly through administrative action or indirectly through the advice of representative and expert bodies which they have appointed or been associated with. Many such statements which have originated with governments are of very recent date. The period when it was only associations of librarians which were interested in this subject is now over.

Standards for public library service produced by certain countries have been revised, often more than once, and some countries have prepared such standards for the first time in the

---

1. International Association of Library Associations, Section of Public Libraries, *Standards for Public Libraries*, Pullach bei München, Verlag Documentation, 1973.

past few years. Many standards are in varying degrees out of date. This survey makes no claims to completeness but it has been possible to obtain full or partial information about such standards in some twenty countries. They have been summarized or described in the second part of this chapter.

It is clear from a study of comprehensive standards from a number of countries that they contain very similar statements about the part the public library should play in the community. The similarity in this and other respects is not surprising since what is being expressed is the essence of good librarianship. This, despite local differences and in many cases differences of ideology, is common to all countries.

After a definition of the purposes served by the public libraries there usually comes a discussion of the desirable administrative structure of the libraries, from the point of view of effective service. Here again much is common to the standards which have been studied, though it is in this area that differences begin to be marked. In particular, the structure of government organization, whether this follows a federal or unitary pattern, and the degree of decentralization of authority determine the pattern and often the standards which can in practice be proposed. There are two themes which run through most, if not all, of these discussions.

There is, in general, agreement about the disadvantages of small units of public library administration and of small independent public libraries, and therefore about the need for units of library administration large enough to provide a comprehensive and efficient library service. If this is impossible to achieve, there is a large area of agreement that the separate library administrations should combine to form 'systems' centred around one or more large libraries, or that public libraries should be wholly or largely provided by the central government (in a federal country by the State government) directly or through national or State libraries or public library boards.

There is also general agreement about the need for co-operation in a number of forms, ranging from local co-operation in 'systems' or 'networks' (as, for example, in Canada, the German Democratic Republic, the Federal Republic of Germany, Hungary, the U.S.S.R. and the United States) or links with regional libraries (as in Scandinavia), with State or provincial libraries (as in Australia and South Africa) or with the national library (as in New Zealand), to nation-wide regional and national inter-library co-operation involving all types of library (as in the United Kingdom and other countries). Even where the units of library administration are large enough to support a good library service—and there have been in recent years in several countries reforms enlarging units of local administration not only for library purposes—co-operation between libraries at all levels is still regarded as essential.

Only when the standards move into the area of library materials, staff and buildings are quantitative standards possible on a large scale. Here, inevitably, local differences occur but the standards bear a great deal of resemblance to each other. The influence of one set of standards on others is apparent. Indeed the standards already promulgated in one country are frequently put forward as a justification for similar standards in another. There are, however, differences which reflect variations in local circumstances, which may be of historical, geographical, economic, political, linguistic and other origin.

A number of key points have been taken and, in the following tables,[1] summaries made of the standards recommended for certain countries. In looking at the resultant information, which is presented principally in figures, it is essential to appreciate that comparisons cannot be made without taking account of the local conditions and of what it is possible to achieve in those conditions in a reasonable period of time. A more reliable comparison may be possible on a 'regional' basis. Even then, there are bound to be differences in circumstances between one country and its neighbours but these are likely to be less extreme. It must be remembered that the facts and figures are often not properly comparable, due to differences in definitions, local conditions, or local practice, and that standards expressed as a simple statement or single figure can be misleading. The actual text of the standard should be referred to.

1. The information contained in the tables can only indicate in broad outline the minimum level of service recommended. It must be read in conjunction with the summaries of the standards included in this chapter and, better still, read with the original standards documents. Moreover, many of the figures quoted, particularly those depending on definition of terms, such as population, *per capita*, volumes, titles, issues, librarian, professional, are frequently not truly comparable.

LIBRARY MATERIALS

Since the library exists primarily to make books and other library materials available to the public, the book stock is of first importance. Traditionally books and other printed material have been the first consideration, although increasing emphasis is now being placed on other media. Tables 10 and 11 summarize the position in a number of countries in respect of total book stocks and annual accessions and periodicals and newspapers.

In general the recommended figures for total book stock per inhabitant, which naturally are higher for small populations than for large ones, range from about three volumes to one volume, or less where there are very large concentrations of population. Exceptionally figures of four volumes are quoted from the United States and the U.S.S.R. (in the latter case also a figure of five volumes for village libraries), with a bottom figure from the United States of two volumes in systems serving over 1 million population.

Information concerning standards for annual accessions is more difficult to compare. One point of comparison is between the one-sixth of a volume per inhabitant in areas of up to half a million population and the one-eighth in areas with over half a million population recommended in the United States, and the one-quarter of a volume recommended generally in the United Kingdom.

It is now rare to find any country considering standards for book purchases in terms of minimum annual expenditure. The most carefully worked out accessions standards are expressed in terms of figures for annual purchases of books and other materials according to calculations about the number and proportions of the different types of books and other material required, the expected life of particular items—in respect of which standards vary considerably from one country to another—and the minimum proportion for replacement annually.

Once again there cannot be any strict comparison between these figures which reflect the annual book production in the main language or languages of the country concerned and the extent to which material has to be obtained from other countries. In the United Kingdom, it was stated in 1962 that, of the approximately 20,000 items of adult non-fiction currently published in that country, some 10,000 to 11,000 were suitable for general use in public libraries, including 5,000 to 6,000 which were suitable for small and medium-sized libraries. In a paper to the IFLA General Council in 1969, a speaker from the Federal Republic of Germany stated that in his country some 25,000 new titles were published every year, of which 10,000 to 15,000 might be relevant for public libraries. In other countries the position is different. In Scandinavia there is a relatively small annual book production in the language of each of the countries and large numbers of books in other languages published abroad have to be acquired. In Malaysia the output of local publishing is still small. In 1970 total Malaysian publications written in six languages, one being English, included only 874 books. Perhaps significant as an indication of the position in some developing countries are the high figures for Malaysia in Table 11 referring to the standards for periodicals and newspapers.

Of increasing importance is the provision of non-print materials, particularly of audio-visual material. Table 12 summarizes some standards which are beginning to emerge on this subject. A number of existing standards are currently being revised to take account, *inter alia*, of the need for standards covering all aspects of the provision of non-print materials.

SERVICE AND USE OF THE LIBRARY

Table 13 gives information about service points and opening hours by which the level of service given in different countries can be judged to a certain extent. The more detailed descriptions of the standards, given in the text, refer almost invariably to the point that a library should be open for as long as possible to suit the convenience of the public, including evening hours, subject to considerations of economy. Since the actual hours and days of opening are so dependent on the local circumstances, the size and nature of the library and of the district served, it is difficult to make comparisons, especially over the hours of service for part-time branches. A point of growing importance, which Table 13 illustrates, is the desirable standards for mobile libraries. There is a difference between countries which regard a fortnightly visit as a reasonable minimum and those which recommend at least one visit every week. There is also the fact that in certain cases the minimum length of the stop is indicated, ranging from a quarter of an hour (United Kingdom) to long enough to give a readers' advisory service (United States).

Included in Table 14 is some information about registered readers and circulation of books. Only a few countries have mentioned the proportions of population expected to become registered readers and the anticipated numbers and nature of issues per head of population. In many countries where public library services are well developed this type of standard is not included. This may be because of doubts about the reliability of the statistics of registered readers and issues as a measure of use, or the fear of the distortion of library service which can follow if there is undue emphasis on these figures. However, these statistics are useful and some such indications may have value especially in countries where the public library service is poorly developed. In any event, some assumptions as to use must be made in planning book purchases, staff and accommodation. Noticeable, however, are the wide variations between the figures assumed.

STAFF

Table 15 gives information about staffing standards proposed in a number of countries. It should not be assumed that the minimum standards all refer to the same range of services or, in a particular country, to what could be described as a full range of services.

In its simplest form minimum total staff (usually excluding manual workers) is most commonly stated in terms of a ratio of staff members to population served or to annual loans. The greater part of the standards studied shows a preference for the population basis. On this basis the figures are, with some exceptions, either 1 : 2,000 or 1 : 2,500. While there is an appreciable difference between these two figures, it is not so great that it cannot be explained by the difficulty of estimating staff requirements rather than by differing views as to desirable standards of service. What is significant is that the figure is of the order of 1 : 2,000 population served and not, for example 1 : 3,000, 1 : 4,000 or 1 : 5,000. Sometimes the standard is based on numbers of readers. In the few cases where the total staff is calculated on the basis of issues the figures used are between 1 : 15,000 and 1 : 25,000 loans. In other cases the standards are related to several factors, e.g. both issues and accessions.

As to the proportions of librarians to other staff, the standards appear to vary considerably. There are references to the proportions being approximately equal. Other proportions mentioned vary from 2 : 3 to 1 : 3. The most common is 1 : 2. But the figures are not all comparable and terms like 'librarian', 'qualified', and 'professional' need interpretation. In one case, New Zealand, there is specific reference to 33 per cent 'professional or intermediate staff' and in another, United States, to 33 per cent 'professional and sub-professional'.

LIBRARY BUILDINGS

The provision of library premises brings into play not only librarians but also architects and other specialists. In view of the extensive library building programmes in many countries, this subject has been given considerable attention in recent years, particularly where capital grants are given by the central government to local authorities towards the cost of new or improved premises.

It is an oversimplification to talk about a standard for total floor areas—as is well brought out in the Danish standards—and, where this is attempted, the figures normally exclude accommodation likely to be particularly variable, such as the provision for cultural and educational activities. With other variables dependent on design and other factors, any total areas quoted are bound to be regarded as guides to be used flexibly. As stated in the South African standards, a thorough study of the community and its needs is the only sure basis on which to determine the total amount of space required. Nevertheless, Table 16 referring to total areas recommended in particular countries, a study of the summaries of the standards contained in this text, and of the original documents, may be of help in planning future libraries.

It is hardly possible to generalize from the few standards which the writer has been able to analyse in respect of the areas occupied by principal departments of the library, referred to in Table 17. The pattern of use and other factors must be taken into account.

This information should be compared with the standards for space requirements for the different facilities provided by public libraries, recommended in the recent IFLA *Standards for Public Libraries*.[1]

A feature of increasing significance in new public library buildings now being erected in many countries is the provision proposed for the use of audio-visual materials and for activities of a cultural and educational nature. These include exhibitions, musical and other recitals, dramatic and other performances, lectures, group meetings and formal adult classes, the public library either acting as or being integrated into a local cultural centre. The scale of the accommodation contemplated by certain countries in their official standards for these purposes is a measure of the increasing importance being attached to this aspect of a public library's work. This is illustrated in the information given in Table 18.

TABLE 10. Book stocks

Country[1] (1) Date of standards (2) Category	Total book stocks	Annual accessions
Australia (1) 1972 (2) B. 1	2 volumes per inhabitant reducing to 1 volume. Minimum 70,000 volumes. 40–45 per cent adult non-fiction; 20–25 per cent fiction; 35 per cent children	Minimum 8,750 volumes, rising to 37,500 at 300,000 population
Belgium (1) 1968 (2) A. 2	2.5/3.0 volumes *per capita* under 2,000 population, reducing to 0.4 above 1 million according to type and size of library. 40–50 per cent adult non-fiction; 30–50 per cent adult fiction (maximum); 10–15 per cent children	

1. In the first column, under 'Country', the date when the standards referred to were established is given, where possible, in item (1). In item (2) the status of the standards is referred to, using the following code:
A. 1. Official-direct; for example by government department as condition of giving financial assistance to local bodies, or as guidelines.
A. 2. Official-indirect; advice of body, for example advisory committee, appointed by the government.
B. 1. Non-official; produced by permanent professional or other functional organization, for example library association.
B. 2. Non-official; advice of body, for example a committee not appointed by the government.

1. *Standards for Public Libraries*, op. cit.

134

Country (1) Date of standards (2) Category	Total book stocks	Annual accessions
Canada (1) 1969 (2) B. 1	Canadian Library Association. Lending collection—from 2 volumes *per capita* reducing to 1.25 volumes. 25–30 per cent children's; 70–80 per cent non-fiction in adult collection. Reference collection, 10–15 per cent	Lending collection—3,500– 5,000 new titles
(1) 1973 (2) A. 1	British Columbia. For small and medium-sized libraries. Under 10,000 population, 3,000 volumes or 3 volumes *per capita*, whichever is the greater. Reference collection, 40 titles. 10,000–50,000 population, 30,000 volumes or 2 volumes *per capita*, whichever is the greater. Reference collection, 100 titles	
Denmark (1) 1967 (2) A. 1 and 2	Adult section, 2.5 to 1.5 volumes per adult, minimum 8,000 volumes. Children, 4 volumes per child (0–13 years). All suitable titles in Danish plus other material	Adult section, from 400 (under 5,000 population) to 1,300 (25–50,000) new Danish titles plus replacements. Children, formula, see text
France (1) 1972 (2) A. 1	1.5 volumes *per capita* (5,000 popu- lation) reducing to 1 volume (75,000 population)	
German Democratic Republic (1) 1968–71 (2) A. 2	Municipal libraries, 2.5 volumes (3,500 population) to 1.65 volumes (over 1 million) *per capita*. Children's literature, average 30 per cent. Trade union libraries, 3 to 4 volumes per employee	For replacement— non-fiction, 7.5 per cent; fiction, 5 per cent; children, 13 per cent
Federal Republic of Germany (1) 1964–73 (2) B. 2	2 volumes *per capita*; minimum, 10,000 volumes. Adult, 67 per cent increasing to 88 per cent with size of collection. Children, 33 per cent decreasing to 12 per cent. Branch library, minimum 10,000 volumes. Mobile library, capacity 2,500–4,000 volumes	12 per cent of existing stock for replacements, excluding reference, plus 3 per cent for extension of collection

135

Country (1) Date of standards (2) Category	Total book stocks	Annual accessions
Hungary (1) 1971–72 (2) A. 1	Basic grade, 5,000; medium grade, 20,000; high grade, 100,000 volumes Children, 10–12 volumes per child reader in certain types of children's library	Basic grade, 350–400 titles; medium grade, 2,500–3,000 titles; high grade, 3,500–4,500 titles Children, see text
Japan (1) 1969 (2) A. 2	See text	
Malaysia (1) 1968 (2) B. 2	Aim to reach a minimum of 1 book per head of population within 20 years. Each central state library, minimum 100,000 volumes, 40 per cent for children and 10–15 per cent for teenagers (13–19 years)	Central state library, once basic collection achieved, additions at rate of 1,000 new titles annually, withdrawals averaging 5 per cent
Netherlands (1) 1970 (2) A. 2	Each central or branch library, 2.5 volumes per head of population served below 2,000, reducing to 0.5 over 1 million population	15 per cent of total book stock, plus 3 per cent addition until required stock is reached
New Zealand (1) 1966 (2) B. 1	Minimum standards. Access to 100,000 titles in non-fiction and foreign languages; 7,500 fiction; 7,500 children and young people—plus reference collection, 4,000. Local provision, minimum 6,000 volumes, at least 25 per cent juvenile	Minimum stand. New titles, adult non-fiction 5,000; fiction, 500; children and young people, 750; reference, 400 Volumes: adult non-fiction accessions $7\frac{1}{2}$ per cent of stock on open shelves; other—in proportion to issues, between 8–10 per cent

Country (1) Date of standards (2) Category	Total book stocks	Annual accessions
	Provisional standards. 1.4 to 2 volumes *per capita*. Children and young people, 40–50 per cent. Both standards exclude rental collections	Provisional stand. Minimum of 0.15 volumes per head of population served, 33 per cent for children and young people, and 100 volumes basic reference
Norway (1) current (2) A. 1	Under 6,000 population, 2 volumes *per capita*; over 6,000, 1.5 volumes	
Poland (1) 1968 (2) A. 1	Up to 25,000 population, 3.3 to 2.2 volumes *per capita*; 25,000 to over 200,000, 2 to 1	
Singapore (1) 1967 (2) A. 1	Regional branch library, 1.5 volumes *per capita*	
South Africa (1) 1968 (2) B. 1	3 volumes *per capita*, under 50,000 literate population, reducing to 1 volume above 250,000. 25 per cent non-fiction	
Sweden (1) 1965 (2) A. 1 (1) 1972 (2) A. 2	A. 1, 3 volumes *per capita*. A. 2, total stock of current interest, including audio-visual media, 2.5 to 3 items per inhabitant	
United Kingdom (1) 1962 (2) A. 1 and A. 2	No standards of general applicability. Interpretation of data suggested minimum 1.5 currently useful volumes *per capita* for areas under 40,000 population, without several small branches	Basic library service, up to approximately 30,000 population. Minimum 7,200 volumes, adult non-fiction, 2,000 titles (2,600 volumes); adult fiction, 3,000 volumes; children's, 1,500 volumes.

Country (1) Date of standards (2) Category	Total book stocks	Annual accessions
		Libraries giving more than basic service. 250 volumes per 1,000 population, including 90 volumes adult non-fiction. Non-fiction titles, basic 2,300 plus 500 every 10,000 population between 30,000 and 100,000. Other titles—see text
United States of America (1) 1966 (2) B. 1	ALA Standards (1966). Total systems collection (population 150,000 to 1 million). 4 volumes *per capita*, reducing to 2 volumes. Juvenile, minimum 25 per cent, maximum 40 per cent	One-sixth volume *per capita* up to 500,000 population; one-eighth above 500,000. Up to 33 per cent for children and at least 5 per cent for young adults
(1) 1962 (2) B. 1	Interim standards—small public libraries (1962). Under 5,000 population—access to minimum of 10,000 volumes or 3 volumes *per capita*, whichever greater. 5,000–50,000 population, minimum 2 volumes *per capita*	
U.S.S.R. (1) 1968 (2) A. 1	Urban libraries, 4 volumes *per capita*, minimum 3,000 volumes. Village library, 5 volumes *per capita*, minimum 1,500 volumes. Trade union library, 7 to 11 volumes per reader, minimum initial stock 1,000 volumes	

TABLE 11. Periodicals and newspapers

Country[1] (1) Date of standards (2) Category	Periodicals	Newspapers
Australia (1) 1972 (2) B. 1	*Population* *Subscriptions*[2] 35,000–50,000 150–200 50,000–100,000 200–300 100,000–200,000 300–400 200,000–300,000 400–500	
Belgium (1) 1968 (2) A. 2	*Population* *Subscriptions* *Retention* 20,000 90–110 10 years 50,000 190–260 20 years 100,000 600–675 20 years	

Canada
(1) 1969
(2) B. 1
	Canadian Library Association.
	From 200–400 to 1,000 newspaper
	   and periodical subscriptions,
	   excluding duplicates or
	   replacements.
	50–75 per cent to be kept in back
	   files
		Included with periodicals

(1) 1973 (2) A. 1	British Columbia *Population* *Subscriptions* under 10,000 20 10,000–50,000 40	

*German
Democratic
Republic*
(1) 1968–71
(2) A. 2
	Combined figures, subscriptions.
	Municipal and district libraries
	   and big city libraries, 160–170.
	Municipal and sub-district
	   libraries, 110–120.
	Rural central and small
	   municipal libraries, 30–35.
	Village libraries, 14
		Included with periodicals

Federal Republic of Germany (1) 1964–73 (2) B. 2	Grade II libraries, 500 subscriptions in German	
Hungary (1) 1971–72 (2) A. 1	Combined figures, subscriptions. Basic grade, at least 50. Medium grade, 230–300. High grade, 450–500	Included with periodicals

1. See footnote 1, Table 10.
2. Serials, i.e. annuals und continuations excluded.

Country (1) Date of standards (2) Category	Periodicals	Newspapers
Japan (1) 1969 (2) A. 2	From 30 to over 300 subscriptions	Urban and rural prefecture and city libraries, over 10 national newspapers; also local newspapers
Malaysia (1) 1968 (2) B. 2	Combined figures, subscriptions. From 20 (under 5,000 population) to 2,500–3,000 (over 500,000)	Included with periodicals
Netherlands (1) 1970 (2) A. 2	Combined figures. 150 titles; approximately 10 per cent of budget available for books	Included with periodicals
New Zealand (1) 1966 (2) B. 1	Access to 500 titles in runs of 5–10 years. This requires subscriptions to minimum 750 titles, including indexing and bibliographic services	Local newspapers, and other newspapers justified by use
South Africa (1) 1968 (2) B. 1	Every library, 5 titles, plus 1 for every 200 population to reasonable maximum	Every library, 3, plus 1 for every 1,000 population to reasonable maximum
United Kingdom (1) 1962 (2) A. 2	Minimum, 50 titles of general interest plus specialist and local periodicals	Minimum, 3 major daily papers
United States of America (1) 1966 (2) B. 1	ALA Standards (1966). Minimum one current title for each 250 in service area.	
(1) 1962 (2) B. 1	Interim standards (1962). 2,500–50,000 population, 25 to 150 periodical and newspaper titles. Files kept up to 10 years	Included with periodicals

Table 12. Non-print materials

Country[1] (1) Date of standards (2) Category	Standards, referring mainly to audio-visual materials
Canada (1) 1969 (2) B. 1	Discs and tape recordings, 750 to 5,000. Discs and tape recordings added annually, 125 to 500. Films, filmstrips, film slides, etc., added annually, 25 to 75
Norway (1) 1972 (2) A. 1	Size and nature of collections, see text. Annual additions and maintenance, not more than 10–15 per cent of total media budget Apparatus (examples): record players, up to 10,000 population, 1–3; 10,000–20,000, 3–5; over 20,000, 5–8. Radio/television: over 10,000 population, 1
South Africa (1) 1968 (2) B. 1	In libraries serving populations above 40,000 special allocation for audio-visual materials. Other libraries to rely on provincial library systems
United States of America (1) 1970 (2) B. 1	Collections, standards (examples): sound recordings, one for each 50 persons in service area, minimum 5,000 discs/reels of which 20 per cent non-musical; films, 16 mm, over 5,000 population, total 3,000, annual additions 200. Minimum 20 per cent materials budget for audio-visual materials. Repair and replacement, 10–15 per cent annual audio-visual materials budget

1. See footnote 1, Table 10.

Table 13. Service points and hours of opening

Country[1] (1) Date of standards (2) Category	Service points and weekly hours of opening
Australia (1) 1972 (2) B. 1	Low density of population. Over 5,000 population: full-time branches, not less than 40 hours; 2,500–5,000: part-time branches, not less than 15 hours; up to 2,500: mobile library or deposit station. At least 30 per cent service hours outside users' normal working hours
Canada (British Columbia) (1) 1973 (2) A. 1	Small and medium-sized libraries. Population (minimum hours): under 1,000, 8; 1,000–2,499, 15; 2,500–4,999, 20; 5,000–9,999, 30; 10,000–24,999, 40; 25,000–39,999, 50; 40,000–50,000, 60

1. See footnote 1, Table 10.

Country (1) Date of standards (2) Category	Service points and weekly hours of opening
Denmark (1) 1965 (2) A. 1	Population (minimum hours): full-time libraries, under 10,000, 20 (5 days); 10,000–20,000, 30 (5 days); over 20,000, 10 a.m. to 8 p.m. weekdays, earlier Saturdays. Part-time libraries, 2 hours over 2 days to 10–14 hours over 4 days
Federal Republic of Germany (1) 1964–73 (2) B. 1	Main libraries, 40–60 hours including Saturday. Grade I libraries, small communities, 30 hours on 5 days. Average branch library, 35 hours. Mobile libraries, visits weekly; stops 'for a sufficient length of time'
Hungary (1) 1971–72 (2) A. 1	Sub-standard, 8 hours; basic grade, 20–24 hours at least 4 days; medium grade, adult 48 hours, children 30 hours; high grade, 48 hours
Malaysia (1) 1968 (2) B. 2	Below 5,000 population, bookmobiles, half-hour stop. Part-time branches, 5,000–10,000, 10 hours; 10,000–25,000, 15 hours. Full-time branches, 25,000–50,000, 24 hours; 50,000–100,000, 36½ hours; central libraries, 100,000–250,000, 60 hours, over 500,000, 72

Netherlands

(1) 1970
(2) A. 2

Population	Hours	Days	Evenings
Up to 1,500	10	2	1
5,000–10,000	20	4	2
50,000–100,000	40	5	3
Over 200,000	60	6	5

New Zealand (1) 1966 (2) B. 1	Libraries open as long as consistent with economy. Lending services normally six days a week. Large libraries to be open on Sundays, in winter months at least, for reading and study. Branch libraries only in compact areas, population above 5,000

Norway

Population	Main libraries		Branch libraries	
	Hours	Days	Hours	Days
Up to 1,000	6	2	2–4	—
1,000–5,000	6–15	2–4	4–15	2–4
5,000–7,000	15–20	4–5	15–20	4–5
above 7,000	20	5	20	5

(1) 1972
(2) A. 1

South Africa (1) 1968 (2) B. 1	Libraries open at times best suited to needs of users. Those serving populations above 4,000 should open six days a week, including evenings and Saturday. Mobile libraries—visits weekly; stops not less than 30 minutes

Country (1) Date of standards (2) Category	Service points and weekly hours of opening
United Kingdom (1) 1971 (2) A. 2	Major service points. Central libraries and administrative headquarters, at least 60 hours; district libraries, at least 60 hours. Other service points. Under 4,000 population, 15–20 hours; over 4,000, 30 hours. Mobile libraries, serve populations less than 1,500 and between 1,500 and 4,000. Minimum service, fortnightly visits, stop 15 minutes.
United States of America (1) 1966 (2) B. 1	Minimum standards for public library systems. Central resource library, at least 66 hours; community libraries, 10,000–25,000, 45–66 hours; over 25,000, 66–72 hours
(1) 1962 (2) B. 1	Interim standards for small public libraries. Under 2,500 population, 15 hours; 25,000–50,000, 60 hours. Mobile libraries, minimum service, fortnightly visits, adequate stop for readers' advisory service

TABLE 14. Registered readers and circulation

Country[1] (1) Date of standards (2) Category	Standard	
	Percentage of registered readers	Volumes borrowed annually (per head population served)
Belgium (1) 1968 (2) A. 2	25 per cent of population 20 per cent of population over 15 years 40 per cent under 15 years	—
Federal Republic of Germany (1) 1964 (2) B. 1	15 per cent of population	4.5 volumes
Hungary (1) 1972 (2) A. 1	Up to 8,000 population, 25 per cent (7 per cent children) Over 8,000 population, 21 per cent (6 per cent children)	—
New Zealand (1) 1966 (2) B. 1	40 per cent	8–10 volumes (excluding rental collections), at least

1. See footnote 1, Table 10.

Country (1) Date of standards (2) Category	Standard	
	Percentage of registered readers	Volumes borrowed annually (per head population served)
		3 from children's/ young people's collections. Issues from rental collections—see text
Poland (1) 1968 (2) A. 1	From 40 per cent under 2,500 population, to 30 per cent over 20,000	—
South Africa (1) 1968 (2) B. 1	—	6 volumes, 25 per cent non-fiction

TABLE 15. Staff

Country[1] (1) Date of standards (2) Category	Standards for non-manual staff
Australia (1) 1972 (2) B. 1	Minimum 1 member of staff to 2,500 population served. Unless centralized services provided by state library authority, at least one-third librarians
Belgium (1) 1968 (2) A. 2	Excluding chief librarian, staff at rate of 1 to 800 readers or 3,200 inhabitants; additional for specialized services (e.g. children ,audio-visual)
Canada (British Columbia) (1) 1973 (2) A. 1	Under 10,000 population. Librarian plus 1 member of staff for first 4,000 and 1 for every 2,000 population. 10,000–50,000. At least 1 member of staff for every 2,000 population, including at least 1 librarian for every 10,000
Denmark (1) 1967 (2) A. 2	One member of staff for every 2,000 population, except where annual issues exceed 8 volumes per head or there are additional services, including branches
France (1) 1972 (2) A. 1	Average of 1 member of staff per 2,300 population; approximately one-third should be librarians
German Democratic Republic (1) 1955–56 (2) A. 1	One member of staff for every 500 readers. In children's libraries 1 for every 300. Librarians and other staff in equal proportions. Additional staff, mainly librarians, in libraries with regional functions, etc.

1. See footnote 1, Table 10.

Country (1) Date of standards (2) Category	Standards for non-manual staff
Federal *Republic* *of Germany* (1) 1964–69 (2) B. 2	1964. Based on book circulation and accessions. For readers' services, 1 librarian for 30,000 annual issues. For other duties, 1 librarian for every 7,500 accessions. 2 non-professional assistants for every librarian
(1) 1973 (2) B. 2	1973. Total staff, 1 per 2,000 population served
Hungary (1) 1971–72 (2) A. 1	Based on book circulation and accessions—see text. Children's service, higher levels, for every 500 readers a full-time children's librarian
Japan (1) 1969 (2) A. 2	Librarians (minima): prefecture libraries, 24; city/ward libraries above 100,000 population, 7; town and village, 3+; city/town/village, 7+, with additions according to circumstances. Other staff equal, or exceed, trained librarians
Malaysia (1) 1968 (2) B. 2	One member of staff for every 4,000 population served; ratio 1 professional to 4 non-professional. Minimum of 1 qualified librarian for every 50,000 population served
Netherlands (1) 1970 (2) A. 2	Total staff (excluding managerial and specialized staff) calculated on basis of population served and size of required book stock. Proportion of professional to non-professional staff approximately equal
New Zealand (1) 1966 (2) B. 1	Minimum standards. One member of staff for every 2,000 population served; at least 33 per cent professional or intermediate staff. Provisional standards. For libraries up to 10,000 population —see text
Norway (1) 1970 (2) A. 2	Largely based on number of population served and of annual issues; population per staff member from 3,400, when issues 3–5 per head, to 1,300, when issues 9
Singapore (1) 1967 (2) A. 1	One member of staff for every 4,000 estimated population
South Africa (1) 1968 (2) B. 1	Alternative standards. (a) One member of staff for every 2,500 literate population served; (b) Based on annual issues from, under 10,000 population, 1 staff to 25,000 issues to, over 250,000 population, 1 staff to 15,000 issues
Sweden (1) 1972 (2) A. 2	One staff member for every 15,000 issues annually. Proportion between librarians and other staff 1 : 1.7

Country (1) Date of standards (2) Category	Standards for non-manual staff
United Kingdom (1) 1962–71 (2) A. 2	Minimum of one member of staff per 2,500 population served; 40 per cent librarians in towns up to 100,000 and in counties, 33 per cent in urban areas of concentrated population, possibly lower in largest cities, minimum 25 per cent
United States of America (1) 1966 (2) B. 1 (1) 1962 (2) B. 1	ALA Standards. One member of staff for every 2,000 population served, professional and sub-professional 33 per cent. Aspects of service for which professional staff required indicated Interim standards for small public libraries. One staff member for every 2,500 population served, professional and sub-professional approximately 33 per cent
U.S.S.R. (1) 1948 (2) A. 1	Numbers of staff depend on the size of the collection, the volume of work and the structure of the library

TABLE 16. Library buildings (total floor areas)

Country[1] (1) Date of standards (2) Category	Total floor areas (Population in thousands. Areas in m² per thousand population, normally excluding conference, exhibition or other meeting rooms)				
Australia (1) 1972 (2) B. 1	Population 10–20 Area 42 (as IFLA Public Library Building Standards 1959) Reduced areas where library materials and professional services centrally provided	20–35 39	35–60 35	60–100 31	over 100 28
Belgium (1) 1968 (2) A. 2	Population 3 Area 61–74	10 41	20 37	50 28	100+ See text

Canada (British Columbia) Small and medium-sized libraries:

(1) 1973 (2) A. 1	Population up to 1 Area 12	1–2.5 12–69	2.5–5 69–65	5–10 65–56	10–25 56–48	25–40 48–50	40–50 50–46

Denmark (1) 1967 (2) A. 2	Population 5 Area 109 Standards include lecture and meeting rooms but exclude book stack and circulation, etc., areas	10 76	15 72	20 67	25 61

Excluding conference and meeting rooms areas are:
81   61   58   54   49

1. See footnote 1, Table 10.

Country (1) Date of standards (2) Category	Total floor areas (Population in thousands. Areas in m² per thousand population, normally excluding conference, exhibition or other meeting rooms)							

France
(1) 1972
(2) A. 1

Population	5–6	6–10	10–20	20–30	30–45	45–60	60–75
Area	70–58	77–46	65–33	57–38	51–34	42–31	34–27

Federal
Republic
of Germany
(1) 1968
(2) B. 1

Population	15	20	25	30	40	50	60	80	100
Area	37	35	34	33	42	42	41	44	42

Figures exclude areas for circulation and services

Hungary
(1) 1972
(2) A. 1

Libraries serving up to 30,000 population:

Population	up to 3.5	5–8	8–12	over 12
Area	55	50	44	36

Libraries providing central and high-grade services:
55 m² per 1,000 inhabitants directly served plus 2 m² per
1,000 inhabitants of total area

Japan
(1) 1969
(2) A. 2

Prefecture libraries—see text.
City/ward libraries, from (approximately) 70 to 25 m² per
1,000 population

New Zealand
(1) 1966
(2) B. 1

From 65 m² per 1,000 population (up to 15,000) to 56 (15,000–50,000).
Libraries serving less than 10,000, 20 per cent area for children

Poland
(1) 1968
(2) A. 1

Population	under 2.5	2.5–5	5–10	10–15	15–20	20–25
Area	87	104–74	124–68	80–61	64–53	57–51

Areas stated exclude conference and meeting rooms but include rooms
for adult classes in libraries over 5,000 population

Singapore
(1) 1967
(2) A. 1

Total library space, 23 m² per thousand estimated population

South Africa
(1) 1968
(2) B. 1

Population	1	4	8	10	10 to 1 million
Area	185	93	72	64	65 to 28

Sweden
(1) 1965
(2) A. 1

50 to 100 m² per 1,000 inhabitants (probably includes areas for
cultural, etc., activities)

United States
of America
(1) 1962
(2) B. 1

No floor areas given in main standards document. Figures given in
interim standards for small public libraries are:

Population	under 2.5	2.5–5	5–10	10–25	25–50
Area	74	65	65	65	56

TABLE 17. Library buildings (areas occupied by various departments)

Country[1]
(1) Date of standards
(2) Category — Areas occupied by various departments (Population in thousands. Areas in m² per thousand population)

Belgium
(1) 1968
(2) A. 2

	Population			
	3	10	20	50
Adult lending (Area)	19.0	14.7	13.6	10.9
Children's lending	11.7	6.3	6.1	3.7
Reading room	8.3	4.4	4.4	2.6

Denmark
(1) 1967
(2) A. 2

	Population				
	5	10	15	20	25
Adult lending (Area)	21.6	17.1	15.6	14.0	12.6
Youth section	3.6	2.1	1.6	1.4	1.2
Adult reference and reading rooms	14.4	8.7	8.8	8.0	7.4
Children's lending	12.0	9.0	8.4	8.1	7.9
Children's reference, study, etc., rooms	12.0	7.5	7.2	6.5	6.0

France
(1) 1972
(2) A. 1

	Population						
	5-6	6-10	10-20	20-30	30-45	45-60	60-75
Adult lending (Area)	26-22	27-16	24-12	17-11	11-7	8-6	6-5
Adult reference and reading	—[2]	—[2]	—[2]	8-5	6-4	7-5	6-5
Children, lending and reference	16-13	20-12	14-7	7.5-5	5-3.3	3.3-2.5	3.3-2.7

Poland
(1) 1968
(2) A. 1

	Population				
	2.5-5	5-10	10-15	15-20	20-25
Adult lending (Area)	22-18	19-12	13-10	10-9	8-6
Adult reading, including periodicals	24-21	23-11	15-10	11-9	10-9
Children's lending	—	7-3	4-3	3	4
Children's reading	—	14-7	9-6	6-5	5-4

1. See footnote 1, Table 10.
2. Combined with adult lending.

Country[1] (1) Date of standards (2) Category	Space for cultural and educational activities (Population in thousands. Areas in m².)						

Belgium
(1) 1968
(2) A. 2

	Population	3	10	20	50
Meeting rooms[2]	Area	40	80	100	150
Gramophone record library		28	28 +45³	56 +45³	64 +45³
Children's story hours		30	45	45	45
Workshop, free expression		45	45	45	45

Denmark
(1) 1967
(2) A. 2

	Population	5	10	15	20	25
Exhibition and conference rooms	Area	60	84	108	132	156
Rooms for study groups		36	60	60	90	90
Audio-visual/music room		—	—	30	30	30
Study rooms (carrels), adult		6	6	12	18	24
Study room (homework), children		—	—	18	24	30

France
(1) 1972
(2) A. 1

	Population	6–10	10–20	20–30	30–45	45–60	60–75
General activities rooms (meetings, exhibitions, etc.)	Area	40	50	70	80	120	140
Gramophone record library		—	20	40	50	70	70

Sweden

Libraries designed as cultural centres, see text

United States of America
(1) 1970
(2) B. 1

Libraries and library systems serving over 150,000 population. Within the system at least 1 meeting room large enough for audio-visual programmes for groups of 100 or more.
Branches—a suitable space for this purpose

U.S.S.R.
(1) 1970–74
(2) A. 1

Standards provide areas for group studies and lectures and for auditoria

1. See footnote 1, Table 10.
2. At 1 m² per person.
3. Listening room for 30 persons.

Australia

The Library Association of Australia, in 1969, set up a committee to prepare standards for public libraries and the document produced, *Interim Minimum Standards for Public Libraries*,[1] was approved by the association and published in 1972. The committee had the benefit of standards drafted earlier by the association's Public Libraries Section, but not formally adopted, of standards of book provision[2] and siting and design of public library buildings[3] published by the Library Board of Western Australia, of public library objectives and standards, issued by the Library Board of New South Wales in 1969,[4] and of a report of the Library Council in Victoria to the state government on the public library service in that state, including proposed minimum standards,[5] published in 1972. The committee adopted, where possible, or adapted, the standards recommended for Victoria.

The committee aimed to produce a document which could be used in each state and as a basis for planning and of evaluation of existing library services in the states of the Commonwealth, but they recognized that the detailed standards of library provision appropriate to one state were likely to differ from those appropriate to another, and that certain standards were not applicable in Western Australia[6] nor perhaps to those other states (South Australia, Tasmania and Queensland) making, in whole or part, centralized provision of book stocks and professional services.

The committee, in preparing the standards, were handicapped

1. Library Association of Australia, *Interim Minimum Standards for Public Libraries*, Sydney, 1972.
2. Library Board of Western Australia, *Book Provision and Book Selection: Policy and Practice*, Perth, 1966.
3. Library Board of Western Australia, *Siting and Design of Public Library Buildings: Notes for Guidance of Local Authorities and Architects*, Perth, 1962.
4. Library Board of New South Wales, *Public Library Objectives and Standards*, Sydney, 1969.
5. Library Council of Victoria, *Public Library Service in Victoria: A Report to the State Government*, Melbourne, 1970 (Appendix I: Minimum Standards for Public Libraries).
6. In Western Australia the population, outside the metropolitan area of Perth (approximately 500,000), is very sparse. Local authorities, large in area but small in population, could not provide effective library service on their own or with any reasonable level of financial aid from the state. A library system has been devised whereby elements requiring large financial resources, such as books and central professional services, are provided by the state library board, while elements better contributed and organized locally, as premises and staff, are local responsibilities.

by the lack of statistical information on individual library services in some states and by the absence of informed and critical comment on existing public libraries. They referred to the need for federal aid, the case for which had been argued in a report of the Australian Advisory Council on Bibliographical Services,[1] and said that services in Australia were unlikely to achieve the standards proposed without help from the Commonwealth Government.

The following is a summary of the minimum standards proposed.

PROVISION AND ADMINISTRATION

Everyone should have access to public library services without charge. The cost should be shared by the state and the local community, the contribution of the state being in cash or in books and service or in a combination of both.

In association with local authorities, the state government should work towards the provision of library service according to the standards. To this end they should promote the organization of libraries into systems as part of a state-wide plan for efficient and adequate public library service.

State governments should provide a programme of services in support of their public libraries, including, for example, (a) study, review and promotion of legislation in support of public library development; (b) supervision and evaluation of existing public libraries; (c) provision of advisory and consultative services to local authorities and librarians concerning public library planning and operation; (d) provision of technical and bibliographical services and of in-service training and continuing education of library staff; (e) encouragement of improvement by means of subject specialization, co-operative storage, union catalogues and a centre for reference inquiries, inter-library lending and promotion of library co-operation generally.

The public library should be an integral part of local government, and on this assumption (not equally valid in all states, notably Western Australia), advice was given about such matters as supervision by statutory library committees or governing bodies;

1. Australian Advisory Council on Bibliographical Services, *Libraries for the Public: A Statement of Needs*, Canberra, 1968.

regular reports on the operation and needs of the libraries; definition of functions of library committees and staff, and, with regional systems, the incorporation of such definitions in legal agreements between constituent authorities; appointment of chief librarians (who should attend all meetings of library committees) as chief administrators with responsibility for personnel selection and management, the development of programmes and services, and the selection of books and related materials, equipment and furnishings.

Each public library should have a defined policy, reviewed at regular intervals. This should outline the aims of the library, having regard to local requirements, and define such matters as responsibilities of senior staff, selection policy for books and related materials, adoption of the Library Association of Australia's *Statement on Freedom to Read*, the provision of material and services for special groups and co-operation with other institutions and groups, as well as employment policy.

Economic provision of public service being dependent on a population able to provide the necessary financial support, the smaller the population unit the higher the *per capita* expenditure on the services. A population unit of less than 35,000 was considered in general unable to support an effective public library service. Therefore, except where the state library authority provided centralized services, it was proposed that public library systems should be created to provide units of adequate size.

The state library authority should provide the greater part of public library services when the local authorities, whether singly or together, could not provide service, such as in areas where sparse population, geographical factors, lack of communication or the absence of identity of interest precluded independent service.

The number of service points would be affected by both size and density of population. The advantages of large book stocks, of more senior, better qualified and of specialized staff must be weighed against the disadvantages of distance of readers from libraries, particularly children.

Except in high density population areas, the following basis for service points was suggested; over 5,000 population, full-time branch operated and supervised by professional librarian and open not less than 40 hours a week; 2,500 to 5,000 population, part-time branch, operated by non-professional staff and open not less than 15 hours a week; up to 2,500 population, a bookmobile service, or (as a last resort) deposit stations in premises not exclusively used as a library.

Service points should be fully integrated and supervised by senior professional staff through regular visits. They should operate effective reference and request services. There should be inter-availability of borrowing facilities in the state and desirably in the Commonwealth. Service points should be open for the same hours each day, avoiding closure for such as meal breaks; at least 30 per cent of the service hours should lie outside the normal working week of the population.

All public libraries should lend freely to each other and to other kinds of libraries. Where no adequate state-wide lending organization existed, co-operation within an area between special, school, college, university and public libraries would ensure access to all material available locally before requests were made to other municipal or state, national or international centres. Co-operative selection, storage, and technical services should be developed, and staff should meet with staff of other types of library in an area, in professional organizations, workshops and conferences, to exchange ideas and establish joint programmes.

Public libraries should record, analyse and report essential information about their service, and evaluation of the service was essential.

SERVICE TO USERS

Public libraries should collect and organize books and related materials and make these available for use at home and in the libraries. Conditions of loan should be adequate to allow use of material borrowed. No charges should be made for loan of library material for home use. Advisory services should be provided to assist readers in the selection and use of material.

Public libraries should provide an adequate reference and information service from their own resources, or other sources such as the state reference library. They should serve groups and organizations with advice on resources available, provision of materials related to group programmes, organize visits to the library and provide speakers on library topics. They should serve individuals and groups with special needs, notably the underprivileged, including the economically, educationally and culturally disadvantaged, the physically handicapped, patients and inmates of hospitals and other institutions, old people, newcomers with limited knowledge of the language and customs of the area, groups or individuals engaged in specialized programmes, such as adult education. Public libraries should promote or sponsor group activities, such as local history and film societies. They should develop a programme of public relations and publicity and promote the establishment and use of other libraries in their area.

Children's libraries, with a children's librarian, should be an integral part of the public library service, the requirements of children being considered in planning and provision. There should be as few restrictions as possible, no minimum age limit and children should be able to use the adult section on the basis of need and individual development.

Public libraries should co-operate with school libraries in their area. Public and school library services should be complementary. While there would necessarily be duplication of some material, the school library would in general provide material related to the teaching programme, which it was not the public library's primary role to provide.

BOOKS AND MATERIALS

Public libraries existed to make available books and related materials required for information, education and recreation. Australian libraries purchased the bulk of their printed material from the United Kingdom, the United States and Australia. The total publishing output of these countries in 1969 was about 46,000 titles, more than two-thirds being adult non-fiction. From this approximate figure of more than 30,000 titles, Australian public libraries had to select to provide as wide a coverage as possible. The lowest annual acquisition providing a reasonable selection of newly published materials and maintaining a collection of 70,000 volumes (regarded as a necessary minimum) was 8,750 volumes per annum. This was based on an average life expectancy of a public library book of eight years and referred to a public library or system of public libraries maintained by one

TABLE 19

Minimum population	Minimum book stock	Minimum volumes acquired annually	Approximate allocation according to nature of community served (%)
35,000	70,000	8,750	40–45 adult non-fiction;
60,000	100,000	12,500	20–25 adult fiction;
100,000	150,000	18,750	35 children, of which:
200,000	250,000	31,250	10 picture and beginning books,
300,000	300,000	37,500	15 junior fiction, 10 junior non-fiction.

local authority. Where there was a centrally provided book stock for the whole state, the standards expressed by the state authority should obtain.

The minimum recommended book stock was as shown in Table 19.

The stock should reflect the needs and interests of the community served and every public library service should have a written statement of policy defining criteria for the selection and maintenance of its collection. The annual acquisition rate must be large enough to provide a reasonable selection of the annual publication output. In each service point, at least 10 per cent of total adult acquisitions should be replacements, and at least 5 per cent of its total adult acquisitions should be duplicates. In a children's library with a basic collection of children's books, annual purchases should contain no more than 30 per cent of new titles; at least 70 per cent should be replacements and duplicates of basic titles and standard works. The minimum book stock available at service points should be one volume per head for over 10,000 population, increasing to one and a half for between 5,000 and 10,000, and to two for between 2,500 and 5,000.

Other materials appropriate to the library should be part of the collection, and correspondingly accessible. A collection of periodicals, including newspapers, should be maintained on the following basis:[1]

1. Serials, i.e. annuals and continuations, are excluded.

towns with a population of 35,000–50,000 should have 150–200 titles; 50,000–100,000, 200–300; 100,000–200,000, 300–400; 200,000–300,000, 400–500.

A representative collection of periodicals should be available at every service point. Provision should be made for storage of back files.

Policy regarding preservation, discarding and local and central storage of periodicals should be determined co-operatively with other libraries and with the state library authority. Each public library should acquire and preserve periodicals within its subject specialization.

The collection of printed materials should include maps, charts and other graphic materials. Audio-visual materials, including pictures, films, slides, filmstrips, music scores, recordings, video-tapes and various forms of micro-reproduction, properly constituted part of the collection.

Open access stock must be maintained in an attractive physical condition. Material obsolete in form or content should be constantly deleted, and allocated to stack, offered to co-operative storage or other libraries, or discarded. There should be public catalogues of the total collection at all service points within the library system, with a separate catalogue for the children's collection.

STAFF

The public library system must have staff of competence and integrity, to render effective service and to function as an unbiased source of information. The number should be sufficient to provide efficient service when the library was open and to perform the duties involved in making available the library materials. Local factors, the service given and the opening hours all bore on the composition of staff.

Library positions should be clearly defined and differentiated in terms of qualifications, duties and responsibility. Positions should be distinguished as professional, sub-professional and clerical. One member of non-manual staff per 2,500 population was the minimum to provide reasonable service. The smaller the population the more staff per head would be required. Unless centralized staff services were provided by the state library authority, at least one-third of staff should be librarians.

Professional duties, which should include the selection of books, should be carried out by librarians. Each full-time service point should be in charge of a librarian. In addition to the chief librarian, a deputy chief librarian, a children's librarian and branch librarian, as appropriate, were essential appointments for all services of 35,000 or more population.

Library authorities should provide good conditions of employment to attract and retain staff of high calibre and should support the initial and continuing education of librarians by various means, including sending staff to library schools and professional meetings, and sending qualified staff to other courses.

BUILDINGS

The public library building should create the environment most conducive to the use and enjoyment of the library's resources. It should be located centrally in respect of population density and public transport facilities, main local traffic routes, ease of pedestrian access, schools, and should be in the main commercial area, near a public car park or have its own parking area. Exterior identification should be readily seen.

The site should be large enough to have all public areas on the entrance floor and should allow for economic use and future expansion. It should be level, or capable of being levelled at low cost, so that no steps will be required. The frontage should have minimum sun exposure and protection from prevailing winds.

The size of the building should be related to the total population to be served and the scale adopted by the International Federation of Library Associations was recommended, namely: with a total population to be served of 10,000–20,000, 450 ft² (42 m²) per 1,000 population; 20,000–35,000, 420 ft² (39 m²); 35,000–65,000, 375 ft² (35 m²); 65,000–100,000, 335 ft² (31 m²); over 100,000, 300 ft² (28 m²).

For populations over 100,000 the size of the building might be less than 300 ft² (28 m²) per 1,000 population, but special weight should be given to a number of variable factors, e.g. the population of the area served by the building and the number of other service points.[1]

For a building other than the central building in a system the ratios proposed should be applied to the population expected to be served by that building. For buildings serving less than 10,000 population the ratio 450 ft² (41.8 m²) per 1,000 population should be applied with a minimum area of 1,500 ft² (139 m²).

The library building should be designed for efficiency, flexibility and future expansion. Accommodation likely to be required was listed, including (as well as the traditional lending and reference provision) exhibition and display areas, listening and viewing areas for audio-visual materials, and meeting rooms for local groups and activities. Attention should be given to the functional relationship of accommodation. Ease of access, especially for the physically handicapped, must be considered.

Interior finishes, furniture, fittings and mechanical equipment of appropriate and adequate quality and quantity should be provided in the building. Advice was given regarding minimum light intensities and light-reflection factors and attention recommended to acoustic control. Air-conditioning should be used where necessary. Furniture and fittings should be durable, easily maintained and in harmony with the architecture. They should contribute to efficiency and provide a comfortable, inviting environment.

Seating should be provided on the minimum basis of one and a half to two readers' seats per 1,000 population served, except for libraries serving less than 10,000 population, two to three seats per 1,000.

Areas provided for extension activities might have direct access

---

1. In an appendix were given the following minimum public library building standards approved by the Library Board of Western Australia, of interest where library materials and professional services are centrally provided:

Design population (i.e. estimated population 7–10 years ahead, of the defined service area of the library)	Floor area per 1,000 population (excludes reading rooms, study areas, staff accommodation, entrances, stairs, passages, etc.)	
Up to 10,000	200 ft²	18.6 m²
10,001 to 15,000	195 ft²	18.1 m²
15,001 to 20,000	190 ft²	17.7 m²
20,001 to 25,000	185 ft²	17.2 m²
Above 25,000	180 ft²	16.7 m²

from the exterior of the buildings; access to public toilets, kitchen facilities, cloakroom; a flat floor with stage or dais; means of partitioning into smaller areas. Equipment should include display screens and tables; record players, tape recorders and players, slide and film projectors and screens.

Belgium

In Belgium the present library administration is based on a law of 1921, and comes under the ministers of culture, of whom there are two, one for each of the linguistic communities, the Minister of French Culture and the Minister of Flemish Culture. There are also two ministers of education, but a unified Ministry of Education and Culture, one section of which, called Service des Bibliothèques Publiques, is responsible for the development of the public libraries. The information given below refers particularly to the French-speaking parts of the country. The arrangements are not all the same in the Flemish-speaking areas.

Grants are given annually by the ministry to all approved public libraries towards the cost of books, chosen in accordance with the advice of the Public Libraries Department. In addition, the government pays a proportion of the salaries of chief librarians and of an assistant librarian. The grants are based on a sliding scale and vary in accordance with the nature of the area and other factors, including an inspector's assessment of the efficiency of the library.

To qualify for government grants, a first grade or important library must have a comprehensive book stock of at least 10,000 volumes, lend 30,000 books annually, have a reading room and employ a librarian and at least one assistant.

A more important category of library receives an additional grant, the total grant being a maximum of 50 per cent of running costs. This class of library must meet the following requirements. It must possess a comprehensive stock of at least 20,000 volumes, lend at least 50,000 books annually, be open to the public thirty hours a week during six days, have a reading room and reference library and employ a librarian and several assistant librarians.

Mobile libraries receive a grant according to the number of books lent and the number of places visited. Other grants, between 40 and 50 per cent of the expenditure, are available for other purposes, such as towards the cost of renewing and improving equipment, the organization of sections for young people, and for the establishment of record and film libraries.

These are very rudimentary standards by which the efficiency of a library can be judged. More significant are the requirements of the government when it agrees to pay 60 per cent of the cost incurred by local authorities in the construction, extension and repair of public library buildings, and the purchase of equipment, and standards for public library buildings have been produced by the Flemish Section of the National Advisory Council for Public Libraries in 1968 and subsequently adopted, with minor changes, for the French area by the French section of the council and approved by the council.[1]

The minimum standards are being applied by the government and, if they are not currently reached by the local authority applying for a capital grant for new or improved buildings and equipment, the responsible local authority is required to provide over the next ten years sufficient funds to reach the standard.

The council lays down certain general principles on which the provision of library buildings should be based, such as that the building should be functionally designed, taking account of the specific requirements of the activities carried on in a public library, and that new or enlarged buildings should anticipate the needs of the next ten years, and should not be confined to immediate requirements. It then proceeds to lay down minimum standards for the construction and equipment of public libraries, stressing that the minimum can be exceeded if the additional provisions can be justified.

Two introductory notes are of particular interest. There must be 'open access' and the minimum accommodation for a public library in a town of 10,000 inhabitants is expected to include, as well as the traditional accommodation (lending library, reading room, children's library, staff and storage accommodation) a room for meetings, a gramophone record library, a film library (if desired), and toilet accommodation for library users.

1. Conseil Supérieur des Bibliothèques Publiques, *Normes de Construction des Bibliothèques Publiques* [Building Standards for Public Libraries], Brussels, Ministère de la Culture, 1968 (produced in French and Flemish, mimeo).

BOOK STOCKS

The report lays down minimum standards for book stocks and certain conditions which bear on the quality of the service such as:
Approximate percentages of the collection to be held in the various types of books, namely: adult non-fiction, 40–50 per cent minimum; adult fiction, 30–50 maximum; books for children, 10–15 minimum; and reference books and periodicals 5–15 minimum.
In libraries serving over 10,000 population, the children's library should be a separate space, specially planned and situated, preferably close to the adult section and almost all the children's section should be 'open access'.
Tables are given illustrating the total numbers of books required according to the number of inhabitants and status of the library, based on a sliding scale of which the following are the lower and upper figures:
Local libraries: from under 2,000 inhabitants, 2.5 to 3 books per inhabitant; to over 100,000 inhabitants, 1 to 1.3 books per inhabitant.
Regional libraries: from under 25,000 inhabitants, 1.0 books per inhabitant—minimum 30,000 including the local collection; to over 100,000 inhabitants, 0.33 books per inhabitant—minimum 50,000 plus local collection.
Provincial libraries: from under 250,000 inhabitants, 0.8 books per inhabitant—minimum 100,000; to above 1 million inhabitants, 0.4 books per inhabitant—minimum 500,000.
Examples of the resultant figures of total book stock are given in Table 20. These figures relate to the total book stocks of the central library. For branches, the size of the book stocks would

TABLE 20

Population	Number of books	Population	Number of books
1,000	2,500–3,000	50,000	65,000–80,000
10,000	18,000–22,000	75,000	97,500–105,000
20,000	30,000–37,000	100,000	120,000–135,000
30,000	42,000–54,000	125,000	137,000–165,000
40,000	54,000–70,000	150,000	150,000–195,000

TABLE 21

Population	Sub-division[1]	Population			
		From	Percentage	To	Percentage
20,000	A	18,000	60	22,000	60
	B	4,200	14	4,500	12
	C+D	5,400	18	7,600	20
	E	1,500	5	1,800	5
	F	900	3	1,100	3
50,000	A	35,800	55	40,000	50
	B	5,000	8	5,000	6
	C+D	17,800	27	26,800	33
	E	2,600	4	3,000	4
	F	3,800	6	5,200	7
100,000	A	42,000	35	43,200	32
	B	5,000	4	5,000	4
	C+D	57,200	48	69,300	51
	E	3,800	3	4,000	3
	F	12,000	10	13,500	9

1. A, open access not counting duplicates; B, for children not counting duplicates; C, reserve; D, in book stack; E, reference books; F, periodicals.

need to be determined in relation to the size and age composition of the population served, the social and cultural needs of the community served, account being taken of the book stocks of the central library.

Figures are also given for central libraries serving different numbers of inhabitants showing the minimum number and percentages of volumes there should be in different categories (see Table 21).

The figures for periodicals represent copies retained for ten years, if population served is less than 50,000, and for twenty years, if more. Thus, in an area with 20,000 population, the 900 to 1,100 volumes represents 90 to 110 subscriptions.

READING ROOMS, READING CORNERS
(WHERE NO SEPARATE READING ROOM)
AND BROWSING AREAS (IN LENDING LIBRARY)

Advice is given about reading rooms, which are obligatory for adults in libraries in areas with more than 10,000 inhabitants and may be provided in libraries serving less than this number. The

TABLE 22. Area of reading rooms (minimum 25.2 m²)

Number of inhabitants	Places	Table areas (m²)			
		1 place 4 m²	2 places 2.5 m²	4 places 2.25 m²	average 2.9 m²
3,000	8 (minimum)	32	25	25	25
10,000	15–20	60	38	34	44
20,000	30–40	120	75	68	90
50,000	60 (minimum)	—	150	135	—
100,000	No areas recommended; special study required in each case				

area of the reading room will vary according to local circumstances. As a general rule, space should be provided in the reading room on the basis of 1–1½ reading spaces per 1,000 inhabitants, and in the lending library 1 seat for 400 books on open access.

Recommended areas for reading rooms are given in Table 22.

Corners for reading and quiet (coins de lecture et de repos) *in lending libraries*

Guidance is given on the number of seats required and space to be provided in lending libraries and how it is to be used on the basis of 1 seat per 400 volumes on open access. Where there is a separate reading room the seats provided may be deducted, as shown in Table 23. The provision of the maximum possible number of seats, without unduly increasing the distance between the shelves, is recommended.

TABLE 23. Number of seats required

Number of inhabitants	Books on open access with duplicates	Seats	Area (m²)		
			With tables	Without tables	Average
3,000	6,500	15 (minimum)	30	19	24
10,000	18,000	45—15 = 30	60	39	50
20,000	26,500	66—30 = 36	72	47	60
50,000	45,000	102—60 = 42	84	55	70
Up to 150,000	55,000	125—60 = 65	130	82	106

Numbers of readers

It should be assumed that 20 per cent of the population over 15 years of age, and 40 per cent of the population less than 15 years will be registered as readers, equivalent to a figure of 25 per cent of all inhabitants.

Staff accommodation

Excluding the chief librarian, it is recommended that professional, technical and administrative staff should be employed at the rate of 1 for every 800 registered readers or 3,200 inhabitants. Each specialized service—children, gramophone records—would justify at least one extra member of staff. The chief librarian's office requires a minimum of 24.2 m^2 and each member of the staff 8.2 m^2.

Total area of premises

A table of areas is given based on the recommended book stocks for a library open 40 hours a week, and on the following units of measurement:

Average distance between the shelves on open access, 2.76 m.

Average distance between shelves in book stack, 1.36 m.

Capacity of books on open access plus 20 per cent for the counter, etc., 122/m^2.

Capacity of books in book stack, 300/m^2.

Area per person in the reading room, 2.90 m^2.

Area per person in the lending library, 1.60 m^2.

The report finally suggests total areas for libraries (Table 24) serving different populations on the basis of minimum areas for the basic accommodation to be found in all libraries, together with standard areas for additional accommodation, not to be found in all libraries, e.g. for meeting rooms, gramophone record library, children's story hours.

The modification of the 1921 public libraries law has been under discussion for some years and a new draft law was submitted to ministers in 1969 but was not enacted. Since that date, committees of experts of the two *Conseils supérieurs* (French and Flemish) proceeded with a study of the main points of the draft law in order to prepare measures for its implementation. However, as a result of a modified constitution creating cultural councils, any new organization of public libraries will not be governed by a single law but by decrees from each cultural council.

TABLE 24. Library areas (m^2) in relation to population

Services	Population				
	3,000	10,000	20,000	50,000[1]	100,000+
Entrance hall and cloakrooms	18	45	60	90	
Lending (adults)	57	147	272	543	
Catalogues	—	—	—	54	
Lending (children)	35	63	121	186	
Book stacks	10	14	30	110	To be treated
Reading room	25	44	87	143	individually
Librarian[2]	24	24	24	24	according to
Staff	8	24	56	128	local circumstances
Refectory[2]	16	16	22	27	
Circulation and technical installations (heating, lighting, etc.)	30	40	60	80	
TOTAL	223	417	732	1,385	

Possible additions of special services

	3,000	10,000	20,000	50,000	100,000+
Gramophone record library:					
General	20	20	40	40	
Staff	8	8	16	24	
Room (listening)	—	45	45	45	
Meetings room[3]	40	80	100	150	
Individual listening	9	9	9	9	To be treated
Committee room	9	9	9	9	individually
Room (children's story hours)	30	45	45	45	according to
Workshop (free expression)	45	45	45	45	local circumstances
Staff (work with young people)	8	8	8	8	
Small workshop	10	10	10	10	

1. Calculated on basis of library open 60 hours weekly, not 40.
2. In full-time libraries.
3. On basis of 1 m^2 per person.

The proposed reforms involve the establishment of a structure for public libraries comprising local, regional and provincial public libraries, mobile libraries, special public libraries (e.g. for handicapped persons) and a national centre for 'public reading for each cultural community'. Also envisaged is a better distribution between the State, the provinces, and the local authorities of the expenditure involved in the establishment, modernization, development and operation of the public libraries. The staff of libraries would have the backing of a more progressive library law and facilities for their training would be improved.[1]

Canada

Early Canadian public library standards, like early United States standards, recommended minimum expenditure figures as a basis for providing a satisfactory library service. In 1933, in the first major survey of Canadian libraries, an annual expenditure of $1 per head and a minimum total budget of $3,000 was recommended.[2] After the Canadian Library Association was established in 1946, work on standards was undertaken in several fields and *Suggested Standards of Service for Public Libraries* was published in 1955.[3] The committee preparing the standards had been guided by the American Library Association's *Post-War Standards for Public Libraries*, but not governed by this; their objective had been to set up standards which would 'provide good to optimum public library service to Canadians'. The standards were 'targets at which to aim . . . not binding rules and regulations'.

The 1955 standards were designed for the individual library, while encouraging regional libraries and urging small libraries to consider the advantages of co-operation with a larger unit. Quantitative standards suggested referred, for example, to the desirable number of volumes *per capita* for various populations, the percentage of adult and juvenile borrowers, and circulation figures. One professional librarian was recommended for every 5,000 to 7,500 population served. An annual expenditure per head of $1.50 for minimum service, $2 for reasonably good service,

1. Information supplied by Ministry of Culture, Service des Bibliothèques Publiques, Brussels.
2. Commission of Enquiry, *Libraries in Canada: A Study of Library Conditions and Needs*, Chicago, Ill., American Library Association, 1933.
3. Canadian Library Association, *Suggested Standards of Service for Public Libraries in Canada*, Ottawa, Canadian Library Association, 1955. Issued with revisions as *Standards of Service for Public Libraries in Canada*, Ottawa, Canadian Library Association, 1957.

and $2.50 for superior service was proposed. With slight revisions the standards were reissued in 1957.

The library scene changed considerably in the next ten years due to a number of factors including the work of the Canadian Library Association, the existence of Canada's new National Library (established in 1953) and the influence of the 1955 standards. Larger units of organization had become generally accepted in government and social life, and critics had pointed out the needless duplication of holdings and processing in small libraries. Canada, with a large area and comparatively sparse population, had long looked with interest at regional libraries, of which a demonstration project had been set up in British Columbia in 1930, and the Commission Report of 1933, previously referred to, had recommended a regional organization. Standards for such systems had been inherent in public library standards in 1955 and were to be a basic tenet of the new *Public Library Standards* which was prepared in the second half of the 1960s and published in 1967.[1] As Professor Florence B. Murray has said,[2] recording also the leadership of the federal government as a factor in the preparation of these standards:

It is a statement of the requirements for total library service for the nation, in qualitative, not quantitative terms. . . . Local libraries are to provide the first level of service and are to be linked together to form a system. Co-operation is to be established between university and special libraries on the basis of mutual benefit, and between public and school libraries. Each province or territory should have a programme of library service, and this should be complemented by the Government of Canada. . . .

Stress is placed on the government and organisation of the public library, its financial support, the functions and duties of the public library board and the chief librarian, the employment of professional librarians and the number and qualifications of non-professional employees. The library's collection. . . should include all types of material that are required to achieve the library's objectives and should reflect a variety of views. In a bilingual or multilingual country materials must be available to meet the requirements of all the people. . . .

The only quantitative statement in the document is that a population base of at least 50,000 to 100,000 was required to support an acceptable level of public library service at a reasonable cost.

1. Canadian Library Association, *Public Library Standards*, Ottawa, Canadian Library Association, 1967.
2. In her article 'Canadian Library Standards', *Library Trends*, October 1972, p. 298–311, to which the writer is greatly indebted.

The *Appendix to the Public Library Standards*, published in 1969,[1] contained some quantitative standards related to library collections of both printed and non-printed materials, based on the minimum population for effective public library service as specified in the 1967 standards. These are summarized below:

Printed materials

Circulation book collection: (a) book stock *per capita*—from $1\frac{1}{2}$-2 to $1\frac{1}{2}$-$1\frac{1}{4}$ for highest population; (b) new titles added annually (excluding duplicates or replacements)—from 3,500 to 5,000; (c) percentage of children's books—25 to 30 per cent; (d) percentage of non-fiction in adult collection—70 to 80 per cent.

Reference collection (excluding bound periodicals)—10 to 15 per cent; 50-75 per cent in back files.

Newspaper and periodical subscriptions—200 to 1,000 titles.

Non-print materials

Discs and tape recordings—750 to 5,000.

Discs and tape recordings added annually—125 to 500.

Films, filmstrips, film slides etc., added annually—25 to 75.

The committee preparing the appendix considered that certain quantitative standards should be formulated at the provincial rather than the national level.

The document provided model statements for use by each public library about its purpose and general objectives, and about its policy—relating its programme of service and its objectives—and a typical organization chart. Also discussed were library budgeting, personnel policy, salary structures, public library buildings, and the orientation of new library trustees, for whom a selected list of books and pamphlets was provided.

The Canadian Library Association now regards the 1967 standards, and appendix, as out of date and plans to develop new standards within the next few years.

Included in the list of books and pamphlets for librarians and trustees referred to above was *Quantitative Standards for Public Libraries*, published in 1968 by the Library Development Com-

---

1. Canadian Library Association, *Appendix to the Public Library Standards*, Ottawa, Canadian Library Association, 1969.

mission for British Columbia, a province in which there has long been leadership from the government and the provincial library association, and where real interest in standards has been shown. This document was designed to supplement the qualitative criteria of the national standards, and set out the lowest grade of acceptable library service for small- and medium-sized libraries. The commission expected these standards to be soon replaced by figures representing an adequate rather than a minimal service, and indicated a date, 31 March 1971, after which any library or library system falling short of the minimum standards might be obliged to forego all or part of its provincial support until the deficiency had been remedied.

The standards have now been replaced by *Quantitative Standards for Public Libraries* (1973).[1] In the new standards the Library Development Commission stated that the former standards were considered minimal for 1971 and that between 1968 and 1971 many libraries had achieved them and were eligible to receive maximum provincial support. The revised standards would be effective on 1 April 1976. The commission considered the further three years should be sufficient time for every library board to upgrade its service to meet the new standards. These are shown in Tables 25 and 26.

TABLE 25. Quantitative standards for small and medium-sized libraries in British Columbia

	Libraries serving under 10,000 population	Libraries serving 10,000–50,000 population
Book stock—currently useful		
Minimum book stock	3,000 volumes or 3 volumes *per capita*, whichever is greater	30,000 volumes or 2 volumes *per capita*, whichever is greater
Minimum expenditure for books, binding, periodicals, etc.	$1 *per capita*	$1 *per capita*
Minimum reference collection	40 titles (not volumes) from the commission's list	100 titles (not volumes) from the commission's list
Minimum number of periodical subscriptions	20 from the commission's list	40 from the commission's list

(Continued)

1. Library Development Commission, *Quantitative Standards for Public Libraries*, Victoria, British Columbia, 1973.

	Libraries serving under 10,000 population	Libraries serving 10,000–50,000 population
Personnel		
Person in charge	*For future appointments* Must have following minimum qualifications: Under 5,000 population, high-school graduation (some university desirable). 5,000–10,000, 2–4 years university (some library service training desirable)	*For future appointments* Must be a professional librarian
Minimum staff (includes pages but not maintenance personnel)	Additional staff, preferably paid, on basis: 1 for first 4,000 population and 1 for each additional 2,000 in service area, for the period the library is open	Must be at least 1 full-time person for every 2,000 population, including at least one professional librarian for every 10,000 population

Service	Population	Hours weekly (minimum)	Population	Hours weekly (minimum)
Hours of opening	Under 1,000	8	10,000–24,999	40
	1,000–2,499	15	25,000–39,999	50
	2,500–4,999	20	40,000–50,000	60
	5,000–9,999	30		

Every library serving over 2,500 population must have a listed telephone

Finance	Every public library association must receive $2.50 *per capita*, but not less than $2,000 annually from municipal funds	Minimum local support per library: population 10,000–24,999, $3 *per capita*; 25,000–50,000, $4 *per capita*

TABLE 26. Facilities

Population	Total floor space (ft², m² in parentheses)	Population	Total floor space (ft², m² in parentheses)
Up to 999	1,300 (120.77)	10,000–24,999	5,000–13,000 (464.51–1,207.74)
1,000–2,499	1,300–1,850 (120.77–171.87)	25,000–39,999	13,000–21,600 (1,207.74–2,006.70)
2,500–4,999	1,850–3,500 (171.87–325.16)	40,000–50,000	21,600–24,500 (2,006.70–2,276.12)
5,000–10,000	3,500–6,000 (325.16–557.42)		

Denmark[1]

The Scandinavian countries have among the highest and most uniformly even standards of public library service in the world, and Denmark shares with Sweden the reputation for providing the best service.

In Denmark not only have the State subsidies been favourable—fixed proportions of local expenditure are paid without any maximum being prescribed—but the denser population, the relative compactness of the area and better communications have meant that a more tightly knit library system could be established.

A basic problem has been—and to some extent still is—the existence of many small local authorities (communes) with independent library authorities, many of them with very small populations. Up to 1970 there were some 1,200 communes and an equal number of library authorities, of which only about 110 had more than 5,000 inhabitants and only 9 more than 50,000. About 440 had less than 1,000 each. In 1970 the number of communes was reduced to 277 and the library authorities (1972) have been reduced to 256, some libraries serving more than 1 commune. Of the new communes 164 have less than 10,000, 36 less than 5,000 inhabitants. Of the communes 156 (with about 4 million inhabitants) are served by libraries with full-time professional staff, 120 (about 900,000 inhabitants) by part-time libraries run by non-professional staff (mainly teachers).

A system of regional central libraries based on the libraries in the larger towns has been established and these libraries, with additional State and county aid, supplement the book provision made locally by the smaller libraries and help them in other ways. The number of these libraries—one in each county—has been reduced from thirty-three to fourteen.

1. The first part of this survey is based on an article in *Scandinavian Public Library Quarterly*, Vol. 2, No. 2, 1969, by Aase Bredsdorff and V. Klingberg-Nielsen, Library Inspectors at the Danish State Inspection of Public Libraries, and the second on the report *Public Library Buildings: Standards and Type Plans for Library Premises in Areas with Populations of Between 5,000 and 25,000*, op. cit., see footnote 2, page 173. Acknowledgments are made of the help given by the Danish State Inspectorate and the English translator of the report, Oliver Stallybrass.

Under the Danish Public Libraries Act 1964,[1] the purpose of the libraries is defined as 'to promote the spread of knowledge, education and culture by making books and other materials available free of charge'. More detailed definitions of satisfactory library service are left for Regulations which the Minister of Cultural Affairs has power to make containing 'detailed provisions concerning the establishment, organization and running of public libraries, including general guidance about premises, staff and book stock etc., for the various types of library'.

Two regulations have been made under this act. One, in 1965[2] (which was revision of previous regulations), deals with the general activities of the public libraries and can be described as setting qualitative standards. The other, in 1966,[3] which had two predecessors under earlier legislation, deals with the size of book stocks and annual accessions (i.e. quantitative standards).[4] No regulations have been made for library premises but guidance is given in a report described later.

The State Library Inspectorate, as in all the Scandinavian countries, exercises a considerable influence, and there are in Denmark probably the most comprehensive and detailed public library standards in the world, due largely to work undertaken by committees appointed by the Danish State Inspection of Public Libraries, or the minister.

One committee was set up in 1953 to 'work out standards for library buildings and related problems'. This committee, with Robert L. Hansen, the Director of the State Inspection of Public Libraries, and later his successor, E. Allerslev Jensen, as Chairman, and Sven Plovgaard, one of the Library Inspectors, as Secretary, issued a preliminary report in 1958 on standards for and the

1. *The Danish Public Libraries Act, 1964,* Copenhagen, Bibliotekstilsynet (Danish State Library Inspectorate), 1965 (English, French and German).
2. *Bekendtgorelse Nr. 169 af 13. Maj 1965 om Folkebiblioteker. Bibliotekslovene* [Announcement No. 169 of 13 May 1965 on Public Libraries, Library Laws], 10th ed. with notes, ed. by Ole Koch, Copenhagen, Danish State Library Inspectorate, 1969, p. 22–46.
3. *Bekendtgorelse Nr. 368 af 24. Oktober 1966 om Vejledende Retningslinier for Bogbestand og Tilvoekst i Folkbiblioteker* [Announcement No. 368 of 24th October 1966 on Guiding Principles for Book stock and Acquisitions in Public Libraries. Library Laws], 10th ed. with notes, ed. by Ole Koch, Copenhagen, Danish State Library Inspectorate, 1969, p. 47–55.
4. The book standards must be regarded as obsolete because the actual book stocks and accessions of the libraries are now exceeding the standards and the national book production, especially of books for children, has increased remarkably.

planning of public libraries in areas with 5,000 and 10,000 inhabitants.[1] In 1967 a further definitive report was issued on the same
subject, dealing with areas up to 25,000 inhabitants. This report
is very highly regarded and has been translated into English by
the British Library Association.[2]

Another committee was appointed in 1965 to put forward
suggestions for book standards for libraries in independent areas
of greatly differing sizes, but supplemented by a regional library
service and a national inter-library loan system. Since the space
required for library buildings is so largely dependent on the numbers of book stocks and accessions, it is more convenient to discuss
the report on book standards first.

STANDARDS FOR BOOK STOCKS

Reference should first be made to the standards in general terms
referred to in the 1965 regulation, which demand high quality
and complete objectivity. Paragraph 21, Sections 1 and 2 state:

The purpose of public libraries is to promote the spread of knowledge, education
and culture, by making books and other suitable material available free of charge.
These requirements shall be fulfilled by quality, comprehensiveness and current
usefulness in the choice of the material placed at the disposal of the public by the
municipal libraries. In the field of fiction, the libraries shall be able to provide
their readers with access to the best of the literature in Danish. The choice of
literature is to be decided by the literary value of the book alone and not by
the religious, moral or political views contained therein. The composition of the
bookstock of non-fiction literature is governed by corresponding requirements in
that, while taking due account of the size and nature of the service area concerned,
the bookstock shall include both elementary and more advanced works within all
fields.

The library stocks of periodicals and newspapers shall be composed on corresponding lines.

1. *Normer og Planer for Folkebiblioteksbyninger. I. Teknisk Vejledning samt Forslag til Planer
for det Mindre Købstadtbibliotek (5,000–10,000 indb)* [Standards and Plans for Public
Library Buildings. I. Technical Guide, with Proposals for Plans for Smaller Municipal
Libraries (5,000–10,000 Population], preliminary ed., Copenhagen, 1958.
2. Sven Plovgaard (ed.), *Folkebiblioteksbygningen. Normer og Typeplaner for Bibliotekslokaler
i Omrader med 5,000 til 25,000 Indbyggere* [Public Library Buildings. Standards and
Typical Plans for Library Premises in Districts with 5,000 to 25,000 Inhabitants],
Copenhagen, Copenhagen State Library Inspectorate, 1967.
  Sven Plovgaard, *Systemplaning von Buchereibauten Danische Normen und Typenplane für
Buchereiraume*, Wiesbaden, Harrassowitch, 1970 (Beitragg zum Bucheriewesen. Reihe
A. 9); *Public Library Buildings: Standards and Type Plans for Library Premises in Areas
with Populations of Between 5,000 and 25,000*, London, The Library Association, 1971.

Apart from the small size of the library units for which they then had to prescribe minimum standards, the committee on book standards had to take into account the small scale of Danish book production compared with the rest of the world. Despite the considerable use of material in English and other foreign languages (for which numerical standards could not then be devised) the libraries must depend basically on material in Danish.

The committee considered what should constitute the minimum standards for the 'basic service' of the library. This is defined in the Regulation subsequently made in 1965, as:

... placing at the disposal of the public an up-to-date, comprehensive and well kept collection of books for lending and reference, of a size bearing a reasonable relation to the number of inhabitants served ... the establishment and running of permanent or mobile branches, and the purchase of books in foreign languages, printed music, newspapers and periodicals.

The committee found it impracticable to set minimum standards for certain parts of this basic service, including book stocks for branches and foreign language books and periodicals. Books and other printed material required for services outside the basic (such as special collections and the requirements of education establishments) would be additional to the minimum. Considered separately were (a) the total size of book stocks and (b) annual accessions.

TOTAL BOOK STOCKS—ADULTS

The total size of book stocks was considered less important than the scale of addition of new books. This view was possible in a small country with good communications and an efficient inter-library lending system. None the less minimum standards for total book stocks were agreed to be necessary. For the adult

TABLE 27

Inhabitants[1]	Volumes	Inhabitants[1]	Volumes
5,000	8,000	20,000	22,500
10,000	15,000	50,000	56,000

1. Includes both adults and children; adults 75 per cent on a national average.

sections of the libraries figures were recommended, within the range of 2.5 to 1.5 volumes per adult, with a minimum of 8,000, the number of volumes per adult decreasing as the population increases—see Table 27 for examples.

These standards are for 'effective book stock', i.e. after the exclusion of all worn-out, outdated and seldom-used books. The committee considered a reasonable rate of discarding due to wear and tear to be one copy per seventy loans. No detailed guidance could be given for the rate of discarding obsolescent and little-used books. The committee, however, considered that large reserves of books in the stacks were undesirable.

The standard seemed to some librarians modest compared with the book stocks actually existing. But, when taking account of the fact that they concern the effective book stock and as such presuppose a discarding procedure which is both consistent and effective, they could in reality be said to be rather radical.

ANNUAL ACCESSIONS

The committee departed from the principles which had been followed in a 1951 instruction, but, as in the British Roberts Committee Report (1959), it based standards for annual accessions on the annual book production of the country. While in the United Kingdom and certain other countries, a very high proportion of the material published annually is not required in many of the public libraries, in Denmark it was found that the contrary was the case and a very high proportion of all the titles published in Danish were necessary, though it was necessary to reduce the number progressively, the smaller the population served.

The question of duplicates has special significance in a country like Denmark, where the book production is small, and the committee considered a high ratio of copies required. It also discussed replacements of discarded books, and suggested replacement of 30 per cent, a high figure also affected by the absence of suitable alternatives in Danish.

The committee finally recommended standards for annual accessions on the following basis:

The accessions consist of a given number of titles from the year's book production, with a greater purchase of duplicates

TABLE 28

Total number of inhabitants adults and children	Number of titles	Total annual accessions, per 100 adults[1] (volumes) (minimum 600)
Under 5,000	400	25
5,000–10,000	500	24
10,000–15,000	900	23
15,000–20,000	1,100	22
20,000–25,000	1,200	21
25,000–50,000	1,300	20

1. Adults = persons aged 14 and over.

than has hitherto been the practice. To this must be added a certain number of replacements of discarded books. The number of titles per inhabitant must be graduated according to the population served, with a minimum. The number of volumes per inhabitant must be larger in the smaller library (see Table 28).

The standard applies only to the new Danish books published each year, together with a small number of replacements of older books; it also presupposes the library has at its disposal an effective book stock of the size recommended. Thus, any purchases to fill the gaps in the collection should be additional. Recommended figures relate to the basic service and should be increased for branch book stocks, books in foreign languages, printed music, periodicals and newspapers, and for any special local needs.

PART-TIME LIBRARIES

The standards for book stocks and accessions for the adult departments refer to full-time libraries. Figures recommended for part-time libraries are half that for the full-time libraries.

The book standards so far described refer only to books for adult departments of libraries. Separate consideration was given to 'standards for library service to children'. This term is used, rather than book stocks in children's libraries, because recommended standards for this purpose, since they were first issued in 1953, have included the book stocks of children's and school libraries of the *folkeskoler*—elementary schools providing a ten-year course of schooling—within the service area of a particular library.

BOOK STOCKS—CHILDREN

The post-1953 standards for children's libraries required that there should be, within a library service area, ten volumes per child at elementary school at the disposal of the school libraries and the children's department of the public libraries. Distribution between the two types of library was a local matter.

The committee put forward proposals for a completely new standard for book stocks in children's sections of public libraries which has been accepted by the government and embodied in the 1966 regulation. This is that the book stock in a children's library is to be built up to four volumes per child (up to 13 years of age) in the service area of the library. As such children total about 25 per cent of the population, the stocks of public libraries for children will become in all about one volume per inhabitant. (School libraries have, since 1965, had independent standards for their book stocks, but in the comparatively few cases where schools have not a lending library, the public library standard is increased to six volumes per child.)

The children's library standard is the same for both full-time and part-time libraries. The national production of children's books in 1965 was so small—only some 200 titles a year—that all libraries, full-time or part-time, central or branch, were expected to contain all suitable titles published.[1] The standard is only enough for the basic service but, unlike the standard for adult book stocks, can also cover the demand for children's books in any branch library. Any special local responsibility, such as providing for a children's institution, calls for extra purchases, as also does the provision of music and foreign language material. This standard is considered valid up to at least 100,000 population. Beyond that only a slight reduction in the number of volumes available per child is expected to be called for.

ACCESSIONS

The committee decided that even the smallest library must purchase all suitable titles of children's books published in Danish.

1. Children's book production has increased since that date.

TABLE 29

Number of children aged 0–13	Number of volumes	Total annual accessions	
		Purchases by reason of wear and tear	Increase[1]
1,000 1,500 2,000 2,500 3,000 4,500 6,000 7,500 9,000 10,500 12,000	Approximately 200[2]	One-fortieth of the annual loans but at least 20 volumes per 100 children annually	Approximately 60 per cent ↑ ↓ Approximately 20 per cent

1. The increase is 20 per cent in all libraries where the number of loans is over 12 copies per child.
2. 1965 figure, now increased.

As with the adult departments, it considered that duplication had to be high, that replacements needed to be 40 per cent of discarded titles (compared with 30 per cent for adults), and that children's books should be discarded because of wear and tear after an average of forty loans (as against seventy for adult books).

A formula was used to arrive at total figures for annual accessions in children's libraries which had been developed to four volumes per child (up to 13 years of age)—see Table 29.

EXAMPLE OF A BOOK BUDGET
IN A DEVELOPED LIBRARY

Wear and tear: 50,000/40 loans = 1,250 volumes, plus increase (approximately 40 per cent) 500 volumes, giving a total acquisition of 1,750 volumes. To this must be added periodicals, printed music and foreign literature.

STANDARDS FOR LIBRARY PREMISES

The 1967 report *Public Library Buildings: Standards and Type Plans for Library Premises in Areas with Populations of Between 5,000 and 25,000*[1] is a considerable work resulting from close collaboration between librarians and architects and represents many years of research. It is a combination of detailed planning advice and detailed space standards derived from elaborately presented data. It is difficult to distinguish between planning principle and requirements and library standards. Indeed it appears to be the theme of the report that there is no such distinction. Many statements, such as those included in the section 'General Requirements of Library Buildings' are in both categories, as shown below.

Allowance should be made at planning stage for the needs which will arise from population growth, increased use of the library and new forms of activity. The layout of a public library, which is to be appropriate to the needs of today, must first and foremost be purpose-oriented, but it must also be functionally oriented. (The report stresses the importance of the various departments of the library being on the same level.)

However, comprehensive principles and detailed requirements are clearly to be identified as being in the area of library standards and they are illustrated in practice in the type plans included in the book. The report is emphatic that the standards are only general guides and that each library building needs to be designed with a number of variable local circumstances in mind, affecting the exact space requirements.

The emphasis in the report is on the space requirements of libraries serving populations of between 5,000 and 25,000, of which there are many in Denmark, and many of the standards are prescribed in numerical terms in relation to five hypothetical libraries serving populations of 5,000, 10,000, 15,000, 20,000 and 25,000. But the committee states that the principles of library planning are, in essentials, valid for somewhat larger libraries. It also concludes that the space requirements of the regional central libraries are not in principle greatly different from other comparable libraries, and that, where they differ, this can easily be allowed for. The committee also consider the needs of part-time

1. Op. cit.

libraries, defined as serving populations below 5,000, and give minimum space requirements for certain areas.

The committee goes into great detail into the categories of rooms required in full-time libraries for different purposes, dividing them not only into the traditional groupings by functions (of service to the public, administration and other internal operations and storage) but breaks this down so meticulously that there are in all some thirty categories of rooms detailed. An indication is given of which of these many spaces should normally be found in the libraries of the various sizes described, and sizes are suggested for these spaces in the typical libraries.

The 'average standard book stock' for each of the libraries can be calculated according to the standards which have already been described, and the committee recommends how these books should be divided between different parts of the library, including a theoretical apportionment of the required book stocks for children between the public library and school library or libraries. It, however, stresses that the dimensions of rooms must be determined by the size of the book stock actually required and not mechanically by the size of the population.

Advice is given about the kind of audio-visual material for which accommodation needs to be provided but the committee could give no detailed space requirements.

Minimum space requirements for the different types of accommodation are calculated in a variety of ways. Those in adult and children's lending areas are on the basis of about 65 and 55 volumes per square metre respectively. Requirements for reading areas are calculated according to function, adult reading room about 4 m² per reader, newpaper room and youth section 3 m², and children's reading room 3.5 m². A minimum number of fixed seats is recommended for these rooms in each of the typical libraries, e.g. for a library serving 25,000 people a total of 70 seats is required, 24 in adult reference, 10 in both newspaper room and youth section, and 26 in children's reference.

The capacity of conference, exhibition and meeting rooms is considered and it is proposed that each library within the population range under discussion should have meeting rooms of more than one size, group rooms for study circles and similar activities, and a larger room for meetings and exhibitions, etc. It is recommended that the number of rooms for small groups should be not less than 1 per 5,000 to 6,000 inhabitants in the case of the smaller libraries, holding up to 25 people. The large conference room should hold between 50 and 170 people. The actual space requirements could, it is stated, be roughly calculated at about 2 m² per person for the group rooms (including gangways and space for leader or speaker) and 1 m² per person for the large conference room (including gangways and space for speaker's desk or dais).

The number of staff required in each of the typical libraries was calculated on the basis described later (1 per 2,000 population) and accommodation for them was worked out on the basis of: (a) librarian's office—18 to 36 m² according to the number of people likely to attend meetings in the room (e.g. book selection meetings); (b) other staff—minimum size of individual rooms, 12 to 15 m²; (c) shared rooms—8 to 10 m² per assistant.

With population figure, standard book stock and 'normal activity' as starting points, and with the analysis of standard measurements, etc., discussed in the report as the basis, a mean value has been estimated for the space requirements of every room. The results are shown in Tables 30 and 31; but the figures quoted do not include a requirement for the main book stack, on account of the number of variables affecting the size of this. Nor do they include for other variable areas, such as entrances, corridors, stairs, lifts and service installations, for which an increase which might vary from 20 to 50 per cent of the area for the spaces calculated with the aid of the standards. For this reason no gross figure of floor area required for a given type of library or total floor area per 1,000 population is suggested.

TABLE 30. Standard book stock allocated (volumes)

	Population				
	5,000	10,000	15,000	20,000	25,000
Adult lending	7,000	11,000	15,000	18,000	20,000
Adult reference	1,000	1,500	2,000	2,500	3,000
Children's lending	3,000	5,000	7,000	9,000	11,000
Children's reference	500	750	1,000	1,250	1,500
Near stacks	1,500	2,750	4,000	5,250	6,500
TOTAL	13,000	21,000	29,000	36,000	42,000

TABLE 31. Standards for premises of full-time libraries (m²)

Department/unit	Minimum space needed (net) for population				
	5,000	10,000	15,000	20,000	25,000
Library core					
Adult department					
Lending	108	171	234	279	315
Youth section	18	21	24	27	30
Reference (seats)	48	60	72	84	96
Study rooms (carrels)	6	6	12	18	24
Newspaper reading seats	18	21	24	27	30
Local collection	—	—	24	30	36
Children's department					
Lending	60	90	126	162	198
Reference (seats)	48	60	72	84	96
Study room (homework)	—	—	18	24	30
Younger children's corner	12	15	18	21	24
Shared area					
Service (counter)	9	12	15	18	21
Sorting area	6	7	8	9	10
Near stack(s)	12	18	27	36	45
Conference unit					
Exhibition and conference hall	60	84	108	132	156
Store for the above	9	12	15	18	21
Seminars (rooms for study groups)	36	60	60	90	90
Audio-visual room (music room)	—	—	30	30	30
Administration unit					
Librarian	18	18	24	36	36
Lending librarian	—	—	15	21	27
Reference librarian (near stack)	—	—	18	18	18
Children's librarian	—	12	15	21	27
Cataloguing, etc.	18	24	36	48	60
Secretary	—	—	—	12	12
Dispatch and delivery	6	6	12	12	12
Staff rooms	18	24	30	36	42
Unallocated space					
Available on main floor	36	42	48	48	48
Prescribed functional area (net)	546	763	1,085	1,341	1,534

OTHER STANDARDS

Staffing

No detailed staffing standards have been recommended in Denmark. All that can be said is that the Public Libraries Act 1964 requires that in libraries serving an area with a population of more than 5,000, a full-time librarian and the requisite clerical staff be appointed before 1 April 1969, and that if the work of the library is carried out by one or more full-time staff, the head of the library shall be a professionally qualified librarian.

Some staffing standards are, however, assumed by the committee which drew up the 1967 premises standards. In its report it says that as there are so many uncertain factors involved, it has not been possible to draw up any standards in this field but, as it was necessary to make recommendations as to space requirements for staff, on the basis of existing material and with support from an investigation made by the Committee for Better use of Libraries, it decided to use a simple rule of one member of staff per 2,000 inhabitants. This assumes ordinary forms of work in normally developed full-time libraries with annual issues (to adults and children) of eight volumes per head of population. Where this figure is exceeded, or there are additional services (including branches), more staff would be necessary.

Opening hours

The requirements for opening hours are to be found in the 1965 regulations. The most important are:

Minimum opening hours in full-time libraries: less than 10,000 inhabitants, 20 hours per week, 5 days a week; 10,000–20,000 inhabitants, 30 hours a week, 5 days a week; over 20,000 inhabitants, weekdays from 10 a.m. to 8 p.m., earlier on Saturday.

Minimum opening hours in regional central libraries: weekdays from 10 a.m. to 8 p.m., earlier closing on Saturday but not before 2 p.m.

Part-time libraries: the requirements for opening vary from 2 hours a week spread over 2 days to 10 to 14 hours spread over 4 days, depending on the number of inhabitants.

Audio-visual materials

Danish public libraries are under a legal obligation also to provide audio-visual materials, but no standards for this type of materials have been drawn up.

France

As well as being a great agricultural area, with wide expanses of rural areas and large numbers of small towns and villages, France is a rapidly growing industrial country. With its still increasing population of over 50 million, it has a large proportion—some 18 per cent—of young people under 20 years of age. This has considerable significance for its educational institutions which nearly a quarter of the whole population attend, and for its public and other libraries. France is at the same time a country with a long and historic past and a legacy of rare books and manuscripts, well preserved in learned libraries. But it has been slow in providing general reading services for the whole population, though the position in this respect is now improving as a result of measures taken in recent years and in prospect.

The basic unit of local government, to which one would normally look for the provision of public libraries, is the *commune*, of which there are as many as 38,000. While many *communes* contain a considerable population, like the large cities of Marseille and Lyon, most populations are small and many very small. Some 60 per cent of the population in 1968 lived in places of less than 20,000 inhabitants, an inadequate basis for an efficient independent library. The total number of *communes* with more than 20,000 inhabitants at the same date was 334, so the 700 municipal libraries under the control of the Minister of National Education include many which are small.

Of long standing, however, are the municipal libraries, which owed their existence in large measure to the opportunity to the municipalities early in the nineteenth century to take custody of the books and manuscripts of the religious houses and the noble families, confiscated at the time of the French Revolution. Some fifty of these libraries have been designated as *bibliothèques classées*, on the basis until quite recently of the antiquity and value of their collections of rare materials, and the Minister of National Education has since 1931 appointed a chief librarian and, in some cases, other librarians. These *conservateurs*, totalling 124 in 1972, are members of a corps of State librarians. Nominated by the minister, the municipality contributes to their salaries to the extent of 40 per cent to 60 per cent, according to the population of the towns, the smaller towns getting the larger contribution from the State. A second grade of librarian, the *sous-bibliothécaires* are appointed and paid wholly by the municipalities.

The basis of classification is changing, the central government now classifying the libraries for the interest they show in *la lecture publique*, the popularization of general reading through libraries, and the library's initiative in developing this work.

The existence of these old and valuable collections in the municipal libraries has led to the municipal libraries being developed as learned libraries frequented by a scholarly élite. This strong tradition of scholarship still persists in these libraries and has delayed and hindered the development of a public library service in France conducted on modern lines.

There is no legal obligation on the local authorities to provide a public library service and no immediate prospect of this being imposed. The central government has therefore had to proceed both by indirect and direct means to encourage development of public libraries.

In 1945, the Direction des Bibliothèques et de la Lecture Publique was established as part of the Ministry of National Education. Of this body John Ferguson has said that it is 'the corner stone of the French library movement and must remain its hope for the future'.[1] The *direction*, from the outset, was called upon to administer the learned libraries (the national libraries, certain large specialized collections and the State university libraries), to control in different degrees the various municipal libraries, and to organize and administer *la lecture publique*.

The central government has assisted the municipal libraries with small annual grants, the rate of which has increased with the rate of expenditure by the local authorities, and with books. It has given substantial capital grants—previously 35 per cent, recently

1. John Ferguson, *Libraries in France*, London, Clive Bingley, 1971, p. 9. The writer is indebted to this book for background information and also to an unpublished essay by Miss Madeleine de la Haye on 'The Post-war Development of Libraries in France'.

increased to 50 per cent—to encourage the municipalities to build and equip new central libraries and branch libraries, as well as to provide mobile libraries in both highly populated and less populated areas. The *direction*'s most striking development has been the establishment, from 1946 onwards, of the central lending libraries, the *bibliothèques centrales de prêt* or BCP, for the benefit of the people in the smaller towns and villages. Originally BCP served localities with less than 15,000 people but recently this figure has been increased to 20,000. These central lending libraries are largely financed by the State and administered by the *direction*. They are organized on the basis of the *départements*, the largest units of local government, and by 1971 they had been provided in sixty-one out of the ninety-five *départements*.

BCPs are separate library organizations, with their own premises and staffs. They supply mobile library services and circulate supplies of books for deposit in small local centres, usually schools, under the supervision of an unpaid local librarian, most frequently a schoolteacher. Apart from the schools, centres are established in places such as the town hall, or *mairie*, run as an additional unpaid duty by a member of the staff. Deposit collections, changed frequently, are also placed in educational institutions, hospitals, youth clubs, cultural centres, etc.

But despite the efforts of the central government through the *direction*, the work of certain of the more progressive local authorities, as well as of the French public librarians and the Association des Bibliothécaires Français, the progress made was far from adequate to meet the rapidly growing and changing needs of the situation. In 1966 an inter-ministerial committee, presided over by M. Georges Pompidou, then Prime Minister, initiated an inquiry into the position of the public libraries and the means of improving them. A working party, under the chairmanship of M. Etienne Dennery, head of the *direction* and also administrator of the National Library, studied the position closely and reported in 1968.[1]

The working party's report confirmed the extreme poverty of the situation. In the areas served by the central lending libraries provided directly by the State, only some 2 per cent of adults were using the service and 50 to 75 per cent of the schoolchildren, in all

---

1. *La Lecture Publique en France. Rapport du Groupe d'Études*, Paris, La Documentation française, 1968; *Notes et Études Documentaires*, No. 3459, 1 February 1968. Also published in *Bulletin de Bibliothèques de France*, No. 3, March 1968, p. 105–34.

less then 10 per cent of the total population concerned. In the municipal libraries the position, though different, was little better. New libraries and mobile libraries, the working party said, were only one of many needs. Buildings were often obsolete and staff insufficient. The municipal libraries, which together served over 15 million people, had little more than 500,000 registered borrowers, representing only 3 per cent of the population concerned. The most favourable estimates for the municipal libraries, including Paris and the Département de la Seine, were 4.6 per cent of the population.

The working party discussed the reasons for this situation, having particularly in mind the wealth of literature and the high level of literacy in France. They considered whether it was not only possible but desirable that France should be brought in line with other countries where the system of public libraries was more highly developed. They rejected a number of arguments against developing the service, including one that, in a new world of mass communication, libraries were an anachronism. They agreed that the role of audio-visual information was considerable and would continue to grow, that world-wide television would soon, using communications satellites, enable everyone to participate in an enormous mass culture. They considered that just for that reason reading would become more than ever indispensable, serving as an antidote and permitting the individual to rediscover himself. A means of personal enrichment, they also considered reading a condition of social advancement. Reading enabled social gaps to be bridged. At a time when the process of learning was becoming more democratic, reading gave to lifelong education its sense and its dimension.

The report of the working party was concerned primarily with diagnosis and with administrative recommendations designed to bring about a rapid improvement of the service. But, in addition, the report contains a number of other general statements which can be considered to lay down modern standards for public library service in France. These statements are especially significant as they indicate a rapid transition from the standards of a past age to modern and progressive thinking about the role of the public library in present-day society.

The working party considered that many people in France did not appreciate the true meaning of the term *lecture publique*, saying

. . . it is necessary to understand the 'public' reading in the sense that one had previously used for 'public' education. Just as one offers to everyone freely the means of instruction, the state considers it has a duty to provide for every citizen access to works, the reading of which can be pleasant or useful in enriching his personality and preparing him in a better way for his role in society.

New functions, the working party said, must be added to—and even in the majority of localities might have to replace—the traditional functions of conserving, augmenting and making available a large, old and valuable collection, functions which, however, retain their value and in a certain measure their importance in connexion with the wider conception of 'public reading'.

With both open access to the shelves and the growth in the number of publications, the readers needed guidance, particularly if it was for reasons of social and professional improvement that the library was being used. The librarian should put the reader at his ease on his first contact with the library and establish with him a bibliographical relationship so that the reader could make the best use of the materials available and avoid a waste of his time.

Essentially a documentation centre, the public library, in the opinion of the working party, was also a centre of social and cultural life. A few words exchanged over a book or about an author were sufficient to establish a similarity of taste and a new personal relationship. But to play such a role the library should attract and retain a public which too often ignored it. It should do this by means of extension activities such as:

The display of books related to current events, national, regional and local.

Exhibitions, not only about writers and their works but on any subject likely to arouse interest.

The organization of lectures based on these exhibitions.

Readers' circles, discussion groups, readings, with or without sound or visual illustrations, of a book, studies of a theme.

Meetings with writers and interpreters of works for the theatre and cinema.

Concerts (with commentary), musical hours, films.

Publicity for and use of television programmes devoted to literature. Even the partial realization of such a programme required the librarian to be out of the library much of the time, to be at the service of others during their leisure periods, and to collaborate with other bodies, public and private, which required his assistance.

Where other socio-cultural organizations existed, the librarian should collaborate with them and harmonize his work with theirs.

To undertake adequately all these activities, both traditional and new, required staff with good general education—at least to the level of the *baccalauréat* and professional training bearing on library techniques and on the spirit and techniques of extension work. By their character and personality, the staff should be able to advise courteously and organize extension work unobtrusively, both tasks requiring tact and a keen sense of human relations. The enlarged functions of the library required aptitudes and special knowledge different from, yet at the same time complementary to, those up to that time asked of the staff. Members of the staff should nevertheless be able to discover their role in the new structure. The *conservateurs* to whom would fall the responsibility for the public libraries, would need initiation courses in the techniques of extension work; the *sous-bibliothécaires* should be able to proceed by promotion to a new corps of *bibliothécaires de lecture publique*. The last named body of librarians would have to be established, recruited, trained and fitted in to the present organization of library staffs.

The working party envisaged that this new category of librarian should be trained in the new university institutes of technology, and that they would need courses lasting not more than two years. The functions of these new librarians would have an educational character, the importance of which would gradually grow as the institutions contemplated for the development of lifelong education (*l'éducation permanente*), in which the public libraries would play a major role, were established.

While recognizing that the decision as to what public library facilities should be provided in the larger areas rested with the municipalities, the working party considered it useful to define what, in a modern town, was the most desirable form of organization for the library service. Some of the points which they made are given below.

As with the post office and town hall, everyone should know where the public library was. Its whereabouts should be clearly indicated. The main library building should be in a central position and its design should be such as to make it easy of access and inviting to use.

Direct access to the shelves was a prime requirement. The traditional arrangements of a large book stack and a small reading room should be reversed by the elimination of well-used and out-of-date material no longer in demand.

According to the size of towns and of their resources, additional library accommodation should be provided, set aside, for example, for children. In the large towns the branches of the municipal library should be as numerous as possible. They should be simple in design and situated at well frequented points near the shops or bus-stops, sometimes having a large room for meetings and other activities. In some circumstances deposits of books could be made in factories and offices.

Municipal libraries might often benefit by the use of mobile libraries, particularly in the districts on the perimeter of the towns.

In many urban areas there were districts which were socially deprived and where it was urgent that there should be a public library. This referred to the suburbs described as cultural deserts, notably (with some exceptions) around Paris, as well as to the many large new areas of urban development. In respect of these areas special steps should be taken to reserve sites for libraries on the basis of about 500 m² for every 5,000 houses or housing units. A library should figure expressly among the social equipment considered necessary for a new district.

At least on an experimental basis, branch libraries should be established in the *maisons de la culture* and there should be an extension of the practice of depositing books in youth clubs and centres, the public librarians assisting with the exploitation of the books.

Opening hours of libraries should permit their widest possible use.

Conflicting views were received on the question of membership charges, which are levied in many places. The working party thought it wise not to make a definite ruling and, while advising that charges should not be made, proposed that the municipalities should continue to make their own decision on this point.[1]

With regard to the small towns and rural areas, the working party said that it had been accepted that the *maisons de la culture* provided for in earlier national plans could not be developed indefinitely and that less important areas should seek to provide simple

---

1. Membership charges are usually nominal. In Grenoble, for example, they are 2 francs a year, no charge being made to children.

comprehensive cultural establishments.[1] The public library was well suited to this role, as had already been demonstrated. By adding a gramophone record library and organizing in a special room exhibitions, conferences, concerts or theatrical productions, it was relatively easy to augment its own traditional influence, since all cultural work ended in the book.

But many small towns and most villages could not establish a proper library. For them it was desirable to encourage the use of books by a complete network of central lending libraries, designed for the purpose. The mobile library was only effective if it was possible to borrow from it directly, by choosing a book from the shelves as in a true library. The rural population would certainly value the chance of intellectual parity with those of the urban areas. It had, when the mobile library came to its area, the very real feeling that it had not been forgotten.

The mobile libraries of the rural central libraries need not give up entirely the deposit centres, either in the smallest communes or in the towns of 5,000 to 20,000 inhabitants. The prospect of additional supplies of books should encourage the local librarians to modernize their methods, and deposit collections could be envisaged in other organizations, such as places of employment or of leisure.

Many of the administrative measures proposed by the working party, including more generous grants from the central government for both capital and maintenance expenditure, have been adopted and for the current (1972–75) Sixth National Plan more funds have been placed at the disposal of the *direction* for their work.[2] There has been a considerable increase in the size of the municipal library building programme and the rural library programmes are moving forward at a faster rate. At the time of the report only thirty-nine *départements* in metropolitan France had a public library service. This figure had by 1973 reached sixty-six.

While national figures may not yet record a great increase in the number of libraries and of their use, the improvements currently being brought about in the localities directly concerned—particularly where new library buildings have been provided or are

---

1. *Rapport Général de la Commission de l'Équipement Culturel et du Patrimoine Artistique (5ᵉ Plan)*, Paris, La Documentation Française, p. 96, undated (special number of *Notes et Études Documentaires*).
2. Alice Garrigoux, *La Lecture Publique en France*, Paris, La Documentation Française, 1972 (*Notes et Études Documentaires*, No. 3948, 15 December 1972, Annexe No. IX).

under construction—are beginning to make their mark on the French public library scene, particularly in regard to the quality of the service, and further prospects are encouraging.

The *direction*, in connexion with its library building programmes and for other purposes, has for some time worked to a number of progressive standards of a quantitative nature. The standards currently operative—which are used flexibly—are quoted in Tables 32 to 35 below. The writer is indebted to the *direction* for making this information available and for other assistance.

TABLE 32. Municipal libraries—books

Library serving population	Total volumes per head of population	Adult lending open-access volumes	Reading and reference open-access volumes	Children's open-access volumes	Separate book-stack volumes
5,000–6,000	1.5	6,000–7,000 Combined space		1,500–2,000	—
6,000–10,000	1.5 to 1.4	7,000–10,000 Combined space		2,000–4,000	—
10,000–20,000	1.4 to 1.1	10,000–16,000 Combined space		4,000–6,000	—
20,000–30,000	1.7 to 1.4	14,000–18,000	6,000–8,000	4,000–6,000	10,000
30,000–45,000	1.5 to 1.2	14,000–18,000	7,000–9,000	4,000–6,000	20,000
45,000–60,000	1.4 to 1.2	18,000–25,000	9,000–11,000	4,000–6,000	30,000
60,000–75,000	1.2 to 1.0	18,000–25,000	10,000–12,000	6,000–7,000	35,000
Branch ibrary, 15,000	—	8,000–12,000 Combined space		4,000–6,000	—

Source: Bibliothèques Municipales. Normes en Surfaces [Municipal Libraries. Building Standards], Paris, Ministère de l'Éducation Nationale, Direction des Bibliothèques et de la Lecture Publique, Service de la Lecture Publique, December 1972 (ref. SLP 211).

Library serving population (thousands)	Service points other than central library		Books (volumes) (thousands)	Staff					
	Branches	Mobiles		Total	Librarians	Assistant librarians	Non-professional	Drivers	Manual
10–20	—	—	20–28	6	1	1	4	—	—
20–30	—	—	34–42	10	1	2	6	—	1
30–45	1	1	58–72	17	2	4	9	1	1
45–60	2	1	87–110	23	2	7	12	1	1
60–75	3	1	107–135	32	3	10	17	1	1
75–90	4	1	132–164	38	4	12	20	1	1
90–105	5	1	155–191	43	4	14	23	1	1
105–120	6	1	177–217	50	6	16	26	1	1
120–135	7	1	194–235	58	6	19	31	1	1
135–150	8	2	211–253	65	6	22	34	2	1
150–165	9	2	228–271	71	7	24	37	2	1
165–180	10	2	245–289	76	7	26	40	2	1
180–195	11	2	262–307	84	7	29	45	2	1
195–210	12	2	279–325	90	8	31	48	2	1
210–225	13	2	296–343	95	8	33	51	2	1
225–240	14	2	313–361	100	8	35	54	2	1
240–255	15	2	330–379	109	9	38	59	2	1
255–270	16	2	347–397	114	9	40	62	2	1
270–285	17	2	364–415	119	9	42	65	2	1
285–300	18	3	381–433	130	10	46	70	3	1
300–315	19	3	398–451	135	10	48	73	3	1
315–330	20	3	415–469	140	10	50	76	3	1
330–345	21	3	432–487	146	11	52	79	3	1
345–360	22	3	449–505	157	11	55	84	3	1
360–375	23	3	466–523	162	11	58	89	3	1
375–390	24	3	483–541	171	12	61	94	3	1

1. Standards accepted as a basis for evaluating the provision required for securing the efficient working of municipal libraries, within the framework of the sixth plan.
Source: Bibliothèques Municipales. Normes en Livres et en Personnel [Municipal Libraries. Standards for Books and Staff], Paris, Ministère de l'Education Nationale, Direction des Bibliothèques et de la Lecture Publique, Service de la Lecture Publique, March 1972.

TABLE 34. Municipal libraries—building standards

Library serving population (municipal libraries) (thousands)	Adult lending		Reading room and reference			Children			Gramophone records (m²)	General activities rooms (m²)	Work areas offices, storage, workshop, garage, etc. (m²)	Separate book stack (a) books (b) area (m²)	Circulation services, toilets, etc.—add (%) (m² in parentheses)	Total area (m²)
	Volumes (thousands)	Area (m²)	Volumes[1] (thousands)	Seats	Area (m²)	Volumes[1] (thousands)	Seats	Area (m²)						
5-6	Combined space		6-7	10	130	1.5-2	30	80	—	—	70	—	+25 (70)	350
6-10	Combined space		7-10	14-18	160	2-4	40	120	—	40	80	—	+25 (100)	500
10-20	Combined space		10-16	20-30	240	4-6	40-45	140	20	50	110	—	+25 (140)	700
20-30	14-18	330	6-8	30-35	160	4-6	40-50	150	40	70	110	(a) 10,000 (b) 60	+30 (280)	1,200
30-45	14-18	330	7-9	35-45	180	4-6	40-50	150	50	80	310	(a) 20,000 (b) 120	+30 (380)	1,600
45-60	18-25	350	9-11	50-60	300	4-6	40-50	150	50	120	320	(a) 30,000 (b) 180	+35 (510)	2,000
60-75	18-25	350	10-12	60-70	340	6-7	50-60	200	70	140	345	(a) 35,000 (b) 210	+35 (545)	2,200
Branch library, 15	Combined space		8-12[2]	10	180	4-6	40	140	In combined space	40	40	—	+25 (100)	500

1. Open access.
2. Books and records.

Source: Bibliothèques Municipales. Normes en Surfaces, op. cit.

TABLE 35. Municipal libraries: standards for site areas and mobile libraries

Library serving population (thousands)	Area (m²)		Mobile libraries
	Central libraries	Branches[1]	
10–20	700	—	—
20–30	1,200	—	—
30–45	1,600	500	1
45–60	2,000	1,000	1
60–75	2,200	1,500	1
75–90	—[2]	2,000	1
90–105	—[2]	2,500	1
105–120	—[2]	3,000	1

1. 500 m² per branch. One branch for every 15,000 population above 30,000.
2. Above 75,000 population areas are established according to local circumstances.
Source: Bibliothèques Municipales. Normes en Surfaces, op. cit.

German Democratic Republic

What follows is based on material supplied by the Zentralinstitut für Bibliothekswesen (Central Institute for Librarianship).

The development of the public libraries (staatliche Allgemeinbibliotheken) of the German Democratic Republic, like other sections of the library system, is taking place on the basis of the Library Decree of 31 May 1968,[1] as well as of its regulations, particularly the fifth regulation on tasks, methods, and structure of the public libraries controlled by the local councils.[2] The library decree,

1. 'Verordnung über die Aufgaben des Bibliothekssystems bei der Gestaltung des entwickelten gesellschaftlichen Systems des Sozialismus in der Deutschen Demokratischen Republik vom 31. Mai 1968 [Decree on the Functions of the Library System in the Formation of the Developed Social System of Socialism in the German Democratic Republic, of 31 May 1968]', *Gesetzblatt der Deutschen Demokratischen Republik*, Vol. II, No. 78, 1968, p. 565–71.
2. 'Fünfte Durchführungsbestimmung zur Verordnung über die Aufgaben des Bibliothekssystems bei der Gestaltung des entwickelten gesellschaftlichen Systems des Sozialismus in der Deutschen Demokratischen Republik—Aufgaben, Arbeitsweise und Struktur der den örtlichen Räten unterstehenden staatlichen Allgemeinbibliotheken vom 27. Januar 1971 [Fifth Regulation for the Library System in the Formation of the Developed Social System of Socialism in the German Democratic Republic—Functions, Methods and Structure of the Public Libraries under Local Councils, of 27 January 1971]', *Gesetzblatt der Deutschen Demokratischen Republik*, Vol. II, No. 24, 1971, p. 209–12.

which lays down the principles on which the library work is based, regulates the co-ordination of libraries on a co-operative basis and thereby aims at a more precise delineation of the tasks of different types of library, their functions and methods as a preliminary condition for co-operation. The adoption of the fifth regulation in conjunction with the accompanying directive,[1] has, for the first time, introduced principles which must be followed by public libraries.[2] This makes fundamental demands on the libraries and makes statements on fields such as use, stock building, cataloguing, technology, accommodation and equipment. It has thereby established a basis for similar regulations for other sections of library work, such as special libraries.

In the German Democratic Republic there already exists an extensive network of public libraries. In 1971 the more than 8,800 municipalities had 10,822 libraries, including 942 full-time libraries with 731 branch libraries and 1,803 lending centres, as well as 7,346 part-time libraries (all in municipalities with fewer than 5,000 inhabitants).

The services rendered by public libraries have, in the course of the development work of the last twenty years, achieved a notable level. At the end of 1971 the libraries concerned, whose services are without exception given free, contained about 22.5 million volumes or 1.3 volumes per head of population, had some 3,332,000 readers (19.5 per cent of the population) and had lent approximately 60.3 million volumes and other materials (3.5 volumes per head). The trade union libraries are not included in these figures.

The further development of the socialist society makes increasing demands on the libraries. Therefore, beyond the regulations previously referred to, criteria have been devised in the shape of indices by which can be assessed the extent to which regional and

1. 'Richtlinie zur Fünften Durchführungsbestimmung zur Verordnung über die Aufgaben des Bibliothekssystems bei der Gestaltung des entwickelten gesellschaftlichen Systems des Sozialismus in der Deutschen Demokratischen Republik. . . Vom 24. Februar 1971 [Directive concerning the Fifth Regulation for the Implementation of the Decree on the Functions of the Library System in the Formation of the Developed Social System of Socialism in the German Democratic Republic. . ., of 24 February 1971]', *Verfügungen und Mitteilungen des Ministeriums für Kultur*, No. 3, 1971, p. 22–7.
2. Wolfgang Schumann, 'Die staatliche Allgemeinbibliothek—der regional wirksame Bibliothekstyp der siebziger Jahre [The Public Libraries—The Regionally Effective Type of Libraries of the Seventies]', *Der Bibliothekar*, Vol. 6, No. 25, 1971, p. 395–402.

local conditions exist for the continued improvement of the libraries and whether optimum effectiveness, as to numbers of readers and circulation figures, can be obtained by using the stocks in hand.

BOOK STOCKS

The more than 22.5 million volumes which were held in 1971 by the public libraries do not suffice to secure the considerable expansion, which is envisaged, of the scope of public libraries. The Zentralinstitut für Bibliothekswesen has consequently worked out standards which will establish principles for the enlargement of book stocks. These standards (Tables 36 and 37) envisaged for public libraries total stocks of at least 1.65 to 2.5 volumes per head.

Graduations and differences in the standards result, in the first place, from the functions performed by the library, the number of persons catered for and the existence of further public or special libraries within its area. Thus a municipal and sub-district library (*Stadt- und Kreisbibliothek*), exercising local and regional functions, has at its disposal stocks for the inhabitants of the sub-district capital, stocks for the satisfaction of specialized and more varied demands by the population of the sub-district (*Spitzenbestände*), and stocks to supply the part-time libraries in the villages. The standard values for such over-all stocks must necessarily differ from standards applied to town libraries without regional responsibilities.

THE BOOK STOCK STANDARD—TOTAL
VOLUMES PER HEAD

Municipal libraries

For the local supply function libraries serving populations less than 3,500 are required to provide a stock of at least 8,700 volumes. In larger areas the standard ranges between 1.65 and 2.5 volumes per head, as shown in Table 36.

TABLE 36

Population	Volumes per head	Population	Volumes per head
3,500–7,000	2.5–2.2	100,000–250,000	1.94–1.85
7,000–20,000	2.2–2.1	250,000–500,000	1.85–1.75
20,000–40,000	2.1–2.0	500,000–1,000,000	1.75–1.65
40,000–100,000	2.0–1.94	over 1,000,000	1.65

TABLE 37

Population of district	Volumes per head	Population of district	Volumes per head
Under 25,000	0.35–0.32	75,000–100,000	0.20–0.17
25,000–50,000	0.32–0.25	over 100,000	0.17–0.11
50,000–75,000	0.25–0.20		

Stock of literature of high standard (Spitzenbestände) *in municipal and sub-district libraries*

Libraries operating in the sub-district centre and serving the area of the sub-district should build up high standard stocks for the satisfaction of specialized and more varied demands both from the centre and from the sub-district in relation to the population of the combined area (see Table 37).

Stocks in municipal and sub-district libraries and rural central libraries

One of the tasks of municipal and sub-district libraries, as well as of rural central libraries, is the supply of literature to part-time libraries in their areas which have only small stocks of their own. The basis for an adequate mobile supply service is provided by raising the stocks in the municipal and sub-district libraries, as well as in rural central libraries, to such a level that they are capable of supplying the inhabitants of the villages within their areas, according to their size, with between 2.7 volumes per head in the smallest villages to 0.8 volume per head in the larger villages.

The standard invariably includes children's literature, the proportion of which should average 30 per cent (excluding the higher standard book stocks of the municipal and sub-district libraries).

Newspapers and periodicals, bibliographic reference works

According to the functions of the libraries concerned and the number of people living within their area, the following standards apply:[1]

Municipal and district libraries (*Stadt- und Bezirksbibliotheken*), and big city libraries: 160–170 titles (about 3,700 to 3,800 marks).[2]

Municipal and sub-district libraries (*Stadt- und Kreisbibliotheken*), 110–120 titles (about 2,400 to 2,600 marks).

Rural central libraries and small municipal libraries, 30–35 titles (about 600 marks).

Village libraries (part-time), 14 titles (about 240 marks).

Public and trade union libraries, according to their functions and the number of people living within their area, or the size of their book stocks, are required to include in their stocks basic bibliographical reference works.[3]

WEAR AND TEAR

The useful life of books varies. It is expected to amount to 13 years for non-fiction, 20 years for fiction and 7.5 years for children's books. Annual wear and tear is calculated on this basis and, for the main sections of book stock, the standard is as follows: non-fiction—about 7.5 per cent; fiction—about 5 per cent; children's books—about 13 per cent.

This has been laid down in Section 4 of the Decree of

1. *Zeitungen und Zeitschriften im Bestand der staatlichen allgemeinen öffentlichen Bibliotheken. Empfehlungsliste* [Newspapers and Periodicals in the Stock of the Public Libraries. Recommended Titles], Berlin, Zentralinstitut für Bibliothekswesen, 1970, 21 p.
2. Mean requirement, in each case, for an annual subscription for the titles concerned.
3. 'Anweisung über den Bezug bibliographischer Nachschlagewerke in den allgemeinbildenden Bibliotheken. Vom 7. Januar 1965 [Instruction on the Acquisition of Bibliographical Reference Works in the Public Libraries, of 7 January 1965]', *Verfügungen und Mitteilungen des Ministeriums für Kultur*, No. 2, 1965, p. 18–9.

10 December 1970, on the financing according to performance of the public libraries,[1] as well as in the Directive of
20 September 1963 on stock revision in public libraries.[2]

CIRCULATION

The public libraries aim to reach circulation figures which, in
relation to the whole territory of the German Democratic Republic,
are approximately 5 books per head. In 1971 the figures reached
were 3.5. Where other libraries, such as trade union and special
libraries, exist within the area served, the mean value can be altered
upwards or downwards, regionally as well as locally.

STAFF

In 1955 and 1956 the Ministry of Culture issued two directives for
the staffing of public libraries run on a full-time basis.[3] These provided for the existence of public libraries on a full-time basis
in all municipalities with more than 5,000 inhabitants. For every
500 readers (in children's libraries for every 300 readers) one

1. 'Anordnung über die Leistungsfinanzierung in den staatlichen allgemeinen öffentlichen Bibliotheken vom 10. Dezember 1970 [Instruction on Performance Financing
in the Public Libraries, of 10 December 1970]', *Gesetzblatt der Deutschen Demokratischen
Republik*, Vol. II, No. 2, 1971, p. 20–3.
   Edith Schurzig, Klaus Geerdts and Wolfgang Schumann, 'Die Leistungsfinanzierung in den staatlichen allgemeinen öffentlichen Bibliotheken [Performance Financing
in the Public Libraries]', *Der Bibliothekar*, Vol. 4, No. 25, 1971, p. 243–67.
2. 'Richtlinie über die Bestandssichtung in allgemeinbildenden Bibliotheken. Vom
20. September 1963 [Directive on Stack Revision in Public Libraries, of 20 September, 1963]', *Verfügungen und Mitteilungen des Ministeriums für Kultur*, No. 9, 1963, p. 49.
3. 'Anordnung zur Einführung eines Rahmenstellenplanes für allgemeine öffentliche
Bibliotheken in Gemeinden von 5 000–100 000 Einwohnern. Vom 30. September 1955
[Instruction on the Introduction of an Outline Staffing Plan for Public Libraries in
Local Authorities of 5,000–100,000 Population, of 30 September 1955]', *Gesetzblatt der
Deutschen Demokratischen Republik*, Vol. II, No. 54, 1955, p. 354–6.
   'Anordnung zur Änderung der Anordnung zur Einführung eines Rahmenstellen-
planes. . . Vom 23. Oktober 1956', *Gesetzblatt der Deutschen Demokratischen Republik*,
Vol. II, No. 44, 1956, p. 372.
   'Direktive zur Einführung eines Rahmenstellenplanes für allgemeine öffentliche
Bibliotheken in Städten über 100 000 Einwohner und in Bezirksstädten [Directive on
the Introduction of an Outline Staffing Plan for Public Libraries in Towns of Over
100,000 Population and in County Towns]', *Verfügungen und Mitteilungen des Ministeriums für Kultur*, 1956, 2, Sonderdruck, p. 3–6.

member of staff is required. The staff consists of librarians and others (mainly library assistants) in equal proportions.

The number of readers and circulation figures have more than doubled in the past fifteen years. This, together with the extension of the library networks in the rural areas and the introduction of rationalization measures in library work, has had two results. In many municipalities with less than 5,000 inhabitants full-time libraries now exist; these are the rural central libraries, which operate in each case as supply and administrative centres for a number of neighbouring part-time village libraries. In most of the full-time libraries there are more than 500 registered readers (300 in children's libraries) per member of staff. This is in excess of what the directives of 1955 and 1956 provided for.

In addition, two to five persons, mainly librarians, are employed in public libraries with a regional function, dealing with the extra work arising according to the number of people in the area to be provided for, and additional positions are provided in training libraries (*Ausbildungsbibliotheken*), for special institutions attached to larger libraries and for libraries in holiday centres.

TRADE UNION LIBRARIES

In addition to the public libraries there exist other libraries of a public nature, in the first place the trade union libraries which are maintained by the trade unions and operate in places of employment. These libraries fulfil for the working people similar functions to the government-run local public libraries. They include 577 full-time libraries with 159 branches and 2,619 lending stations, as well as 1,858 part-time libraries operated on a voluntary basis. At the end of 1971 some 6,820,000 volumes were stocked in the trade union libraries, with more than 900,000 readers borrowing about 11,250,000 books.

The minimum standards for trade union libraries for book stocks and staff were laid down in 1968 in a decision adopted by the Federal Executive of the Confederation of Free Trade Unions[1] and are shown in Table 38.

1. 'Die Aufgaben der Gewerkschaftsbibliotheken im entwickelten gesellschaftlichen System des Sozialismus. Grundsätze für die Tätigkeit und Leitung der gewerkschaftlichen Bibliotheken. Beschluss des Präsidiums des Bundesvorstandes des FDGB vom

TABLE 38

Number of employees	Book stock volumes	Volumes per employee	Library staff
1,000	3,500	3.5	1.0
1,000–1,500	6,060	4.0	1.5
1,501–2,500	10,000	4.0	2.0
2,501–4,000	15,000	3.5	3.0
4,001–5,000	18,000	3.5	3.5
5,001–7,000	22,000	3.0	4.0
7,001–10,000	30,000	3.0	6.0

Book stocks should consist of fiction (including children's books) and non-fiction in equal proportions. In establishments with more than 10,000 employees additional staff should be employed as required.

Federal Republic of Germany

The public library service in the Federal Republic of Germany, in comparison with that of certain other countries, is seriously under-developed. There are many reasons for this. There is no central direction by the federal government, since public libraries are the responsibility of the local communities. There is little financial support of local libraries by the individual states or *Länder*. There is no library legislation requiring a service to be established or, if established, to conform to any particular standards, though legislation has been drafted in a few *Länder*. The local authorities which provide public library services are numerous, including the smallest communities in the villages and rural districts. In 1971 there were some 9,000 separate communities maintaining about 8,500 stationary libraries, compared with some 8,000 public library systems in the United States and about 500 library authorities in the United Kingdom. Only 77 per cent of the total popu-

8. November 1968 [The Functions of the Trade Union Libraries in the Developed Social System of Socialism. Principles for the Staffing of Trade Union Libraries. Decision of the Praesidium of the Federal Board of the FDGB, of 8 November 1968]', *Kulturelles Leben*, Vol. 16, No. 1, 1969, Beilage, 4 p.

lation of 61 million in the federal republic was served by public libraries, and half the stock of the books was concentrated in only 259 communities. In 15,000 communities, mainly rural, not served by public libraries, there existed small libraries established by the Roman Catholic or Protestant Churches—some 8,000 Catholic libraries with some 9 million books and 4,500 Protestant libraries with about 2 million books. (The corresponding figure for public libraries provided by local authorities was about 22 million.) Such parochial libraries provided by the churches, existed also in areas served by public libraries. Also provided in all the major firms are well-organized works' libraries for the use of employees.

The pattern of library provision for the general public in the federal republic is more complex than in many other countries where the public library service is entirely in the hands of local authorities, with assistance in varying forms and degrees from provincial, state and central governments. In the Federal Republic of Germany the states maintain state libraries (*Landesbibliotheken*) in fifteen cities. These are reference libraries serving a scholarly minority. As a result it is not uncommon to find the public library service provided by a large municipality without a central lending and reference library, as the state library fulfils this purpose to a large degree for the city and neighbourhood. About one-fifth of the state libraries serve also as the main university library. However, in many large cities, especially where the state and university library is not centrally situated, the municipal authorities are developing their own central libraries for lending and reference purposes.

Two other factors which tend to diminish the use of the public libraries are that in certain public libraries small charges are made for the borrowing of books, though these charges are being progressively abolished, and the German people, by tradition, are book buyers and book owners.

Taking all these facts into account, but perhaps more particularly the excessively large number of library authorities, many too small to provide an efficient service, it is not surprising that book collections are inadequate in most libraries, and that library statistics show a relatively low use of public libraries. In 1972 only 10 to 12 per cent of the population in the communities served by public libraries were registered readers, though in certain places 10 per cent to 20 per cent was being achieved. Despite this a great deal of progress has been made since the end of the Second World War, judged by circulation and expenditure figures and by the amount of new library building, and librarians, the library associations and other bodies concerned have been active in pointing the way to improved service and greater use of the public libraries.

A number of important documents have been issued proposing ways of reorganizing public library services, and standards which should be achieved.

The first publication, *Kommunale Öffentliche Bücherei*[1] was published in 1964 by the Kommunale Gemeinschaftsstelle für Verwaltungsvereinfachung, a local government organization which is concerned with efficiency. This body, in consultation with the Arbeitstelle für des Büchereiwesen, (Study Centre for Public Libraries), subsidized by the federal and state governments but maintained by the Deutscher Büchereiverband (German Library Association), set up a committee of local government experts and librarians of communities of different sizes to consider the organization of public libraries in towns with over 10,000 population. This committee set down for the first time a number of standards for public library service, which took into account both international standards and the state of library service in the federal republic. For communities with populations over 10,000 the following broad general requirements were stated:

A public library should be headed by a qualified librarian.

The book stock should be adequate in number and quality.

The library materials should be made accessible and be presented professionally and there should be readers' advisory and reference services.

Public libraries should allow open access to their collections.

Bibliographical tools as well as periodicals should be available to the library users.

There should be reading and study rooms or areas.

Public libraries should participate more in inter-library lending.

Opening hours should be long and convenient for the public.

Some other, including quantitative, standards were proposed, including the following, and it was suggested that the standards should be reached within five or ten years.

---

1. *Kommunale Öffentliche Bücherei* [The Public Library Maintained by the Community], Cologne, Kommunale Gemeinschaftsstelle für Verwaltungsvereinfachung (KGSt-Gutachen), 1964.

A new edition, a development of the *Kommunale Öffentliche Bücherei*, entitled *Öffentliche Bibliothek* was published in 1973, including some revised standards.

REGISTERED READERS AND USE

For the purpose of the standards it was assumed that 15 per cent of the population would be registered readers and that each reader would borrow 30 volumes a year, or 4.5 volumes per head of population.

BOOK STOCKS

In the new edition the revised standard is at least two volumes per head, with a minimum collection of 10,000 volumes, excluding special collections and audio-visual material. The figures in Table 39 of adult and children's books were subsequently suggested as a guide in *Flachenbedarf Öffentlicher Büchereien*.

To replace worn-out or outdated books, 12 per cent of the existing number of books (excluding reference stocks) should be added each year together with a further 3 per cent for the extension of the book collections. This does not apply to new branches or to branches in suburbs.

Public libraries need to increase their holdings of learned literature, even if there exists a university or state library within the city boundary.

TABLE 39

Total volumes (thousands)	Adult books		Children's books	
	(thousands)	(%)	(thousands)	(%)
15	10	67	5.0	33
20	13	67	6.7	33
25	16	67	8.3	33
30	20	67	10.0	33
40	28	70	12.0	30
50	38	76	12.0	24
100	88	88	12.0	12

It may be necessary to provide books for other institutions in the community, such as schools and colleges, hospitals, old peoples' homes.

Public libraries should be within easy reach. In general, no one likes to travel more than 15 minutes (1 kilometre) to the nearest service point, but, in outer suburbs with less dense building, the distance can be increased to 1.5 kilometres. The same distance applies to the stopping places of mobile libraries.

The main library should be open for 40–60 hours a week, including Saturdays, and the average branch library for 35 hours a week.

Branch libraries should be established for areas of not less than 10,000 people and should offer a book collection of not less than 10,000 volumes, of which 3,000 might be children's books.

Mobile libraries should visit at least once a week for a sufficient length of time. They should have a capacity of 2,500 to 4,500 volumes and a total collection of 10,000 to 15,000.

Public libraries should make their resources available to the public, including persons who do not live in the community, without charge except for overdue books.

Other libraries, such as those provided by industrial firms or churches, may supplement but cannot substitute for a public library.

STAFF

In the smallest library unit there should be at least 1 professional librarian and 1 non-professional assistant.

Staff requirements begin with qualified staff. The requirements for other staff depend on local organization of duties and other factors.

For staff generally, the number of loans and the number of accessions are the principal factors. Local circumstances, such as opening hours, organization of the library and services provided, design of the building, are secondary factors.

As an average standard for readers' services, 1 qualified librarian for every 30,000 loans a year can be taken. But this cannot be strictly applied. Also different standards may apply to branch libraries according to circumstances.

For other regular duties, staff needs are determined principally by the rate of accessions and, with an annual accessions rate of 15 per cent, one librarian is required for every 7,500 accessions. In general, 2 non-professional assistants are required for every qualified librarian. If certain duties are centralized in a library system or other forms of co-operation, the ratio might be reduced to 1 : 1. But further provision must be made if specialized libraries and reading rooms exist.

To achieve the highest quality of book selection at a time when more and more learned literature is purchased by public libraries, librarians should be employed as specialists for main subject areas, such as pure science, technology, the humanities, the social sciences, fiction and children's literature. Libraries in smaller communities should seek to benefit from larger systems or to join with other communities.

Each mobile library should be staffed by one librarian, 1 library assistant (the driver), with 1 library assistant working at the base.

A second document prepared by the Arbeitstelle für das Büchereiwesen (Study Centre for Public Libraries) at the request of the Standing Joint Committee of the Ministers of Cultural and Educational Affairs of the eleven federal states, was issued by the Deutscher Büchereiverband und vom Verein Deutscher Volksbibliothekare, in 1966, entitled *Grundlagen für die bibliothekarische Regionalplanung*.[1] This contained some basic proposals and standards for the formation of library systems and library regions, and elaborated some of the standards included in the first document. This recommended the local authorities and other bodies providing public libraries which satisfied certain requirements to combine to form 'library systems' which should serve a population of about 500,000. These systems would maintain stationary and mobile libraries; the larger libraries in the system would make their resources available for inter-library loan and might send out circulating collections to smaller libraries or provide facilities for mobile libraries. One library in each system, providing an open-access collection of

---

1. *Grundlagen für die bibliothekarische Regionalplanung* [Fundamentals for Regional Planning of Libraries], Wiesbaden, Harrassowitz, 1966.

at least 50,000 volumes, should act as a central library and a clearing house for external inter-library loans. Each system would need a headquarters linked with the central library, or another main library in the system, at which there would be the 'system's librarian'.

In addition to the 'systems', numbering possibly 150, the document proposed the establishment of a small number of 'regions', which might be identical with a federal state or with one of the regions of the existing German inter-library loan structure. The regions would try to provide most of the literature requested from their own resources and would establish union catalogues to facilitate inter-library lending. They would provide books through the national inter-library loan scheme or from abroad, would be responsible for the education of librarians and would provide a centre for the advancement of library methods by the exchange of ideas and information.

A third document published by the Deutscher Büchereiverband, Arbeitstelle für das Büchereiwesen, in 1968 entitled *Flachenbedarf öffentlicher Büchereien—Bedarfsberechnungen*[1] gives recommended building standards for accommodation required to meet the book stock and other recommendations in the 1964 document *Kommunale öffentliche Bücherei*.

This document is too detailed to be more than briefly referred to

TABLE 40

	Square metres per 1,000 volumes			
	Reference	Non-fiction	Fiction	Children
Shelf spaces and access area	52.5	14.0	12.6	15.0
Working spaces for users	13.6	5.0	2.5	8.0

The resultant net areas are as follows:

Total volumes (thousands)	15	20	25	30	40	50	60	80	100
Area (square metres per 1,000 population)	37	35	34	33	42	42	41	44	42

1. *Flächenbedarf öffentlicher Büchereien—Bedarfsberechnungen* [Space Requirements for Public Libraries: Calculations of Needs], Berlin, Deutscher Büchereiverband, Arbeitsstelle für das Büchereiwesen, 1968 (Bibliotheksdienst, Beiheft 37).

here. On the basis of assumptions about total stocks of the various types of library materials, staffing, hours of opening, figures of actual loans, areas are calculated for all sections of the library premises. Total net areas (excluding circulation and services) in square metres per 1,000 volumes held (which on the basis of 1 volume per inhabitant corresponds also to square metres per thousand population) are suggested. These calculations are based on areas considered to be required for each different purpose. Two examples of these bases are given in Table 40.

Model estimates are also given for special libraries and special services, including a music library with 30,000 volumes, 3,000 records and a reference library, and a mobile library centre, together with data about shelving under different library conditions.

In January 1969, the Deutscher Büchereiverband issued a further document entitled *Bibliotheksplan I. Entwurf für ein umfassendes Netz allgemeiner öffentlicher Bibliotheken und Büchereien.*[1] This contains standards for developing individual libraries and a comprehensive library network, building on the earlier statements referred to. In particular it refers to three levels of library, indicating their respective roles and expected standards of service.

'Grade I libraries', which will serve small communities, such as branch libraries in larger systems or community libraries in rural areas, with holdings of 1 volume per inhabitant and a minimum stock of 10,000 volumes and a basic stock of reference works. These must be open on 5 days a week for at least 30 hours and run by a full-time professional librarian. They should be part of a system and connected with the central library of the system for book selection, book processing, loan transactions, information services and other forms of assistance.

'Grade II libraries' offering a higher level of service would be those in large towns or towns in association with rural areas which form the central library and headquarters of the library systems, and local libraries in larger communities. They require a central library and adequate stock to assist Grade I libraries affiliated to them. These libraries should provide a comprehensive service and

1. *Bibliotheksplan I. Entwurf für ein umfassendes Netz allgemeiner öffentlicher Bibliotheken und Büchereien* [Library Plan 1. Model for a Comprehensive Network of General Public Libraries].

services for other libraries in their system, including a union catalogue and participation in inter-library lending.

National and State libraries, university and other major libraries in the library region are regarded as 'Grade III libraries'. They would co-ordinate joint activities within the region, making books and other materials available to users throughout the State through local public libraries and the inter-lending arrangements. They should organize and control the regional inter-library lending and should collect all the literature which cannot be stored in the library service of the region. They should render bibliographical and other services to libraries in their region.

The plan is based on the assumption that the libraries of the first and second grade take care of German language and literature and translations. Foreign language literature is expected to be mainly in the third-grade libraries at present, since the smaller libraries have to meet the standards in the German collections before going further.

In all libraries a reference and information collection of different dimensions should be provided. Estimates are given of the initial cost of the reference materials required for the three levels of libraries namely: DM.11,000; DM.75,000; and DM.145,000 (at then current prices). The plan proposed that in libraries of the second grade 500 periodicals in German should be available. For the third-grade libraries mention is made of a duty to build a comprehensive stock of books and periodicals with no language preferences.

In 1970 a further document was published *Grundsätze und Normen für die Büchereigesetzgebung in den Ländern der Bundesrepublik*. These were elaborated by a joint commission of the Deutscher Büchereiverband (German Library Association) and the Verein der Bibliothekare an Öffentlichen Büchereien (Association of Librarians in Public Libraries).[1] The document consisted of a list of all the matters to be covered by public library legislation in order to guarantee the uniformity and equivalent value of the literature and information service to the population of all the states in the federal republic.

---

1. 'Grundsätze und Normen für die Büchereigesetzgebung in den Ländern der Bundesrepublic Deutschland [Principles and Standards for Public Library Legislation in the States of the Federal Republic of Germany]', *Bibliotheksdienst*, Vol. 5, May 1970, p. 234–40; also published separately in Berlin by Deutscher Büchereiverband, 1970.

One of the two 1973 documents *Öffentliche Bibliothek*[1] introduces a new formula for calculating staff requirements. Both German and foreign experience suggested that there should be one librarian for every 2,000 inhabitants, with staff divided: General 40 per cent; processing 30 per cent; lending 30 per cent. Space standards are discussed.

A second Bibliotheksplan, *Bibliotheksplan '73*,[2] was published in 1973 by the Deutsche Bibliothekskonferenz (German Library Conference—a federation of all the German library associations), an enlarged and revised edition of the first. This refers even more than the first plan to libraries other than public libraries, aiming at a closer integration of the academic and research (state and university libraries, etc.) into the system and to adapt the whole plan to the developments of the last few years. In this plan the most outstanding libraries are included in a Grade IV. This plan contains a considerable amount of new, or consolidated standards material, which considerations of space make it impossible to summarize.

Plans have thus been laid and standards of service indicated, which if implemented would ensure that, through co-operative networks integrating all libraries and adequate inter-library loan facilities, the public libraries—and indeed all libraries in the federal republic—could meet the demands made on them.

Hungary

What follows is based on material provided by the Centre for Library Science and Methodology of the National Szechenyi Library.

Although there is a long history of public libraries in Hungary it was not until after the Second World War that effective measures were taken to develop public libraries systematically. A comprehensive libraries act of 1956, dealing with all types of libraries, established networks of libraries performing similar functions, with general supervision by the largest library among them. In

---

1. *Öffentliche Bibliothek. Gutachen der kommunalen Gemeinschaftsstelle für Verwaltungsvereinfachung (KGSt)* [The Public Library. Report of the Community Office for the Simplification of Administration (KGSt)], Berlin, Deutscher Bibliotheksverband, Arbeitsstelle für das Bibliothekswesen, 1973.
2. *Bibliotheksplan '73—Entwurf eines umfassenden Bibliotheksnetzes für die Bundesrepublic Deutschland* [Library Plan '73—Model for a Comprehensive Library Network for the Federal Republic of Germany], Berlin, Deutsche Bibliothekskonferenz, 1973.

addition there was extensive provision for control and assistance by the central government through the Ministry of Culture and other government departments concerned. The act provides for the making of regulations regarding, for example, the establishment, maintenance and development of libraries, employment of librarians, library training and co-operation between libraries and library networks. The Ministry of Culture is authorized to issue further regulations about such matters as the organization of library networks, acquisition policies, and inter-library lending. There is a National Council for Librarianship and Documentation—the members being the directors of selected libraries and library networks and other library experts—which has two sections of special library and information activity for (a) social sciences and (b) science, technology, agriculture and health, and a third section of public and school libraries. This is an advisory organ of the Ministry of Culture. There is also an organization within the National Library, responsible to the Ministry of Culture, the Centre for Library Science and Methodology. This is in many respects comparable to the State Inspectorates of the Scandinavian library systems, though its functions are mainly technical. It has a wide range of functions designed to aid the development of the library services, including a Department for Network Development concerned mainly with public libraries. Frank Gardner says of this body: 'The organization of the centre is most impressive and is obviously an important factor in the high standards of the public library system of Hungary.'[1]

Among the networks of libraries established under the act are public libraries, organized on a territorial basis. This has made possible a more methodical and closely knit organization. A second network is provided for trade union libraries with which the public library network is grouped, thus making for co-operation.[2] The territorial organization has created opportunities for co-operation on a local basis, inter-library committees, consisting of representatives of the various types of library being set up to deal with problems on a county basis. As Gardner also says: 'A basis is thus

1. Frank M. Gardner, *Public Library Legislation: A Comparative Study*, Paris, Unesco, 1971, p. 141–8. For fuller information see: Jenö Kiss, *Libraries in Hungary*, Budapest, National Széchényi Library, Centre for Library Science and Methodology, 1972.
2. The public also has access to libraries related to special fields of interest, through the networks of national and other special libraries, which are open to all.

laid for a truly national service, operating at both national and regional level with obvious advantages.'[1]

The territorial network of public libraries is established around the nineteen counties into which Hungary is divided and Budapest, the capital. Within the counties the district and village libraries are independent, although they co-operate with each other, and the supervision exercised by the county and district librarians over the smaller libraries is only advisory. Budapest, however, has a unitary system with a considerable degree of decentralization and local district committees. The result, particularly in the rural areas, is that there is an excessive number of small service points.

For some time past there has been a process of fusion and concentration of small public libraries, a process greatly assisted by a recent general re-organization of local administration. Some of the separate communities have become part of other districts or have been merged into larger territorial units around a city centre. These changes have helped the development of public library networks, the library resources available being concentrated in larger districts and in the towns. By building up a system of branches, central libraries in these enlarged areas are becoming increasingly responsible for providing a library service to the smaller communities.

These administrative changes have given an impetus to the preparation of standards for public libraries as an aid to their planning and development. This work has been undertaken by the Centre for Library Science and Methodology, which has produced guidelines and standards for public libraries. These have been approved by the Ministry of Culture and published for the benefit of the county councils and other local councils responsible for maintaining the libraries.[2] The following summary of the document is based on material provided by the centre.

1. In 1970 the 9,251 public libraries and trade union libraries in Hungary, with 25 million holdings (about 2.5 volumes per inhabitant), lent 54.8 million books (5.3 volumes per inhabitant) to 2.2 million readers (21.6 per cent of the population)—(*IFLA Annual 1971*).
2. 'Szakmai irányelvek a tanácsi közművelődési könyvtárak távlati fejlesztéséhez [Professional Guiding Principles for the Future Development of Hungarian Public Libraries], *Művelődésügyi Közlöny*, 11.sz., 1972, p. 315-20. For standards for trade union libraries see: 'Alapelvek és követelmények a szakszervezeti könyvtárak távlati tervezéséhez [Basic Principles and Requirements for the Future Planning of Trade Union Libraries—Central Council of Hungarian Trade Unions]', *SzOT Elnökségi Tájékoztató*, 2.sz., 1971.

ORGANIZATIONAL STANDARDS
FOR LIBRARY PROVISION

The work of library institutions is to be organized by counties and within these areas by service levels in three categories—basic, medium and high grade. These three levels of service together furnish a unified service, with close connexions with national and university libraries and through all effective channels to individual users.

Basic-grade library provision

This supplies a rural community with 3,000 to 5,000 inhabitants or several villages united in one administrative unit, or an urban area of a similar size within a radius of 1 to 1.5 kilometres. If the community consists of several small villages there is only one basic grade library in the central village; in the other villages there are sub-standard service points.

Total stock. Minimum, 5,000 volumes.

Annual accessions. Books: at least 350–400 titles. This means the best part of Hungarian book publishing and is recommended by the central acquisitions advisory service to be acquired as a core. Periodicals: at least 50.

Staff. Minimum, 1 qualified librarian.

Opening hours. Minimum, 20–24 hours weekly, open on at least 4 days.

Services. Lending, reference and children's service; readers' advisory service and inter-library loans.

Medium-grade library provision

Supplies several villages and towns with more than 10,000 inhabitants within a normal radius of 10–15 kilometres. Number of people served: up to 50,000, sometimes more.

Total stock. Minimum 20,000 volumes.

Annual accessions. Books: 2,500–3,000 titles (the whole of Hungarian book-publishing recommended by the central acquisitions advisory service, as well as a selection of the most important general reference books published in world-wide languages). Periodicals: 230–300 titles (a comprehensive selection of Hungarian newspapers and periodicals and a representative selection of periodicals published in major foreign languages and languages of national minorities in Hungary). Music: sound recordings and printed music, 250–300 titles (classical and folk music, books on music).

Staff. Staff varying in number according to extent and nature of work, with a librarian of high qualifications in charge.

Opening hours. Adult service, minimum 48 hours weekly. Children's service, minimum 30 hours.

Services. Lending; reference reading room, including collection of reference books representing Hungarian book publishing since 1945; reference service; inter-library loans; listening to music; activities popularizing literature, music and science.

High-grade library provision

Supplies a group of communities, minimum population 200,000, maximum 500,000, generally comprising a county, including towns and villages with their library institutions.

Total stock. Minimum 100,000 volumes.

Annual accessions. Books: 3,500–4,500 titles—all essential titles published in Hungary and a selection of foreign material (including material for national minorities), non-fiction and fiction. Periodicals: 450–500—a generous selection of Hungarian newspapers and periodicals and a selection of periodicals published in major foreign languages and languages of national minorities in Hungary. Music: 400–500 titles of recorded music (records, tapes) and other audio-visual materials—the whole range of Hungarian gramophone record production—and music scores and other printed material relating to music. Non-traditional material: standards, maps, micro-films, etc.

Bindery. For the requirements of the library and its network.

Staff. Each library should have a staff organized according to the amount and nature of the work, including a number of qualified librarians and a chief librarian, all with high grades of qualification from university or college.

Opening hours. Both adult and children's service, minimum weekly of 48 hours.

Services. Lending; reference reading, including reference collection representing Hungarian book publishing in the twentieth century; information on special literature in conjunction with the national information system and national special libraries; inter-library lending; reprography; translating and abstracting; audio-visual service (including provision for listening and re-recording in the library); activities popularizing literature, music and science.

Sub-standard service points

In addition to the three levels of library described, providing a library service to a recognized standard, there are other circum-stances in which library service of a lower standard may be justified by local conditions and social needs. The need may be in an institution, such as a school, club or cultural centre, or in a village for the time being still independent of the basic or higher-level library services. Such library services are sometimes merely delivery stations or circulating library deposits. They receive their book material to a lesser degree from local sources but increasingly from larger libraries. A typical example is given of such a library in a community or scattered settlement with less than 2,000 inhabi-tants, provided in a public or other institution for culture or general entertainment.

Stock. Selection of 1,000 volumes (some general reference books, classics of the world and Hungarian literature, children's and juvenile literature, popular scientific works).

Accessions. Two hundred volumes or more, as a deposit, changed regularly, periodicals—10 titles.

Opening hours. Minimum weekly of 8 hours.

Services. Lending and advice on reading.

Staff. An honorary library worker, who receives a small payment.

Standards for the planning of book stock and library staff

Development of stock

In order to satisfy readers' demands and to provide for normal replacement and development of the basic collection, the stock should be increased by 2 per cent of the total average number of volumes lent annually. In the case of the sub-standard service points, part of the stock can come from a central library and be changed frequently. In such cases the 2 per cent figure above can be reduced to 1 per cent. This is financially advantageous to the authority directly providing the local service.

At the sub-standard service points, the book stock should, if possible, come entirely from the deposit collection. The central library should provide each deposit library with at least fifty new books a year.

Staff

Staff should be provided in the main areas of library work on the basis: shown in Tables 41 and 42.

TABLE 41. Readers' service (advisory service, information)

Number of volumes loaned annually (thousands)	Staff required (non-manual)			
	Professional		Non-professional	
	Full-time university grade qualified librarian	Full-time middle grade qualified librarian	Full time	Part time
15–20	—	1	—	1
20–30	—	1	—	1
30–40	1	—	1	—
40–50	1	1	1	—
50–60	1	1	1	1
60–70	1	2	1	1
70–80	2	2	2	—

TABLE 42. Accessioning, recording, processing, storage

Yearly increase (volumes or other items)	Staff required (non manual)			
	Qualified librarians		Non-professional	
	University grade	Middle grade	Full time	Part time
600–1,200	—	—	—	1
1,200–1,500	—	—	—	1
1,500–2,500	—	1	—	—
2,500–4,000	1	1	—	—
4,000–6,000	1	1	—	1

In libraries more extensively used, one middle-grade qualified librarian and one part-time non-professional worker should be employed for every additional 20,000 issues.

It is desirable to employ in the departments of music and periodicals one middle-grade qualified librarian, in addition to the numbers referred to above.

It is reasonable to employ in all libraries one storage worker for every 100,000 issues, if less than this a part-time worker. It is also reasonable to employ one librarian with university qualifications to carry out duties requiring local knowledge in connexion with the processing of the local history collection as well as other bibliographical work. In libraries where the yearly increase is less than 1,200 volumes, the staff requirements for these categories of work should be considered together with those for the service to readers.

Library network—supply of deposit collections,
methodological advice and professional supervision
For work in connexion with deposit collections one middle-grade qualified librarian should be employed for every twenty to twenty-five service points. To provide methodological advice and professional supervision, one librarian with university qualifications should be employed at the central institution for every forty to forty-five libraries and service points. For less than this number it is advisable to plan the professional supervision in association with other kinds of work.

Administration and management
Management responsibilities can only be regarded in the highest grade of library as full-time work. In other cases the chief librarian should take part in other professional duties, and this should be reflected in the total number of staff required.

STANDARDS FOR LIBRARY BUILDINGS

Recommended areas for library buildings are deduced from two basic indices, the estimated number of readers as a percentage of total population and the total number of volumes aimed at per inhabitant. It is assumed that, in communities of up to 8,000,

TABLE 43. Basic indices for public libraries in cultural centres or in independent buildings—areas and volumes

Population served	Area required per 1,000 population (m²)	Books required (volumes) Per 1,000 population	Books required (volumes) Total (to nearest 500 population)	Area for readers' services (open access lending; information; reading room) Total (m²)	Area for readers' services Children (included in total) (m²)	Area of service rooms and stacks (m²)	Total area of library, excluding staff accommodation and circulation space (m²)	In an independent building located separately Addition for: entrance hall, cloakrooms, club and lecture room(s) (m²)	In an independent building located separately Total area (m²)
Under 1,000	55	3,000	3,000	55	—	—	55	—	55
1,000–1,500	55	3,000	4,000	82	—	—	82	—	82
1,500–2,500	55	2,500	6,500	138	—	—	138	—	138
2,500–3,500	55	2,400	8,500	143	—	20	163	30	193
3,500–5,000	50	2,300	11,500	170	—	35	205	45	250
5,000–8,000	44	2,100	17,000	240	70	50	290	62	352
8,000–12,000	36	1,900	23,000	280	80	70	350	82	432
12,000–20,000	36	1,700	34,000	480	120	120	600	120	720
20,000–30,000	36	1,600	48,000	750	150	150	900	180	1,080

TABLE 44. Provision for readers in reading rooms

Population served	Expected number of readers Adults	Expected number of readers Children	Expected number of readers Total	Minimum number of readers' places Adults	Minimum number of readers' places Children	Minimum number of readers' places Total
Under 1,000	—	—	250	—	10	10
1,000–1,500	270	105	375	—	13	13
1,500–2,500	470	175	625	14	8	22
2,500–3,500	540	210	750	16	10	26
3,500–5,000	900	350	1,250	18	14	32
5,000–8,000	1,200	480	1,680	28	22	50
8,000–12,000	1,800	720	2,520	36	24	60
12,000–20,000	3,000	1,280	4,200	60	40	100
20,000–30,000	4,500	1,800	6,300	68	45	113

25 per cent of the population (of which 7 per cent will be children) and, in communities of over 8,000, 21 per cent (6 per cent children) will be readers. The expected figures for volumes per inhabitant range from 3 for a population of 1,500 to 1.6 for 30,000.

For readers' places, calculated on the basis of percentage of adults and children enrolled, the recommended standards are as follows: up to 3,000 inhabitants, 3 per cent adults, 5 per cent children; up to 20,000, 2 per cent adults, 4 per cent children; over 20,000, 1.5 per cent adults, 3 per cent children.

Total useful surface areas (excluding corridors, services, etc.) required per 1,000 inhabitants for a library established in an independent building or in a cultural centre are calculated as follows: up to 3,500 inhabitants, 55 m²; 5,000–8,000 inhabitants, 50 m²; 8,000–12,000 inhabitants, 44 m²; above 12,000 inhabitants, 36 m².

Detailed standards, both for areas and for equipment, for libraries up to 30,000 population have been prepared and the principal figures are set out in Tables 43 and 44. Figures are included for libraries serving 1,000–2,000 inhabitants. In these small villages library premises will remain; they will later on function not as independent libraries but as service points.

For libraries providing central and high-grade services detailed standards have not been prepared. The size of these libraries is best determined individually. For a preliminary calculation approximate figures can be used. For the number of inhabitants in the area directly served, 50–55 m² per 1,000 inhabitants; in addition 2 m² per 1,000 inhabitants can be added for the total area served. The necessary conditions for the service envisaged should be established on the basis laid down in the general standards.

PUBLIC LIBRARY SERVICE FOR CHILDREN
AND ADOLESCENTS

In addition to the general public library standards, the Ministry of Culture has issued guiding principles and standards for library service for readers under 18[1] aimed at providing networks of

1. 'Irányelvek a 18 éven aluli ifjuság könyvtári ellátásának javitására [Guiding Principles for the Improvement of Library Services to Young Readers under 18]', *Müvelödésügyi Közlöny*, 24.sz., 1971, p. 392–5.

children's library services through schools and public libraries. This statement includes detailed standards for school libraries and for public library children's services. It also discusses the provision of library services for adolescents, without giving quantitative standards. Recognizing that library services for these groups cannot be provided through public libraries alone, the ministry expects close co-operation between public and school libraries, especially in connexion with children of school age.

Children's library service is regarded as an integral part of public library service, even if provided outside the premises of the public library, and libraries with central responsibilities, whether county, town or urban district libraries, are required to provide for the maintenance of children's services within their systems. Libraries exclusively serving children may be regarded as branch libraries and, as such, responsible to their central libraries.

In major towns it is proposed that each area with 15,000 to 20,000 population should be served by a separate children's library and that in other areas a children's section should be developed in each public library serving a community of 8,000 to 10,000 people. The public libraries are encouraged to send deposit collections to day and boarding schools, to children's homes and to establish points in children's wards of hospitals.

Provision is made for the establishment of joint children's libraries and school libraries in small urban centres or in residential areas of a larger district. These would operate as school libraries during school hours and afterwards would provide a general children's library service. Such libraries are regarded as school libraries under the control of the head of the school, with the librarian a member of the teaching staff. Such joint libraries are established to serve residential areas where young readers would have to walk between one and one-and-a-half kilometres to the nearest children's library.

Suggested standards for public library children's service

Children's library service, like adult service, may be provided at different levels. There are four categories. Type A (including central county libraries); Type B (including sub-centres); Type C; and Type D (providing supplementary services). The basic principles relating to children's service may be summarized as follows.

Requirements for the provision of children's service in Type A libraries

Stock. This must comprise ten to twelve volumes per child reader; the total stock must not be fewer than 10,000 to 15,000 volumes. As regards the contents of the collection, endeavours should be made to achieve a complete coverage of children's books and youth literature, including periodicals, issued in the Hungarian language. In addition there should be well-selected material from adult literature for readers under 14, children's literature and periodicals in foreign languages to help studies in modern languages, manuals, reference books and tools for children's service, scientific literature on psychology and dealing with the pedagogy of reading, and books on the history of children's literature, its theories and criticism. Children's literature treated from the points of view of bibliophilism may form a part of the stock for adult readers, but a separate register should be kept of it in the children's library catalogues. Gramophone records (music recordings, recorded texts in Hungarian and in foreign languages), tape recordings, slides, 16 mm films, audio-visual equipment for reproduction (record players, tape recorders, projectors, etc.), if useful for work with children, must be acquired for the music collection of the adult service but also made available for children's service. The children's library collections must include visual aids, e.g. graphic materials, such as pictures showing prominent historical and public figures, townscapes, landscapes, sporting events, natural phenomena, current events of interest, etc.

Accessions. These must cover all publications in the Hungarian language, both of books and periodicals, for readers between 6 and 14 and must total yearly about 500 to 600 titles, in sufficient number of copies to meet readers' demands. Books representing 3 per cent of the total circulation should be added to the acquisitions to allow for wear and tear. There should also be thirty to forty periodical titles, reference books, and literature on children's books dealing *inter alia* with the pedagogical aspects of reading.

Staff. This must consist of a children's library team, working under the guidance of a fully qualified teacher or librarian, assisted by librarians with middle and high-level qualification. For every 500 child readers there should be a full-time children's librarian; over 800 readers the librarian should have the help of a clerical assistant to attend to loans administration.

Accommodation. There must be a minimum area of 250 to 300 m² set apart for children's service. Shelving area, allowing free access to books, should be commensurate with the stock size and the number of readers, but must be at least 150 to 200 m². There must be a study/reading room, and a separate room for group activities.

Library hours. These should be at least forty-eight hours weekly enabling maximum use of the library for child readers, including pupils attending schools with alternating classes.

Services. These should include lending, facilities for reading on the premises, reference service, children's library programmes and games, provision of audio-visual aids.

Methodological and bibliographical activities. It is the responsibility of Type A libraries—which function in the county centres—to provide methodological guidance to children's libraries and sections in every part of the county, to organize continual training courses for children's librarians, and to prepare bibliographical guides for local needs. For this last activity, at least two highly qualified children's librarians are required.

Requirements for the provision of children's service in Type B libraries
There must be separate accommodation for the children's service, set apart from adult service.

Stock. This must consist of ten to twelve volumes per child reader, minimum 6,000 volumes. It must be an appropriate collection, including books, periodicals, manuals, slides, gramophone records and tapes, for users between 6 and 14.

Accessions. This should be about 500 titles yearly of books in the Hungarian language, with sufficient copies to meet needs, together with replacements amounting to 3 per cent of total issues to provide for wear and tear, and twenty-five to thirty periodical titles.

Staff. For every 500 readers there must be a full-time professional librarian with middle or higher qualification; for over 800 readers a clerical assistant is needed.

Library hours. These should be at least thirty hours weekly, apart from time devoted to school classes visiting the library and to group activities arranged in the library.

Services. These should include lending, reading facilities on the premises, reference service, group activities.

Accommodation. The children's library should be housed in a room of its own of at least 100 m². Children's services provided in schools and maintained jointly by the school and the public library belong to this category.

Requirements for the provision
of children's service in Type C libraries
Stock. Of the total collection, minimum 5,000 volumes, at least 2,000 volumes should be children's books and an additional 1,000 should be books used by children as well as adults. Of the yearly accessions at least 200 titles must be children's books in sufficient number of copies; there should also be replacements amounting to 3 per cent of total issues.

Staff. In this type of library a single librarian is usually assigned to carry out the joint services for adults and child readers. But if there are two qualified librarians, one of them should work exclusively with young readers.

Library hours. It is desirable that library hours for children should differ from those for adults, but they must not be fewer than for adult readers, i.e. twenty-four hours weekly, spread over at least four days.

Accommodation. In cases of joint accommodation for adults and children there must be a separate area for the children where they have free access to their books and to reference material. If the children's department is housed in a separate room, children must also have access to the adult reference library.

Requirements for supplementary children's services
provided by Type D libraries
These services include provision of deposit collections for schools, colleges, day-time homes for pupils, day-time study groups and for children's wards at hospitals. The collection for this purpose should comprise at least 1,000 volumes, including fiction, non-fiction, periodicals, and reference books. The deposit collections should contain at least 100 volumes and exchanges must be made frequently.

Services. These should include lending and guidance to readers.

Staff. This should consist of a librarian working part time in more than one library or a librarian engaged for work in one library for an hourly or sessional payment.

Youth service provided in public libraries

In promoting the interests of youth it is necessary that public libraries should provide library service for the 14 to 18 age group, even though libraries at present may not be in the position to secure separate premises for this purpose. Youth service must be performed by competent librarians with a natural gift for and adequate practice in educational work. Their scope of activities should be clearly defined and organized accordingly in all libraries where it seems desirable that youth service be, to a certain extent, separated from adult service. Because of lack of experience in providing library service to this age group, no definite numerical standards could be recommended. The necessary conditions for the service envisaged should be established on the basis of the principles laid down in the main standards document.[1]

Japan

Libraries have existed in Japan from the early part of the seventh century, but, until the Meiji Restoration of 1868, they belonged mostly to private persons and few were open to the public. After this a modern system of libraries was introduced from the United Kingdom and the United States, but not until after the Second World War did people begin to appreciate the value of public libraries. Since then libraries in Japan have come to play a positive role in social education and to attract growing interest among the people at large.

In 1971 there were 885 public libraries in Japan distributed as follows:

Main Libraries: 58 prefecture; 493 city; 231 town and village; and 30 private.

Branch Libraries; 22 prefecture; and 51 city.

This gives a total of 80 prefecture, 544 city, 231 town and village and 30 private.

Japan is divided into forty-seven prefectures, each including a number of cities, towns and villages. The prefectures are empowered to provide library services throughout the whole of

1. See footnote 2, page 213.

their area. They maintain mobile and temporary library services in many of the localities, but most of their purpose-built libraries are in large cities. In these cities there is often a prefectural central library as well as a central library maintained by the city itself. This concurrent exercise of library powers makes it possible to retain large units for the more specialized services essential in metropolitan and county areas, and yet permits the smaller units to operate the general library services.

Japanese public libraries are primarily reference libraries, but of recent years they have played a more active part as lending libraries. Lending use is, however, very low, except in a few areas. But the number of books issued is rapidly increasing. The number of branch libraries is very small, the great bulk of the public being served only by small collections of the more popular books in mobile libraries or provided on bulk loan to groups of various kinds. The provision of audio-visual materials tends to be considerable and performances held in the libraries are well attended. Special rooms are set apart in purpose-built libraries for such traditional cultural activities as the tea ceremony and flower arrangement.[1]

In 1950 a library law was enacted:

... to provide for necessary matters concerning the establishment of libraries and to promote a sound development thereof, and thereby to contribute to the enhancement of the education and culture of the nation. . . .

This law is concerned with community libraries provided by local public bodies (public libraries) and also with similar libraries provided privately (private libraries). Some provisions touch on general principles of the kind normally found in documents about standards.

Under 'Library Service' it is said that:

Libraries shall endeavour . . . to realize . . . the following . . . taking into consideration local situations and the wishes of the general public and . . . to aid school education.
(1) Books, archives, audio-visual materials, and other necessary data and materials shall be collected and offered to the use of the general public . . .;
(2) The library materials shall be properly classified and arranged . . . ;

1. George Chandler, 'Libraries in Japan', *Times Educational Supplement*, 20 August 1971.

(3) . . . the library personnel may obtain adequate knowledge of the library materials and may give advice to library users;
(4) Close contact and co-operation shall be made between libraries and with the National Diet Library . . . and libraries attached to schools by such as inter-library loans;
(5) Branch libraries, reading centres and book circulating centres may be established and the service of book-mobiles and itinerant lending libraries may be offered;
(6) Reading circles, seminars, appreciation meetings, showing of films, exhibitions of data and materials etc. shall be sponsored and encouraged;
(7) Information and reference materials concerning current problems shall be introduced and offered to the general public;
(8) Close contact and co-operation shall be made with schools, museums, citizens' public halls, research institutes etc.

Under 'Personnel', the law requires that the heads of public libraries which receive subsidies from the State should normally have minimum qualifications, details of which are specified.

Public libraries are precluded from making any admission charges or any charges for the use of library materials.

Provision is made for the establishment of representative library councils to advise the heads of libraries about their operation.

The law provides that the major city libraries in metropolitan areas (e.g. Tokyo) and the prefectural libraries may invite the local Boards of Education—the bodies responsible for providing the public libraries—of the cities, towns and villages to co-operate over preparation of union catalogues, the service of mobile lending libraries and the mutual lending of library materials.

The law is, however, mainly administrative and on the question of what at any given time constitutes a satisfactory level of library service provides that:

(1) The Minister of Education shall, in order to promote the sound development of libraries, formulate desirable standards for the establishment and the operation of public libraries and make them available to the [local] Board of Education, for guidance and, in addition, make them known to the general public;
(2) The minimum standards required for receiving the promotional subsidies under the provision of Article 20 from the State shall be prescribed by regulations of the Ministry of Education.

Implementing the first of these provisions, the Sub-Committee of Facilities of the Social Educational Council of the Ministry of Education produced in 1969 a set of standards indicating

desirable levels for establishing and managing public libraries.[1]
    A summary of the current standards is given below. These
standards are at present being revised.

ORGANIZATION

The document states that:

The urban and rural prefectures are responsible for establishing
    public libraries in the prefectures.

The municipalities (including special municipalities) are respon-
    sible for establishing public libraries in their areas. The size of
    the library should be increased in areas with more than
    100,000 population, by reason of total population, population
    density, topography, traffic density and other factors.

The towns and villages should establish libraries. But, where they
    find it difficult to set up separate libraries, joint libraries should
    be established by the union of neighbouring municipalities,
    towns and villages.

Among the principal standards indicated in the document are
    the following:

Activities

The libraries are responsible for the establishment or provision of
services for young people and children as well as for adults;
reference services, reading guides and copying services; branch
libraries and stations for lending books in relation to demand; a
network of services in co-operation with private libraries, public
halls[2] and schools, and mobile lending libraries.

    They should also establish co-operative arrangements between
libraries (whether provided by the same or different authorities),
for the co-operative acquisition of materials, reference services,
and for inter-library lending.

    The urban and rural prefecture libraries should be responsible,
in co-operation with city, town, village and private libraries, for

---

1. *Report of Sub-Committee of Facilities of Social Educational Council. Standards for establishing
   and managing public libraries*, Tokyo, Ministry of Education, 1969.
2. Public halls, available to the general public for cultural purposes, exist in almost all
   municipalities in Japan. If there is no separate public library building, there is a small
   library in the public hall.

making contact with the libraries within the prefecture and promoting a co-operative relationship between them; regulating the acquisition, preparation and preservation of materials within the prefectures; giving help to local libraries in compiling union catalogues, in lending materials and in respect of reference services; acquiring local government materials for use in their work by staff and elected or appointed members of local authorities, as well as local publications and to preserve them for practical use; providing local services to districts not covered by city, town and village libraries by means of mobile lending libraries.

Where more than two libraries are to be established in the same municipality, one of these should be responsible for regulating the others to promote the service among the libraries.

Materials

The total volumes and the volumes purchased annually in the library should be as follows:

Urban and rural prefecture libraries

For libraries serving up to 1 million population, total volumes should be over 200,000 and volumes purchased annually should be over 10,000; both figures should be increased in relation to the amount of library extension work, assistance to city, town and village libraries.

For libraries serving over 1 million population, the following formulae should be applied to obtain the basic figures.

Total volumes = $0.05 \times$ (population — 1 million) $+200,000$
(Example: population 2 million; total volumes = 250,000.)

Volumes purchased annually
$= 0.003 \times$ (population — 1 million) $+10,000$
(Example: population 2 million; volumes purchased annually = 13,000.)

Where the population served exceeds 5 million, the minimum number of volumes to be purchased annually for the population over 5 million should be calculated using a factor of 0.0016 instead of 0.003. (Example: population 7 million, volumes purchased annually 22,000 (the figure for 5 million) $+0.0016 \times 2$ million, i.e. total of 25,200.)

City and ward libraries

For libraries serving up to 100,000 population, total volumes should be over 50,000 and the volumes purchased annually should be over 4,000: both minima to be increased in consideration of library extension work, the number of libraries in the city or ward, and other regional requirements.[1]

For libraries serving 100,000 to 300,000 population, total volumes should be at least $50,000 + 0.4 \times$ population over 100,000. (Examples: 90,000 for 200,000 population; 130,000 for 300,000 population.) Annual additions should be $4,000 + 0.015 \times$ population over 100,000. (Examples: 5,500 for 200,000 population; 7,000 for 300,000 population.)

For higher populations similar principles are followed, but the factors for additional population are diminishing ones, e.g. 300,000 to 500,000 (0.2 and 0.01); 500,000 to 1 million (0.12 and 0.008); over 1 million (0.08 and 0.003) (see Table 45).

Town and village library

Total volumes should be over 20,000, and the volumes purchased annually should be over 1,500 in town and village libraries and in town-village joint libraries; total volumes should be over 50,000 and the volumes purchased annually should be over 4,000 in the city-town-and-village joint libraries.

Audio-visual materials. Libraries are responsible for acquiring not only those made for classroom use but also photographs, charts, gramophone records, sound and video tapes, film-strips and films. The libraries are also responsible for recording them, acquiring reference data and preserving them.

TABLE 45

Population	Minimum total stock	Minimum annual additions
500,000	170,000	9,000
900,000	218,000	12,200
1,500,000	270,000	14,500

1. Ward libraries only exist in special municipalities, of which there are twenty-three in the metropolitan area of Tokyo.

Newspapers. In urban and rural prefecture libraries and in city libraries, over 10 national or similar newspapers should be acquired as well as local newspapers, especially those published in the nearby districts with which the prefecture or the city has close relations industrially and good communications.

Periodicals. Representative periodicals in every field should be acquired. This should include governmental and technical publications, including foreign material. Over 300 periodicals should be acquired in urban and rural prefecture libraries, and in the city library serving over 1,000,000 population; over 100 in city (or ward) libraries and in city-town-village joint libraries; over 30 in town and village, and town-village joint libraries. Governmental periodicals should not be included in the figures.

Personnel

The library should be provided with a chief librarian who has both expert knowledge of the library and administrative ability, with trained librarians who have knowledge and ability in selecting, acquiring, processing, preserving and interpreting the materials, and with other staff.

The standards for staffing are as follows:

Trained librarians
In urban and rural prefecture libraries. Over twenty-five trained librarians should be provided as a minimum and the figure should be increased in consideration of the total number of volumes, the number of volumes purchased annually, library extension, and other activities.

In a library serving over 1,000,000 population additional qualified staff should be appointed on the following formula:

$$25 + \frac{0.04}{10,000} \times (\text{population} - 1 \text{ million})$$

(Example: population 2 million; minimum number of trained librarians, 29.)

In city (or ward) libraries. In libraries serving up to 100,000 population, over seven trained librarians should be provided as a

TABLE 46

Population served	Formula	Population	Number of trained librarians
Up to 300,000	$7 + \dfrac{0.3}{10,000} \times \text{population} - 100,000$	300,000	13
Up to 500,000	$13 + \dfrac{0.25}{10,000} \times \text{population} - 300,000$	500,000	18
Up to 1,000,000	$18 + \dfrac{0.15}{10,000} \times \text{population} - 500,000$	1,000,000	26
Over 1,000,000	$26 + \dfrac{0,05}{10,000} \times \text{population} - 1,000,000$	2,000,000	31

minimum and the figure should be increased in consideration of the number of libraries, annual increases in library materials, library extension and other activities.

For larger libraries the formulae shown in Table 46 should be applied to obtain the basic figure.

In town and village libraries. In town and village libraries and town-village joint libraries over three trained librarians should be provided, and over seven in city-town-village joint libraries.

Other staff

The number of the other staff should be the same as or more than that of trained librarians.

Buildings

The library buildings should be provided with the following facilities, large enough to fulfil their functions and with the necessary equipment for reading and lending; reference services; library extension; processing and preserving materials; lending and use of audio-visual materials, copying services; reading and preserving micro-film and for the work of inter-library co-operation; meetings and exhibitions; users' rest and staff recreation; and administration.

The standards for the total floor area of the buildings are as follows, the total floor area to be increased in consideration of the increase of the number of volumes held and the scope of the activities of the library.

In urban and rural prefecture libraries
Up to a population of 1 million there should be a minimum total floor area of 4,000 m². For a library serving over 1 million population, the following formula should be applied for the basic figure:

$$4{,}000 \text{ m}^2 + \frac{5 \text{ m}^2}{10{,}000} \times \text{population} - 1 \text{ million}$$

(Example: population 2 million: area 4,500 m².)

In city (or ward) libraries
For libraries serving under 100,000 population the total floor area should be over 1,200 m². For libraries serving over 100,000 population, the formulae shown in Table 47 should be applied for the basic figure.

In town and village libraries
The total floor area of town and village libraries and town-village joint libraries should be over 330 m² and in city-town-village joint libraries over 1,200 m².

Equipment
The report also indicates the range of equipment which libraries need to carry out the various functions which are specified.

The foregoing account of the Japanese public library standards is based on material supplied by the Japan Library Association.

TABLE 47

Population served	Formula	Population	Minimum area required (m²)
Up to 300,000	$1{,}200 \text{ m}^2 + \dfrac{50 \text{ m}^2}{10{,}000} \times \text{population} - 100{,}000$	300,000	2,200
Up to 500,000	$2{,}200 \text{ m}^2 + \dfrac{40 \text{ m}^2}{10{,}000} \times \text{population} - 300{,}000$	500,000	3,000
Up to 1,000,000	$3{,}000 \text{ m}^2 + \dfrac{20 \text{ m}^2}{10{,}000} \times \text{population} - 500{,}000$	1,000,000	4,000
Over 1,000,000	$4{,}000 \text{ m}^2 + \dfrac{10 \text{ m}^2}{10{,}000} \times \text{population} - 1{,}000{,}000$	2,000,000	5,000

Malaysia

Since its foundation as the Malayan Library Group in 1955, the Malaysian Library Association (Persatuan Perpustakaan Malaysia) has made efforts to improve public library services in that country. A memorandum on public libraries was prepared by the group in 1956 at the request of the Adult Education Association of the Federation of Malaya, pointing out the lack of such a service and proposing the establishment of a nation-wide library system to cater for all needs of the whole population, fully supported by public funds. Conditions did not favour immediate action on the lines suggested.

In 1965 a Standing Committee on Public Libraries was set up by the Malaysian Library Association to encourage the organization and development of public libraries at all levels and in 1967, in conjunction with the Singapore Library Association, a joint conference on Public Libraries in National Development was organized. One of the main recommendations of this conference was the drawing up of a blueprint for public library development in Malaysia. The proposal was immediately implemented by the Malaysian Library Association, with the financial assistance of the Asia Foundation. The association had the support of the Federal Minister of Education who, with the co-operation of the Government of Singapore, obtained the services of Hedwig Anuar, Director of the Singapore National Library, to undertake the survey. Her report, *Blueprint for Public Library Development for Malaysia*, was published in 1968.[1]

The report surveyed the position of public libraries, described as 'at different stages of development, ranging from the non-existent or minimal to those which have achieved state-wide coverage of their services'. It contained detailed proposals for their development up to 1975, more particularly between 1971 and 1975, the period of the next five-year national development plan. A major objective of the report was to put forward proposals for public library development which could be incorporated into the next and successive national plans. Also included was an interim plan for 1969–70, to lay the basis for the beginning of the main plan. Both

1. *Blueprint for Public Library Development in Malaysia*, Kuala Lumpur, Persatuan Perpustakaan Malaysia (Malaysian Library Association), 1968.

the Interim Plan and the first Five Year Library Plan were accompanied by recommended standards.

The blueprint proposed that the development of the public libraries should be integrated, as far as possible, with that of a national library for Malaysia, expected shortly to be established, which would gradually take responsibility for the planning and integration of public library services, including the periodic revision of standards. Ultimately the report contemplated the national planning of all library services being undertaken by a national library advisory board, headed by the director of the National Library.

As local authorities, with few exceptions, would not have sufficient resources to provide for professional staff and book funds essential to a good service, and as administrative barriers would hinder expansion outside the areas of the local authorities to other areas, including rural areas, the report recommended a single library authority for each state through the agency of an independent public library corporation, to which existing libraries provided or partly financed by local authorities should be transferred. Fundamental to the success of the proposals was the enactment by each of the thirteen states forming the Federation of public library legislation establishing such bodies. A model public library bill, designed to this end, was included as an appendix to the report, together with model rules for public libraries. It was not contemplated that such legislation would be made mandatory on states until there were greatly increased numbers of trained staff available to run libraries on the scale required.

Whatever may prove to be the ultimate outcome of this plan for public library development, it is one of few examples where detailed standards have been prepared for use in a developing country. For this reason both the blueprint and the standards are worthy of close attention.

INTERIM STANDARDS FOR PUBLIC LIBRARIES, 1969–70

The standards, expressed almost entirely in general qualitative terms, were provided in order to assess existing services and to serve as guidelines for evaluation and immediate action, where necessary. They are briefly summarized below.

Structure and government

The public library should be governed by a library committee or board and by capable and interested officials. Members of the committee should include representatives of the federal, state and local governments, as well as members of the public.

Services

The public library service should be free and should be available to all. The library must maintain well planned hours of service, minimum hours proposed being shown in Table 48.

The period of loan for most materials and the number of items lent should be as liberal as possible. There should be a printed or typed guide to the materials and services of the library.

The library should record and report regularly to its governing body information concerning the amount and kind of services rendered. It should have a telephone or quick access to one.

Collections

There should be a written statement of policy concerning selection and maintenance. Material added should meet high standards of quality in content, expression and format, and should meet the needs and interests of the individual community. Gifts should be

TABLE 48

Population	Minimum hours per six-day week	Type of library
Below 5,000	Half-hour stop[1]	Mobile library
5,000–10,000	10	Part-time branch
10,000–25,000	15	Part-time branch
25,000–50,000	24	Full-time branch
50,000–100,000	$36\frac{1}{2}$	Full-time branch
100,000–250,000	48	Central library
250,000–500,000	60	Central library
Over 500,000	72	Central library

1. At regular intervals no greater than two weeks.

in keeping with the library's selection policies. The character and emphasis of the collection should be influenced by the existence of other library collections in the community or area. All materials should be actively used, with systematic weeding and discarding of materials no longer useful. (In appendixes detailed advice is given on book selection policies and policy for weeding and discarding.)

Staff

All public libraries should have at least one permanent paid member of non-manual staff. All libraries should be under the guidance of a professional librarian from a neighbouring library or the central library of the state.

Organization and control of materials

The collection should be organized logically, appropriate catalogues and shelf-lists provided, and records of the materials kept up to date. The library should issue without charge regular lists of new books added. Materials should be arranged so that they can be found easily, and kept in usable and attractive condition.

Physical facilities

The library building should be attractive and well maintained and should be easy to use. Furniture and equipment should be clean and usable, adequate lighting provided and glare avoided. Toilet facilities should be provided, with adequate supervision. There should be work and storage areas not visible to library users. Libraries in buildings also serving another purpose must have their own entrance and control their own water, lighting and air-conditioning.

MINIMUM STANDARDS FOR PUBLIC LIBRARIES, 1971–75

The standards were drawn up on the assumption that there would be a national library giving support to the public library service, which would, in accordance with the recommendations of the blueprint, be provided by a single library authority for each state. The standards considerably amplified the principles of good library organization described in the interim standards, adding quantitative standards in regard to library collections, staff and space requirements as follows:

Size of the collections

In relation to the State as a whole, the aim should be to reach a minimum of one book per head of population within twenty years.

Central public library within each state

This library should have a minimum of 100,000 volumes, of which 40 per cent should be for children, 10 to 15 per cent for teenagers and the remainder for adults. Once the basic collection has been achieved, additions should continue at the rate of 1,000 new titles per annum. Annual withdrawals from the basic collection should average 5 per cent of the total collection.

Periodicals

Each library service point should have a collection with a minimum number of periodical and newspaper titles as shown in Table 49.

Staff

There should be approximately one-quarter of a member of staff for every 1,000 population in the service area, a minimum provision of one qualified librarian for every 50,000 population served, and a ratio of professional to non-professional staff of one to four.

TABLE 49

Population	Number of titles	Population	Number of titles
Under 5,000	20	50,000–100,000	200–400
5,000–10,000	20–40	100,000–250,000	400–1,000
10,000–25,000	40–100	250,000–500,000	1,000–2,000
25,000–50,000	100–200	Over 500,000	2,500–3,000

TABLE 50

Population	Type	Staff	Maximum total
10,000–25,000	Part-time branch	1 probationer librarian 1–2 clerical staff	5
50,000–100,000	Full-time branch	2 qualified librarians 2–3 probationer librarians 3–6 clerical staff (including 2 typists) 5–9 library attendants	20
250,000–500,000	Central library	4–7 qualified librarians 3–8 probationer librarians 8–10 clerical staff (including 3 typists) 13–17 library attendants	42

A schedule giving categories and minimum and maximum numbers of staff for different types of service at different population levels (excluding maintenance staff) was provided (see Table 50).

Accommodation

The minimum space requirements for libraries are determined by size of population and of book collections. The following standards should act as a guide: 1 reader seat per 1,000 population; 1 seat requires 25 ft^2 (2.32 m^2); 15 books per square foot of book stack space; 1 staff office space requires 100 ft^2 (9.29 m^2).

The recommendations of the blueprint can be said to have been accepted in principle by the government, as its National Library Committee set up a sub-committee to study it and make recommendations. This endorsed the recommendations and proposed limited objectives for approval and implementation during the Five Year Plan Period 1971–75. These included the establishment of state central libraries in every state with the necessary new library legislation; financial provision for public library development; and the public libraries to be run by independent public library corporations on a state basis with representation of federal, state and local government interests. The cabinet approved the recommendations and authorized the National Library to implement them. Three states, up to the end of 1973, had passed the necessary public library laws and draft legislation was under consideration in others. The 'interim standards' proposed to be reached by 1969–70 could not, in practice, be implemented and have been carried over to the First Five-Year Plan period.

Netherlands

The following account of the public libraries position in the Netherlands, with particular reference to the question of standards of library provision, is based on material supplied by the Rijksinspectie der Openbare Bibliotheken (State Inspectorate for Public Libraries).

GENERAL

Since the beginning of the century, through two world wars and the loss of a large colonial empire, the Netherlands has changed from a country whose economy was based on agriculture and on trade, banking, shipping and related industries to one with almost half its working population employed in industry. At the same time its population has grown from 5 million to 13.5 million and it has become one of the most densely populated countries in the world and highly urbanized.

The general level of education is now comparatively high. Education is compulsory from 6 to 16 years of age and illiteracy is virtually nil. General and professional educational institutions above the level of the elementary school are attended by more than 1 million full-time students. The universities are overcrowded. The promotion of adult education of all kinds has been an important item in the programmes of successive governments and, in this rapidly and fundamentally changing society, public libraries have been modestly playing their part and gaining in strength, particularly in the 1950s and 1960s.

PUBLIC LIBRARIES—THEIR DEVELOPMENT
AND PRESENT STATE

The social and economic life of the Netherlands is based on three pillars, Protestantism, Roman Catholicism and Humanism (liberalism and socialism), which have pervaded and still pervade all areas of public activity. Each pillar has its own political parties, educational, cultural and social organizations, trade unions and other economic associations though, under the influence of industrialization, urbanization and secularization, the strength of these influences has been decreasing in recent years.

The first public library was introduced in the Netherlands in 1898. The first grant from a municipal authority was received in 1905 and from the government in 1908. Such was the strength of the influences mentioned above that a monopoly of general public libraries was out of the question. The first denominational public libraries were founded in 1911, one Roman Catholic and another Protestant, and these had to be recognized by the government and to receive the same support as the general public libraries. There are, therefore, to the present day general, Roman Catholic and Protestant public libraries. Sometimes two or three different public libraries operate in one municipality, though they are all united in one national organization and are subject to the same regulations, as conditions for the receipt of state grants. In recent years the differences between the three kinds of public library have diminished and there has been a process of amalgamation and secularization. All these public libraries have been governed, since 1921, by a decree of the Minister of Education, Rijkssubsidievoorwaarden—1921, voor Openbare Bibliotheken (State Regulations 1921, containing conditions for the subvention of public libraries), which have been repeatedly amended in the course of the years.

The Dutch public library system is based on the existence of independent local public libraries, active within the territory of one municipality or two or more adjoining municipalities. The libraries are predominantly privately owned, their legal status being that of an association or a foundation whose board decides upon the local library policy, although the municipal authorities have a considerable influence. A local public library may consist of a main library and one or more branch libraries and mobile libraries. It may contain a number of specialized departments, a technical library, a music department, a gramophone record department, a library service for schools, and for the aged and infirm. Every main library and branch library offers services both to adults and to children. Audio, visual and audio-visual media, apart from gramophone records, are as yet rarely found in the collections of the libraries.

PROVINCIALE BIBLIOTHEEKCENTRALES
(PROVINCIAL CENTRAL LIBRARIES)

In the 1950s and early 1960s there were set up in every province one or more new library organizations, *Provinciale Bibliotheekcentrales*, whose task is to establish and support public libraries in the smaller communities—the municipalities with up to 30,000 inhabitants. Normally these central libraries give no services to the public in their own premises. They provide the libraries in the smaller communities with books and other materials, catalogues and staff, as well as with other forms of assistance and advice. They organize and provide library services to schools, homes for the aged, hospitals, etc., for and in co-operation with the small public libraries, and offer supplementary library services in villages where no public library exists. For this purpose a number of mobile libraries are in use. The libraries in the smaller municipalities are not obliged to make use of these provincial central libraries, but the great majority do so. The provincial central libraries, of which there are currently fourteen in the eleven provinces (including two of different denominational origin in each of three provinces), are building up background collections consisting of those books and other materials too infrequently used to justify their presence in the smaller libraries, but which should be available on request.

LANDELIJKE BIBLIOTHEEK CENTRALE
(NATIONAL CENTRAL LENDING LIBRARY)

Books and other material which may be expected to be available from any public library can be borrowed by local public libraries and the provincial central libraries from the National Central Lending Library. They can also obtain block loans of books which they do not possess or else have in insufficient numbers, such as books for foreign workers and to meet exceptional demands, e.g. after the opening of a new library, or by classes for specific books.

REGIONALE STEUNBIBLIOTHEEK (REGIONAL SUPPORTING LIBRARIES)

In 1969 ten important public libraries and three provincial or regional learned libraries were designated to fulfil the function of a regional supporting library. These were to relieve the heavy demands of public libraries and private individuals on the existing inter-library loan scheme, based on co-operation between the Royal Library, the libraries of the universities and many other learned and special libraries whose holdings are accessible through a number of union catalogues. Each of the regional supporting libraries was to be, for its region, a first tier in the inter-library loan system, and for this purpose they are required to extend their holdings of literature of a learned or specialized character in accordance with the needs of the region. They have to bring together a collection of bibliographies, reference books, handbooks and periodicals at the appropriate level for persons who have no easy access to a university library. These thirteen libraries receive a special annual grant from the government for the purchase of books and periodicals and for a limited number of additional staff members.

FINANCE, PRESENT STANDARDS AND STATISTICS

The 1921 regulations, as amended, stipulate that the local public libraries should receive annual grants from the local authorities and the state, and the provincial central libraries from the provincial authorities and the state. For each branch library, mobile library, etc., the basic grants are augmented by a percentage.

These arrangements do not constitute an adequate basis for the development of the local public libraries and of the provincial central libraries for a number of reasons. There is no legal obligation on any municipality or other body to establish and maintain

243

TABLE 51

Library serving inhabitants	Minimum book stock within 3 years				Opening hours weekly			
	Main library		Branch library/mobile		Main library		Branch library	
	Adults	Children	Adults	Children	Adults	Children	Adults	Children
10–15,000	3,000	1,000	1,000	500	6	4	5	3
100,000 and over	20,000	3,000	2,000	1,000	30	12	13	8

a public library service. The amounts of the grants, prescribed by the regulations on a sliding scale, are dependent only on the number of inhabitants of the municipality or province; they are not related to local circumstances, nor to the quality and extent, and cost, of the activities of the library concerned. Furthermore the standards laid down in the regulations are so low that they do not act as a stimulus to the improvement and extension of library activities. This is illustrated by the examples of minimum standards given in Table 51. Hardly any library in recent years has started with as few books as prescribed as a minimum by the regulations. The minimum standards are generally regarded as too low to enable a public library to establish its position in cultural and social life. Despite this the public libraries in the Netherlands have developed considerably in the twenty years between 1952 and 1972, as the following figures show. (The figures given are for 1972 with figures for 1952 in parentheses.)

Service: Public libraries (main libraries), 378 (101); branch libraries, 398 (63); mobile libraries, 73 (—); provincial central libraries, 15 (4).

Bookstocks: 16 million (3 million).

Library use: readers, 2 million (300,000); loans, 78 million (10,750,000).

Expenditure (florins):[1] books, 15 million (0.7 million); staff, 51.5 million (2.5 million); accommodation, 13.5 million (300,000).

Grants (florins):[1] municipal, 42.5 million (2.4 million); provincial, 8 million (200,000); state, 29 million (500,000).

1. Account should be taken of changes in the value of money, which has fallen by approximately 54 per cent.

PROPOSED NEW LIBRARY LEGISLATION

In view of the inadequacy of the existing system of regulating public libraries, new arrangements have been under consideration since the early 1960s. An outline of a proposed law on public libraries was published by the Minister of Culture in 1967, followed in 1972 by a draft of the legislation. A bill was introduced into Parliament late in 1972. Several stages in the consideration of this bill were completed by early 1974 and, at the time of writing this, it was hoped that the bill would be soon enacted and come into force in 1975.

The legislation would do no more than provide a legal framework and lay down general principles. More detailed requirements would be indicated in regulations made by Orders in Council. The objects of the new law can be summarized as to provide (a) an equal and acceptable public library service in every part of the country and to make new developments possible; and (b) a sound legal and financial basis for the public libraries and their work.

No important changes are proposed in the structure of the public library system as described above, except that libraries in municipalities with less than 30,000 inhabitants would be obliged to accept the assistance of a provincial central library or an adjoining large urban library, and that provincial central libraries would be responsible for the library service in municipalities with less than 5,000 inhabitants without the intervention of a local library association or foundation.

The most important parts of the proposed new law are (a) a procedure, expected to lead to an evenly spread network of library services all over the country, under which the Minister of Culture would lay down a national plan for successive three-year periods referring, *inter alia*, to existing public libraries and to new libraries to be established and indicating the municipalities and provinces which would be held responsible for the establishment and maintenance of the libraries mentioned; (b) the financial provisions under which the municipalities would be obliged to bear the total net cost of the local libraries, and the provinces similarly the cost of the provincial central libraries. For its part, the State would reimburse the municipalities and provinces 100 per cent of the cost of staff and 20 per cent of other costs. Such provisions call for the establishment of standards to guarantee a minimum scale and quality of library service and to define the elements of cost to be reimbursed by the State.

PROPOSED NEW STANDARDS

In 1965, the Minister of Culture set up a Rijksnormencommissie voor Openbare Bibliotheken (State Commission on Standards for Public Libraries). This consisted of a number of experienced working librarians and three members of the State Inspectorate, the head of which was chairman of the commission. The proposals of the commission are likely to constitute the basis for those parts of the Order in Council, supplementing the proposed new library law, which would define both quantitatively and qualitatively the public library service to be provided.

In 1970 the commission published its final report, *Voorstel voor de normering van het Openbare Bibliotheekwerk in Nederland*.[1] The proposals of the commission can be summarized as follows.

LIBRARY AREAS—WORKING DISTRICTS

The basis of the proposed standards is the size of the population served by the library, the 'working district'.

For a main library operating without the assistance of a provincial central library, i.e. in municipalities with 30,000 inhabitants or more, the total territory and the total population of the municipality concerned is regarded as its working district.

A provincial central library is to be regarded as a main library for the province, excluding the municipalities with 30,000 or more inhabitants. The population of these municipalities is to be deducted from the total number of inhabitants of the province to establish the working district of the provincial central library.

The working district of a branch library is to be arrived at separately in each case depending, *inter alia*, on socio-geographic

1. Ministerie van Cultuur, Recreatie en Maatschappelijk Werk, Rijksnormencommissie voor Openbare Bibliotheken, *Voorstel voor de normering van het Openbare Bibliotheekwerk in Nederland* [*Proposals for the Establishment of Standards for Public Library Activities in the Netherlands*], The Hague, 1970.

conditions. The same applies to libraries in the municipalities with less than 30,000 inhabitants, affiliated to provincial central libraries.

BOOKSTOCKS AND OTHER LIBRARY MATERIALS

The minimum size of the book stock required for each main library or branch library is calculated on a sliding scale—see Table 52.

These standards assume that, in districts with up to 100,000 inhabitants, 20 per cent of the population of the working district will make use of the lending facilities of the library, that each reader will borrow on average forty books a year and that the average circulation of a book will not exceed seven times a year.

An urban main library, serving a district of 30,000 inhabitants or more, acts at the same time as a local service point for the centre of the town. A provincial central library, serving a large area mainly of a rural character and whose premises are not accessible to the public, does not itself act as a service point. For that reason the minimum number of volumes required, as stated in the table, should be reduced by 40 per cent when applied to a provincial central library.

Mobile libraries should have separate book stocks, with a minimum of 8,000 volumes for the first and of 5,000 for each subsequent mobile. A mobile library should be able to carry at least 1,800 volumes.

In some cases it might be desirable to establish a separate children's library, with a minimum of 3,000 volumes.

TABLE 52

Population of library area	Required stock per inhabitant	Total volumes required	Population of library area	Required stock per inhabitant	Total volumes required
Up to 2,000	2.5	5,000	75,000	1.3	97,000
3,000	2.0	6,000	100,000	1.2	120,000
5,000	2.0	10,000	200,000	1.0	200,000
10,000	1.8	18,000	300,000	0.9	270,000
20,000	1.5	30,000	400,000	0.8	320,000
30,000	1.4	42,000	500,000	0.7	350,000
40,000	1.35	54,000	1,000,000	0.5	500,000
50,000	1.3	65,000			

The commission did not suggest any standards for proportions of fiction and non-fiction, nor for books for adults and for children, etc., considering that librarians are sufficiently experienced and have sufficient knowledge of the needs of their areas to adjust their holdings to the needs of the population served. Moreover, the high quantitative standards proposed, as compared with the present position, would make possible an important qualitative improvement in the holdings.

Within the complex of a main library and its branches or a provincial central library and its affiliated libraries, the librarian should be permitted within certain limits to adapt the number of volumes in each library to actual needs, provided the total number of volumes required is available within this complex.

A special music department should have at least 10,000 volumes/scores. A special record library should have at least 3,000 records or tapes, this standard to be regarded as provisional, the introduction of audio, visual and audio-visual media in the holdings of a public library being the subject of further research. The commission recommended that directions in regard to collections in other specialized departments should be given by the Minister of Culture.

The minimum number of periodicals recommended for both main and branch libraries is 150, including daily newspapers and weekly magazines. A useful guide would be to spend 10 per cent of the money available for books on the purchase of periodicals.

In libraries established at least ten years, 15 per cent of the total book stock should be withdrawn annually and replaced by new books. In addition, the book stock should be increased by 3 per cent of the total number of volumes until the required stock is reached. For libraries established less than ten years, the percentage of annual withdrawals has not been fixed. If this is less than 15 per cent, the difference is to be added to the proposed 3 per cent annual growth. These percentages refer to the total holdings of a main library and its branches, or a provincial central library and its affiliated libraries, with the exception of permanent parts of the collection.

Public libraries

STAFF

The commission distinguished the following categories of staff: managerial staff; staff engaged on the collection of library materials, with making them accessible and with direct service to the public (librarians); non-manual clerical staff; manual staff (binders, janitors, drivers, etc.); and staff for special functions (the staff of special departments—both librarians and clerical staff).

The standards proposed are to be regarded as maxima in view of the proposed reimbursement of the total cost by the State.

The maximum number of staff with managerial responsibilities in a main library or provincial central library should depend on the size of the population served and the proposed figures are shown in Table 53.

If the branch libraries or affiliated libraries of the main library or provincial central library serve a population of more than 80,000, an extra head of department is allowed.

The maximum number of staff engaged on the collections of library materials, etc. (librarians), together with the maximum number of non-manual clerical staff, should be dependent on the size of the book stock and should be calculated on the formula:

$$\frac{\text{Total book stock prescribed by standards} + \text{existing book stock}}{7,500}$$

$=$ Number of non-manual staff required, other than managerial

The proportions between librarians and clerical staff should be approximately 1 : 1. The formula is to be applied to any library, provincial central library, main library, branch library or mobile

TABLE 53

Population	Chief librarian	Deputy chief librarian	Head of clerical staff	Head of departments
30,000–50,000	1	—	—	—
50,001–100,000	1	1	1	2
100,001–200,000	1	1	1	4
200,001–500,000	1	2	1	8
500,001 and over	1	2	1	9

249

library. For librarians the commission suggests a subdivision according to rank or grade.

By taking into account the existing book stock as well as the future book stock required by the standards, the commission had in mind a size of staff adapted to the needs of an expanding library. It advised that the standard should be applied flexibly and that changes in working methods, mechanization, etc., should not adversely affect the financial compensation from the State in respect of the cost of staff.

No standards are proposed for manual staff nor for staff employed in specialized departments.

If the book and staff standards are applied to a typical situation, for example, in a town with a population of 60,000, having a central library and one branch library serving a population of 20,000 and a book stock which satisfied the minimum standards, the results are as follows:

Book stocks. The central library should have 78,000 volumes ($1.3 \times 60,000$) and the branch library 30,000 volumes ($1.5 \times 20,000$).

Staff. As regards managerial staff, the library might have a chief librarian and a deputy chief librarian, one head of clerical staff and two heads of library departments. It might also have twenty-one additional non-manual staff ($(78,000+78,000)/7,500$), and the branch library eight ($(30,000+30,000)/7,500$).

TABLE 54

Population of working district	Number of hours open	Distribution over working days	Days open during evening hours
Up to 1,500	10	2	1
1,501–5,000	15	3	2
5,001–10,000	20	4	2
10,001–20,000	25	4	2
20,001–30,000	30	5	3
30,001–50,000	35	5	3
50,001–100,000	40	5	3
100,001–200,000	50	6	5
200,000 or more	60	6	5

The total number of twenty-nine non-manual staff should be divided approximately equally between librarians and clerical staff: fourteen or fifteen each.

OPENING HOURS

Both main libraries and branch libraries should be open as many hours a week as possible. Hours of opening should be adapted to local needs and customs so as to promote the maximum use of the library. They should be at least as those shown in Table 54.

ACCOMMODATION

Public libraries require sufficient space to enable them to discharge their functions efficiently and in particular to enable the requirements as to library materials and staff to be fulfilled. They should be situated as centrally as possible in the districts they serve and should be clearly recognizable as libraries. The buildings should be easily accessible and adapted, as far as possible, to the needs of persons physically handicapped.

Main libraries should contain provision for the following:

1. Housing the stock of adult books on a basis of fifty books per square metre, including space for the lending and catalogue areas.
2. Study or reading rooms for adults, possibly combined with the area mentioned in 1 above, seating as many persons as required by local circumstances. In its interim report, the commission suggested a minimum of ten and a maximum of 150 seats, with an average of one seat per thousand of the population served. There should be 3 m² per person available, not including the space required for reference books and periodicals.
3. The stock of children's books, on a basis of forty books per square metre, including space for the lending and catalogue areas.
4. A reading room for children, possibly combined with the room mentioned in 3 above, seating as many children as required by local circumstances.
5. Possibly, depending on local circumstances, other rooms where extension activities can take place, for example, visits of school children, lectures, etc.

6. A director's office, serving also as a boardroom.
7. Offices and workrooms for staff.
8. Stack and/or storage room.
9. Bindery or repair shop.
10. Sufficient sanitary facilities, kitchen with canteen, and cloak-rooms for visitors and staff.
11. Bicycle shed and, possibly, parking space.

Accommodation standards recommended for branch libraries and libraries affiliated to the provincial central libraries are largely the same as for central libraries, with the difference, however, that the separate children's accommodation might be combined with that envisaged for adults, and that a librarian's office might not be required.

Provincial central libraries should have available as a minimum a room for the convenient arrangement of the book stock on the basis of 125 books/m², and a stack on a basis of 200 books/m², a director's office serving also as a boardroom, offices and workrooms for the staff, a room for the dispatch of books, adequate sanitary, kitchen and cloakroom facilities and, possibly, a garage and parking space.

The commission has provided relatively few quantitative standards. In its view buildings will be greatly influenced by local conditions. In areas where there is little accommodation for other social and cultural activities, the library may act as host for such activities and adapt its building programme for this purpose. Alternatively, a library may be housed in the same building as other institutions active in social and cultural fields and the library may use part of the accommodation of others for its own extension activities. The presence, or absence, of specialized departments affects the building as a whole, e.g. in regard to the number of books in the general lending department. So do the working methods adopted by the library. There is a tendency to centralize activities like book processing and cataloguing and to introduce mechanized and electronic administrative procedures, affecting the space requirements for offices and workshops.

The commission regarded its standards proposals as a first step and recommended that these should be subject to constant evaluation and re-appraisal.

New Zealand

The standards for public libraries published in 1966 by the New Zealand Library Association,[1] currently being revised, are modelled on those of the United States in their form and style, adopting the same method of general principles and detailed standards. The document is, of course, very different because of local conditions. For example, New Zealand is one of the few countries left in the world where a certain part of the library book stock is commonly organized on a payment basis in the form of a 'rental collection'. The existence of these rental collections has some effect on the way in which quantitative standards are expressed, i.e. free books and rental books, and may have some effect on the standards for free books compared with other countries without the rental system.

The New Zealand Library Association has adopted the United States standard that the minimum unit for an efficient service is 150,000 population, and similarly, therefore, it encourages the formation of regional library services, which would enable library service to be given over wider areas than that of a single local authority. It recognizes, however, that small library units must continue, in many cases not co-ordinated in a library system. So the association, in addition to the minimum standards based on the requirements for a minimum level of adequate library service to all citizens wherever they live, has proposed a set of provisional standards reflecting the best practices of public libraries in New Zealand. These provisional standards are mostly quantitative and can be applied to any size of population. But only in the largest libraries will adoption of these provisional standards result in minimum standards being reached.

Like so many of its kind, the document starts with a statement of the purposes of the public libraries, which it likens to the articles of a public librarian's faith. It includes a model statement of objectives of the kind it hopes the individual local authorities will adopt under headings such as: to be an instrument of democracy and good citizenship; to be a powerful instrument for supplementing

---

1. New Zealand Library Association, *Standards for Public Library Service in New Zealand*, Wellington, 1966.

education in schools and sustaining the desire to learn; to contribute to the economic life of the community; to present art and imaginative literature in abundance.

PUBLIC LIBRARY GOVERNMENT AND UNITS OF SERVICE

Under this heading the statement discusses the following: (a) that public library service should be free and universally available; (b) public library service is essentially a function of local government; (c) the functions of the local authority and of the librarian should be clearly distinguished; (d) the informed interest of the library committee is essential; (e) finance should be the joint responsibility of local and central government and there is a minimum level of financial support for adequate library service; (f) in terms of total book supply, New Zealand will be one unit for many years to come; (g) the development of public library service and the building of regional collections must be based on larger units of service; and (h) a regional pattern of public library service should be the prize objective of the future.

PUBLIC LIBRARY RESOURCES

Under this heading there are quantitative and qualitative standards, both for the minimum standards and the provisional standards. Illustrating the principle that the quality of a library's service depends principally on the size, quality, range and balance of its stock of books and periodicals, the following standards are stated:

Book stocks

Minimum standard
The minimum standard requires that borrowers should have access to at least:

100,000 titles in non-fiction and foreign languages; 7,500 fiction titles; 7,500 titles for children and young people, not also in the adult collection, and 500 periodical titles in runs of 5–10 years.

This range of material should be available from regional centres. The minimum number of free books in a library or branch library, including books on loan, should be 6,000 books, of which at least 1,500 should be for children and young people, plus 1,500 rental books.

Provisional standard

The provisional standard requires the total free book stock to be 140–200 books per 100 population served. Books for children and young people should be between 40 and 50 per 100 population served. This standard requires in addition that borrowers should use the National Library of New Zealand Request and Information Service and the inter-loan system as a matter of course.

Annual purchases

Minimum standard

For the minimum standard these should be at least:

Non-fiction—5,000 new titles to maintain a collection of 100,000 non-fiction titles.

Fiction—500 new titles to maintain a collection of 7,500 fiction titles.

Children's and young people's—750 new titles, not bought also for the adult collection, to maintain a collection of 7,500 titles.

Periodicals—subscriptions to a minimum of 750 periodicals, including duplicate subscriptions, as well as indexing and bibliographic services etc.

To maintain the physical quality of any lending collection (exclusive of non-fiction), accessions measured by the number of books must be in proportion to issues. Assuming a regular programme of rebinding, one book must be bought in each section for the number of issues each year as follows: (a) fiction, every 90–100 issues; (b) children's fiction, every 50 issues; (c) children's non-fiction, every 75 issues; (d) young people's books, every 75 issues.

For adult non-fiction stock as a whole, annual accessions should equal, as a minimum, $7\frac{1}{2}$ per cent of stock on the open shelves. Some more popular sections may require a higher rate.

The free fiction, children and young people's book stock should not fall below 8–10 per cent of the annual issues for each section: this applies also to the more popular sections of non-fiction.

Provisional standard
The provisional standard requires that at least fifteen books per 100 population served should be purchased for the free collection each year by any library, one-third of them being for children and young people. Libraries (including branches) which are serving 10,000 people or less, should have at least 2,000 new free adult titles appearing on their shelves each year, increasing to 4,000 titles a year for libraries serving 40,000 people. All these libraries should receive on loan, from a central stock or Country Library Service,[1] sufficient new titles to reach this figure. The smaller the library, the smaller will be the proportion of its accessions to titles borrowed.

Qualitative standards
Qualitative standards are indicated in comments on such matters as: (a) high standard, in content and presentation, of material added to the collection; (b) a balance among the major sections of the collection, and the components parts of these sections; (c) the need to hold material giving both sides of controversial questions; (d) acquisition policy being influenced by the existence and contents of other libraries in New Zealand and in the immediate area; (e) use to be made of national resources to satisfy the specialized needs of readers; and (f) material asked for frequently to be purchased by the library.

Reference material

The following standards are recommended.

Minimum standards
Trained staff, ready access to the basic collection of at least 100,000 non-fiction titles and to a non-circulating collection of at least 4,000 books, excluding stack room stock, maintained by 400 new books per annum (excluding pamphlets). The children's library must have its own reference collection at a suitable level, in addition to access to the adult reference collection.

---

1. The Country Library Service is a division of the National Library of New Zealand which provides, from three regional offices and subject to certain conditions, state aid to libraries serving up to 75,000 people. This aid is primarily in the form of books in bulk exchanges, subject collections and individual requests.

Provisional standards
Provisional standards for the smallest library require a collection
of 100 volumes of basic reference books, including a number of
stated items. For libraries serving more than 10,000 people, the
range of the stated items in the adult reference library is enlarged
and recommendations are made concerning items of reference
material required for the children's library.

Other standards
These include the following: (a) selection of material should not be
limited by format; it may include non-book written material and,
for example, recordings, slides, films; (b) all collections should
contain current periodicals and newspapers; (c) larger libraries
should maintain lending collections of recordings, art prints, litho-
graphs and original paintings, and of miniature and playing scores;
(d) systematic withdrawal of material is essential; (e) historical
material of value to the community should be collected and
preserved.

On the nature of the public library services to be provided the
document refers to:
Service being provided free to all persons within the local authority's area, with the exception of the rental collection of light
reading.

Under this heading it deals with the question of charges,
concluding that fees should not be charged for use of inter-loan
or request service or for postage, for reservation of books (except
rental books) or for borrowing from record or picture collections.
Opening hours, as long as consistent with economical administration; lending libraries to be open normally on six days a week;
large libraries to be open on Sundays, in the winter months at
least, for reading and study.
Library material to be organized efficiently for convenient use and
the library to aim at the most complete use of its resources by the
community (e.g. lending policy to be as generous as possible);
no limits to the number of items that may be borrowed for a
serious purpose; loan periods to be varied to meet special
demands.
The simplest measure of a lending service is the number of books
issued a year. A good library service will issue eight to ten free
books a head of population served each year, at least three of

these being from the children's and young people's collections.

Organization of the lending service: with re-registration at three yearly intervals, at least 40 per cent of people in the area should be registered members. Large centres should be served by branches and bookmobiles. Establishment of a branch should be considered only in a reasonably compact area which has a natural centre and a population of 5,000 or more.

Organization of the reference service: a minimum of four subject areas (e.g. music and fine arts, social sciences and humanities, commercial and technical, and New Zealand), each staffed by two subject librarians, is necessary for adequate service.

A reference and inquiry section especially directed to the needs of industry and commerce is required and a qualified librarian with a technical background and experience for this kind of work is desirable.

Organization of children's and young people's libraries: public libraries should place no restriction on the use of their facilities by students, but the formal educational needs of these students should be met by the libraries of their own institutions.

The children's librarian and staff must be familiar with their stock in a way which is not possible with wider adult stock.

For the transition from the children's to the adult library, a special collection of books should be provided; there should be no impediment to the use of the adult subject collections by this age group if they so desire.

General: libraries should provide a readers' advisory service. Libraries need to know their community and to work closely with any group which can make good use of the library's resources.

The rental collection: standards are recommended indicating the ephemeral nature of the material. Books which will not average at least twenty issues a year should not be purchased for these collections. The rental collection should not dominate the library; issues from it should not be more than 40 per cent of the total adult issues. Receipts should be approximately $2\frac{1}{2}$ times the cost of the books purchased calculated over a three-year period. Rental collections should not be exploited to increase the library's income, nor be subsidized at the expense of the free service.

STAFF

Three general principles are stated: (a) that adequate library service requires professional librarians with intermediate and clerical assistance; (b) that staff conditions of appointment and employment should ensure work satisfaction; and (c) that all posts should be established and organized as part of a career service.

New Zealand professional training leads to the diploma or certificate of the New Zealand Library School, which may be followed after at least three years' satisfactory service by the standard professional qualification, the Associateship of the New Zealand Library Association. The standard intermediate qualification is the Certificate of the New Zealand Library Association.

In addition, the following quantitative standards are recommended.

The library should employ one full-time library worker per 2,000 people in the area served. At least one-third of the library staff (excluding maintenance staff) should have completed the New Zealand Library School course or the New Zealand Library Association Certificate course (i.e. professional and intermediate staff).

Minimum standard
The minimum standard requires a staff of qualified administrators, together with persons who have special qualifications and training for reference services, service to children, advisory service to readers, lending services and cataloguing.

Provisional standard
The provisional standard for libraries serving up to 10,000 people, where qualified staff is not available, requires a librarian with a knowledge of books and an understanding of people, who is willing to undertake training through the Country Library Service short courses or through the New Zealand Library Association's Certificate course. Leave with pay while training should be provided.

PREMISES

Standards for public library buildings were issued by the New Zealand Library Association in 1949 and 1958. The 1966 document gives statements of principles and detailed standards based on the previous standards. Matters dealt with include the following.

A good standard of library service must be assured when a new building or extensive modification is planned. A fine building does not make a fine library and public bodies should not erect library buildings unless council responsibility for library service is assured.

The site should be in the busiest part of the town, on the main street in a small borough and in the heart of the shopping or business area in the larger towns. All libraries which serve a population of 4,000 or more should be planned as separate units, and not as a subordinate part of a civic centre, or as part of a building or block to be used for other purposes.

The planning of the interior arrangement, including the design and placing of the shelving and furniture should be completed before the exterior is designed.

The library building should be flexible and allow for expansion. The needs for the next twenty years should be considered when planning the building. A single-storey building should be preferred; a mezzanine may be practicable for workrooms and staff rooms. The building should be planned on a modular principle with a minimum of solid interior walls and internal pillars. It should be capable of adaptation for future changes in service.

In discussing the internal arrangement of the libraries, standards are proposed. For example: special provision should be made for children and young persons in all public libraries; in libraries serving a population under 10,000, at least one-fifth of the total public service area should be allocated to children's reading and browsing. Libraries serving a population of 10,000 or over will require a closed access stack for reserve stock and less used material, the amount of which will depend on the access to regional and other large collections. Larger libraries should provide a separate meeting room suitable for educational groups. All libraries should have toilet facilities for children and such facilities for use by adults and children is recommended for larger libraries.

In an appendix to the document is given a table (see Table 55) relating to building standards for premises serving populations up to 50,000. Some examples from this are given below.

TABLE 55. Library building standards in New Zealand

	Population served		
	6,000–8,000	10,000–15,000	25,000–50,000
Size of book collection	12,000 volumes plus 2 books per head of population over 6,000	20,000 volumes plus 2 books per head of population over 10,000	62,000 volumes plus 2½ books per head of population over 25,000
Linear feet of shelving	1,500 ft (457.2 m) add 1 ft (0.305 m) of shelving for every 8 books over 12,000	2,500 ft (726.0 m) add 1 ft (0.305 m) of shelving for every 8 books over 20,000	7,750 ft (2,362.2 m) add 1 ft (0.305 m) of shelving for every 8 books over 62,000
Amount of floor space	1,200 ft² (111.5 m²) add 1 ft² (0.093 m²) for every 10 books over 12,000	2,000 ft² (185.8 m²) add 1 ft² (0.093 m²) for every 10 books over 20,000	6,200 ft² (557.4 m²) add 1 ft² (0.093 m²) for every 10 books over 62,000
Reader space	900 ft² (83.6 m²) add 5 seats per 1,000 over 6,000 population at 30 ft² (2.79 m²) per reader space	1,500 ft² (139.4 m²) add 5 seats per 1,000 over 10,000 population at 30 ft² (2.79 m²) per reader space	2,250 ft² (209.0 m²) add 3 seats per 1,000 over 25,000 population at 30 ft² (2.79 m²) per reader space
Staff workspace, cloakrooms, etc.	900 ft² (83.6 m²)	1,500 ft² (139.4 m²)	3,000 ft² (278.7 m²)
Estimated additional space needed[1]	1,200 ft² (111.5 m²)	2,000 ft² (185.8 m²)	3,550 ft² (329.9 m²)
Total floor space	4,200 ft² (390.2 m²) or 0.7 ft² (0.065 m²) per head, whichever is greater	7,000 ft² (650.3 m²) or 0.7 ft² (0.065 m²) per head, whichever is greater	15,000 ft² (1,393.5 m²) or 0.6 ft² (0.056 m²) per head whichever is greater

1. Additional space is for heating equipment, cleaning materials, stairways, public lavatories and other purposes not included specifically under headings.

EXPENDITURE

In another appendix estimates are given (as at 1965) of the cost of providing a library service giving the minimum standards and, for libraries too small to provide an independent service of that level, estimates of the cost of providing services at the level of the provisional standards. Local authority expenditure in the smaller areas is supplemented by the value of the aid in kind provided by the Country Library Service, thus reducing the gap for smaller libraries between provisional and minimum standards. Library service at the level of the provisional standards is considered to reach the minimum standards in a system serving about 150,000 people.

Norway

Few countries can have more physical difficulties in maintaining a public library service than Norway, a country with only a small population, about 4 million, a low density of population, 11.5/km², only three towns of over 100,000 population, and 1.5 million people living in rural communes. Divided into nineteen counties and 450 local authority units, Norway is a country of small communities and of small library units. Despite the handicaps these conditions have imposed, an effective public library service has to a high degree been achieved with the aid of a series of public library laws dating from 1935 to the latest enacted in 1971. These laws define in general terms the responsibilities of the local authorities and of the State in this field and four administrative features are of particular significance in this partnership. First, there have been the statutory duties imposed on the local authorities to provide a library service of a certain minimum level, almost invariably surpassed; second, the powers and duties imposed on the State and exercised through the State Library Directorate (Statens Bibliotektilsyn), a department of the Ministry of Church and Education which has to apportion the State grants and thereby has the opportunity to influence the general planning and development of the libraries; thirdly, the establishment, based on a particular municipal library, of regional central or county libraries (fylkesbiblioteker), with the encouragement of favourable and flexible State grants. The duties of these regional central or county libraries include service not only to their own immediate areas but to persons living within a larger area (in most cases the administrative county), supervision of and support of all kinds to independent libraries within this area, and the provision of travelling and other forms of circulating libraries (mobile libraries, including book boats, book boxes for small local libraries, adult classes, lighthouses, etc.). Fourthly, there is the National Library Supply Agency (Biblioteksentralen), controlled jointly by the local authorities and the State, through which the public libraries purchase books and have binding done advantageously. This also operates many technical services, e.g. cataloguing, on a centralized basis, which would otherwise be impossible for many of the small libraries, with their limited qualified staff and financial resources, to carry out properly. In his account of the legislative and administrative arrangements (on which the above note is based), Frank Gardner has recorded the improvement over twenty years up to 1968, measured by a tenfold increase in State grants and by an even higher rate of increase in local expenditure.[1] The effects of changes in the value of money account for only a part of these increases. One result of the new libraries act of 1971 was to increase the State grant from 9 million kroner to 30 million kroner in 1972, the State now paying almost half the total expenditure for books and salaries.

The following statement about recommended standards for library service in Norway has been provided by the State Library Directorate.

Norway's new libraries act came into force on 1 January 1972. According to this:

Public libraries shall have as their responsibility the promotion of information and other cultural activity by making available books and other appropriate material free of charge to all who live in the country.

BOOK STOCKS

Quantitative standards for books will most likely not be worked out as regulations under the new act. In the regulations worked

1. Gardner, op. cit., p. 60–74.

out so far, requirements are described in general terms including such statements as:

All the public libraries shall, in addition to books for loan, have a reasonable choice of handbooks, reference books and periodicals.

However, the State Library Directorate, in advising local authorities on book expenditure and in dealing with proposals for new or improved library premises, works on the principle that libraries in areas with less than 6,000 inhabitants must have a book stock of at least 2 volumes of current literature per inhabitant, and in larger areas of 1.5 volumes per inhabitant.

AUDIO-VISUAL MEDIA

The State Library Directorate has tentatively worked out the following advisory standards:

Suitable audio-visual media

Records/tapes (collections of music and other audio materials); collections of pictorial art, slides, filmstrips, etc.

Conditions for establishing audio-visual collections

The usual total media budget for the purchase of books, other printed materials and audio-visual materials of the municipal public library must be a minimum of 25,000 to 30,000 kroner. The structure of the population and of the libraries can necessitate a larger media budget, so that in municipalities with many library units there will be a reasonable budget for books and periodicals. If a municipality wants to establish both a collection of music and a collection of pictorial art, the total media budget ought to be minimum 50,000 kroner. To establish collections of audio-visual media it will also be desirable to have an extra grant for the acquisition of a basic collection, possibly over a period of, say, three years.

The book stock of the municipal public library must be in accordance with the standards in force.

The comments of the county library on the plans must be obtained before establishing collections of audio-visual material.

Purchase and maintenance of the collections

For annual additions and maintenance not more than 10–15 per cent of the total media budget ought to be spent.

The size and nature of the collections

Records/tapes (collection of music and other audio materials):
Linguaphone records/tapes, literary records/tapes. For audio materials in connexion with slides, filmstrips, etc., see below.
Linguaphone records/tapes, library records/tapes should be acquired by most libraries and bought independently of the standards given above. Music records/cassette-tapes. To be acquired in accordance with the standards given above; when a library commences lending records, it must have a collection corresponding to the size of the population in the area, and not less than 200 records.

TABLE 56. Recommended apparatus for public libraries according to size of municipality

Type of apparatus	Population		
	Up to 10,000	10,000–20,000	20,000+
Record players with necessary number of amplifiers	1–3[1]	3–5	5–8
Places for listening with listening devices	2–6	6–10	10–16
Loudspeakers	1	1	1
Tape recorders	(1)	1	1
Radios	(1)	1	1
Cassette tape recorders with listening devices	1	1	1–2
Reading apparatus for microfilm	1	1	1
Projectors	—	1	1
Screens	—	1	1
Episcopes	—	1	1
Film projectors, 16 mm	—	—	1
Overhead projectors	—	1	1
Television	—	1	1

1. Tape recorder and/or radio may be used as amplifier.

Pictorial art, slides, filmstrips, etc.:

Slides, filmstrips, etc.: slides and filmstrips, if necessary with relevant audio materials, should be acquired according to the demand for such media, and to the extent it cannot be met by loans from other institutions. To be acquired independently of the standards given above.

Posters, reproductions for study purposes, graphic arts (printed after plate made by the artist), drawings, paintings in water colour: photography as art. To be acquired in accordance with the standards given above. The collection should primarily comprise reproductions, posters and graphic art. Paintings in water colour, drawings, pictures, collages, etc., can be obtained to the extent allowed by the library budget.

Microfilm, primarily newspapers: requisitions of newspapers on microfilm should be made in co-operation with, and in accordance with a plan prepared by, the county library.

Films. Films are not expected to be bought to any great extent.

Table 56 shows the apparatus which public libraries in municipalities of various sizes are recommended to acquire. The question of acquiring television ought to be seen in connexion with the provision of adult and other education by television and ways in which the libraries can take part in these activities. The same applies to overhead projectors.

TABLE 57

Inhabitants in service area[1]	Main libraries		Branch libraries[2]	
	Hours per week	Divided between number of days	Hours per week	Divided between number of days
Up to 1,000	6	2	2–4	—
1,000–2,500	6–10	2–3	4–8	2
2,500–5,000	10–15	3–4	8–15	3–4
5,000–7,000	15–20	4–5	15–20	4–5
Above 7,000	20	5	20	5

1. Should the library have a branch, the number of inhabitants in the area of the branch must be excluded from the reckoning.
2. The same opening hours ought to apply to both main libraries and branches. The minimum requirements for branches are indicated as follows: (a) in all libraries open more than two days a week, the opening period on at least one day must be in the morning; (b) main libraries and branches with part-time staff should keep open for at least 42 weeks in the year. Libraries with full-time staff should keep open for at least 46 weeks in the year; (c) the opening periods of the main library and branches must be co-ordinated so that the public is best served.

Opening hours

The minimum requirements in the regulations following the passage of the new act are shown in Table 57.

SPACE REQUIREMENTS

These are based very much on the Danish standards (q.v.). The size of lending departments is worked out on the basis of the desired number of volumes, as previously indicated, and required areas are calculated on the basis of 70–75 volumes/m². For reading room areas they normally calculate 2–3 seats per 1,000 population in respect of smaller libraries, but each project has to be considered on its merit having regard to factors such as degree of dependence on the library of the schools and other institutions in the area. A basic figure of 3.5 to 4 m² is used per seat.

However, according to the requirements of the act, standards have to be worked out, standards that the municipalities must follow in order to get state grants for their library service.

STAFFING

The statement does not refer to staffing. According to the library law local authorities with more than 8,000 inhabitants must appoint a full-time trained librarian, who has successfully completed the course at the State Library School. There are no other official standards.

However, staffing was the subject of a report issued in 1970 by the Norwegian Rationalization Committee.[1] This committee was set up by the State Library Directorate in 1966 and contained representatives of local authority and library interests, under the chairmanship of the State Library Director. The report was based on detailed surveys of work done in libraries and other studies.

Comparing the results of a survey of work done by 150 staff in eight selected county libraries over a period of three weeks with the results of similar Swedish and Danish investigations (in

1. Norwegian Rationalization Committee, *Report on Work Distribution and Staff Requirements in Norwegian Public Libraries*, Oslo, Statensbibliotektilsyn (State Library Directorate), 1970 (mimeo).

the first of which county library work was excluded), the committee concluded that there was a certain conformity in the composition of library work. Its investigation showed that 45.53 per cent of all library work was carried out by qualified librarians, while the office staff comprised 34.80 per cent. The rest of the work was carried out by trainee-librarians (10.01 per cent), part-time librarians without professional qualifications (4.99 per cent), and manual workers 4.69 per cent. The smallest libraries had the highest proportion of qualified librarians.

Also analysed was how the working force was distributed and an attempt was made to reach a practical distribution of work among the different categories of staff. Grouping work operations according to the American Library Association's *Professional and Non-professional Duties in Libraries*, and using the work classification table used in the Swedish and Danish rationalization investigations (which were based on the American definitions), the committee established which duties should be assigned to the different staff categories and arrived at certain percentages of work distribution. Adjusted to take into account additional factors, it concluded that library work of the average composition would be distributed among the staff categories in the following way:

Librarians, 37 per cent.

Library functionaries (sub-professionals, i.e. office staff with practical or theoretical knowledge of special working methods of libraries), 20 per cent.

Library helpers (office staff requiring no professional qualifications, only a limited practical training), 37 per cent.

Drivers, caretakers, etc., 6 per cent.

The committee stressed that these average figures should not be taken as standards and said they were unlikely to be applicable to small libraries. It recommended the establishment of these staff categories in individual libraries and of a training system for library assistants and part-time librarians, providing opportunities for individual advancement.

The committee was required to provide standards for staff requirements in libraries. Obtaining statistics from full-time libraries with a staff of two or more librarians, it found a clear connexion between issues and size of staff. While average numbers of inhabitants per staff members varied greatly and were generally less in the small- or medium-sized towns than in the larger towns and in county libraries, the average number of issues annually per inhabitant was substantially greater in the smaller towns. As a result, issues per staff member showed no great variation. The committee therefore concluded that, as was the method used in Sweden, the number of inhabitants as well as issues must be considered in calculating staff requirements.

The committee considered that in Norway an issue figure per staff member higher than 12,000 would not be justifiable. With this as a starting point, and based on a national average of 3.5 issues per inhabitant per year, it drew up the following table for staff requirements for varying issues. With reservations this was recommended for adoption as a provisional method of calculating staff requirements. Issues figures below the national average should not be used. The figures did not apply to the staffing of the county libraries' rural service points, nor could they be indiscriminately applied to authorities with populations below 15,000, where the character of the municipality necessitated a strongly differentiated library service. Particular attention was also drawn to the libraries in university towns, where the need for long opening hours in reading rooms, etc., necessitated a larger staff than indicated by the standard figures (see Table 58).

The committee also issued a report in 1970 on the county libraries' mobile library service in which advice is given, *inter alia*, on staffing. It considered that a mobile library with an annual issue of 40,000, required a librarian and a driver on the vehicle, as well as supporting staff at the base library.[1]

TABLE 58

Issues per inhabitant	Inhabitants per staff member	Issues per inhabitant	Inhabitants per staff member
3.5	3,400	7	1,700
4	3,000	8	1,500
5	2,400	9	1,300
6	2,000		

1. Norwegian Rationalization Committee, *Report on the County Libraries' Mobile Library Service*, Oslo, Statensbibliotektilsyn (State Library Directorate), 1970 (mimeo).
    For information about the reports of the Norwegian Rationalization Committee, the writer is indebted to the article written by the secretary of the committee, Magne Hauge, 'Investigation into Rationalization in Norwegian Public Libraries', *Scandinavian Public Library Quarterly*, No. 3/4, 1971.

Poland

In 1971 Poland had 8,666 public libraries containing over 59 million volumes, an average of 1.81 per inhabitant, and 20.8 per cent of the population borrowed books. In addition to normal activities in book circulation, large numbers of book exhibitions, meetings with writers and lectures were organized in the libraries.[1]

A number of quantitative standards were prescribed by the Polish Government in May 1968, on the advice of the Department of Cultural and Educational Work and Libraries of the Ministry of Culture and Fine Arts, in connexion with the building, extension or modernization of public library premises.[2] These indicate the following:

The scale of total book stock to be provided in terms of volumes per inhabitant for all sizes of library, and total numbers of

TABLE 59. Books (in volumes)

Population[1]	Total number	Adults (open access lending)	Open access reference	Children (open access)	Total book stock in stack
1,000	3,300	2,250	300	750	—
2,000	6,600	3,600	1,200	1,200	600
3,000	9,000	4,900	1,650	1,650	800
4,000	11,000	6,000	2,000	2,000	1,000
5,000	12,500	6,750	2,250	2,250	1,250
10,000	22,000	12,000	4,000	4,000	2,000
15,000	33,000	15,000	4,800	4,500	8,700
20,000	44,000	18,000	6,000	6,000	14,000
25,000	55,000	20,000	10,000	10,000	15,000

1. For populations over 25,000 the following figures are given for the number of volumes per inhabitant: 25,001–35,000, 2 volumes; 35,001–80,000, 1.75; 80,001–150,000, 1.50; 150,001–200,000, 1.25; over 200,000, 1.0.

1. *Biblioteki publiczne w liczbach x 1971 r Cz.1. Informacja statystyczna* [Public Libraries in Figures in 1971. Part I. Statistical Information], Warsaw, Biblioteka Narodowa, Instytut Ksiazki i Czytelnictwa, 1972, s. 62, tab. 10.
2. 'Nr. 26 Ministra Budownictwa i Przemyslu Materialow Budowlanych z dnia 11 maja 1968 r.w. sprawie ustanowienia normatywu technicznego projektowania bibliotek publicznych [Regulation of the Ministry of Architecture and Materials for the Building Industry, Relative to the Establishment of Technical Standards for the Construction of Public Libraries, 11 May 1968]', *Dziennik Budownictwa Dziennik Urzedowy* (Warsaw), No. 6, 17 September 1968.

books in smaller libraries up to 25,000 population divided into adult lending and reference on open access, children's reference books on open access and total numbers in the stack—see Table 59.

The number of places to be provided in reading rooms, for adults and children and in newspaper/periodicals reading rooms. Also included in this table is the percentage of registered readers to be provided for, ranging from 40 to 30 per cent—see Table 60 following.

Of particular interest are the space standards prescribed for all the different areas to be found in small and medium-size libraries—serving up to 25,000 population—see Table 61 following.

The Institute of Books and Reading of the National Library subsequently prepared standards for the addition of new publications for the years 1971–80. These have been given effect to by an order of the Minister of Culture and Art issued 2 February 1971, which provides as follows: (a) the minimum number of new publications added annually to the stock of a library shall not fall below 13 volumes for every 100 inhabitants of the area served by the library; (b) in libraries where the size of the book stock is less than 1.5 volumes per inhabitant, or the number of readers greater than 21 for every 100 inhabitants, a higher minimum should be expected, namely, at least 18 new additions for every 100 inhabitants, the number of new acquisitions should reach a minimum of 20 volumes per 100 inhabitants.

TABLE 60

Libraries serving number of inhabitants	Percentage of registered readers to be planned for	Number of places in reading room			
		Total	Adult	Children	Newspapers/periodicals
Under 2,500	40	16–20	6–10	10	—
2,501–5,000	40–35	22–40	10–20	12–20	—
5,001–10,000	35–30	38–70	18–35	20–35	—
10,001–15,000	30	93	40	38	15
15,001–20,000	30	100	40	40	20
20,001–25,000	30	110	40	45	25

TABLE 61. Areas (in square metres) of rooms (required areas are stated for all spaces; the following are the major areas prescribed and total areas)

Libraries serving	Populations					
	Under 2,500	2,501–5,000	5,001–10,000	10,001–15,000	15,001–20,000	20,001–25,000
Lending (adults)	50	55–90	97–120	130–150	150–180	180–200
Reading (adults)	55	59–106	115–105	150–156	135	155
Lending (children)	—	—	34	38–44	44–63	72–96
Reading (children)	—	—	68	87	92	104
Periodicals	—	—	—	—	35–41	48–58
Catalogue	6	7–9	10–12	13–15	16–18	21
Staff in reading room	6	6	12	12	18	18
Stack room	—	6–9	11–16	16–33	41–51	55–88
Room to organize books for branches	—	—	12	12	12	12
Classrooms (adult classes)	—	—	23–41	41–46	46	46
Administration area						
Chief librarian	—	—	—	12	12	12
Workroom	6	6	12	12	12	18–24
Office— secretarial and accounts	—	—	—	—	8	8–12
Organizer of branches	—	25	32	42	42	48
Toilets—staff, public	4	4–8	8	10–15	15–18	18
Floor						
Total area—net	168	193–285	471–527	615–703	731–820	875–990
Communications +30 per cent	50	58–86	141–158	185–211	219–246	263–297
Total area— gross[1]	218	251–371	612–685	800–914	951–1,066	1,138–1,287
Total floor area per 1,000 population	87	104–74	124–68	80–61	64–53	57–51

1. This includes adult classroom areas, but excludes lecture halls and other meeting rooms.

Singapore

The National Library of Singapore combines the functions both of a national and of a public library. As the public library it is responsible for providing a free library service to all members of the community, making library materials in the main languages used in Singapore, Malay, Chinese, Tamil and English, available for reference and for lending.

'Library material' is defined in the National Library Act as:

. . . any form of written or graphic record, including manuscripts, typescripts, books, newspapers, periodicals, music, photographs, maps, prints, drawings and other graphic art forms, films, filmstrips, gramophone records, tape recordings and other recordings on paper, film or other material and reproductions thereof.[1]

Although no quantitative standards have been laid down, a duty to provide books and other materials has been set forth in the following terms:

To provide books for men and women as workers. In Singapore, which is changing the basis of its economic and social life, the public library must help people in occupations that have previously been confined to expatriates, in trades and skills that are needed as the economy develops, in management as the republic becomes industrialized, and it must provide for the needs of the new professional groups.

To provide books for men and women as home-makers.

To provide books for men and women as citizens. The task of the library is to provide access to a wide range of the best books on social, economic and political problems of this generation. People must have access to the facts, to the history of political theory and development.

To provide books for the fruitful use of leisure time; on Asian history, art and culture; for children below the age of 15 (forming almost half the total population); for teenagers between 14–19 years (the population group with the highest rate of increase in Singapore).[2]

During its thirteen years of service as the combined national and public library of Singapore, the National Library has developed

---

1. 'National Library Act', *Singapore Statutes*, Chapter 311 of 1911.
2. *Functions of the National Library*, 16 April 1969 (mimeo).

from a small library providing limited reading materials for a limited clientele to one with a membership of over 200,000, providing reading material in the four official languages, with an annual circulation of over 1 million. Because of the library's rapid growth and the increasing demand for library services, with the increase in literacy (now estimated at 80 per cent), the National Library Board has recommended decentralization of the library's home reading service through the establishment of full-time branches and the extension of the mobile library service.

In 1967 a document, *Outline Policy on Optimum Size and Number of Branch Libraries in Singapore*, was prepared by the National Library. This has not been published and has been partly superseded by further developments.

It explained the economic arguments for the establishment of large branches serving larger units of population and suggested the following minimum guidelines for the establishment of branch libraries in Singapore, recommending also that sub-branches and deposit stations giving an extremely limited service should not be provided.

Regional branches, acting as reference and administrative centres for groups of smaller branches and having book stocks of 200,000 volumes or above.

Major branches, open for 48–66 hours per week and serving 35,000–70,000 population; offering lending and reference service for adults, children and young people, and extension services such as talks, discussion groups, reading programmes, etc.

Community or neighbourhood branches, open for 30–48 hours per week, serving populations of from 10,000 to 35,000, within a one-mile radius; providing adult, children's and reference services; expected to answer 10,000 information enquiries a year and to lend 75,000 to 100,000 books a year.

Bookmobiles, serving populations of up to 1,000 by means of regular visits at least once every two weeks. These would introduce library service to unserved areas, give continuing service to areas that could not support permanent library buildings, e.g. rural areas of scattered and low density population, and determine desirable locations for branch library buildings.

The 'Outline Policy' proposes to increase mobile library service points, which would continue to be used in the rural areas, but to aim to do away entirely with the mobile library service by the end of 1985 through the provision of additional community or major branch libraries.

The document also sets out guidelines for estimating basic library requirements for a regional branch library serving an estimated maximum population of 160,000 as follows:

Total library space: 250 ft² (23.2 m²) per 1,000 estimated population.

Reader accommodation: reader seats (2 per 1,000 estimated population); reader space (25 ft² (2.3 m²) per seat).

Staff: 0.25 employee per 1,000 estimated population.

Staff accommodation: 100 ft² (9.3 m²) per employee.

Book collection: maximum book collection (1,500 books per 1,000 estimated population); accommodation for collection (15 books/ft² (0.3 m²)).

South Africa

GENERAL

South African public library standards show clear signs of the influence of the United States and United Kingdom standards, and present some aspects different from other comparable standards, which may be of interest to other countries. The first, *Standards for South African Public Libraries*, was published in 1959, and the current document is a revised edition issued in 1968 with extensive changes necessitated by the rapid growth of public libraries in that country in that short period.[1]

The document defines library standards as the criterion by which public library services may be measured and assessed and puts forward, as a general guide only, norms of service either already attained in leading public libraries in South Africa or recommended for general implementation.

The introduction points out that the choice of a suitable population basis for South African library standards is complicated by the fact that large population groups exist whose standards of

1. South African Library Association, *Standards for South African Public Libraries*, Potchefstroom, 1968.

literacy are low.[1] To these groups the concept of a free public library service is something new; from them very little spontaneous demand can be expected. Furthermore, the pattern of library service to the Whites and for a lesser degree the Coloured is uneven—in most cases it is rudimentary or non-existent. While the literacy level of the community is the key factor in determining the extent to which the standards should be applied, no differentiation in the standard of public library service to the various population groups is visualized. Where standards are based on population, literate population is meant.

The document establishes a dividing line of 40,000 population between those public libraries which can operate economically and efficiently as independent units, and those which are too small to do so. Public libraries serving communities with populations under 40,000 are recommended to affiliate to a provincial library service; those serving communities with population in excess of this figure, it is suggested, should receive financial support rather than direct service.

In practice the provincial administrations provide a direct service to the rural areas and a number of smaller urban centres are affiliated to the provincial system. Only nine urban centres have large enough populations to enable them to maintain independent library systems. Affiliation to the provincial library services works like this. The local authority provides a building, which must be approved by the provincial library authorities, and financial support for the library based on an amount per head of population served, which varies according to the regulations of the particular provincial library service and according to the size of the small urban area concerned. From the provincial library service, the affiliated library service receives supplies of books (pre-catalogued), cards to form a temporary catalogue, advice on all aspects of running a library, assistance in the initial reorganization of the library if required, and a request service with the entire book stock of the provincial library system to draw on. The library service to the readers is free, the abolition of subscriptions and deposits being a condition of membership of the provincial library service. Such affiliated libraries are not centrally controlled. Local

1. The population (1970 estimated figures) is 21,448,000 of which 3,751,000 are Whites (people of European descent), 15,058,000 are Bantu (comprising a number of different ethnic groups), 2,019,000 are Coloured (mixed race), and 620,000 Asians.

committees are formed acting in an advisory capacity, staff is appointed by the local authority, and every effort is made to encourage local pride and local interest in the library.[1]

The traditional and conventional qualitative standards are described in the document in sections on 'Objectives', 'Government and Administration', and 'Service', the last beginning to enter into quantitative matters.

OBJECTIVES

The basic objectives are stated as being to make books and associated material freely available to all members of the community; provide information services for the use of all citizens; advance the intellectual and cultural status of the community; promote and encourage the informal self-education of all citizens; provide supplementary informational material to those pursuing formal educational courses; provide the means for promoting aesthetic appreciation; conserve books and other library material for future generations; promote the material development of South Africa and, in particular, to meet the special needs of commerce and industry; meet the recreational needs of the individual, the family and other community groups and to encourage sound use of leisure time.

The objectives, it is said, should be attained by:

Making available from public funds library materials of a predetermined standard to all who can benefit from their use. Books are most important but the provision of other library material, such as periodicals, films, records, art prints, newspapers, pamphlets, and micro-film should be considered.

Organizing, presenting and housing library material so that it can be employed to the best advantage.

Employing qualified staff, only thus can library resources be properly exploited.

Providing functional buildings and equipment, with generous allowance for expansion.

Bringing to the notice of all members of the public the resources and value of the library.

1. This general information is based on Loree Elizabeth Taylor, *South African Libraries*, London, Clive Bingley, 1967.

Offering opportunities for self-education by serving as an adjunct
to formal education. The role of the public library in education
is an important one; guidance in the use of educational material
must be provided and the library must promote the maximum
potential use of books and other media which are of outstanding
merit and value. Often the library is the only institution through
which adult education organizations can work.

Giving special service to those who are physically handicapped
or who for some other reason are unable to come to the library,
e.g. hospital patients, prisoners, the partially sighted, seamen
and those who reside in remote areas.

Providing the means for promoting civic enlightenment, a matter
of vital concern in the complex South African social structure.

GOVERNMENT AND ADMINISTRATION

The provincial administration should initiate, support and co-
ordinate public library services, either by means of subsidies to
urban library authorities, if required, or direct services to smaller
communities and should foster co-operation between all public
library agencies, urban and rural in the province. The central
government, in subsidizing the provincial administration, should
make adequate provision for public library services to all population groups, finance national bibliographical services, financially
encourage individual public library authorities towards specialization in approved subject fields, and co-ordinate library services
on a national scale to ensure complete coverage of recorded
knowledge in the national book stock and to avoid unnecessary
duplication of library material. Such co-ordination should be on
a voluntary basis.

SERVICE

General

Each public library should have a written statement of its objectives. To achieve these objectives there should be, *inter alia*:

A lending service with enough service points to reach the whole
community.

The services of a readers' adviser in lending sections of all libraries serving populations in excess of 10,000.

Some provision for the special needs of young adults in all libraries. In urban libraries a specialist should be appointed who is familiar with the needs of this group.

An effective inter-library loan service that is brought to the attention of readers.

Service to and co-operation with bodies engaged in adult education on a local, provincial and national level.

Hours of opening

The library should be open at those times best suited to the needs of all its patrons. Those serving populations in excess of 4,000 should be open six days a week. Service should be given in the evenings and on Saturdays. Hours of opening should be reconsidered periodically to meet changing local conditions. Mobile libraries should maintain regular schedules of visits. Intervals between visits should be no greater than one week. Visits should be not less than thirty minutes duration.

Statistics

Libraries should keep regular statistics of services rendered, expenses incurred and revenue received.

BOOK STOCK AND AUDIO-VISUAL MATERIALS

Selection principles

The selection of books and other materials should be governed by interdependent factors, the objectives of the library, considerations of quality of the materials selected and the needs and interests of the community served.

All libraries should maintain:

A collection of basic and up-to-date works of reference; this will vary with the size and characteristics of the community served but a minimum collection of some twenty-five ready reference titles should be available for consultation in the smallest public library.

A comprehensive range of non-fiction books, in extent at least
25 per cent of the total book stock.

A collection of fiction conforming to generally accepted minimum
literary standards, including attractive editions of the classics
and standard twentieth-century authors.

A collection of books for children, quality of production and
content being of the utmost importance.

Due consideration must be given to the provision of books and
audio-visual materials in both official languages (English and
Afrikaans) and, where a demand is made, in the vernacular Bantu
languages and foreign languages.

Quantity

The smaller the library the larger the number of books is required
per head of population. The minimum number of volumes immediately available proposed is as follows: above 250,000 population,
from 1.5 to 1 volume per head of population; from 100,000 to
250,000, from 2 to 1.5; from 50,000 to 100,000, from 2.5 to 2; and
under 50,000, from 3 to 2.5.

In a small independent public library there is a limit to ultimate
availability, whereas the same library, if a member of a large library
system, is limited only by the total book stock of that system. If
communications between the public library and the system are
good, immediate availability is relatively unimportant.

At least 5 per cent of circulating stock should be withdrawn from
the open shelves annually. Out-of-date superseded textbooks and
reference books should be discarded. Provincial library systems
should provide storage for little used and redundant material from
affiliated libraries. Replacements should be acquired in terms of a
definite policy; up-to-date editions of standard texts should be purchased to maintain the balance of stocks.

Circulation

Total annual circulation of libraries conforming to the requirements of the standards should be not less than six books per head of
population served. In a well-balanced and adequately housed collection under the care of an enlightened librarian, the circulation
of non-fiction books should be not less than 25 per cent of the total

annual circulation. Circulation statistics should be kept for books borrowed by adults, young adults and children and should be recorded separately for fiction by language and for non-fiction in each group.

Audio-visual materials

All libraries should provide audio-visual materials (i.e. films, speech and music records and art reproductions), and, in libraries serving populations above 40,000, a special amount should be set aside for the purchase of such materials. Smaller libraries should be able to draw upon provincial library systems for the loan of this material. For films, filmstrips and slides for use by groups, a public library should draw freely on established collections.

Newspapers and periodicals

Newspapers and periodicals should be provided for use in the library. Every library should receive a minimum of three newspapers and one additional newspaper for every 1,000 population up to a reasonable maximum. Selection must be related to the nature of the community, adequate representation of both official languages, provision of newspapers in the Bantu vernaculars, and proximity to large centres where a number of newspapers are published daily. Except for the smallest libraries, subscriptions should be placed with leading newspapers from other provinces and from overseas. Every library should receive a minimum of five periodicals plus one additional for every 200 population, up to a reasonable maximum. Advice is also given about local collections, pamphlet material and ephemera, and special collections.

INTER-LIBRARY CO-OPERATION

The section concludes with a recommendation that the entire book and other public library resources of the republic should be at the disposal of readers and all libraries should participate in the national inter-library loan system, except those affiliated to provincial library systems, which should do so through their respective provincial library authorities.

TECHNICAL PROCESSES

Provided satisfactory standards of accommodation, staffing and management are maintained, a satisfactory standard in technical processing should be observed. Certain requirements are listed in the areas of catalogues and processing. Work areas are briefly discussed, stress being laid on the contribution of pleasant and functional working areas to efficiency.

STAFF

The staff must be of the temperament and have the education, training and experience for the successful selection and organization of materials and be able to promote their use to the fullest advantage of the community.

There should be one staff member for every 2,500 population (maintenance staff excluded). The application of this standard is subject to a number of local factors—the percentage of borrowers, number of branches, opening hours, etc. An alternative method of determining the size of staff based on the amount and type of work carried out is suggested. Norms found to be applicable are: 25,000 books issued per staff member per annum in community of less than 10,000 population; 20,000 books issued per staff member per annum in communities of between 10,000 and 250,000 population; 15,000 books issued per staff member in communities of more than 250,000 population. (Figures based on a loan period of fifteen days; all members of staff, except maintenance staff, included.)

In populations of less than 40,000, 40 per cent of the staff should have professional or sub-professional qualifications. In larger towns or cities 33 per cent may be regarded as satisfactory. Professional is defined as a person with the following or equivalent qualifications: diploma of the South African Library Association; university degree and a post-graduate diploma in librarianship; degree in librarianship.

Two years of full-time post matriculation study towards a lower diploma or certificate in librarianship is regarded as a sub-professional qualification.

In libraries serving over 10,000 population a qualified librarian should always be available.

Other staffing standards include: (a) library staffs must be adequately remunerated; (b) equal salaries for men and women should be paid; (c) libraries should maintain a well-organized system of in-service training for both professional and non-professional staff; (d) as far as possible, professional staff should be engaged on professional duties and non-professional duties assigned to clerical staff.

BUILDINGS

Planning

A number of planning standards are stated, including:
The library should be planned and equipped as a modern, educational, cultural and intellectual centre.
The building should be planned to allow for maximum flexibility of internal arrangement. The exterior architectural features should be secondary to the functional relationship of departments.
The library entrance should be on street level, allowing for maximum visibility from the street outside, giving an immediate suggestion of accessibility.
A single-storey building is to be preferred, except for the larger library.
Every effort should be made to make the library as beautiful and inviting as possible with particular attention to the comfort and convenience of users.
Special care should be taken to provide good lighting.
Modern methods should be applied to noise control.

Location

The location of the public library and its branches should be determined with great care to ensure the utmost accessibility. The library should be sited where people meet, near shopping and traffic centres, and where it will be seen. It should not be in a park or other open space. Sacrificing accessibility to save expenditure is false economy. An urban public library and its branches should be situated so that all users are within easy reach of a service point; it should be possible for children and old persons to reach such a point unaccompanied.

Communities with more than 10,000 inhabitants should consider the provision of a branch where a separate shopping centre has evolved at some distance from the main shopping area.

Area

There must be accommodation apart from public rooms, for (a) book storage; (b) storage of materials and equipment; (c) work or office space; (d) staff rooms and facilities for the staff to prepare drinks or light meals.

In determining the total floor space required, a practical method is to relate this to the size of population. The minimum size for a public library building is considered to be 1,000 ft² (92.9 m²). Sizes are recommended for main libraries between 1,000 and 10,000 population on a sliding scale: 1,000 population, 2,000 ft² (185.80 m²); 4,000 population, 4,000 ft² (371.60 m²); 8,000 population, 6,200 ft² (575.99 m²); 10,000 population, 7,000 ft² (641.02 m²).

In a population range from 10,000 to 1 million, the minimum *per capita* space allocation will range from 0.7 ft² (0.065 m²) for the smaller communities, to 0.3 ft² (0.028 m²) for the largest; but a study of the community and its library needs is the only sure basis on which to determine the amount of space required.

In analysing the use made of the floor area of a library, provision should be made for the following functions: service, administration and group activities. An allocation of service area is suggested in Table 62.

TABLE 62

| Population | Percentage of total | | |
	Adult lending	Juvenile	Reference and reading
Under 5,000	45	33	22
5,000–10,000	45	30	25
10,000–15,000	45	27	28
15,000–20,000	45	25	30

In libraries serving over 20,000 population, the reference and reading area will gradually increase and the lending area proportionately decrease in area.

In addition to the service area, space should be allocated for administrative offices and special collections, where these exist.

Space for group activities will include lecture rooms, committee rooms, exhibition area, listening rooms, etc., to make allowance for the library's adult education programme. As local needs vary, no percentage of the total library area required for each of these functions is indicated.

FINANCE

Specimen budgets of existing public libraries in South Africa serving communities of various sizes and characteristics are given with comments. No generally applicable cost figures per head of population are proposed because the constitution and literacy level of the population varies too widely from place to place.

Sweden

In his comparative survey of public library legislation, Frank M. Gardner has described the background in which the question of desirable minimum standards for public library service in Sweden has to be considered.[1] Describing the Swedish public library system as the most highly developed in Europe and possibly in the world, with its many post-Second World War library buildings 'of a lavishness and a technical and architectural perfection which is the envy of all librarians', he has traced the steps by which since 1965, in contemplation of the reduction in the number of local authority areas (and consequently of separate public library authorities) from some 1,000 to 278 by 1974, the central government's responsibilities in regard to public libraries have been changed from largely supervisory to advisory. No longer in a position to enforce certain minimum standards as a condition of obtaining State grants towards the cost of all library expenditure

1. Frank M. Gardner, op. cit., p. 94–104.

(since such grants had been abolished) or State approval to library buildings projects, the National Board of Education, through its Library Division, had become more concerned with information, consideration of developments and work on the extended functions of public libraries: adult education, hospital libraries, libraries for the blind, libraries as cultural centres, public relations. The present library legislation, Gardner has said, was not directed at creating a public library service, as that had been done. It was not directed at improving standards of library service, except under special circumstances. It was considered that improving standards could safely be left to the local authorities.

Gardner has pointed to 'probably the key to what is happening to public libraries in Sweden', that:

> ... more and more ... the public library is seen not as an isolated institution, but as the core and centre of a cultural complex, in a single building or group of buildings. The new libraries are designed as cultural centres, with space for concerts, art exhibitions, a youth centre and even ... dance hall and restaurant. ... Such a conception is only possible in a highly organized, advanced and affluent society where education is no longer a privilege, where access to knowledge is a basic right, and where finance is no longer a barrier to the provision of cultural services as a communal, not a private enterprise.

However high a standard the best library services achieve, there are two causes of unevenness. Even with the reform of local government completed, there will still be many communes with less than 10,000 inhabitants. These areas are not capable of giving the kind of library service provided by the larger authorities. Although in each county one of the large commune libraries receives additional county and State funds to enable it to assist smaller libraries, this does not provide a satisfactory alternative. Secondly, while many libraries spend as much as 40 kronor *per capita*, others spend only 2 or 3 kronor. 'The disparities', Gardner pointed out, 'are much greater than in England or Denmark, and no detailed minimum standards have been formulated as in those two countries.'

Despite this, there are certain standards which can be used as guidelines by the local authorities, as in other countries where the legal position is much the same as it is now in Sweden.

Minimum standards were recommended in a report of a special committee representing the Board of Education, the Swedish Union of Local Authorities and the Swedish Library Association, published in 1960, in which objectives and other guiding principles were discussed.[1] The committee recommended minimum provision of books and staff on the following basis:

Books: Total stock—2 to 3 volumes per inhabitant; annual accessions—twice annual issues divided by 80.

Staff: 1 employee per 20,000 loans in the following proportions: librarians 1; clerks 1.2; and caretakers 0.2. These quantitative standards have been rendered largely out of date by subsequent events.

The legislation of the 1960s, which re-organized the structure of local government and made fundamental changes in the relations of the local authorities to the central government, abolished the system of grants in aid of all public libraries in favour of a system of general grants weighted to help the poorer areas. At the same time it introduced a system of special development grants from the central government to local authorities willing to expand their public library activities over a five-year period to achieve certain minimum standards laid down by the Board of Education. The grants were intended to cover half the cost of the development over the period and the minimum standards included the following:

Books: Total stock—3 volumes per inhabitant.

Staff: 1 employee per 14,500 loans.

Opening hours: 55 hours a week.

Buildings: 50–100 m² per 1,000 inhabitants.[2]

These development grants have achieved a considerable measure of success but have been short-lived. By a subsequent decision of Parliament they are being progressively discontinued, no new grants being started after the end of 1972. Although this form of State grant will no longer exist, the standards applicable to the development libraries will remain as guidance to local authorities as to what should be provided and they will continue to be used by the Library Division of the Board of Education in its advisory and other work.

Because the very considerable developments in Sweden since 1960 had rendered many of the recommendations of the special

1. *Organization och arbetsmetoder vid kommunala bibliotek. Betankande avgivet av särskilda kommitterade* [Municipal Libraries: Organization and Working Methods. Report by a Special Committee], Stockholm, 1960.
2. Based on information supplied by the Library Division, Board of Education, Stockholm.

committee out of date, and because running through the theory of library administration in that country was the principle of rationalization and standardization (which Gardner has described as 'the idea of more and better library service at a lower price') a new committee was set up in 1969 to revise the earlier recommendations. On this the Board of Education, the Swedish Union of Local Authorities, the Swedish Library Association and the appropriate trade unions were represented. The committee reported in 1972.[1]

The committee made a 'rationalization survey' in 1970. This consisted primarily of an investigation into the composition and distribution of library work in a number of libraries selected at random so as to give a suitable cross-section of conditions existing, and of two special studies, one of branch and mobile library services and the other of services to disadvantaged groups. The proposals made by the committee did not cover all aspects of library service and were not intended to establish standards or norms to be followed inflexibly, but rather to serve as guidance for the local authorities. In the same way as the standards used in connexion with the discontinued development grants can continue to be used by the Board of Education in its advisory work, the guiding principles contained in the proposals of the rationalization survey can be referred to as standards in the broadest sense. Very few of the proposals in the report were capable of being quantified. But there were two exceptions: library materials (total stock of current interest—2.5 to 3.5 per inhabitant, including audio-visual media. No recommendations were made about accessions); staff (one full-time employee per 15,000 loans per annum, the recommended proportion between librarians and other members of staff being 1 : 1.7).

The report contained other recommendations, notably those concerning programme activities and extra-mural services. The former, which include for adults exhibitions, film, theatre and music programmes, debates, lectures, 'book-talks' and author presentations, and for children story-telling, films, puppet theatres, music programmes, book clubs and playing activities, should be

1. *Bibliotekarbete. En oversyn av verksambeten vid kommunala bibliotek. Betankande avgivet av 1970 ors rationaliserings-utredning vid folkbiblioteken* [Library Work. A Review of the Activities of Municipal Libraries. Report by the 1970 Rationalisation Committee for Public Libraries], Lund, 1972.

regarded as a normal part of the work of the library and should be developed as part of its informative activities. The latter, which include not only services to welfare institutions (including hospitals and prisons) but also 'shut-in' services and library services at factories and other places of work, should be given high priority.

The committee also discussed the problem of decentralization and provided some guiding principles for the organization of branch and mobile library services. Certain small branch library units, particularly in the rural areas, should be replaced by mobile library services, while other branch libraries should have better library resources, and the mobile library should carry out as large a part as possible of the total library service. Having regard to the recent local government reforms in Sweden, leading to larger local units of population often including vast rural areas, these recommendations are of great importance.

In the absence of a translation of this report, the author's remarks concerning it are based on information supplied by the Library Division of the Board of Education.

U.S.S.R.

Since the October Revolution of 1917 and particularly in the fifty years since the establishment of the Union of Soviet Socialist Republics, there has been a phenomenal increase in the number and use of libraries in Russia. This reflects the importance attached from the outset to libraries and to their work. From an extremely low base, and despite the grave set-back during the war years of 1941–45, a nation-wide organization of libraries has been established so extensive that it can be said that:

Any Soviet person of whatever nationality, wherever he lives and works, can now use any of the 360,000 libraries with their total stock of 3,300 million volumes. . . . There is not a town or village in any part of the Soviet Union where library books cannot be found. . . . There is also a well developed network of independent children's and school libraries—a total of 6,500 and 161,400 respectively—in the Union republics . . . used by over 40 million children [as well as scientific, specialized, technical and educational libraries].[1]

1. I. K. Nazmutdinov, 'Biblioteki 100 nacional'nostej SSSR', *Bjulleten' UNESKO dlja bibliotek*, Vol. 26, No. 6, 1972, p. 336–42; I. K. Nazmutdinov, 'Libraries of the U.S.S.R's One Hundred Nationalities', *Unesco Bulletin for Libraries*, Vol. XXVI, No. 6, November-December 1972, p. 307-14.

These library developments have been carried out under strong central direction and the Lenin State Library has provided the writer with a survey of the most important documents affecting the question of standards of service, governing the work of Soviet libraries. The survey is concerned for the most part with the libraries controlled by the U.S.S.R. Ministry of Culture, and with the libraries provided by trade unions and in schools. These three categories account for the overwhelming majority of Soviet libraries and the documents which provide guidelines for the libraries of other systems (technical libraries, libraries of colleges and universities, the libraries of the U.S.S.R. Academy of Sciences, etc.) are, in their basic aims, in line with those issued by the Ministry of Culture.

The documents referred to in the survey are, for the most part, included in the manual entitled *Instructional Materials in Librarianship. A Handbook.*[1] Other documents are represented by their citations in the text and in the footnotes.

In the text which follows, and which is based closely on the material supplied by the Soviet authorities, information is given about a number of general standards for library service to adults and children and in respect of library premises and equipment. Owing to limitations of space the writer has had to be selective, in particular it has not been possible to include material concerning the standardization of library procedures or the organization of catalogues in the U.S.S.R.[2]

Attention is drawn to the fact that this section, included in the chapter on public libraries, contains some information appropriate to the chapters on national libraries and on school libraries, and that the standards related to buildings and equipment do not exclusively relate to accommodation for public libraries. This indicates that it is not always possible to look at different types of library as if they are different in all respects.

1. *Rukovodjaščie materialy po bibliotečnomu delu. Spravočnik* [Instructional Materials in Librarianship. A Handbook], Moscow, Kniga, 1968, 270 p.
2. Attention is, however, drawn to *International Standardization of Library and Information Techniques*, p. 201–5, Paris, Unesco, March 1972 (mimeo; ref. COM/WS/257).

GENERAL STANDARDS

General research libraries controlled
by the U.S.S.R. Ministry of Culture

The Soviet Union has developed a unified system of general research libraries. This includes the Lenin State Library in Moscow (the national library of the U.S.S.R.); the Saltykov-Shchedrin State Public Library in Leningrad; the State libraries of fourteen Union republics;[1] the republic libraries of the twenty autonomous republics; 119 territorial (*krai*) and regional (*oblast*) libraries, eight regional (*oblast*) libraries of the autonomous regions, and ten district (*okrug*) libraries of the national districts. These libraries are open to all and make no charge to readers. All are major library institutions of nation-wide importance, holding the largest stocks of pre-Soviet, Soviet and foreign literature, as well as being centres of the inter-library networks.

The activities of these libraries are regulated by the following documents: *The Statutes of the Lenin State Library for 1973*,[2] *The Statutes of the Saltykov-Shchedrin State Library*,[3] and the corresponding statutes of the State libraries of the Union republics and of the regional, district, and republic (A.S.S.R.) libraries.

The functions of all these general libraries are the same. Each is a repository of a comprehensive collection of pre-Soviet, Soviet and foreign printed publications; the largest public library in its area; a centre of information and bibliographic activities; a research and methodological centre; and a centre for co-ordination and co-operation in the work of the libraries controlled by the U.S.S.R. Ministry of Culture.

The Ministry of Culture's general research libraries aim, in particular, to meet the requirements of specialist readers, arising from their professional and research work and from the need for the education and training of personnel for employment in all

---

1. The Soviet Union is formed by fifteen Union republics, but the largest of them, the Russian Soviet Federative Socialist Republic (its capital being Moscow), has no separate national ('State') library: the V. I. Lenin State Library of the U.S.S.R. in Moscow is at the same time the Russian Federation's national library.
2. *Ustav Gosudarstvennoj biblioteki SSSR imeni V. I. Lenina. 1973* [The Statutes of the Lenin State Library for 1973], Moscow, 1973.
3. *Ustav Gosudarstvennoj biblioteki imeni M. E. Saltykova-Ščedrina* [The Statutes of the Saltykov-Shchedrin State Library], Leningrad, 1956, 14 p.

areas of the national economy and of cultural life. At the same time the libraries serve their readers' general educational needs. They maintain day-to-day contact with public libraries, study and help them in their work, develop the inter-lending system, draw up lists of recommended reading and aids to research, hold seminars and conferences and give practical instruction to library staff.

Differences in the character and extent of the work of the general research libraries largely reflect historical distinctions in the nature of their stocks, the composition of their reference material, and the conditions of their service to their users.

The largest stocks are to be found in the U.S.S.R. Lenin State Library (over 26 million volumes) and the Saltykov-Shchedrin State Public Library (about 18 million volumes). These libraries receive deposit copies of all Soviet printed production, enjoy currency allocations for purchase of foreign literature and participate in extensive international exchange of publications. The State libraries of the Union republics, as well as the regional (*oblast*), and territorial (*krai*) libraries, and the libraries of the autonomous republics, form regional links in the library network. The special features of their work depend on the functions of the central libraries of the different areas.

The State libraries of the Union republics represent qualitatively a new type of national library. Their establishment and rapid progress have been part of the country-wide implementation of Lenin's plan for advancing national cultures. Since their inception the libraries have helped to raise cultural standards and bring the republics to new scientific and cultural levels.

In the post-war years the State libraries of the Union republics have been formed into a unified system of major research libraries, connected both with each other and with the general and specialized libraries of national standing in the U.S.S.R. The resources of the State libraries of fourteen Union republics (the Russian Federation not included) total 50 million volumes, the number of readers nearly 350,000, and annual book issues 18.5 million volumes. In most of these libraries the number of users varies between 25,000 and 30,000.

Among the specific tasks of the State libraries of the Union republics is the organization of their holdings and library and bibliographic information about the literature of the U.S.S.R. and the literature concerning the particular republic, information on inter-disciplinary problems involving branches of production and fields of science and technology, as well as the humanities.

The Soviet regional (*oblast*) libraries contain over 86 million volumes and have about 2.5 million users. The formation and development of these libraries has been part of the whole country's advance, both economic and cultural, and the libraries have combined their cultural and educational activities and their methodological research functions with meeting the professional needs of specialist readers. The regional libraries still differ significantly in the size of their holdings, in their organization and in the content of their service to specialists. Despite this they have common aims and prospects.

Public libraries

Public libraries occupy an important place in serving the reading needs of the Soviet people. The role of the libraries in the intellectual, social and moral education of the population has been increasing every year. Between 1965 and 1970 the number of readers at the State public libraries has increased by almost 15 million. In 1970, readers borrowed from these libraries 350 million more books than five years earlier. By January 1971 the holdings of the libraries exceeded 750 million volumes.

The library system has been expanding on a planned basis. In recent years, in the library system of the Ministry of Culture alone, 16,100 new libraries have been opened, including 12,200 in rural areas. Now the Soviet Union has 125,000 public libraries with great possibilities for meeting the people's book requirements and for raising their cultural and professional standards.

From its inception the Soviet Government has attached great importance to the proper location and organization of a system of public libraries which would secure the best possible conditions for library service to the whole population. Considerable research and organizational work aimed at studying the state of, and developing new principles for, the organization, location and planning of the library system resulted in the publication of 'Basic Rules for the Organization of a Network of Public Libraries'.[1]

1. 'Osnovnye položenija organizacii seti massovyh bibliotek.—V spravočnike Rukovod-jaščie materialy po bibliotečnomu delu [Basic Rules for the Organization of a Network of Public Libraries]', *Rukovodjaščie materialy. . .*, op. cit., p. 111–15.

Soviet public libraries are located for the most part on the territorial principle, readers being served where they live. In each area the library service is ensured by a system of republic, regional, central city, city, town, district, children's and village libraries. In each library area a permanent library serves the people living or working there. The division of the country into library areas is designed to enable the urban and rural population of any part of a town or other inhabited area to use a library or one of its branches not more than 10 to 15 minutes walking distance from home or work in towns, or not more than 30 minutes in the countryside. The size of the service area depends upon the number and density of the population and on other local conditions.

The official standards and principles of organization and location of the library system are laid down in 'Model Rules for the Organization of a Single Network of Public Libraries'.[1] It is envisaged by these standards and principles that all public libraries with general collections should form a single system, whatever department of government they are responsible to. This unified library network is based upon general principles concerning the location of the libraries, co-operation and co-ordination of their efforts and of their material resources.

One standard requires that a city or district ('rayon') library has a book stock of at least 3,000 volumes, calculated at four volumes per inhabitant, and a village library at least 1,500 volumes reckoned at five volumes per inhabitant. These standards apply both to adult and children's libraries. A city and a district library should employ one member of library staff per 1,000 population and 20,000 annual book issues, and a village library one member of staff per 600 library users and an annual issue of 10,000. These standards are under revision with a view to reducing the staff's work load. Union republics may adopt somewhat different, and lower, standards, depending on geographical, economic and other factors.

Rural libraries

In rural areas, each village council has in its territory at least one public library. The village council may have several libraries,

1. 'Primernye položenija organizacii edinoj seti massovyh bibliotek.—V spravočnike: Rukovodjaščie materialy po bibliotečnomu delu [Model Rules for the Organization of a Single Network of Public Libraries]', *Rukovodjaščie materialy. . .*, op. cit., p. 108–11.

depending upon the total number of inhabitants, the number and size of populated centres and the distances between them. A library should serve at least 1,000 inhabitants and the distance between libraries should be at least 1 kilometre, except in the far north, highly mountainous and other less accessible areas, where the standards for population are lowered.

If the village council has several libraries in its area, one is made central, organizes the library service for the whole of the population and co-ordinates the work of the other libraries. If the total population of a village council's area contains 500 or more school children of Grades 1 to 8 (aged 7–15 years), and pre-school children of 6 years of age or more, the village library must set up a children's department.

The book stock required by a village library is calculated on the basis of five books per reader and that of a central village library five books per inhabitant of the service area served by the central library plus 0.5 book per inhabitant of the village council seat. The initial book stock for a village library should be not less than 1,500 volumes.

The library service to adults and children who live in a district's administrative centre is provided by the district's central library for adults and its central library for children. These libraries act as centres of bibliographical and reference work, of organizational and methodological aid to village libraries and of the inter-library loan service of the district's libraries. Depending on the size of its population and territory, the district centre can have several public libraries run in factories and offices. The district library co-ordinates the work of all libraries in the district.

Urban libraries

In urban areas, in each city or town, administrative district of a city, or workers' community there is organized at least one library, not counting libraries in factories or offices.

One library is required for every 10,000 inhabitants in cities and for every 4,000 inhabitants in small towns with single-storey houses. Trade union libraries are set up in factories and offices with a staff of not less than 500. Smaller factories and offices are served by mobile libraries, book issuing centres and branches of nearby libraries.

Where urban centres have several public libraries one is usually made the central library. Urban centres divided into administrative districts set up central district or supporting libraries. These become centres for bibliographic and inter-lending services, methodological and organizational aid and co-ordinate all public libraries in their city, town or district.

Book stocks in urban public libraries are provided on a basis of four books per inhabitant of the area served. In the central district and central urban libraries there is added 0.5 book per inhabitant of the whole of the administrative area, city or town. The initial book stock of an urban library should be not less than 3,000 volumes.

In trade union libraries required book stocks are calculated on the basis of seven to eleven books per reader and the minimum initial book stock 1,000 volumes.

Every urban library must have at least two members of staff. Further additions to staff are required in accordance with the official 'Standard Staff Regulations for Public, Urban, District and Children's Libraries',[1] depending upon the size of the collections, the volume of work and the structure of the library.

The 'Model Rules for the Organization of a Single Network of Public Libraries' also govern the setting up of public libraries. A factory or office wishing to open a library must provide a minimum number of books, a regular source of finance, special library premises suitably equipped and at least one member of staff for the library.

All existing and new public libraries must be registered with the cultural department of the district, city or town, the regional cultural board or the Ministry of Culture of the respective autonomous republic.

The 'Model Rules for the Organization of a Single Network of Public Libraries' require that, in each Union republic, the Ministry of Culture and the councils of trade unions must work out a basic organization for the republic's library system, having regard to its national, physiographic, economic, demographic and cultural features. Experts have made a study of the existing library system

---

1. 'Tipovye štaty massovyh gorodskih, rajonnyh i detskih bibliotek [Standard Staff Regulations for Public, Urban, District and Children's Libraries]', *Rukovodjaščie materialy po bibliotečnoj rabote* [Instructional Materials for Library Work], Moscow, Goskul'tprosvetizdat, 1948, p. 131.

and their findings have provided a basis for standards for the public library system in each republic. Over the country as a whole the existence of these standards has enabled order to be brought into the existing public library system and has facilitated planning for its further advance.

In seeking further improvement in the library services to the population emphasis is currently being placed on the centralization, through a system of affiliation, of the network of State public libraries in urban and rural areas.

Unification of public libraries within a city or town or a rural area, of their collections, staff and other resources, holds out prospects of raising the level of library service through a more rational use of resources.

Library service for children

Under the Soviet system every child from 6 to 15 years of age is provided with library books without charge. The children are served by school libraries, children's libraries and children's departments attached to adult libraries. In all they are served by some 250,000 libraries of different types.

In practice almost every school child uses at least one library. More than 95 per cent of the 40 million pupils from Grades 1 to 8 (age 7 to 15) regularly use school libraries. Fourteen million children are served by the children's libraries controlled by the Ministry of Culture and as many by rural and urban public libraries for adults. The stock of books for children in school and children's libraries total over 576 million volumes or ten to eleven books per reader. School children constitute one of the most active categories of reader in the Soviet Union. Every young user reads on average twenty to twenty-five books yearly in the children's libraries alone and visits the library at least fifteen to twenty times a year.

The activities of libraries serving children are defined in the following documents: 'Model Rules for a Children's Library Controlled by the U.S.S.R. Ministry of Culture';[1] 'Rules for a

1. 'Primernoe položenie o detskoj biblioteke sistemy ministerstva kultury SSSR [Model Rules for a Children's Library Controlled by the U.S.S.R. Ministry of Culture]', *Rukovodjaščie materialy. . .*, op. cit., p. 118–20.

School Library';[1] 'Standard Statutes for the Provincial, Regional and Republic (A.S.S.R.) Children's Library';[2] and 'Model Statutes for the State Children's Library of a Union Republic'.[3]

Each school is required by the 'Standard Staff Regulations for Schools'[4] to set up a library which is to contribute to the intellectual and moral education of the children, fostering in them habits of systematic reading of suitable material.

The network of children's libraries controlled by the U.S.S.R. Ministry of Culture includes (in ascending order of size of area covered) children's libraries of the following kinds: district; urban; central town or city; regional or territorial; autonomous republic; and state children's libraries of the Union republics. All these libraries are institutions in their own right, have their own budgets and are subordinate to organs of the Ministry of Culture. Their staff requirements are defined in 'Standard Staff Regulations for Public, Urban, District and Children's Libraries' (see above).

Children's libraries serve pupils of grades 1 to 8, pre-school children, teachers and Young Pioneer leaders. The libraries supervise children's reading, undertake mass book promotion work and give methodological assistance to the district or town libraries, and to school libraries.

Where adult libraries have more than 500 child readers, but conditions do not permit the establishment of independent children's libraries, children's departments are set up. This department performs all the functions of a children's library.

The regional (*oblast*) and territorial (*krai*) children's libraries, and those of the republics, are research and methodological centres of library work with children in their respective administrative areas. They publish recommended bibliographies, study the state of library work, give publicity to and encourage the adoption of

1. 'Položenie o školnoj biblioteke [Rules for a School Library]', *Rukovodjaščie materialy. . .*, op. cit., p. 120–22.
2. 'Tipovoj ustav oblastnoj, kraevoj, respublikanskoj (ASSR) detskoj biblioteki [Standard Statutes for the Provincial, Regional and Republic (A.S.S.R.) Children's Library]', *Rukovodjaščie materialy. . .*, op. cit., p. 255–8.
3. 'Primernyi ustav gosudarstvennoj detskoj biblioteki Sojuznoj respubliki [Model Statutes for the State Children's Library of a Union Republic]', *Rukovodjaščie materialy. . .*, op. cit., p. 140–6.
4. *Tipovye štaty škol otražajutsja v sbornikah Prikazov i instrukcij Ministersv prosveščenija različnyh sojusnyh respublik (vyhodjat ežemesjačno)*. These are collections of orders and instructions of the ministries of education of the various Union republics; published monthly.

the most advanced methods of library work with children, arrange meetings, seminars, and other forms of theoretical and practical training for staff in children's, school and rural libraries, and participate in the running of refresher and other courses related to library work with children. The State children's library of a Union republic, fulfilling the functions of a national book depository, maintains the national bibliographic record of children's literature in the languages of the republic.

The children's libraries are governed by the following state instructions worked out exclusively for children's libraries: *Tables of Library Classification for Children's Libraries;*[1] *Minimum Library Techniques for School Libraries of the Ministry of Education of the R.S.F.S.R. (Instructions and Forms of Assessment);*[2] 'Rules for the Use of a Children's Library'[3] and others. In addition, certain instructions applicable to all public libraries are relevant: *Minimum Library Techniques in Public Libraries. Instructions and Forms of Assessment;*[4] *Unified Rules for the Description of Printed Works and the Organization of an Alphabetical Catalogue for Small Libraries,*[5] etc.

Participation of the public in library activities

In the Soviet Union, one of the most important principles underlying the organization of libraries is the extent to which the population are attracted to library work. This has a long tradition and takes many forms, the most widespread of which is the activity of library councils. Of the 2 million readers who play an active part, more than 500,000 are members of these councils.

A library council is organized at each public and research library. 'Rules for Library Councils'[6] defines the role of the councils

1. *Tablicy bibliotečnoj klassifikačii dlja detskih bibliotek* [Tables of Library Classification for Children's Libraries], Moscow, Kniga, 1964, 86 p.
2. *Minimum bibliotečnoj tehniki dlja bibliotek škol Ministerstva prosveščenija RSFSR* [Minimum Library Techniques for School Libraries of the Ministry of Education of the R.S.F.S.R. (Instructions and Forms of Assessment)], Moscow, Uchpedgiz, 1963, 38 p.
3. 'Pravila ispol'zovanija detskoj biblioteki [Rules for Use of a Children's Library]', *Rukovodjaščie materialy. . .*, op. cit., p. 149–50.
4. *Minimum bibliotečnoj tehniki v massovyh bibliotekah. Instrukcii i učetnye formy* [Minimum Library Techniques in Public Libraries. Instructions and Forms of Assessment], Moscow, Kniga, 1969, 126 p.
5. *Edinye pravila opisanija proizvedenij pečati i organizačii alfavitnogo kataloga dlja nebol'ših bibliotek* [Unified Rules for the Description of Printed Works and the Organization of an Alphabetical Catalogue for Small Libraries], Moscow, Kniga, 1970, 316 p.
6. 'Položenie o sovete biblioteki [Rules for Library Councils]', *Rukovodjaščie materialy. . .*, op. cit., p. 150–1.

as organs of collective direction of the library's activities and one of the means by which the working people exercise control. The council is made up of the library's most active readers elected for a term of one year at an annual meeting called to discuss the work of the library. The council of a children's library is formed of teachers, representatives of town and district public education authorities, school librarians, Young Communist League workers, and parents.

The U.S.S.R. Ministry of Culture has an advisory body, an inter-departmental library council, whose functions are set out in 'Rules for the Library Council under the U.S.S.R. Ministry of Culture'.[1] Members of the council are library experts and bibliographers. It sets up sections and commissions for research in which experts who are not members of the council participate. The council's decisions are circulated as recommendations. The Union and autonomous republics, territories and regions, cities, towns and districts also set up inter-departmental councils for library work. Their activities are governed by the 'Model Rules for Public-run Library Councils'.[2] The councils consist of representatives of public organizations, and of government departments controlling libraries, of factories and offices, and of library workers.

The Council on Library Acquisitions assists library systems and all government departments on a voluntary basis. This is set up under the 'Model Statute for a Council on Library Acquisitions'.[3]

Evidence of the growth of the voluntary principle in library work is the extensive use of volunteer substitutes for regular library staff to deputise on a permanent basis. More often than not, libraries with one paid worker have a regular volunteer deputy librarian who acts for the librarian when the latter is absent on business, on holiday or on sick leave.

A significant factor in raising the level of library work has been the help given by non-official methods experts, departments of culture and method centres, established on a voluntary basis. In this way many librarians themselves become voluntary workers.

1. 'Položenie o sovete po voprosam bibliotečnoj raboty pri Ministerstve kultury SSSR [Rules for the Library Council under the U.S.S.R. Ministry of Culture]', *Rukovodjaščie materialy*. . ., op. cit., p. 107–8.
2. 'Primernoe položenie ob obščestvennom sovete po bibliotečnoj rabote [Model Rules for Public-run Library Councils]', *Rukovodjaščie materialy*. . ., op. cit., p. 151–2.
3. 'Primernoe položenie o sovete po komplektovaniju bibliotek [Model Statute for a Council on Library Acquisitions]', *Rukovodjaščie materialy*. . ., op. cit., p. 154–5.

LIBRARY BUILDINGS AND EQUIPMENT

More than 4,000 new libraries are opened in the Soviet Union every year and many existing libraries have new premises. In designing and building modern libraries account is taken of the specific tasks facing libraries of different types and the need to give readers convenient conditions for effective work. Librarians and architects are assisted by the publication of rules and manuals such as *The Foundations of Library Planning;*[1] *Library Equipment;*[2] *Public Libraries in Towns (The Structure of the Network, Internal Accommodation and Buildings);*[3] *The Planning of Technical Libraries at Enterprises*[4] and others.

Detailed specifications for designing libraries of the various types are currently being worked out as well as 'Instructions' for the planning of public and research libraries, from whose standards are taken the examples given below.

SPACE STANDARDS

Libraries are major cultural and educational institutions, either housed in special buildings or in a non-library building, intended for the use of readers working with printed source material. They are also the repositories for various forms of printed and audio information. Library planning is based on *The Nomenclature of Basic Types of Libraries*, a manual which is approved by the Ministry of Culture of the U.S.S.R. (see Table 63).

Libraries, apart from their types, differ from each other according to their size, characterized by their stacks capacity and the number of stationary seats for readers, standards for which

1. *Osnovy proektirovanija bibliotek. Sbornik. Sost,* redaktor arhitektor G. V. Mejendorf [The Foundations of Library Planning. A Collection of Articles, ed. by G. V. Meiendorf], Moscow, Ministry of Culture of the U.S.S.R. Chief Library Inspectorate, 1967, 466 p.
2. *Bibliotečnoe oborudovanie* [Library Equipment], Moscow, 1967.
3. Ju. P. Obrosov and F. N. Paščenko, *Massovye biblioteki v gorodah (Struktura seti, pomeščenja i zdanija)* [Public Libraries in Towns. (The Structure of the Network, Internal Accommodation and Buildings.)], Moscow, Strojizdat, 1973, 176 p.
4. *Proektirovanie tehničeskih bibliotek predprijatij* [The Planning of Technical Libraries at Enterprises], Moscow, 1966, 62 p. illus. (GPNTB U.S.S.R. (State Public Scientific and Technical Library of the U.S.S.R.), Aids for Employees of Technical Libraries series).

TABLE 63

Book stock (000)	Number of readers' seats	Total working floor space of library (m²)
5	10	50–60
10	20	90–110
15	30	140–170
25	40	220–260
30	50	300–350
50	75	450–500
75	90	600–700
100	100	1,000–1,150
150	150	1,500–1,650
200	200	2,000–2,200
300	300	3,000–3,200
500	400–500	4,000–4,250
750	525–625	5,500–5,850
1,000	650–750	7,000–7,400
1,500	775–875	9,500–10,000
2,000	800–900	12,000–12,500

are given in the *Provisional Instructions on the Design of Buildings and Accommodation for Public and General Research Libraries.*[1]

Standards for calculation of areas in reading rooms
(for public and other types of research library)

Special reading rooms with open access to reference literature: (a) with individual reader's tables, 3 m² per reader; (b) with tables for two readers, 2.70 m²; (c) with multi-seating tables (seats one side only), 2.55 m².

General reading rooms: (a) with individual reader's tables, 2.70 m² per reader; (b) with two- or three-seat tables (seats one side only), 2.40 m²; (c) with multi-seated tables (seats both sides), 2.10 m².

Reading rooms with shelving arranged in alcoves, and with special supplementary literature in open access, and seating for readers in the alcoves (alcoves one stack high, 1.8 m between axes of stacks, with 180–200 volumes per m²): Area occupied by stacks and tables, 4.2 m² per reader.

Current periodicals reading room: for reading newspapers *in situ* at individual tables, 3.0 m² per reader.

1. *Vremennye ukazanija po proektirovaniju zdanij i pomeščenij massovyh i universal'nyh naučnyh bibliotek* [Provisional Instructions on the Design of Buildings and Accommodation for Public and General Research Libraries], Moscow, Stroīzdat, in press.

Readers' places for work with large format material: in situ at individual tables, 4.20 m² per reader.

Loan and book issue points in reading rooms

The space occupied by the foyer and lending department of the library, including the areas directly in front of issue desks, is regarded as a reading area. In small- and medium-sized libraries this includes the area taken by catalogues available to readers, exhibitions and readers' tables (for browsing and reading journals). Each seat for readers at such tables will require 1.80 m² and the number of seats provided in such cases should be 8 per cent to 10 per cent of the estimated number of readers simultaneously using the foyer or lending division.

The reading area of the lending department and foyers in public libraries, minus the area occupied by open access shelves, is calculated at 2.0 m² (1.75 m² for central city libraries) per reader and in general research libraries and in foyers of all types of research and academic libraries on the basis of 1.5 m² per reader.

The estimated number of readers in public libraries who can simultaneously use the reading area of the lending section, expressed as a percentage of all stationary seats in their reading rooms, is as follows:

Small libraries with stocks of 10,000 to 25,000 volumes, 25 per cent.

Small libraries with stocks of 25,000 to 50,000 volumes, 20 per cent.

Small libraries with stocks of up to 200,000 volumes and some medium-sized libraries (central city libraries) with stocks of up to 500,000 volumes, 15 per cent.

Medium-sized libraries (general research libraries) with stocks up to 1 million volumes, 5 per cent.

The estimated number of readers who can simultaneously be in the foyers of central city and research libraries of all types is 20 per cent of all stationary seats, irrespective of the size of the libraries.

The working space required for the issue desk and area behind it is, in public libraries, 4 m² per librarian on duty and, in central city and academic libraries 6 m².

The area occupied by open access shelves and passages is calculated on the basis of 200–250 volumes/m² of floor space, with five or six shelf stacks respectively. Groups of open access shelves should not exceed 50,000 volumes.

AREAS FOR GROUP STUDIES AND AUDITORIA

These are planned on the following bases: (a) group studies—at a common table for 10 to 20 persons, 1.80 to 2.10 m² per person; (b) lectures—groups of 20–40 persons seated at reading desks, 1.20 m²; (c) auditoria—with folding desks, 0.90 m²; (d) auditoria—without desks—for over 100 persons, 0.80 m².

STANDARDS FOR STAFF ACCOMMODATION

Among the standards are the following:

Receipt and unpacking of new accessions—12 m² for one worker plus 6 m² for every additional worker.

Receipt and technical processing of new accessions—4.50 to 4.80 m² per worker.

Cataloguing and classifying material—6 m² per worker.

Bibliographical work, information guides, abstract journals and union catalogues—6 m² per worker.

Typing, either in a special area or as part of general working space—3.2 m² per worker.

ADMINISTRATIVE, WORKSHOP AND AUXILIARY ACCOMMODATION

Room for three persons—4 m² per person. If more than three, 3.5 m² per person.

Private office for two persons (the director and deputy), not less than 12 m². If conferences are held in the room, 1.80 m² per participant should be added.

Bindery—10 to 12 m² per worker with a total floor space of not less than 24 m², including storage space.

Photographic laboratory—minimum of 36 m², plus 12 to 18 m², if there are two rooms.

CALCULATION OF AREAS FOR BOOK STACKS

The arrangement of stacks is more economical in larger libraries. The capacity of book stacks with double-sided cases of standard size with fourteen shelves, each of one linear metre, is calculated on the basis of the following standards per one square metre of space and one cubic metre of storage capacity:

In small- and medium-sized libraries, with stocks of up to 200,000 volumes, an average capacity of double-sided, one-metre-fourteen shelf stack is 700, requiring floor-space of 1.70 m², with 400 volumes per square metre as the standard.

In medium-sized libraries, with a stock of more than 200,000 volumes and up to 1 million, the capacity of each stack will be 725, floor space about 1.63 m², and the standard 425 volumes per square metre of floor space.

In large libraries, with a stock of over 1 million and up to 5 million volumes, and also in the biggest libraries with stocks exceeding this figure, the average capacity of each one-metre stack will be 750, occupying a floor space of about 1.55 m², with 450 volumes per square metre as the standard.

United Kingdom[1]

There is much contained in the major public library documents of the United Kingdom in the last fifty years—notably the Kenyon Committee's report of 1927,[2] the McColvin report of 1942,[3] and the Library Association proposals for the post-war development of the public library service of 1943,[4] which followed directly from this—which can be described as 'standards'. But until recent years such standards were mostly of the qualitative kind, discussing the objects of a public library service, the kind of library service needed, and the need for co-operation and the size of library authority required to provide an efficient service.

Central government interest in this subject was not greatly aroused until, in the wider context of a general reorganization of local government, it was required in 1957 to consider which local

1. This account refers particularly to England and Wales. The position in Scotland and Northern Ireland needs to be considered separately, and is not discussed here.
2. Board of Education, Public Libraries Committee, *Report on Public Libraries in England and Wales*, London, HMSO, 1927 (Cmd 2868).
3. Lionel R. McColvin, *The Public Library System of Great Britain. A Report on its Present Condition with Proposals for Post-war Re-organisation*, London, Library Association, 1942.
4. Library Association, *The Public Library Service. Its Post-war Re-organisation and Development. Proposals by the Council of the Library Association*, London, Library Association, 1943.

authorities, in a reorganized structure, should provide an independent public library service. There were nearly 500 local authorities in England and Wales authorized to provide public library services, ranging from parish councils and municipal and other urban authorities, and even county councils, with very small populations, to boroughs and counties with very large populations. There were forty-nine library authorities serving populations below 10,000 and seventy-four (including one county) below 20,000. At the other extreme there were thirty-one serving over 300,000 population. Moreover, there was very little tradition of co-operation between the library authorities at local level, save over the inter-lending of the more expensive, scarcer and less frequently demanded books.

In 1957 the government set up a committee, whose chairman was Sir Sidney Roberts, to consider the structure of the public library service in England and Wales and to advise what changes, if any, should be made in the administrative arrangements. This was a policy-making committee on which librarians were not strongly represented, Lionel McColvin and Edward Sydney being the two librarian members.

The committee reported in 1959.[1] It expected the number of public libraries and readers, and also the concept of the libraries' responsibilities, to continue to grow and the greatly increased educational provision and numbers receiving scientific and technological training to lead students and others engaged in industry and research to make more demands on the resources of the library, and the general public to make better use of them. Such inventions as wireless and television had also widened the interest of the public in books.

Public libraries, it said, existed to supply to any reader or group of readers the books and related material for which they might ask. This should take precedence over all ancillary services and should include a reference library where the reader might not only consult standard material but specialized books and journals. The public library should not only satisfy but promote the desire for books. This was particularly important in relation to children and young adults. There was need for co-operation between education and library authorities. The public libraries should help

---

1. Ministry of Education, *The Structure of the Public Library Service in England and Wales. Report of the Committee Appointed by the Minister of Education in September 1957*, London, HMSO, 1959 (Cmnd 660).

bodies concerned with adult education, hospitals and similar institutions. They were obvious centres for certain types of cultural
activity. The committee considered that public libraries should be
free libraries, and that freedom to borrow should extend to music,
gramophone records, photo-copies and other related material.

The committee regarded inter-library co-operation as essential.
It was considered no substitute for an adequate basic book stock,
and that no library could be self-sufficient.

The committee, in a questionnaire, asked if there was a figure
of annual expenditure below which an independent library service
could not be provided efficiently by a local authority, and if so,
what the figure was. Replies received were conflicting, the minimum annual expenditure proposed on the provision of books alone
varying between £22,000 and £2,000. The Library Association,
representing both library authorities and librarians, recognized
the desirability of striking a balance between contending views,
since the climate of opinion then was opposed to powers being taken
away from the smaller local authorities unless clearly necessary.

Based on a broad analysis of the approximately 20,000 titles
being published in Great Britain annually, the Library Association
estimated that, of the about 5,500 volumes of general or non-
specialized adult non-fiction, some 3,000 should be bought by
every library authority together with another 3,000 titles of fiction
and children's books. The cost of the 6,000 books was estimated
at £3,600. An additional number of volumes, not specified, would
need to be purchased for duplicates and replacements at an estimated cost of £1,400. Such a book stock, the association suggested,
would constitute a minimum for an efficient lending library.
Further expenditure would be required for reference books, periodicals and other materials. This was not detailed and the association
contented itself with updating its 1949 recommendation of two
shillings per head of population on books[1] to three shillings to
allow for price increases and declared that:

... any autonomous authority spending less than £5,000 annually on books must
give rise to disquiet . . . [and that] in the light of modern needs it would be
difficult for a case to be made out for the retention of autonomous library powers
by some authorities serving populations below 40,000.

1. Library Association, *A Century of Public Library Service. Where Do we Stand Today? The
Library Association Centenary Assessment*, London, Library Association, 1949.

In its report, the committee agreed generally with these views on the subject of a minimum book stock but proposed a slightly lower expenditure figure. It said that,

... if the public in any area was to enjoy reasonable access to books of general significance, the smallest library authority should be able to spend not less than £5,000 a year on the purchase of books of all kinds for the public library, ...

and proposed that the minimum annual expenditure on the purchase of books expected from a non-county borough or urban district as an independent library authority (excluding the cost of binding) should, at 1958 prices, be either £5,000 or two shillings per head of the population, whichever was the greater. It suggested that in urban libraries, non-manual staff should be employed on the basis of a chief librarian and at least one assistant per 3,000 population. In county areas it thought the ratio might be lower 'because the more scattered area is likely to make smaller demands on the personnel of the service'. Of this total staff, is considered that 40 per cent should be qualified.

In March 1961, the Minister of Education set up a working party

... to study the technical implications of the recommendations in the Roberts Report about the basic requirements for an efficient public library service, with particular reference to non-county borough[1] and urban district libraries with populations under 40,000.

This working party, with more technical assistance at its disposal than the Roberts Committee, was able to go into the subject of desirable standards in greater detail. Its report, issued in December 1962,[2] under the heading of 'Objectives and Functions', emphasized the need for public libraries to make adequate provision 'on the spot' of a wide range of books and related material for home reading or for reference in the libraries themselves, and to provide ready access to the wider range of material not immediately to hand, and makes a number of points applicable to all libraries, whether headquarters (or sole) libraries or branches.

1. The material provided must cover a wide range, be well balanced, and include new and standard works suited to the needs of the area.

1. 'Non-county boroughs' were the smaller boroughs, with less powers than the largest towns and cities.
2. Ministry of Education, *Standards of Public Library Service in England and Wales—Report of the Working Party Appointed by the Minister of Education*, London, HMSO, 1962.

2. All libraries should make special provision for children and encourage them to use the libraries. They should also try to cater for the needs of young adults.

3. All libraries should help readers to find books suited to their interests, by providing bibliographical tools, by developing readers' advisory services, and by publishing book lists, bulletins and arranging book displays.

4. The provision of an adequate reference and information service is essential. Information sought ranges from the simple to the highly complex and is increasingly of a scientific and technical nature. Such inquiries call for trained staff and for the provision of varying amounts of bibliographical and other source material. There should be at all significant service points a reasonable amount of quick reference material. To avoid unnecessary duplication public libraries should work in close association with libraries of local technical colleges and of other educational institutions and with other specialized libraries.

5. Public libraries have been one of the principal centres of cultural life in the community, most of them being associated with the schools and other educational institutions and with the educational and cultural work of local societies. The libraries may best provide cultural activities by supporting local societies but, where staff and premises are available, they may also arrange these activities.

6. Public libraries have for a long time been the resort of the student, particularly university and college students, in term-time and vacation, as well as senior pupils in secondary schools, part-time and day-release students at technical colleges, adult students attending evening classes and students working on their own. The libraries provide all these, in varying degrees, not only with room to study, but with many of the books they need. All public libraries must be prepared to play their part in meeting this need.

An appreciation of the quantitative standards proposed in this report depends to a great extent on understanding a concept of the working party of a 'basic library unit' defined thus:

The basic library unit which we have postulated for the purpose of establishing standards and on which are founded the standards to be adopted by larger units or systems at all levels of population, is the smallest unit capable of providing an adequate library service—as we define it—for the population it serves. In some cases this unit will be an independent library authority, while in others it will be a branch of a county system, or of a large city library.

Minimum standards for this 'basic library unit' were proposed by the working party because it was concerned to establish criteria by which the competency of many of the smaller urban library authorities to continue to exercise library powers could be judged. This question had to be considered not in relation to the service the alternative unit, the county council, could provide over the whole of its area, but the standard of service which it could, or was likely to, provide over the area administered by the independent urban library authority.

In addition to these minimum standards for a 'basic library service', the working party recommended standards of general applicability for all library authorities, with the proviso that either the basic standards or the general standards, whichever were the higher, should be met.

The quantitative standards recommended by the working party can be summarized as follows:

THE BASIC LIBRARY SERVICE

This was expressed not only in terms of a standard of annual addition of books, but also of convenient access to books other than those provided locally, of staff, and of the range of facilities necessary if full use is to be made of the library materials. These services could only be made accessible in urban areas by the provision of adequate suitably sited buildings and in rural areas by linking small branches or mobile library units to a larger library. The basic library service involved not only local provision as defined below, but also ready access to books not provided locally and not covered by existing arrangements for regional and national inter-library co-operation.

For the minimum requirement locally a library providing only the basic library service should:

1. Purchase annually the following library materials for lending purposes: not less than 2,000 titles (excluding pamphlet publications) of adult non-fiction from the new and older British publications, American and other English language publications from abroad, and music scores, together with 300 vol-

umes to allow for duplicates and replacements; not less than 300 volumes (excluding pamphlets) to augment or replace existing reference stock; not less than 3,000 volumes of adult fiction; not less than 1,500 volumes of children's books; a basic list of not less than fifty periodicals of general interest, with additional titles reflecting local industrial and business interests, periodicals of a local or regional nature and at least three major daily papers; not less than 100 volumes of fiction and suitable non-fiction books in the most commonly read foreign languages.

2. Maintain in its reference departments up-to-date editions of the majority of the items listed by the Library Association in a selection list of reference books or suitable alternative titles.

Excluding the periodicals, the items listed under 1 above involved an annual addition of a least 7,200 volumes, any provision of library service to schools or other institutions on an agency basis being additional to this.

The criteria proposed in the preceding two paragraphs presupposed that the library had an adequate stock. The stock should also be well balanced—breadth and suitability of subject coverage being no less important than the number of titles. The working party did not prescribe any standards for total book stocks.[1]

LIBRARIES GIVING MORE THAN THE BASIC SERVICE

Volumes added annually

The working party suggested as a complementary standard the purchase of 250 volumes per 1,000 population served (including ninety volumes of adult non-fiction for lending and reference purposes). Authorities should apply this standard, or the basic standard, whichever the higher. For example, a library serving a population of substantially less than 30,000 would be unable from its own resources to provide the total annual additions necessary for a basic library service unless the additions per 1,000 of the

1. The Department of Education and Science, in its Circular 4/65 on the Public Libraries and Museums Act, 1964, commented on this, stating that the evidence referred to in the working party's report indicated that a book stock of not less than 1.5 currently useful books per head of population might be considered reasonable for any authority of under 40,000 population but that an area which required the provision of several small branches would need more than this number of books.

population were increased to a figure higher than 250, with a consequent increase in the *per capita* cost. A library serving a population of 40,000 would normally be expected to add about 10,000 volumes a year.

Range of non-fiction titles added annually

A higher proportion of the adult non-fiction titles published annually would need to be provided than in the basic service. In a community of 100,000 population there would be a sufficient range of demand to justify the provision of most of the 5,000 to 6,000 non-fiction titles published annually suitable for inclusion in the lending stock of any library. Libraries serving between 30,000 and 100,000 population should, therefore, add (in addition to the basic 2,300 non-fiction titles for reference and lending) about 500 titles for every 10,000 population served up to 100,000. These and larger libraries would also need to add a proportion of the wide range of the more specialized British and American publications according to local needs.

Smaller branch libraries

Full-time branches serving a population of under 30,000 should aim to add to their stock annually 250 volumes (including ninety non-fiction) per 1,000 population. The majority of these should be recent publications, and the branches should receive full support from the system of which they formed a part. Such support should include the regular exchange of part of their stock, the supply on loan of material such as music scores, sets of plays and foreign literature and the circulation of special subject collections. Standard works in the main subject fields and the more important authors of adult and children's literature should be permanently represented in their stock in all but the smallest libraries.

OTHER STANDARDS GENERALLY APPLICABLE

The working party recommended the following standards for staff:
A minimum of one non-manual staff member to every 2,500 population served should be aimed at by all libraries.
The Roberts Committee's minimum standard requiring 40 per

cent of the non-manual staff to be qualified librarians was appropriate for municipal libraries serving up to about 100,000 population and for counties. In urban areas of concentrated population a ratio of about 33 per cent could be regarded as a reasonable minimum; in the largest cities the ratio might even be lower but should not be less than 25 per cent. No minimum number of qualified librarians was specified in libraries providing the basic service, but the principal tasks requiring adequate professional personnel were identified.

The view expressed by the Roberts Committee that there should be more specialized posts in libraries and more staff qualified to fill them was endorsed. This applied to reference librarians, children's librarians, readers' advisers, and to a growing extent to technical librarians and other specialists in the larger libraries. The working party considered the increased number of specialist librarians would not be forthcoming unless library authorities recognized the need to make many of these posts a career grade.

Libraries should include on their staff and provide training facilities for their fair share of professional trainees. Up to 10 per cent of the qualified staff recommended could reasonably be trainees who have passed the appropriate examinations but not qualified by length of experience in libraries.

The working party commented on the public library building standards proposed by the International Federation of Library Associations and the Library Association. It also made a number of general observations on the siting of library buildings and discussed the provision of branch and mobile libraries. Since its remarks on these points have been subsequently elaborated by the Library Advisory Councils and since the IFLA standards have been revised, these comments of the working party are not discussed further here.

LIBRARY SERVICE IN WALES

The working party proposed additional standards for libraries in Wales, a bilingual area. When it reported in 1962, Wales had a population of 2.5 million, nearly 700,000 speaking Welsh. There were, however, very wide variations in the proportions of Welsh-speaking to non-Welsh-speaking population in the various areas, ranging from as low as 2 per cent to nearly 90 per cent. The annual production of books in Welsh was low—of the order of 100 titles.

The working party considered that public libraries in Wales had a comparable responsibility for stimulating interest in and demand for Welsh books as for English books and recommended that all public libraries serving areas which included more than 1,000 Welsh-speaking people should buy at least one copy of all Welsh publications, except those clearly unsuitable for public library use. In respect of every 1,000 Welsh-speaking persons served, 50 of the 250 volumes recommended for purchase by every library authority, should be in Welsh. Every library authority serving more than 1,000 Welsh-speaking people should, in addition to the periodicals referred to in the general part of the report, purchase a reasonable proportion of periodicals in Welsh suitable for public library use. To achieve a proper standard of staffing an appreciable increase would be needed both in the number of bilingual librarians and in the total number of librarians employed in public libraries in Wales.

After the issue of the working party's report, and a parallel report by a second working party on the machinery for inter-library co-operation,[1] a new library law was passed, the Public Libraries and Museums Act, 1964.[2] This made great changes in the legal and administrative position of public libraries in England and Wales. Library powers were taken away from the small number of parish councils exercising them and the remaining library authorities given a duty to provide a comprehensive and efficient library service for all persons wishing to make use of it. This duty was defined in the following way:

In fulfilling its duty . . . a library authority shall in particular have regard to the desirability (a) of securing, by the keeping of adequate stocks, by arrangements with other library authorities, and by any other appropriate means, that facilities are available for the borrowing of, or reference to, books and other printed material, and pictures, gramophone records, films and other materials sufficient in number, range and quality to meet the general requirements both of adults and children; (b) of encouraging both adults and children to make full use of the library service, and of providing advice as to its use and of making available such bibliographical and other information as may be required by persons using it, and (c) of securing, in relation to any matters concerning the functions both of

1. Ministry of Education, *Inter-library Co-operation in England and Wales. Report of the Working Party Appointed by the Minister of Education*, London, HMSO, 1962.
2. The Public Libraries and Museums Act, 1964, chap. 75.

the library authority as such and any other authority whose functions are exercisable within the library area, that there is full co-operation between the persons engaged in carrying out these functions.[1]

The act laid a duty on the Secretary of State for Education and Science to superintend and promote the improvement of the public library service and to secure the proper discharge by library authorities of their responsibilities. It set up two advisory councils, one for England and another for Wales, to advise the Secretary of State on library matters, and authorized the Secretary of State to remove library powers from non-county boroughs and urban districts with populations under 40,000, their library powers to be taken over by the counties, and to permit certain urban authorities with populations over 40,000 served by the counties, not library authorities, to exercise independent library powers. Because the question of a general re-organization of local government continued to be under review, no action was taken to transfer library powers from smaller library authorities to county councils or to grant library powers to larger urban areas served by counties. This review resulted in the passing of the comprehensive Local Government Act 1972 under which the pattern of public library authorities will, from 1 April 1974, be radically changed.

In practice the number of separate public library authorities in England and Wales will have been reduced from 385 to some 117, with the addition of any district councils in Wales which are successful in their applications for library powers under the Act. Otherwise library powers outside Greater London will be exercised only by county councils[2] except in the major conurbations (referred to as 'metropolitan areas') in England where they will be exercised by new 'metropolitan district councils'. Both the new counties and the district councils in the conurbations will have large enough populations and resources to provide independently a comprehensive library service, though schemes of library co-operation and

1. Examples of the 'other authorities' referred to are education authorities and welfare authorities.
2. All the new counties exercising library powers will have larger populations than the corresponding existing counties, due to enlarged areas and to the fact that no longer will most of the larger urban areas within the county (including in many cases major towns and cities) be permitted to provide separate libraries, save as agents of the counties. There is provision for library powers in Wales to be granted to district councils applying for them if the Secretary of State for Education and Science considers it expedient to do so. In Greater London the borough councils and the City of London will continue as library authorities.

support service at different levels, local, regional and national will still be necessary.

Since, as a result of these reforms, most library authorities in England and Wales will, after 1974, have populations in excess of 200,000, the recommendations of the working party report as to the basic library service will have relevance only to the level of service provided by a county or district library authority in a metropolitan area to parts of their areas with an identifiable community of about 30,000 for which local provision at this level would be justified.

The rest of the working party's report will continue to have relevance. Although it is a purely advisory document, it has had, and to some extent continues to have, considerable influence on the central government and local authorities in regard to the requirements of an efficient and economical public library service. Future guidance to authorities on the level of provision of library service is, however, likely to be based on further studies or research.

Standards has been a subject in which the Library Advisory Councils for England and Wales set up under the 1964 Act have shown great interest. The councils appointed a joint committee to keep the question of desirable standards of library service under review and to consider what measures could be taken to encourage library authorities to improve the quality of their service. A result of the joint committee's work has been the official publication in 1971 of a document approved by the councils and submitted to the Secretary of State for Education and Science entitled *Public Library Service Points. A Report with Some Notes on Staffing*.[1]

The report of the advisory councils dealt in more detail than the working party with the considerations affecting the nature, location and staffing of service points, with particular reference to the need for the economical use of resources. They thought that, if the public libraries were to fulfil an increasingly educational function, facilities should be concentrated in larger libraries. They differed from the working party as to the distance between service points in urban areas. Given good public transport, car ownership and car parking, in urban areas a longer journey than a mile (the standard suggested) would be acceptable in order to obtain a

---

1. Department of Education and Science, Library Advisory Councils for England and Wales, *Public Library Service Points. A Report with Some Notes on Staffing*, London, HMSO, 1971.

full range of library services. They contemplated invariably in municipal areas, and commonly in counties, a library headquarters associated with the main service point, as well as 'district libraries' providing a full range of services at major focal points, probably serving a population of at least 25,000. Other service points, which would give access to the full range of the library's resources, would be required for those who needed largely recreational reading and might not have the incentive to make a longer journey to a larger library, and for those unable to travel to a library.

As well as commenting on a number of considerations to be borne in mind in planning library buildings, including possible joint provision of school and public libraries, the councils offered guidance about total areas to be provided in libraries serving populations below 10,000.[1] They considered it desirable to provide an area of at least 2,000 ft² (185.8 m²) in libraries open 30 hours a week or less.

Discussing staffing standards generally, the councils considered the working party's recommendations as still the most useful guide, despite the many changes in the conditions under which the libraries were operating compared with ten years previously. But they considered that, if library authorities were to be advised on the staffing levels necessary for the maintenance of an adequate and efficient service, research was necessary, entailing the use of scientific methods of work study, operational research and job evaluation.[2]

The views of the advisory councils on many points concerning the planning and administration of service points have been summarized below.

MAJOR SERVICE POINTS

Central libraries and administrative headquarters[3]

Usually associated with main service point. Usually where most comprehensive book stocks and highly specialized staff concentrated.

1. The standards proposed at that time by the International Federation of Library Associations and the Library Association offered guidance only in regard to populations of 10,000 and above.
2. The Secretary of State for Education and Science has authorized a research project on the lines recommended by the councils. This is being undertaken by the Local Authorities Management Services and Computer Committee and is expected to be completed in 1974.
3. In large authorities some administrative functions may be decentralized to district libraries.

The main provider of reference and information services and other specialized facilities for whole area.

With general responsibility to co-ordinate and supplement the resources of the other service points.

Opening hours not stated, clearly not less than 60 hours weekly recommended for district libraries.

District libraries

In both urban and rural areas, serving population of 25,000 or more.

Associated with shopping centres at major focal points well served by public transport.

With full range of library facilities, including reference and study accommodation on scale appropriate to likely use. May provide accommodation and other facilities of a cultural or educational nature.

Open at least 60 hours a week.

Staff

Central and district libraries—normally qualified staff on duty at all times in all public departments. Concentration of professional work may reduce the man-hours of qualified staff time needed in small branches.

OTHER SERVICE POINTS

Branch libraries

Probably sited close to local groups of shops.

Providing recreational service to adults, a basic collection of quick reference books, study spaces; large part of work may be with children, requiring special bookstock, staff and accommodation.

Book stock only representative in character and proportion changed frequently: (a) serving more than 4,000 population (shelf stock, 6,000; total stock, 8,000; opening hours weekly, 30); (b) serving less than 4,000 population (shelf stock, 5,000; total stock, 5,500–6,000; opening hours weekly, 15–20).

Staff

Branch libraries in urban areas
Work supervised by qualified librarians should include book selection, reference and information service, handling inquiries to be passed on to larger libraries, all aspects of service to children, the training of non-professionals partly involved in work in these categories. Amount of professional work will vary according to circumstances.

Branch libraries in rural areas
Libraries serving population over 6,000; qualified librarian on duty at all times.

Libraries serving populations between 4,000 and 6,000: supervised by qualified librarian, and have ready access to a qualified librarian; may at times be administered by senior non-professional staff.

Libraries serving populations between 1,500 and 4,000: need not normally be a qualified librarian on duty, should be supervised by qualified librarian and equipped with telephone.

Each part-time branch library should be attended by a qualified librarian for at least one-third of its hours of service.

Mobile libraries

Communities of less than 1,500, and many communities of between 1,500 and 4,000 close to large towns most economically served by mobile libraries.

Mobile libraries, including larger trailer libraries, may be necessary in parts of large urban areas.

Minimum stopping period, 15 minutes; more frequent stops preferable to longer stops.

Fortnightly visits normally adequate if sufficient number of books could be borrowed.

Staff: urban areas—under control of professional librarian, service staff need not be qualified; rural areas—normally staffed by qualified librarians.

NOTE ON REFERENCE SERVICES

The Working Party on Standards of Public Library Service was concerned only broadly with the standards for reference and information services and the Library Association in 1969 approved a report of its Reference, Special and Information Section containing detailed standards for reference services in public libraries serving four population groups: under 40,000; 40,000 to 100,000; 100,000 to 300,000; over 300,000.[1]

United States of America[2]

The American Library Association has been concerned with 'standards' since 1917, concentrating first mainly on grading of staff and qualifications of librarians. As early as 1921 it proposed a national minimum financial standard for public library service of $1 per head.

In 1933 the association adopted the first statement in which the phrase 'standards for public libraries' was used. This was largely general but it contained several references to quantitative measurements which were widely used during that period. Continued was the $1 *per capita* minimum library figure with certain qualifications. The exact minimum depended on the size, location and character of the community. The small city must usually spend more than $1 *per capita* to cover essentials, or reduce unit costs by enlarging the area of service and support.

Noteworthy was the introductory statement setting forth the objectives of the public library. Least specific were the attempts

1. Library Association, 'Standards for Reference Services in Public Libraries', *Library Association Record*, Vol. 72, No. 2, February 1970, p. 53–7.
2. Some references to standards for individual states are:
    California: 'Public Library Service Standards in California', *News Notes of Californian Libraries*, Vol. 58, No. 2, spring 1963.
    South Carolina: *Standards for South Carolina Public Libraries*, Public Libraries Section, South Carolina Library Association, 1964.
    Connecticut: *Minimum Standards for Public Libraries in Connecticut*, Connecticut Library Association, 1966.
    Missouri: *Missouri Library Service—A Guide to its Development and Standards of Service*, Missouri State Library, Jefferson City, 1963.
    Oklahoma: *Oklahoma Public Libraries Goals for 1975*, Advisory Committee on Public Library Standards for the Board of the Oklahoma Department of Libraries, 1969.

to define 'reasonably adequate library service' or what constitutes a collection 'adequate to the needs of the community' and 'a professional staff of high quality and adequate number'. The standards provided the basis for minimum standards for many of the states, particularly those working on requirements for grant-in-aid programmes. In 1938, when the document was revised, many important concepts, such as inter-library co-operation, were discussed and endorsed. 'Regional systems' were recommended.

Subsequently, the National Resources Planning Board, part of the Executive Office of the President, gave a grant to the American Library Association for the formulation of working standards for public library service, which would act as a guide to library development during the post-war period. Thus, the American Library Association provided in 1943 the most comprehensive document to date, *Post-war Standards of Public Libraries*.

In the new document the association's Committee on Post-War Planning discussed how it arrived at its recommendations and provided some definitions of terms.

Standard is defined as a qualitative and quantitative measure expressed in general or statistical terms, which may be used as a criterion or test in evaluating the adequacy and efficiency of public library service. Broadly considered, library standards should provide measures of organization and administration, personnel services and book resources, support and operating costs and physical equipment. In all these fields the two concepts of adequacy and efficiency must be emphasized. Library service should be 'adequate' in the sense that its general level is sufficient and suited to community needs; it should also be 'efficient', in the sense that maximum results are achieved with the resources available.

Several methods of stating standards were employed to make them as acceptable to a small community as a very large one. They were expressed in general qualitative terms, in numerical measures, in terms of satisfactory minimum services regardless of population served, in terms of proportions or ratios, and in terms of specific and essential items of public library service.

The committee, while still quoting figures of *per capita* support of $1 for limited or minimum service, $1.50 for reasonably good service, and $2 for superior service, considered that a total minimum budget of $25,000 was necessary to provide those kinds of library services described as essential, regardless of the size of the community, and that exact *per capita* standards of support did not apply to libraries serving populations below 25,000.

The committee published, in 1948, a *National Plan for Public Library Service*, which included much of the data collected in a second stage of evaluating the existing library services, and presented a blueprint for the future, recommending, *inter alia*, the development of larger units of library service, with varying patterns of organization including county, regional, state and or federal units each with a minimum income of not less than $37,500 (an increase from the previously recommended $25,000); and strengthening of state library leadership, financial support, auxiliary and supporting services, and resources towards ' . . . the development of an efficient and integrated system of public libraries.'

In 1950, a further study was published, *The Public Library in the United States*, the summary and final volume of the *Public Library Inquiry* proposed to the Social Science Research Council by the American Library Association and supported by a Carnegie Corporation grant. This was an ' . . . appraisal in sociological, cultural and human terms of the extent to which the librarians . . . were . . . achieving their objectives' and, at the same time ' . . . an assessment of the public library's actual and potential contribution to Americans socially'.

The *Public Library Inquiry* made two significant observations: (a) that adequacy of public library service could not be described in terms of *per capita* support but must be expressed ' . . . in terms of numbers and kinds of staff members, and of types and quantities of new materials needed to provide a modern library service'; and (b) $100,000 was the dividing line between an adequate and inadequate annual budget for a single public library system regardless of size.

In 1956, the American Library Association published a new statement of recommended standards, *Public Library Service*[1] and in the same year the Library Services Act was passed as the first federal grants-in-aid programme for public library purposes. Combined, these two events resulted in a greater impact on the public libraries of the United States than either would singly.

Reflected in the 1956 document are many of the findings, the recommendations and the philosophy expressed in earlier publications already mentioned and in the standards developed by the

---

1. American Library Association, *Public Library Service: A Guide to Evaluation with Minimum Standards*, Chicago, Ill., 1956.

State of California. But the 1956 standards differed from those proposed twelve years earlier; for example, *per capita* expenditures were not included. Over the years administrators had found that, when taken out of context, these figures were all too often misleading. Without a total budget of sufficient proportion, one which will provide the essential services, resources and facilities, no public library can consider itself adequate regardless of *per capita* expenditure. It was also a conclusion of *Public Library Service* that *per capita* costs in smaller places must be at a substantially higher rate than that of larger communities.

Emphasis on quality of service may be considered a major contribution of the 1956 standards. Other emphasized concepts are: availability of total library resources in the local community itself; importance of the educational role of the public library; organizational flexibility in the development of systems; and partnership of local, state and federal resources.

Public Library Service presents some seventy guiding principles, basic to the establishment of standards. Under each of these, various standards were delineated as providing the best possible means of effecting the principles. A total of 191 standards are included. Basic to the understanding of the document is the concept of library systems. The 1956 standards give strong support to the need for and importance of co-operation and joint action as the best means of assuring adequate nation-wide public library service. *Public Library Service* urged libraries to 'band together formally or informally, in groups called "systems" and the standards outlined are for "systems of library service" '. With so many demographic variations in the United States it was not possible, and did not appear desirable, to prescribe a fixed pattern of organization and size for public library systems. Individual states can more readily translate the recommended concept of systems in terms of its own geographic area and population density and more precise individual state standards.

The foregoing history up to 1956 is based on *State Standards for Public Libraries* by Vainstein and Magg, issued in 1960 by the U.S. Department of Health Education and Welfare.[1] This states that, in 1959, twenty states and one territory had formulated their

1. United States Department of Health, Education and Welfare, *State Standards for Public Libraries*, Washington, D.C., 1960 (Bulletin 1960, No. 22).

own standards, eleven states had adopted American Library Association standards or had recommended their adoption, ten were considering the preparation of their own state standards, and nine states and two territories had no standards. Doubtless the position has improved since that date and more state standards are based on or are influenced by current American Library Association standards.

The standards were thoroughly revised and reissued in 1966 under the title of *Minimum Standards for Public Library Systems, 1966,* and the writer thinks that because so much thought has been given to this subject in the United States, an extended account of the current standards will be useful.[1]

The first chapter repeats what was written as an introduction in 1955. This provides what one might call the very first standard in answer to the question: Why should the public library exist at all?

The public library is a way of escape from the narrow area of our individual lives into the field, finite no doubt, but unbounded, of the vision and experience of all mankind. . . . The key to the broader world is the possession of books, but, if the door stands open, there is no need of a key. It is the business of the public libraries to keep the door open and see that no stumbling block lies in the way of those who would enter. . . . This is not to be construed as a suggestion that the library should attempt to set itself up as a pedagogue to the nation. . . . Our need is for a clearer and keener perception of the nature and magnitude of the problems on which our men and women of voting age must pass judgement. . . . This implies the necessity of making access to the truth easy and rapid for anyone who seeks it. For the overwhelming majority, the quickest and easiest access to the world's best thought is through the public library.

The next chapter, headed 'Services and Standards: An Essential Partnership', describes the functions of the library by reference to the materials and services provided and how they should be used: e.g. (a) materials—to facilitate informal self-education of all people in the community; to meet the informational needs of all; and (b) services—the organization of material to make it easily accessible to potential users; lending procedures to ensure that materials may be used at the time and place desired by the public; a programme of public information to make its resources not only available but eagerly sought by its community. It says

1. American Library Association, *Minimum Standards for Public Library Systems*, Chicago, Ill., 1967.

that: 'These minimum functions underlie modern library service, without which the child and the citizen are denied reasonable opportunity to develop.' It refers to the concept of library systems. Finally it describes how the standards can be used 'as a guide to total evaluation of library service'. It explains that the rest of the report contains sixty-six guiding principles, which constitute the substance of the document.

[These] . . . are not standards, but are basic to establishing standards. They require interpretation when applied to individual libraries. They cannot be used like a yardstick which determines the length of an object without requiring any particular skill on the part of the user.

Under the guiding principles are the standards. Some principles have one standard, some several and a few no standards at all.

But wherever a standard appears it is objective, observable and, at least in a broad sense, quantitative. Each provides a measure of achievement of the guiding principle under which it stands.

The report says that the answers to the question: 'Why bother with the principles, why not simply present the standards?' are essential to understanding the nature of the document. The standards alone provide only a partial evaluation of a library and may even, on occasion, provide an erroneous evaluation. The specific standards taken together constitute the minimum public library service to which the people in every community are entitled and are the essential elements found in those libraries which have achieved a reasonable degree of adequacy.

The next chapter, 'Structure and Government of Library Service', describes the organization of library service considered necessary to meet and maintain sound conditions. This contains principles and detailed standards dealing with the following topics: availability and accessibility of public library service; headquarters work, what they should provide; headquarters and local libraries should co-operate; legal basis of establishment, governmental organization and financial support; local library to be an integral part of local government; respective functions of governmental authority and library director; public, school and academic libraries to provide co-ordinated service to students; the role of the state; and the role of the federal government. This chapter necessarily contains few quantitative standards. One worthy of note is that the maximum travel time to the library should be 15 minutes for urban areas and 30 minutes for rural areas.

The chapter 'Service' describes in considerable detail what this should consist of and how it should be organized. A preamble refers to the services performed by the local library as:

Logical organization of materials for convenient use through shelf arrangement, classification and cataloguing; lending of materials so that they may be used in the location and at the time suited to each individual.

It describes what this service should consist of and how it should be organized, as follows:

The services of the system's specialists should be available to the staffs of member libraries and bookmobiles and through them to the users of those agencies. The library system should provide full-time reference service competent to handle inquiries received about general topics and specific subjects important to the life of the community. Modern equipment to secure information should be utilized wherever advisable and advantageous to provide fast, quality service.

The 'principles' and 'standards' derived from them refer mainly to matters which are central to the American 'systems', such as:

Every person whose community (i.e. local) library participates in a system receives experienced service.

The programme of each library system and its member libraries should be focused upon clear and specific objectives.

Library systems must co-ordinate service with other resource centres.

Well planned hours of service must be maintained by all units in a library system.[1]

The public library provides for full utilization of its materials off the premises.

Each library system should provide lending and inter-agency loan

1. The standard under this heading states that: ' . . . the central resource library should be open at least 66 hours a week, and should be open all hours the member libraries are open to give holdings and bibliographical information either by telephone or other medium or communication. Community libraries serving 10,000 to 25,000 population should be open between 45 and 66 hours weekly. Community libraries serving 25,000 population and over should be open between 66 and 72 hours a week.'

practices which make for uniform, co-ordinated service over the whole area served (e.g. inter-availability of tickets and return of material to any library in the system).

Public library service requires the use of all sources of information and all forms of material.

Library systems should provide informational and research services.

The library system provides materials and services for groups and institutions.

The library system serves individuals and groups with special needs.[1]

The public library sponsors group activities inside or outside the library within the framework of its own programme.

Good public library service requires an effective public relations programme.

The next and perhaps the most important chapter, 'Materials: Selection, Organization and Control', deals with such matters as:

Materials—both book and non-book materials—being selected, retained or discarded in keeping with the stated objectives of the system.

Materials acquired meeting high standards for quality in content, expression and form.

Collections being built to meet the needs and interests of people.

Collections containing opposing views on controversial subjects.

> The public library does not promote particular beliefs or views. It provides a resource where the individual can examine issues freely and make his own decisions.

Systematic removal of material no longer useful being essential to maintaining the purposes and quality of resources. Average annual withdrawals from community library collections should be at least 5 per cent. No specific figure is recommended for headquarters libraries.

The community library standing as the first and convenient resource of all readers, calling on larger collections to meet the

---

1. The list of groups under this heading includes not only the conventional ones, such as the physically handicapped, the homebound, inmates of hospitals and institutions, the senior citizens and the retired but also the intellectual and creative persons.

needs of readers with specialized interests and to supplement and enrich its resources for all users.[1]

The character and emphasis of the community library collection being influenced by the existence of other libraries in the area.

A library system having resources covering the interests in the several communities it serves, in reasonable duplication to meet most requests immediately.[2]

There follow standards for materials for systems collections for populations from 150,000 to 1 million. It is assumed that the system serves at least this minimum population, a figure generally agreed to ensure economical use of staff, collections and funds.

Titles

The community library should add the following proportion of new adult non-fiction titles published in English in the United States each year: 10,000–24,999 population, 10–15 per cent; 25,000–49,999, 15–25 per cent; 50,000–99,999, 25–35 per cent. The proportion of juvenile holdings in the total system should be a minimum of 25 per cent to a maximum of 40 per cent. When the total collection is distributed through many facilities, the proportion which is juvenile should be increased. No more than one-half of these should be new titles. In general, two-thirds of the annual additions for children should be replacement or duplicate copies of older works. Even the largest systems should not exceed 1,000 to 1,200 titles annually.

The headquarters collection should contain at least a basic 100,000 adult non-fiction titles and should add approximately 50 per cent of the adult non-fiction trade titles published in English

---

1. At this point is the first set of significant quantitative standards, indicating the percentage of adult non-fiction material which should be locally owned relative to the adult non-fiction requests. The remainder of the requests would be met by inter-library loan. The following are the percentages of adult non-fiction materials locally owned: under 10,000 population, 35–50 per cent; 10,000–24,999, 50–65; 25,000–49,999, 65–80; 50,000–99,999, 80–95. A minimum of 80 per cent of the juvenile material requested should be available locally; the waiting time for reserved materials should not exceed six weeks; reductions of loan periods should not be imposed in lieu of duplication of copies.

2. The comment on this principle is that 'more important than total volume is rate of current acquisitions, particularly in a new library. Quantitative figures to achieve an inclusive collection of this kind will vary, but should not fall below the following levels unless special conditions in a region make some of the usual resources unnecessary'.

in the United States each year in sufficient duplication to meet needs. It should have available a comprehensive collection of older as well as current fiction by American and foreign authors.

Volumes

The total system collection should own resources of at least 2 to 4 volumes *per capita*, and at least 2 volumes *per capita* in areas serving 1 million population.

Maintenance of system collections

Collections should be maintained by annual additions and replacements of not less than one-sixth of a volume *per capita* in areas serving up to 500,000 population; one-eighth of a volume *per capita* in areas serving over 500,000 population. Up to one-third of the volumes added annually should be for children. These should be chosen on the basis of the characteristics and needs of the area. At least 5 per cent of its annual additions should be materials of specific interest to young adults.

Pamphlets

Pamphlet collections should be maintained in system headquarters. Sufficient quantities of more generally useful items should be acquired to serve system needs.

Periodicals

At least one currently published periodical title should be available for each 250 people in the service area. Headquarters collections should receive all current periodicals ordered in *Readers' Guide to Periodical Literature* and the most frequently requested items indexed in other indexing services. Less frequently requested items should be available from a state or regional resources centre.

Indexing services

Headquarters collections should acquire a broad range of indexing services.

Government documents

Systems headquarters will be or have access to a selective United States government documents depository and will acquire local, state and international documents on a selective but systematic basis.

Audio-visual materials

Standards for films and recordings and other material are suggested for systems with access to a resource collection at state or regional level. These, however, have been superseded by a later document.

Other factors

The state or a group of states should help the local library and the supporting library system, by providing research resources. This can be done by making public supported research library facilities, e.g. in universities or large city libraries, available to library systems. Other principles and standards refer to selection, acquisition, and cataloguing, etc., processes and to the organization and control of the material acquired.

In the sixth chapter the report deals with staffing requirements. The principles and the more detailed standards stated refer mainly to points such as positions in the library being part of a career service; positions being clearly defined and differentiated in terms of requirements, duties and responsibilities; staff members to have qualifications for competent performance of their duties; conditions of employment and salaries; qualifications and number of staff.

The more obviously quantitative standards are the following: professional and sub-professional staff should be approximately one-third of the total; professional staff are defined as having five years of formal education beyond secondary schooling including graduation from a library school; sub-professionals should be college graduates and should, preferably, be working towards graduate library education.

One staff member should be the minimum provision for each 2,000 people in the service area.

Professional staff members should be available to provide professional services to the public at all hours when libraries are open. No proportion of the professional to non-professional staff is proposed. Indications are given of the aspects of library service for which at least one professional staff member should be appointed and subject specialists may be required; an example is given of a library system serving 100,000 people requiring at least sixteen or seventeen professional and sub-professional librarians. But, in an addendum issued in 1967, it was stated that for every 6,000 population served, there should be one professional and two clerical. It is also said that the committee was unable to suggest a ratio between professional and sub-professional and recommends further study of this question.

The report recommends that the state library agency should have personnel adequate to provide the leadership, general guidance, planning and specialized information service needed at state level, and that state governments should establish and enforce certification regulations covering professional positions in the libraries.

Finally, the seventh chapter refers to premises, dealing with the following:

What the physical facilities of a public library should express, how a planning team should set about planning a library and what it should be like—inviting and easy to use.

The building should be efficient, flexible and expandable. Appropriate and adequate quality and quantity of lighting and other mechanical equipment should be provided.[1]

Furniture and equipment should contribute to the efficiency of the library, and provide a comfortable inviting environment.

Headquarters building of a library system should be located and designed to provide maximum accessibility and space for the full range of library service needed.[2]

Similar recommendations are made in respect of the premises of a community, or local, library, and reference is made to the

1. The intensity of lighting recommended in most circumstances is 50 foot candles of maintained intensity, defined as about two-thirds of the new installation intensity, on the reading surfaces; air conditioning and humidity control for materials preservation and human comfort to be used where climate conditions have caused such equipment to be used in modern commercial buildings.
2. The site for a public library should have heavy pedestrian traffic; be convenient to public transport, and have conveniently available car parking; the major space in a public library should be allocated to materials, seating and services to adults; multipurpose rooms should be provided for meetings, viewing and listening by groups and individuals. Space must be provided in the library system for the activities of the library extensions programme. A list of spaces, the need for which should be considered, is given.

need to provide mobile stops in smaller centres within reach of all age groups.

Particularly significant is that no recommendations are made about space standards for any purpose, or size of any equipment.

A second currently useful document, was issued in 1962 by the Public Library Association, a division of the American Library Association, called *Interim Standards for Small Public Libraries*.[1] These standards were designed to refer to small libraries, both those within systems and independent libraries with no immediate prospect of joining systems. The production of this document was controversial. Some librarians considered that no separate standards should be established for small libraries which should become part of library systems as soon as possible. Others argued that since two-thirds of the libraries in the United States served populations of under 10,000, these libraries required some standards by which they could evaluate their service. The term 'interim standards' in the title of the document was carefully chosen to indicate that the statement referred to interim goals until the libraries could meet the standards set out in the major document.

'Small library' is not defined but standards are given for libraries serving up to 50,000 population. They refer to libraries with a separate identity with their own governing body, not to branches of a library serving a large area. Forty per cent of the libraries serve population of less than 2,500 and it was the opinion of the drafting committee that libraries in such areas should meet qualitatively the standards set for libraries serving 2,500 population.

In preparing its recommendations, the committee refers to the help derived from the existing standards for libraries which had been prepared by twenty of the fifty states. The standards follow similar chapter headings and approach to those in the main document. The text is greatly simplified and applies only to the requirements of community or local libraries and their relations with the systems to which they may belong. What is particularly important about this document is that a considerable number of quantitative standards of a numerical character are given including, for the first time in the United States, a table of space requirements. The numerical standards are given below.

---

1. American Library Association, *Interim Standards for Small Public Libraries*, Chicago, Ill., 1962.

Opening hours

Minimum opening hours on a sliding scale are proposed: under 2,500 population, 15 hours; 25,000 to 50,000 population, 60 hours. Mobile libraries should visit at least fortnightly with stops of sufficient length to offer a readers' advisory service.

Books and non-book materials

Libraries serving populations from 5,000 to 50,000, a minimum of 2 books *per capita*.
Libraries serving populations up to 5,000, access to a minimum of 10,000 volumes, or 3 books *per capita* (whichever is greater) made up of its own basic collection plus the volume available for changing collections on a sliding scale ranging from: (a) a population of under 2,500, 40 per cent basic collection, 60 per cent changing collection; to (b) 25,000–49,999 population, 90 per cent basic collection, 10 per cent changing collection.

Periodicals

Minimum collection maintained on a sliding scale as follows: from (a) a population of under 2,500, at least 25 magazines and newspapers to be kept for 1–5 years; to (b) 25,000–49,999 population, 100–150 magazines and newspapers to be kept for 1–10 years.

Long-playing discs or recordings

Record collections as follows (if not purchased or given, they can be provided from a resource centre): from (a) a population of 2,500–4,999, a minimum collection of 100–150, with minimum additions or replacements of 35–50; to (b) 25,000–49,999 population a minimum collection of 500–1,000, with minimum additions or replacements of 150–300.

Staff

Many variables govern the size of the staff, such as population, area served and the programme of the library. One staff member (full-time or equivalent) should be the minimum provision for

Table 64

Population	Pro-fessional	College graduate	Library assistant	Clerical	Page	Total
Under 2,500	—	1	—	—	0.5	1–1.5
2,500–4,999	—	1	—	0.5–1	0.5–1	2–3
5,000–9,999	1	1	1–2	0.5–1	0.5–1	3–5
10,000–24,999	1–2	1	2–3	1–2	1–2	6–10
25,000–49,999	2–6	1–2	3–6	2–4	2–3	10–21

each 2,500 in the service area. Table 64 gives a proposed distribution (non-manual staff). Education and training qualifications, and how many professional librarians should be with experience, are prescribed.

Premises

A table is given for shelving space and related floor space; reader space; staff work space; additional space (e.g. for services, staircases, meeting rooms); and total floor space. Examples of space requirements are given in Table 65.

A further United States document is *Standards for Children's Services in Public Libraries*[1] prepared by a sub-committee of the Public Library Association and issued in 1964. This again follows the pattern, philosophy and definitions of *Public Library Service* and amplifies the standards as they apply to children's public library services. These standards assume that children's needs can be satisfied by libraries working in library systems. The document contains only qualitative standards describing how in principle the needs should be satisfied. No strictly quantitative standards are given, it being stated that this was 'because of the temporary validity of quantitative standards and the lack of supporting evidence for them'.

On mobile libraries, the American Library Association issued in 1963 a publication *Standards of Quality for Book Mobile Service*, which gives principles and criteria for evaluating such services.[2]

1. American Library Association, *Standards for Children's Services in Public Libraries*, Chicago, Ill., 1964.
2. American Library Association, *Standards of Quality for Book Mobile Service*, Chicago, Ill., 1963.

TABLE 65

Space requirement	Population 5,000–9,999	Population 25,000–49,999
Size of book collection	15,000 vols. plus 2 books *per capita* for population over 5,000	50,000 vols. plus 2 books *per capita* for population over 25,000
Linear feet of shelving	1,875 linear ft (581 m); add 1 ft (0.30 m) shelving for every 8 books over 15,000	6,300 linear ft (1,920.24 m); add 1 ft (0.30 m) of shelving for every 8 books over 50,000
Amount of floor space	1,500 ft² (139.35 m²); add 1 ft² (0.09 m²) for every 10 books over 15,000	5,000 ft² (464.51 m²); add 1 ft² (0.09 m²) for every 10 books over 50,000
Reader space	Min. 700 ft² (65.03 m²) for 23 seats; add 4 seats per 1,000 over 5,000 population served at 30 ft² (2.79 m²) per reader space	Min. 2,250 ft² (209.04 m²) for 75 seats per 1,000 over 25,000 population served at 30 ft² (2.79 m²) per reader space
Staff work space	500 ft² (46.45 m²); add 150 ft² (13.94 m²) for each full-time staff member over 3	5,250 ft² (487.74 m²)
Additional space needed	1,000 ft² (92.90 m²)	5,250 ft² (487.74 m²)
Total floor space	3,500 ft² (325.16 m²) or 0.7 ft² (0.065 m²) *per capita*, whichever is greater	15,000 ft² (1,393.54 m²) or 0.6 ft² (0.056 m²) *per capita*, whichever is greater

The Film Library Information Council, formed in 1967 by public library audio-visual department heads, immediately set up a standards committee. The American Library Association, Public Library Association, about the same time set up an audio-visual committee which decided that its first priority was the establishment of standards in these media for public libraries. The two bodies have worked together to produce a set of guidelines for audio-visual services, published in 1970.[1] The authors consider

1. American Library Association, *Guidelines for Audio-visual Materials and Services for Public Libraries*, Chicago, Ill., 1970.

that the audio-visual inventions of the past hundred years are comparable to the invention of movable type in the fifteenth century in their implications for librarians and educators and, because the new resources are evolving and changing to such an extent, they recommend that guidelines for audio-visual resources in public libraries must be expanded or revised every three years.

The standards are for public libraries and library systems serving populations of 150,000 or more. The American Library Association does not recommend formation of a library system for a lower population. The form of the document follows that of the *Minimum Standards for Public Library Service, 1966*, with which it may be incorporated in due course.

The document contains advice about local, state and federal levels of responsibility for audio-visual services, and proposes that the newer resources should be lent on inter-library loan like any other material. It gives advice on the organization of the service as a whole, of its material, staff, space and equipment. But most of its recommendations are quantitative and the notes following concentrate on these.

Materials and servicing staff

Not less than 20 per cent of the library's or system's materials budget should be allocated for audio-visual materials. Non-print resources need repair and replacement at the rate of 10–15 per cent per annum of the audio-visual materials budget.

Film collections
Some examples of minimum standards for film collections are given in Table 66.

TABLE 66

Population (thousands)	No. of 16 mm prints	No. of 16 mm prints added each year
150–300	300	30
500–750	600	50
1,000–2,500	2,000	150
5,000 and over	3,000	200

Staff for servicing film collection is based on the following formula: staff per number of 16 mm prints +staff per area in square miles +staff per population equals total staff required, example:

	Population	Area	No. of 16 mm prints	Total staff required
	350,000	700 sq. miles	600	
Staff:	1½	2	1½	5

Sound recordings
One disc, reel of tape, cassette or cartridge tape for each fifty people in the area served, to include the total resources of constituent facilities or member libraries, as well as the systems headquarters collections, but not less than 5,000 discs or reels; 20 per cent of library or system's collection to consist of non-musical tapes or records.

Other media
The present state of development makes it impossible to set standards for certain media but absolute minima are suggested: (a) 8 mm 'single concept' films, 100 in any one format; (b) television, videotape and other electronic media—100 titles; (c) slides arranged in sets arranged by subjects—50 sets.

Space and equipment
For a system or regional service centre serving a population of 150,000 with a staff of three a minimum space of 1,000 ft² (92.9 m²) is needed. Additional space should be allocated or planned to accommodate the growth of collections and staff. Within the system served there should be at least one public meeting room large enough to conduct all types of audio-visual programming for groups of 100 or more. In addition, each branch should have a suitable space available for this purpose.

Statistics
Audio-visual statistics are important in planning budgets, in allocating staff, and in making decisions affecting future service. Standardization is imperative so that statistics may be used for such planning purposes, for comparison with systems and among public libraries nationwide.

In 1972 the Public Library Association, American Library

Association published a further document, *A Strategy for Public Library Change: Proposed Public Library Goals—Feasibility Study*.[1] This examines the development of the public library in the twenty years since the *Public Library Inquiry* (1950), and describes its current status in terms of strengths and weaknesses. The authors make far-reaching recommendations for directing attention to the public library as an agency for meeting the needs of people today and in the future, for a programme of research and investigation to provide a basis for effective performance, for ensuring the wide dissemination of the results of this research, and their application through prototypes and demonstrations and, finally, for an intensive educational effort both within the formal structure of library education and informal continuing education.

In the light of the findings of this study, the American Library Association has been critically reviewing its public library standards. Dissatisfaction had been expressed with them; it was felt that they were not based upon proper research, and that at best they were only goals that had been set by the profession for the profession. It was doubted whether any one set of standards could apply uniformly to all public libraries across the nation; not only do different levels of service exist but local conditions alter the type and degree of service that is required. With these basic premises a new policy is being followed. The Public Library Association's Standards Committee hopes to formulate guidelines based on the users' points of view. No new American Library Association standards are being promulgated until the Committee has developed these guidelines.

A further document showing the ways in which standards and guidelines are likely to develop in the future is 'Community Library Services—Working Papers on Goals and Guidelines, A Progress Report to the Public Library Association from the Task Forces of its Standards Committee'.[1]

---

1. American Library Association, *A Strategy for Public Library Change: Proposed Public Library Goals—Feasibility Study*, Chicago, Ill., 1972.
2. Public Library Association, 'Community Library Services—Working Paper on Goals and Guidelines, A Progress Report to the Public Library Association from the Task Forces of its Standards Committee', *School Library Journal*, September 1973 (papers revised July 1973).

School libraries

General

The survey which follows of school library standards documents from seven widely separate countries is of necessity selective. There are undoubtedly other standards since this is an important growing point in libraries. There will have been 'libraries' of some kind in all schools at all times, but recent curriculum and other developments in education are having an effect on the nature of the role of school libraries and consequently on their work and structure.

In primary and secondary schools, to a greater extent than in most other educational establishments, the work of the library, represented by the activities of its staff and by the materials and accommodation provided, has to be closely related to the formal educational programmes carried out if the optimum use is to be made of the library resources which would normally be provided. The library cannot remain a passive aid to the pupil or the member of the teaching staff who wishes to refer to, or borrow, a book or periodical.

The term 'library resources' is becoming firmly fixed in the vocabulary of librarianship. Increasingly advocates of the positive use of the school library regard it as a 'multi-media resource centre' for the use of the school, teachers and pupils alike. A study of the principal documents referred to in this chapter will show how increasingly, in the words of one commentator, 'there has been a shift from a concern with teaching to a concern with learning'.[1]

---

1. B. J. Enright, *New Media and the Library in Education*, London, Clive Bingley, 1972, p. 64.

Another writer has referred to 'a shift from teacher-oriented whole class instruction, where the text book reigns supreme, to a pupil-oriented environment rich in learning stimuli'.[1]

While changes in teaching and learning methods come about in many ways and for many reasons, they will have been influenced by the technological changes of the past few decades, which have brought new media of communication, principally audio-visual media, into greater use. These media, television, film, discs, tapes, etc., have naturally been increasingly used by the schools, and have moved into the library, by nature the most suitable department of the school to organize the acquisition, conservation and use of the material. Changes in educational philosophy, coupled with the technological changes and, in some countries like the United Kingdom, the increase in the size of secondary schools to cater for pupils of all ranges of ability, has provided an environment in which school libraries are bound to flourish, developing in scope and scale.

As with parallel developments in other libraries, it has been necessary for school librarians and the professional library associations (as well as, sometimes, the organizations concerned with audio-visual means of communication), to state what needs to be done and to be provided if the school library is to play its enlarged role efficiently and effectively.

The newer approach to teaching and learning is reflected in all but one of the documents surveyed by the references to the provision of audio-visual materials, but the extent to which that is emphasized varies. Australian, United Kingdom and United States documents stress the 'learning resources' role of the library most strongly. The Canadian standards, although only six years old, are currently being revised to enable this aspect to be more fully dealt with.

The scale and level of school library provision recommended can be broadly judged by the standards recommended for library materials, staffing and accommodation. The standards, particularly those for materials, vary considerably.

---

1. Shirley L. Blandford, 'The Role of the Professional Librarian in the School', *Library Association Record*, Vol. 71, No. 7, July 1969.

LIBRARY MATERIALS

The Australian Commonwealth Government's 1971 standard for secondary schools is 30 volumes per pupil decreasing to fifteen volumes in the largest schools, with recommended sizes of collection from 1,500 to 15,000+. The Library Association of Australia's earlier 1966 standard was 20 volumes, decreasing to 10 with increasing size of school. The Canadian minimum basic standard for schools with under 300 pupils is 30 volumes per pupil or a basic minimum number of volumes. For over 300 pupils the figure for volumes per pupil is 20. In the Federal Republic of Germany there are short- and long-term targets of 3 and 6 volumes per pupil in primary schools and, in secondary schools, of 6 and 9 for the lower part of the school and 8 and 12 for the higher. In Hungary, 5 volumes per pupil is required in general schools (combining primary and post-primary stages) and 10 in secondary schools. In Singapore 5 volumes per pupil is recommended. In the United Kingdom a minimum of 8 volumes is recommended in primary schools and 10 in middle and secondary schools, with 15 at sixth-form level (age 16–18/19). In the United States, for schools over 250 pupils, a minimum of 10,000 volumes or 10 volumes per pupil, whichever is the greater, is recommended.

LIBRARY ACCOMMODATION

A simple criterion is the scale of provision in reading rooms. Both the Australian Government and Library Association standards recommend 'seating' for 10 per cent of pupils. Canada recommends 'reading areas' for up to 30 per cent of pupils. The Federal Republic of Germany refers to 'working places' for 5–10 per cent of the pupils. Hungary refers to a minimum space for 25–30 users. Singapore refers to 'seating' for 5 per cent of total student enrolment. The United Kingdom document does not give a figure. The United States standards state that the instructional programme in the school might require that one-third to three-quarters of the student population should be accommodated in the media centre. These definitions and figures are clearly not comparable but they give a slight indication of the different approach in the various countries.

SCHOOL LIBRARY STAFF

It is not very profitable to compare recommended figures for school library staff, since the biggest variation is in the number of assistant staff, including media assistants and technicians. The main questions are the point at which a full-time school librarian in charge of the library is required and the education, training and experience needed by such librarians.

The Australian Library Association considers that all schools with more than 250 pupils require a full-time librarian and that such persons should have dual training as teacher and librarian, though not necessarily the full training of a professional librarian. The Australian Government considers that secondary schools with less than 300 pupils should have a part-time librarian and others a full-time librarian, with varying numbers of assistant librarians, media and other assistants. It also considers that school librarians should hold recognized qualifications in both teaching and librarianship.

In Canada a school librarian is recommended for every 300 to 500 pupils. It is stated that they would not all be fully qualified professional librarians. Many would be teacher-librarians with a minimum of library training.

In the Federal Republic of Germany it is stated that a 'qualified librarian' is required in schools with more than 1,500 pupils. In Hungary schools with more than 500 pupils, and more than 16 classes, require a full-time librarian. He must be a qualified teacher who must quickly acquire some library training. Singapore refers to trained teacher-librarians, i.e. a qualified teacher who has completed a recognized course in school librarianship. Junior colleges and secondary schools with pre-university classes will require full-time qualified librarians. In the United Kingdom, the Library Association recommends that schools of 800 and above should have at least 1 full-time professionally recognized librarian, with varying amounts of professional and other assistance. In smaller schools it recognizes that the school librarian is more likely to be a teacher-librarian, who may have some training in school librarianship. The School Library Association, however, regards a full dual qualification as teacher and librarian as ideally desirable but, recognizing that this is impracticable, recommends special courses to train school librarians, involving substantial parts, but not the whole, of both forms of training. In the United States standards a full-time 'media specialist' is recommended for every 250 students, with supporting staff.

Standards documents stress the need for individual school libraries to be backed up by school library services. These are often associated with the public library services, with which there is bound to be a close connexion. The Hungarian document refers to a 'network' of school libraries.

A report of a survey conducted by a committee of the Ghana Library Board, the British Council, and the Ghana Ministry of Education into libraries in secondary schools and teacher-training colleges, published in 1970, recommended that the Ghana Library Board should be empowered to run libraries in secondary schools, and that it should be provided with the necessary financial resources. On accommodation the report stated that ideally the school library should be housed in a separate building but that, where this was not possible, additions and alterations to premises should be made ensuring that the schools should be able to accommodate 10 per cent of their pupils in the library at any one time, allowing 25 ft² (2.32 m²) per user.

The committee recommended the adoption of the United Kingdom standards of 8–10 volumes per pupil with a minimum collection of 5,000 volumes, and that all school libraries should provide some, if not all, of the local papers and the leading journals and magazines dealing with Ghana and West Africa, together with some foreign newspapers and periodicals.

With regard to staff, it stated that a long term objective would be to have the services of a professionally qualified librarian. Until this was possible, the Ghana Library Board should be empowered to provide professional service to groups of schools in a given area or region.[1]

On a lower level of provision, a meeting in 1968 of experts in the development of school libraries in Central America, organized by Unesco in Antigua, Guatemala, recommended that, in order that there should be by 1972 school libraries for 25 per cent of the primary school students and 50 per cent of the secondary school

1. *The Library in Secondary Schools and Teacher Training Colleges* (a survey conducted by a Committee of the Ghana Library Board, the British Council and the Ministry of Education, 1970, mimeo.).

students at a level of 1 book per primary school student and 2 books per secondary school student, 1.5 per cent of their total budgets for education should be spent on the establishment and maintenance of school libraries.[1]

School libraries are, since 1967, being provided in Honduras under the School Library and Library Training Pilot Project for Central America jointly by Unesco and the Honduras Government.[2] School libraries are being provided in four categories of school, 2 categories with over 500 pupils having a full-time librarian and 2 categories of smaller schools between 500 and 100 pupils having a half-time librarian. The minimum number of books to be provided in the collections is based on 1 book per pupil costing on average U.S.$1, 'an amount Honduras can afford'. Sixty per cent are school and reference books, the remainder recreational. Rural schools (70 per cent of all schools) will be served by circulating libraries, administered by the teachers. These schools have less than 100 pupils each. The school libraries planned have enough room to accommodate 5 per cent of the pupils, allowing 2.5 m² per pupil.

Australia

GENERAL

The history of the development of school library standards in Australia in the last ten years is of great interest and significance. In his account of Australian libraries, published in 1966,[3] John Balnaves explained that while tuition at government schools was free, parents must meet the cost of textbooks, uniforms and sports material and, with some assistance from state education departments, of school libraries. Most non-government schools charged fees and only since 1964 had any financial assistance been given to them by the Commonwealth Government. Otherwise the school library in these schools had to be supported entirely by private

1. Unesco, *Final Report of Meeting of Experts on the Development of School Libraries in Central America, Antigua, Guatemala, 1968*, Paris, Unesco, 1968 (mimeo.).
2. Antonieta Ballon, 'Primary School Library System in Honduras', *Unesco Bulletin for Libraries*, Vol. XXIII, No. 6, November-December 1969.
3. John Balnaves, *Australian Libraries*, London, Clive Bingley, 1966.

funds. In all states, the department of education provided advisory services to school libraries and in some states there were central book purchasing and cataloguing services. 'But', says Balnaves, 'in a situation where the basic condition of existence of school libraries is local initiative of headmasters and parents and citizens, systematic development of school libraries is hardly possible.'

Fortunately, the position has dramatically changed, so far as secondary schools are concerned. This is no doubt partly due to action taken in recent years to point out the deficiencies of libraries in the schools. In the Tauber report of 1961,[1] it was stated that 'it would appear that progress in these areas (of children's and school libraries) since 1935 had been minimal'. In 1964 Professor Sara Fenwick of the University of Chicago Graduate Library School surveyed, for the Library Association of Australia, the position of school and children's libraries in Australia. In her report published in 1966, she drew attention to serious deficiencies and identified the chief reasons for the failure to develop both children's and school libraries adequately.[2] But at the time of Professor Fenwick's visit the Children's Libraries Section of the Library Association of Australia had already formulated a set of standards for school libraries and these, under the title of *Standards and Objectives for School Libraries*,[3] were also published in 1966. In 1965, at its General Council, the Library Association of Australia adopted a resolution which led to a two-year programme aimed at obtaining federal aid for school libraries.

These events, together with other developments on the broader educational front, have had their influence on the Commonwealth Government's policy, for in the 1968 budget a $27 million programme for the provision of libraries in government and independent secondary schools throughout Australia was announced. This sum was allocated over a period of three years from 1 January 1969, to assist in raising the level of secondary school libraries throughout Australia to the standard necessary to enable them to be effective centres of the schools' learning programmes. Grants were available

1. Maurice F. Tauber, *Resources of Australian Libraries, Prepared for the Australian Advisory Council on Bibliographical Services with the Assistance of the Librarians of Australia and the Bibliographical Centre of the National Library*, Canberra, AACOBS, 1962–64, 3 vols.
2. Sara Innis Fenwick, *School and Children's Libraries in Australia*, Melbourne, Cheshire, for the Library Association of Australia, 1966.
3. Library Association of Australia, *Standards and Objectives for School Libraries*, Melbourne, Cheshire, for the Library Association of Australia, 1966.

for the erection, alteration or extension of library buildings and for the conversion of existing school buildings to libraries, also for the provision of furniture, equipment, books and instructional materials. In the second period to 1974, a further $30 million has been provided.

A Commonwealth Secondary Schools Libraries Committee was appointed by the Minister of Education and Science to advise on the conditions and standards necessary for the effective development of the new programme in relation to independent schools. This involved recommending desirable standards for library buildings, furniture and equipment, books and materials and also establishing methods by which existing deficiencies in library facilities and services in particular schools may be determined.

As a first step, the committee issued, in March 1969, a preliminary statement about standards for secondary school libraries. The statement gave schools planning libraries, and their architects, advice on the general building standards likely to be accepted for commonwealth grant purposes. Since grants are available for books and other library materials, attention was also given to standards for basic stock. Advice is also included on selection of library materials.

In a foreword to the document the Minister for Education and Science referred to the scheme for financial assistance to secondary school libraries as part of the Commonwealth's aim to provide more facilities and to upgrade the quality of education at a variety of levels, and said:

We want to see the library a centre of learning, the 'hub' of the secondary school programme, in which an extensive collection of various forms of instructional materials is available to students.

The scheme, it is hoped, will achieve in other disciplines what the highly successful science laboratories scheme has achieved in its field. A good library is essential if students are to benefit fully from their schooling.

The Commonwealth has placed education on a high national priority. We must meet education needs if Australia is to advance as it should.

This has now been superseded by *Standards for Secondary School Libraries*,[1] and this, with the Library Association of Australia's 1966 standards are summarized below.

1. Department of Education and Science. Commonwealth Secondary Schools Libraries Committee, *Standards for Secondary School Libraries*, Canberra, 1971.

STANDARDS AND OBJECTIVES FOR SCHOOL LIBRARIES:
LIBRARY ASSOCIATION OF AUSTRALIA, 1966[1]

Foreword

To some the standards may seem Utopian and unattainable; to others they will appear inadequate. It is one of the purposes of the standards to limit this unevenness of service by setting up an irreducible minimum. The standards should be regularly revised (say, every five years). The implementation of the standards and the future of school library development are dependent on the quantity and strength of the officers supervising school library services in each state.

Introduction—why standards?

The unevenness of school library provision alone would, it is said, warrant a charter of minimum standards; so would the system which makes school libraries largely dependent on parental fund-raising efforts. There are other reasons, notably the much needed guidance a standards document gives to those responsible for the provision of school libraries; the attention the document would draw to the important role which school libraries can and should play in education; and the need to bring out the importance of education in and for librarianship and to demonstrate the fallacy of 'anyone can run a library'.

Objectives for the school library

It is not possible to formulate standards in terms of staff, book stock and buildings without first considering the function of the library in the school. This the document does under the following headings:

The library and education
Seven main objectives, which are equally applicable to all types and levels of schools, are stated in general terms and some amplification, more specific references and provisos are given. Two only

1. These standards are under revision, in conjunction with the Australian School Library Association.

are quoted here: to be a source of books and other materials which will support and enrich the teaching-learning programme in the school; to work towards an ideal in which the school library is no longer an aid or an adjunct or simply a service—with the secondary and rather passive role those terms imply—but a centre from which the educational activities of both teachers and children radiate, the heart of the school.

An active policy for the library
This gives specific illustration of what can be done in a school library in encouraging children to read: publicizing the library; the library in teaching and learning; the teacher and the library; reading and study skills.

The administration of the school libraries

This section deals with the staffing of school libraries and of the school library service working within a state's department of education.

Staffing of school libraries

The term school-librarian used in the standards refers to a person with dual training—in teaching and librarianship—and not to a person who carries out both class teaching and library duties within the school. In the school the school librarian is in a key position when the library is the vital force advocated. The educational authorities should provide an adequate supply of school librarians and ensure an equitable distribution throughout the educational system. The duties of the school librarian and assistants are described.

Staffing standards

Librarians
All schools with over 250 children need the services of a full-time school librarian. In large primary and secondary schools there should be one librarian for each 500 children or major fraction thereof. Where the librarian has responsibility for selection and organization of visual aids, one librarian is needed for each 300 children. Schools with less than 250 children should use the services of a part-time librarian.

Assistants
There should be typing and clerical assistance given to librarians in all schools with over 250 pupils.

Salary and status
The salary and status of the school librarian should be the same as that of other teachers in the school and with similar professional education, experience and responsibility. The school librarian should be able to proceed to any position, including headships.

Training for school librarians

This should provide (a) teacher training and successful teaching experience appropriate to the children with whom they are to work; and (b) library training, concurrently with or following teacher training. In either case a minimum of 360 hours (over one or two years) should be spent in library training and at least eight weeks practical experience provided in a school library under a trained school librarian. This would lead either to the full or partial completion of the Australian Library Association's Registration Examination. School librarians should be actively encouraged to improve their qualifications in librarianship, by completing a degree in librarianship or the registration examination or by correspondence and vacation courses.

Library training for all teachers

All student teachers should receive at least 30 hours of library training so that they may be able to integrate the school library into their teaching and understand fully the role of libraries and education.

Staffing of central library services

It is considered that economies can be achieved by the establishment of central library services to schools, dealing with such items as the purchase and provision of a basic book stock to new schools; processing, cataloguing and classifying of new books for schools; issue of detailed book lists or recommended purchases for school libraries; provision of bibliographical information and advice to school libraries; provision of bulk loans of library books to supplement small book stocks in schools with less than 200 pupils; and the provision of a central service for the repair and strengthening of library books.

Such a service would be in charge of a person highly trained in both education and librarianship, capable of giving advice to the educational authority on the implementation of standards. The importance is stressed of this person, described as superintendent of library services, having on his staff highly trained professional officers in adequate number with clerical and general assistants. The professional staff of such a service should represent as wide a range of subject knowledge as possible.

District officers, providing district services (e.g. staffing libraries in schools too small to justify a full-time librarian) should be closely allied with the central office.

Stocking the school library

A well balanced book stock includes a wide range of books on all subjects of possible interest to children. It should reach beyond the confines of the curriculum, to create new interests as well as to enrich and enliven the scope of the formal school subjects. It provides an attractive variety of first rate books of reference, imaginative writing and non-fiction. Schools differ in their needs, but despite this there are certain standards which should be common to all book stocks: small schools should be ensured of adequate supplies of books and not hampered by tiny book stocks through proportionate application of standards; fair allocation of funds must be made for the purchase of fiction, and its educational value in the school recognized; a basic book stock should be provided in all new schools and eventually in all schools; and, in selection, books must be provided to allow both deep and superficial reading in most subjects and allow for the levels of reading interest and ability.

Size of collection

The following standards are recommended: schools with less than 200 pupils should aim at 20 books per pupil and arrange to have their stock regularly augmented by bulk loans from the central authority; all schools having more than 200 pupils should build, within 10 years of starting the library, a minimum book stock of 6,000 to 10,000 books; schools with over 1,000 pupils should have within 10 years of starting the library a minimum of 10 books per pupil.

Two suggested 10 year plans are given for the establishment of libraries in schools with 300 pupils and for schools with an expected enrolment of 1,000 pupils. In both cases, it is assumed that the initial stock is built up over the first 3 years on the basis of 10 books per pupil, i.e. 50 per cent of the ultimate minimum book stock; thereafter there is maintenance and replacement of the existing book stock at 10 per cent per annum and an increase in the book stock and periodicals of an annual order which will bring the total book stock up to the desired total by the end of 10 years. After the tenth year it is assumed that only the 10 per cent increase for maintenance and replacement will be necessary. The plans are costed on the basis of an average cost of a book at $2.

Subscriptions to periodicals should be provided for annually by allowing 10 per cent of the total book grant to magazines, newspapers, etc. If the library is the depository of non-print materials (e.g. audio visual), at least 2 per cent of the library grant should be devoted to new additions and maintenance.

Selection of materials
An average of 30 per cent fiction to 70 per cent non-fiction is considered a reasonable proportion for secondary schools and 40 per cent fiction to 60 per cent non-fiction for primary schools. Advice is given on aids to selection under fiction, non-fiction, ready reference, pamphlets, periodicals and newspapers.

Organization and selection of library materials
Essential school library routines, ordering, classifying and cataloguing, processing and borrowing systems, are discussed. It is recommended that cataloguing should be done centrally by a library service attached to the education authorities in each state.

Finance
The initial stock should be provided by the education authorities when the school is built. As soon as possible all money for current additions should be provided by the authorities through grants. A minimum grant of $6 per student per annum in schools of under 500, and by a sliding scale to $3 per student per annum in schools of over 500, is recommended for current additions.

351

The school library building

Central library
A central library, suitably located, is essential for both primary and secondary schools. It should serve the whole school, both junior and senior years. Small classroom collections provided on loan from the central library, are necessary in primary schools. A book corner in infant and early primary year classrooms is necessary and a special corner for these children in the primary school central library. All children should have access to the central library.

Design and equipment of the central library
This must provide for the following:

Reading room. In both primary and secondary schools, this should be large enough to seat 10 per cent of its pupils. In schools with less than 500 pupils there should be room for 45–55 pupils to be seated at any one time. For every reader, 30 ft² (2.79 m²) should be allowed.

Library annex. When the reading room is used for private study, another area—at least 650 ft² (60.4 m²)—is required where a class or part of a class can work with library books. This should be well lit and soundproof and, if necessary, should provide storage for recordings and viewing machines.

Group study rooms. In schools with 750 students, 2 such rooms are required approximately 12 ft × 12 ft (3.65 m × 3.65 m) for student discussions and study.

Librarian's office and workroom.

Library entrance with room for display case and perhaps informal seating.

Detailed advice is given on lighting, acoustics, ventilation, heating and plumbing of the library premises and on its furnishing and equipment.

Finance and administration

Under finance, it is stated that the provision and equipping of a library building is the responsibility of the state education authority and should not be left to willing parents nor be discharged partly through subsidies; under administration, that when designing and locating the library it should be assumed it will be open at least half an hour before and after school hours; the library should not be used for any purpose other than a library.

Preface

This explained that grants under the Commonwealth Libraries Programme, which began in January 1969, were available to independent schools and to state governments for the library needs of their own secondary schools out of the $27 million available up to 31 December 1971. The states were responsible for the administration of the programme for their own schools within a general programme approved by the Commonwealth Minister of Education and Science. The publication gave information about applications for the grants from independent schools and guidance about standards of provision generally required.

The role of the library in the secondary schools

This section described the relation of the library to the work of the school. Change had been a key process in the twentieth century and education, like other social functions, had felt its effects. Education today emphasized enquiry and was a creative enquiring process. The secondary school enrolled the whole age group and was no longer limited to the preparation of an élite. Less unskilled labour was required and proportionately more people in skilled labour, management, research and innovation.

The variety of communication media available gave the teacher a wider choice of teaching methods and provided students with more varied and appropriate learning situations. The school was concerned with providing a much greater variety of materials, and more flexible groupings, including large group instruction, and individual study. This changed the view of the role of the library and the library became the centre of the school's learning programme. It provided access to the whole range of resource

353

materials, such as books, periodicals, tapes, records, slides, and films, together with specialist staff to organize these materials in the way best suited to the school's educational programme and to guide students and teachers in their use of the wide range of materials. It provided facilities for a wide range of activities involving the use of library materials.

The role of the library staff and relation of facilities were vital to the successful achievement of these purposes.

The role of the school librarian was a dual one. It involved the selection, evaluation and organization of materials to assist the educational programme. It involved co-operation with teachers and guidance to students in developing the best ways of using available material. The librarian had to co-operate with the principal and members of the teaching staff in using the resources of the library to enrich and widen the whole school programme. Equally each teacher should help each student to learn to gather information, appraise it and make judgements. Suitable buildings, a wide range of resources for learning and an appropriately prepared staff were all of equal importance.

The school library should integrate the learning resources of the school, wherever they might be sited or used. Separate subject objectives must be regarded as part of the over-all school programme, which required a central library to support it.

The major purpose in making the library into the resource centre of the school was to make available to the student the full range of information and of media relevant to his needs. A secondary purpose was to provide control and accountability for the varied equipment and material involved. This did not imply that all material and equipment must be housed in the library. It could be housed in other parts of the school, as in a music centre or a mathematics laboratory, but the library catalogue should include all such material.

Listed were the activities which would centre on the library: recreational reading and browsing; study involving the use of library materials by individuals and groups; the use of audio-visual materials by individuals and groups; the use of library resources by teachers; borrowing of library materials by teachers and students for individual and class use; use of the catalogue and other indexes to resources; the instruction of individuals or groups in the techniques of locating and using library materials relevant to their

354

needs; group discussion arising from the use of library materials and from individual and class assignments; guidance in the evaluation of materials.

Planning the library

Advice was given about the siting of the library and the accommodation required, with suggestions about the relationship of the various areas, accompanied by alternative diagrams. An appendix indicated minimum individual space and total area requirements for schools up to 1,000 enrolment, and for schools with 1,050 to 2,000 enrolment. Table 67 gives a number of examples.

In calculating the requirements for a particular school, the secondary enrolment should be increased by doubling the enrolment of classes in the final year of secondary schooling. The total should be taken to the nearest fifty.

The main variable area was that of the reading room. For schools

TABLE 67. Area requirements in ft² (m² in parentheses)

	School enrolment				
	300	500	1,000	1,500	2,000
Reading areas	1,575 (146.32)	1,750 (162.58)	3,500 (325.16)	5,250 (487.74)	7,000 (650.32)
Large seminar room	—	—	750 (69.68)	1,500 (139.35)	1,500 (139.35)
Small seminar room	120 (11.15)	250 (23.23)	500 (46.45)	750 (69.68)	1,000 (92.90)
Teachers' room	120 (11.15)	120 (11.15)	200 (18.58)	300 (27.87)	400 (37.16)
Audio-visual store	Included in workroom	100 (9.29)	200 (18.58)	300 (27.87)	400 (37.16)
Workroom	400 (37.16)	400 (37.16)	400 (37.16)	500 (46.45)	700 (65.03)
Librarian's office	Included in workroom		120 (11.15)	120 (11.15)	120 (11.15)
Bags, cloaks, foyer	200 (18.58)	200 (18.58)	200 (18.58)	300 (27.87)	400 (37.16)
TOTAL	2,415 (224.36)	2,820 (261.99)	5,870 (545.34)	9,020 (837.98)	11,520 (1,070.23)

of 450 and above this was designed to accommodate 10 per cent of the adjusted enrolment area, allowing 35 ft² (3.25 m²) per reader. For schools of 300–450 a minimum of 45 readers and 1,575 ft² (146.32 m²) was allowed. Special advice was given about the library accommodation in schools of less than 300 students.

Provision of resources and facilities

Staff
The number and variety of services indicated that the library staff should include people qualified in a variety of fields: the librarian should hold recognized qualifications in teaching and librarianship; library and media assistants should hold recognized qualifications in librarianship and/or teaching and/or in the production, maintenance and use of audio-visual materials; clerical assistants should be fully trained in office procedures.

Factors which affected the number of staff included the school enrolment, the number of hours the library was open, its educational relevance to the total school programme, and the availability of centralized services. Numbers of staff were recommended as in Table 68.

A librarian in a school with less than 500 should enlist the help of students and parents.

Books
The Commonwealth programme would assist schools to build up a basic book stock, including reference, fiction and non-fiction according to the standards given as examples in Table 69 (grants would not be made for periodicals or newspapers).

TABLE 68. Number of recommended staff

	Adjusted secondary enrolment						
	Less than 300	300	500	550	750	1,050	1,250
School librarian	At least part time	1	1	1	1	1	1
Library and media assistants	—	—	—	1	1	2	2
Clerical assistants	—	—	1	1	2	2	2

Table 69

Adjusted secondary enrolment	Recommended basic stock	Recommended size of collection for adequate library service
50	1,000	1,500
250	3,250	5,500
500	4,500	7,500
750	5,500	11,260
1,000	6,300	15,000
1,250 and above	5,700 for the first 800 students and 300 for each 100 students for basic stock and 15 books per student for adequate library service.	

Financial assistance would be provided to establish the basic stock but the table gave both this and numbers recommended for an adequate library service, the latter ranging from 30 volumes per student in the smaller schools to 15 in the larger. This would require regular funds from the authorities of the school to purchase new materials and replace discarded material.

Advice was given about basic reference books, and the proportion of fiction and non-fiction. This should be in the range 25–75 per cent to 40–60 per cent, the actual proportion being determined with due regard to the structure of the school—schools with more senior students having a higher proportion of non-fiction material.

Non-book materials

What was new was not the use of non-book materials in a school library but the variety of media which had grown out of technological and electronic advances, and the variety of ways in which they could be used to extend the learning situation. Non-book materials included periodicals, newspapers, pamphlets and reprints, illustrative materials, and models and dioramas.

Audio-visual materials would include films, video-tapes, loop films, cassettes, microforms, film-strips, records, tapes and slides, and the necessary equipment for their use.

The library remained the place where the various media were stored and controlled and where listening and viewing by individuals and groups took place. If a school embarked on a programme of multi-media learning, it would have to equip teaching stations or subject centres dispersed throughout the school, using multi-media resources which the library controlled.

Some quantitative standards were given based on standards being implemented in countries where the use of audio-visual materials had reached a degree of sophistication beyond that in Australian schools. The standards were for schools of more than 300 students. This did not mean that the smaller school should not provide non-book materials. Films 16 mm, usually through a general state central collection: loop films, 8 mm, 500 titles; film-strips, 500 titles; slides, 3,000 or 5 per student, whichever the greater. Discs, 1,500 titles; tapes and audio-cassettes and video-tapes—sufficient to cover needs; transparencies, 2,000 items; maps, 200 regional and special maps; prints and charts, 1,000 items; globes—terrestrial, celestial, lunar—one of each; microforms, as relevant to the curriculum.

Furniture was dealt with in considerable detail with drawings and impressive plans and photographs of school library areas.

The document contains an extended bibliography on the role of the library in secondary education and the selection and organization of library materials.

Canada

Until recently, educationalists in Canada relied on the American Library Associations' standards, but the need was felt for Canadian standards and a committee was appointed in 1962, which prepared preliminary standards. These were examined by committees of librarians and educators in each province, by departments of education, and by representatives of interested associations. This led to the publication in 1965 of *Preliminary Standards for School Libraries*. On the basis of decisions taken at a two-day 'workshop', final standards were prepared by an enlarged committee. These were published in 1967 under the title *Standards of Library Service for Canadian Schools*.[1] The Introduction states:

1. *Standards of Library Service for Canadian Schools.* Recommended by the Canadian School Library Association/Association Canadienne des Bibliothèques Scolaires, Toronto, The Ryerson Press, 1967.

This publication is intended to provide guide-lines for administrators, teachers and librarians in the establishment and operation of good school libraries. . . . It points out the necessary requirements for good, but not superior, library service in the individual school, the district and province. It must be emphasized that facilities described in each section of the standards are already existent in some schools in Canada.

The document discusses the role of the library and of the library programme in the school. The role is described thus:

The library is an essential part of the school, composed of quarters, library materials, personnel, with a programme developed to serve the students, teachers and administration. The library collection consists of books, disc records, tapes, pictures, pamphlets, periodicals, filmstrips, film slides, micro-film, charts and museum objects—all materials which might be used to instruct, inspire, as well as encourage and facilitate the learning programme. The librarian, as an instructional materials resource person, works with students, instructional staff, administrators, parents and community agencies to produce a library programme.

Of the library programme, which should permeate the entire educational programme of the school, it is said:

An effective library programme, which in the fullest sense provides the learning experience for every student, requires the support and active co-operation of everyone involved from the superintendent to every member of the staff. To be successful, it needs the endorsement of all levels of educational authority. The library programme is the directed use of library space, staff, equipment and materials to meet specific objectives. A librarian co-operates with the principal and the teaching staff to plan maximum use of existing facilities and budgets. This programme should meet the needs of the curriculum, and provide for the special and individual requirements of the school.

Examining the elements of an effective school library service, three principles are stated, that: curriculum outlines impose on the school library the responsibility for providing adequate materials for learning in depth; every student requires access to varied materials regardless of the total number of his classmates; and each school must provide the necessary learning materials regardless of its size. Therefore, some means of co-operative purchasing and/or central service is necessary to help the smaller schools.

Advice is given about the printed and non-print materials which should be supplied. The importance of pamphlets, which are inexpensive and easily replaced, and of periodicals, as well as of a collection of professional material for the use of the staff, is stressed.

In non-print materials, particular reference is made to the need for all kinds of maps, atlases and globes, film-strips and film slides, records and tapes, museum objects and portable models.

The school library, it is said, should have a well-balanced collection maintained through careful selection, discarding and replacement. The central core of the collection should be ready at the opening of the school as part of the initial establishment. The minimum requirements in any school should, at least, be reached within three years of the opening. Thereafter, expansion and necessary duplication and replacement may be accomplished by annual purchases.

Many points are made about the provision and organization of school library accommodation and equipment. Reference is made to the increasing number of students using school libraries because of the greater emphasis on independent study and the use of educational media. To meet these demands, it is proposed that there should be seating for 30 per cent of the students, at least half of it in individual study carrels, about 20 per cent in small group study rooms, and the remaining 30 per cent by traditional table accommodation with some allowance for lounge furniture. Fewer carrels are required for elementary schools and more lounge and table study area. The library should be capable of being used after regular school hours and provision should be made for its expansion at a minimum of cost and with the least disruption of school work.

Particular attention is given to the library facilities for the student. Facilities hitherto considered adequate have been made obsolete by new trends in education, such as large group instruction, small group instruction and individual research. It is stated that, in some schools stressing individual study, as much as one half of a student's time may be unscheduled and spent in the library.

Small conference rooms holding four to six students, are suggested as small group-viewing/listening areas. Larger rooms for twelve to fifteen students with moveable dividing walls may be preferred. A library classroom adjoining the reading area, for library instruction or for classes brought to the library for special projects, is regarded as essential unless there is a suitable area near to the library. Advice is included about areas for audio-visual purposes.

The dependence of the school library on the adequacy of the

staff is stressed. The fully qualified librarian should be a competent organizer and administrator, a successful teacher, as well as a trained librarian. His special functions are defined as: building and organizing collections of instructional materials; encouraging and assisting staff and students to make maximum use of these materials; training clerical and student assistants and directing their work; and making use of modern publicity and public relations methods to build and maintain a vital library programme.

A fully qualified school librarian, it is recommended, should have university level education in both teaching and librarianship. He should have a university degree and certification as a fully qualified teacher. He should also have a degree in librarianship, with courses taken in children's and young people's literature, non-book materials and school library administration, and should take advanced courses in subjects such as curriculum and audio-visual materials and production.

The document recognizes that not all school librarians will be fully qualified professionally trained librarians. Many will be teacher-librarians giving only part-time service to the library. For such staff, minimum training given through a college of education is recommended in relevant library subjects. For those individuals already educated in the one area, the acquiring of training in the other should be accompanied by experience in that second area. The members of the two professions are urged to co-operate to pool their complementary training and experience.

The work to be undertaken by library clerks is described, and some of the factors affecting the total number of staff members required are stated.

It is recognized that the small school has difficulty in providing adequate library service in terms of staff and collections. Good service requires one librarian for every 300 to 500 students, whether they are in one or more schools. Librarians can either work part-time in one or more schools, or part-time as a librarian and part-time as a teacher in the same school. Alternatively, for a widely scattered area, there could be a mobile district librarian, a central reference and loan collection, a pool collection of materials from which deposit collections can be sent from school to school, and, possibly, a direct mobile library service. One library clerk is recommended for every 500 students.

A section on the school library budget distinguishes between items which should be included in the initial capital cost and the elements in annual expenditure. The annual budget should provide funds for the purchase of one book per student plus replacements of lost and outdated material. The requirements for technical and special schools are considered to be higher because of the wide range and greater cost of special materials.

Staff participation in controlling library expenditure may be secured by organizing a library committee, informal discussions with individual teachers, and by developing advisory groups of teachers in each subject area.

A further chapter 'District and Area School Library Systems: Provincial Services' is based on the principle that no school library can exist by itself. To be completely effective as an integral part of the total conventional programme it must receive support from the district or area level, with provincial government assistance. This section of the document discusses the organization of district and area services by a large school district or combination of school districts, including the provision of a library service centre supplying advisory services, collections of special materials and special services to students and teachers (e.g. an advanced reference service), central purchasing and processing of library materials. Such a district or area service would be administered by a district or area library supervisor who would be qualified both as a classroom teacher and as a librarian.

The responsibilities of the provincial departments of education are also discussed, and co-ordination at provincial level is considered essential if the school libraries are to attain the desired standards. A provincial library supervisor should provide a consultative service to boards of education, and also a direct service to small schools not served by a district library service centre.

A penultimate chapter discusses certain fields where the implementation of standards for good school library service may require special consideration. They are (a) library services to exceptional children, such as those who are physically or mentally handicapped; (b) the problems of organizing a library in a new school and in an established school; (c) library service in the small schools (with less than 150 students)—(i) in a large district, through a central district library; (ii) in remote areas, through direct provincial government aid and/or co-operation between school districts; (d) co-operation with other libraries and learning resource centres;

and (e) the teacher and the library—pre-service and in-service education about the contribution which school library services make to education and relevant aspects of the work of school libraries.

Finally, under the heading of 'Responsibility for School Library Service' the document sets out to define the respective roles of the provincial governments, the boards of education, the superintendents of schools, the principals of the schools, the teachers and the school librarians.

Apart from a few quantitative standards mentioned in the text, which have already been referred to, these have been reserved for an appendix. A further appendix refers to equipment and includes a number of standard specifications and measurements.

In the first appendix these are:

Standards of library materials for a school with 150 or more students

Basic book collection—to be provided in 1 to 3 years from capital grants: elementary school, Grades 1 to 6, 5,000 titles; secondary school, Grades 7 to 13, 5,000 titles; continuation school, Grades 1 to 13, 7,500 titles.

Growth of book collection—from annual expenditure. In schools with 300 students or less, the collection should be expanded to 30 books per pupil or to the basic collection, whichever is the greater. In schools with more than 300 students the library should continue to expand until it has 20 or more volumes per student.

Periodicals. In elementary, secondary and continuation schools, a minimum of 25, 75+ and 75+ subscriptions respectively.

Pamphlets, pictures, maps, film-strips and film slides, recordings and tapes, museum objects. A collection with enough duplicates to meet the needs of the curriculum.

Professional materials. A minimum of 15 professional periodicals is required, together with a book collection of a professional nature.

Films. Films (16 mm) are held in a central pool collection in the district or area. Single-concept films (8 mm) are provided in the individual school in sufficient quantity to supplement the curriculum.

Space requirements, minimum areas

Reading areas for up to 30 per cent of students; 50 per cent in individual carrels; 20 per cent in small groups; 30 per cent in traditional tables; 35 ft² (3.25 m²) per student; no more than 100 students to be accommodated in one room. Reference area—no standard stated. Conference rooms—120 ft² (11.1 m²). Classroom—800 ft² (74.3 m²). Librarians's office—120 ft² (11.1 m²). Work area—300 ft² (27.9 m²). Storage—e.g. shelving for five years back issues of periodicals. Audio-visual—storage, 300 ft² (27.9 m²); co-ordinator's office, 120 ft² (11.1 m²); preparation (if separate) 300 ft² (27.9 m²) (if integrated) 120 ft² (11.1 m²).

Staff requirements

Standards are based on processing of library materials being handled centrally or commercially.

Librarians
Less than 300 students: one-room school, librarian from central services; 30–150 students, part-time librarian from central services; 150–300 students, minimum of half-time librarian.
More than 300 students: one librarian for first 300 students; one librarian for each additional 500 students or major fraction thereof.

Clerks
One clerk for each 500 students or major fraction thereof.

Budget requirements
A minimum capital expenditure to provide initial collections as follows:
Students fewer than 150: a base collection of 1,000 books and other materials: $5,000.
From 150 to 300: a collection of 5,000 titles and other materials: $15,000 to $20,000.
More than 500: a collection of 5,000 titles and other materials: $20,000 minimum (multiple copies needed).

Annual expenditure
Books and other printed materials $5–8 per student; audio-visual materials $2–4.

Supplementation

The collection must be supplemented by reference service and pool collections from a district or provincial service centre.

Suggested minimum standards are given for library service for schools for 300 and 1,000 pupils, based on the recommended figures.

A new edition of these standards is in preparation jointly by the Canadian Library Association and the Educational Media Association, and in the revision special attention is being given to the preparation of standards for non-book material.

Acknowledgement is made to the publishers, the Ryerson Press, Toronto, for permission to quote from *Standards of Library Service for Canadian Schools*.

Federal Republic of Germany

The Deutscher Biblioteksverband, Arbeitstelle für das Bibliothekswesen, published in 1972 a report of its School Libraries Commission (Kommission Schulbibliotheken), entitled *Die Schulbibliothek: Stand der Fachdiskussion*.[1]

This described school libraries and media centres as centres for information, material and study, and said that they should be supported financially by the education authorities according to uniform principles and integrated into the library network. They provided books, periodicals, audio-visual materials and other teaching and learning aids for free use of pupils and staff and, in certain cases, for the general public. Their stocks should be administered by professionally trained librarians, made freely available and arranged with the particular needs of schools in mind.

The document gave as guidelines for adequate performance a number of standards to which school libraries should aspire. Where two figures were given for working stocks (e.g. 3–6 volumes per pupil) the lower figure represented a minimum standard

---

1. Deutscher Büchereiverband, Arbeitsstelle für das Büchereiwesen, Kommission Schulbibliotheken, *Die Schulbibliothek: Stand der Fachdiskussion* [The School Library: the Current Professional Position]. Berlin, Deutscher Büchereiverband, 1972 (Bibliotheksdienst, Beiheft 77).

which should be attainable in the middle term, i.e. the foreseeable future, and the higher figure represented a long-term objective acting as an aid to target planning.

STANDARDS FOR WORKING STOCKS

Standards for the different kinds of school were recommended as follows. Minimum stock for small junior school should be 600 volumes. Where this figure could not be reached there should only be a reference library with other material provided by the public library.

Primary stage: 3–6 volumes per pupil; 3–10 volumes per teacher; audio-visual items—number of items equivalent to about one-third of the book stock.

Secondary stage 1: 6–9 volumes per pupil; 6–10 volumes per teacher; audio-visual materials—number of items equivalent to about half the book stock; class reading material; 40–60 newspapers and periodicals.

Secondary stage 2: 8–12 volumes per pupil; 6–10 volumes per teacher; audio-visual materials—number of items equivalent to about half the book stock; class reading material; 60–90 newspapers and periodicals.

Training and technical schools: 3–8 volumes per pupil; 3–10 volumes per teacher; audio-visual materials—number of items equivalent to about one-third of the book stock; 50–90 newspapers and periodicals.

Stocks for 'free-reading' were not allowed for in the above work stock figures and should be supplied in addition. Preference should be given to non-fiction material, with the proportion of about 20 per cent fiction to 80 per cent non-fiction and according to the requirements of the school and the distance from the public library. As a general average four volumes per pupil was suggested.

Material related to each curriculum subject should be available in either book or non-book material on a basis of equality. But the proportion of the different media would depend on factors such as the school stage and subjects studied; the selection criteria related to the levels of users and the normal pattern of use; an analysis of the curriculum—teaching content, aims and methods; the possibility of supplementing the stocks by means of long-term loans from the libraries of the region.

SELECTION OF MATERIALS

Discussing methods of selection, reference was made to the services of such bodies as the Arbeitkreis für Jugendliteratur (Study Group for Children's Literature), the Einkaufszentrale für öffentliche Büchereien (Supply Centre for Public Libraries) and the Schul-bibliothekarische Arbeitsstelle (Study Centre for School Librarianship). Such bodies and their subject specialists compile lists of recommendations, from model stock lists to special subject lists. The document recommended that school libraries should follow the methods of public libraries with regard to cataloguing, classification and documentation. All the different media should be included. There should be classified, subject and title catalogues. Attention was drawn to the work of the Study Centre for Public Libraries committee on audio-visual material, to international rules for the treatment of music and to other general matters.

ADMINISTRATION OF SCHOOL
LIBRARIES

A further section deals with the various aspects of administration, referring particularly to the study centres for school libraries proposed in each regional central library, whose staff should comprise librarians who would provide leadership, assistant librarians, and library assistants, the last including media technicians. Only with sufficient staff could the work of the study centres, especially the media education duties and the co-operation with teachers, as well as the compilation of book lists, be carried out effectively. For school libraries with full-time qualified librarians there must be close co-operation with the Study Centre over subject specialization services, media education, inter-library loans and planning.

For school libraries also functioning as public libraries there must be institutional integration.

Advice was given as to the steps to be taken locally and regionally in the establishment of study centres for school libraries, including initial discussions with education administrators, teachers and school librarians; introduction to classification, organization and administration; initial and further training of school library staffs; building of model collections; building of central collections and establishment of an express service; centralized administration of technical literature (inter-library loans); taking over from schools of acquisitions and processing; consultations between teachers and librarians over the building of the special collections and their instructional use; regular joint conferences, mutual stock building, etc., for all schools in the region.

SPACE STANDARDS

Location

The school library should be centrally placed in the school, but also accessible from the street without disturbing school activities.

Accommodation and equipment

For the central school library the standards contained in *Flächenbedarf öffentlicher Büchereien*[1] were relevant. The possibility of future increases in the numbers of pupils should be taken into account. The school library should, as far as possible, be functionally and technically independent of the rest of the school. On teaching grounds and because of the variety of media used, provision should be made in all new library buildings for large and flexible rooms.

---

1. Deutscher Büchereiverband, Arbeitsstelle für das Büchereiwesen. *Flachenbedarf öffentlicher Büchereien: Bedarfsberechnungen* [Space Requirements of Public Libraries: Calculations of Needs], Berlin, Deutscher Büchereiverband, 1968 (Bibliotheksdienst, Beiheft 37).

Area requirements

The size of the central school library would be determined by the requirements for work places and stack space, professional working space, and storage space for the preservation of audio-visual media and special collections.

Work places

For work with classes, groups and individual users in the school library, working places for 5–10 per cent of the pupils should be provided. The figures of 30 working places or space for a whole class should be considered as a minimum. Approximately 2 m² per working space should be provided. In addition working spaces would be needed for teaching staff, varying with the size of the institution.

Display of stock

For display of the books, the catalogue and loan areas, at least 0.1 m² per pupil should be allowed with a minimum of 30 m².

Professional working areas

A total of 12 m² per professional member of staff and 8 m² per non-professional would be required.

Storage

Approximately 20 m² per 1,000 pupils would be required. In smaller centres additional storage areas might be dispensed with in favour of storage in cupboards under shelves, etc. In old school buildings it would not be possible immediately to provide appropriate flexible spaces, but at least one central room, each the size of a classroom, should be provided for the central collection and as a study area.

STAFF AND TRAINING

Professional duties

The following should be considered as professional work: provision of library materials; instruction of the pupils in the use of the library and readers' aids; supply of materials to the teachers, pupils and others (e.g. parents); general advice; special advice to pupils (in association with the teachers, or with knowledge of the teaching objectives and material); work in central advisory or subject specialist bureaux.

Numbers of staff

No rigid standards have been recommended for numbers of staff required, but figures have been suggested as guidelines. While numbers in a school are being built up, for approximately every 500 pupils 1 member of staff would be required in the proportion of 1 librarian; 1 assistant librarian; 1 technical assistant. For established schools a pattern of staff was suggested (see Table 70).

If a fully developed study centre for school libraries is not established in the area, these staff requirements would need to be increased, possibly doubled.

Training

Referring particularly to experience in other countries, the document described four possible methods of training library staff for work in schools of various kinds and in central bureaux.

TABLE 70

Pupils	Volumes	Staff
500	Up to 5,000	1 teacher, additional part-time technical assistance
1,000	Up to 10,000	1 assistant librarian, 1 technical assistant
1,500	Up to 15,000	1 librarian, 1 assistant librarian, 1 technical assistant
2,000	Up to 20,000	1 librarian, 1 assistant librarian, 2 technical assistants

Librarians who have specialized in school work and work with children during their training. Such persons would be required for school libraries justifying a professional head, and certainly for those school libraries in functional relationship with a public library.

Teachers who have similarly specialized during their training—e.g. for administering part-time school libraries, or for larger school libraries as a liaison between the library and the teaching staff.

Teachers with supplementary professional library training, e.g. for administering larger school libraries or as assistant staff in central bureaux.

Librarians with supplementary training in education—e.g. for administering larger school libraries or large combined libraries, or as assistant staff in central bureaux.

Hungary

What follows is based on material provided by the Centre for Library Science and Methodology of the National Szechenyi Library.

In Hungary, children have to attend school from 6 to 16 years of age. They all follow the general school course lasting eight years. Schools in the small settlements cater only for the first four years and pupils are then taken daily by motor transport to schools in larger towns where specialist teaching is available, or go to boarding schools. After completing the general school course they may attend secondary schools of various types, the courses lasting up to four years, to about age 18.

Among the networks of libraries performing similar functions established under the comprehensive library law of 1956 is one for school libraries. At the centre, incorporating the long-established library of the Ministry of Education, is the Central Library and Museum of Education. Its field of acquisitions covers pedagogy and the related disciplines and it aims at the comprehensive coverage of children's literature, textbooks and annual reports of schools. It receives large numbers of periodicals, over a half from foreign countries, translates and abstracts journal articles and publishes two abstracting journals. It publishes subject bibliographies, divided into school grades, for the use of schools.

Belonging to this network are the libraries of teachers' training colleges, and of general and secondary schools. In 1971 there were 5,480 general schools, with 1,100,000 students, and 547 secondary schools—gymnasia, technical schools, art schools and vocational schools—with a student body of 233,000. Each school has a library, but the low level of book supply, particularly in the general schools, results in inadequate use of school libraries at a time when greater use is called for by developments in the curriculum. In 1971 only 107 secondary schools employed full-time librarians. In the remainder, and in the general schools, a teacher took charge of the library part-time. To remedy deficiencies and to improve organization, plans for the development of libraries in schools have been prepared and are being implemented.[1]

In the chapter on public libraries, details are given of the Hungarian standards for the provision of public library service for readers under 18. The document, issued in 1971 by the Ministry of Culture, from which these are taken, also included the guiding principles and standards for school libraries.[2] It is impossible entirely to separate the two forms of library provision for young people, in respect of which close co-operation and frequently joint action is required. What follows, therefore, should be read in conjunction with the material contained in that chapter.

Stating that modern school libraries must be developed for the service of both teachers and pupils in all general schools and in all secondary and vocational schools, the following standards are set out as part of a long-term programme for developing school libraries.

GENERAL

The school library must form an integral part of the school under the control of the principal. There should be only one library. Separate libraries for pupils and teachers should be integrated, though literature for teachers' needs may form a special collection.

---

1. For background see Jenö Kiss, *Libraries in Hungary*, National Széchényi Library, Centre for Library Science and Methodology, Budapest, 1972.
2. 'Irányelvek a 18 éven aluli ifjúság könyvtári ellátásának javítására [Guiding Principles for the Improvement of Library Services to Young Readers under 18]', *Művelődésügyi Közlöny*, 1971, 24. sz., p. 392–5.

ACCOMMODATION

In all general, secondary and vocational schools, there should be at least 1 room of class size (about 50 m²) available for library purposes for use by teachers and pupils, with space for 25 to 30 users. New schools should not be built without adequate library premises. Shelving should be provided, allowing at least 250 books per 6 m run.

STOCK

Library development should be speeded up so that, as early as possible, the basic stock for young readers in general schools, allowing for replacements, should be at the rate of 5 volumes per pupil, with a minimum of 2,000 volumes. In secondary schools there should be at least 10 volumes per pupil, with a minimum of 3,000 volumes.

The stock should comprise material both for compulsory and suggested reading at the rates of 1 volume per 5 pupils and 1 volume per 10 pupils respectively. At least 60 per cent of the total stock must be non-fiction literature of use in connexion with the curriculum. Books required by teachers for teaching purposes should be purchased, if necessary, in several copies. A suitable selection of material must be provided to help teachers in their work and to meet their needs for continual training.

The principals of schools, in co-operation with the librarians, should acquire the necessary materials, and funds allocated for this purpose should be available to meet running expenses throughout the year. Periodicals should be provided concerned with pedagogy, methodology and other subjects relevant to teaching, to keep teachers adequately informed and possibly to attract the interest of pupils.

LIBRARY STAFF

In all secondary schools, and in general schools with over 500 pupils and more than 16 classes, there must be a full-time school librarian, who must be a qualified teacher and accorded the same status as a teacher. In general schools with less than 500 pupils and less than 16 classes there must be a qualified teacher to perform the duties of librarian engaged part-time for this work on payment of a monthly salary between 600 and 1,200 forints. The working hours of such librarians must be clearly stated in their contracts. If the librarian's duties are performed by a member of the teaching staff, the quarterly salary for this purpose should not exceed 20 per cent of his quarterly salary for teaching. It is desirable at the present time to assign the work of school librarian to a retired teacher.

The full-time school librarian, within two years of entering the service, must acquire basic school library qualifications and subsequently take part in further training courses in librarianship. The basic minimum qualification and the continual training programme is determined by the Ministry of Culture through the agency of the Central Library and Museum of Education, which also issues detailed directives to help the education departments of the local councils implement the guiding principles and standards issued by the ministry.

LIBRARY ADMINISTRATION

A library run by a full-time librarian must be open at least four hours daily, except on Saturdays. A library run by a part-time librarian must be open at least three times a week for periods totalling a minimum of four hours. The library hours should be provided for in the school time-table.

To interest pupils more actively in their libraries, groups of pupils should be formed to assist the librarian and to carry out certain library duties. Under the guidance of the librarian, these groups might be formed into library circles which would help to organize further library work with young readers.

Singapore

A recommendation of a Seminar on School Libraries, sponsored by the Ministry of Education, the British Council and the Library Association of Singapore and held in February 1970, led to the establishment of a Sub-Committee on Standards by the Ministry of Education Standing Committee on Libraries (Ministry and Schools) to draw up a set of standards relating to school libraries in Singapore to serve as a guide and a goal for the organized development of school libraries over a period of five years. Secondary school libraries were first dealt with as most secondary schools had some minimum provision. The compilation of *Recommended Minimum Standards for Secondary School Libraries* was completed by the beginning of 1972 and approved by the Ministry of Education in October, 1972.[1] The standards have been circulated by the Ministry of Education to secondary schools in Singapore and the following is an abridged version of the document.

BASIC PHILOSOPHY

A school library must be centrally developed, encompass many kinds of material that enrich and support the educational programme. It should be geared to the educational philosophy and the needs of the changing curriculum and educational innovation. It cannot therefore be confined to book materials alone.

SCHOOL LIBRARY COLLECTIONS

Printed materials

Book collections. An attractive, imaginative and well balanced book stock selected with both quantity and quality in mind, including books on as wide a range of subjects as possible so as to add books beyond the limitations of the curriculum and to create new interests.
Size of book collection. A basic book stock of five volumes per pupil should be started in all schools, to be built up over a period of five years (present average in most schools, 2.5 volumes per pupil).
Book selection. Should be related to the needs and interests of individual schools, whether technical or academic; should reflect

1. *Recommended Minimum Standards for Secondary School Libraries*, Internal document circulated to principals of secondary schools, 31 October 1972.

the different reading abilities of students; preference should be given to paperbacks to increase purchasing power; responsibility for book selection should be shared by the principal and the teaching staff; the same standard of selection should apply to gifts of books.

Proportion of fiction to non-fiction. In collections for lower secondary classes the proportion should be 40 per cent fiction and 60 per cent non-fiction and for upper secondary classes 30 per cent fiction and 70 per cent non-fiction; for pre-university classes the proportion should be 25 per cent fiction and 75 per cent non-fiction.

Periodicals and newspapers. Schools with secondary 1 to secondary 4 classes should subscribe to 20 to 50 periodicals and schools with pre-university classes from 50 to 70 in all languages used in the school concerned, excluding those distributed free; each school should subscribe to at least 1 local newspaper in each of the languages used in the school.

Government publications, pamphlets, newspaper cuttings, etc. These should be included in the collection.

Teachers' collection. There should be an up-to-date staff collection including essential books for use by the teacher-librarian.

Non-printed materials

Audio-visual materials should also form part of the collection, including pictures, charts, maps, globes, realia, slides, film-strips, loop films, tapes, records, transparencies for overhead projectors and drills for language laboratories. Special problems with regard to security and maintenance of the materials and operating staff will need to be overcome. Ideally, the teacher-librarian should be trained in the use of audio-visual materials as well as of books.

Schools should subscribe to the ETV Instructional Materials Library at an annual rate of $60, so they may borrow audio-visual material.

All schools should have the following items of audio-visual equipment: 1 16 mm sound projector, 3 portable screens; 1 overhead projector; 1 film-strip/slide projector; 1 8 mm loop projector; 2 record players; 1 tape recorder; 1 cassette tape recorder; 2 television sets; 1 episcope; 6 slide viewers; 1 copying machine for making transparences for overhead projectors.

ORGANIZATION AND MAINTENANCE OF COLLECTION

The school library collection should be organized for efficient use so that it is accessible to pupils and staff with the minimum of procedural routine. The collection should be catalogued according to a simple but consistent set of rules and the Dewey Decimal Classification adopted as the standard system of book classification to train pupils and staff to use library materials systematically.

Books and other printed materials should be regularly weeded, discarded or replaced in order to keep the collection fresh and up to date. Materials in poor physical condition should be repaired and rebound as necessary.

STAFF

Teacher-librarian

A trained teacher-librarian should be in charge of the school library. (A teacher-librarian is defined as a qualified teacher who has completed a recognized course in school librarianship and has the status of a specialist teacher.) In the junior colleges and in secondary schools with pre-university classes, a full-time qualified librarian should be in charge of the library.

Duties and responsibilities of the teacher-librarian: the teacher-librarian should be given no more than 15 teaching periods a week, the remaining 15 periods to be devoted to the school library; should not be in charge of other extra-curricular activities; where possible should be exempt from being a form teacher, being in charge of any games or club activities.

The teacher-librarian would be responsible for: over-all supervision of the administration of the library; allocation of budget for books, equipment, furniture, etc.; co-ordination of book selection; ordering books and other library materials; promotion of the use of the library by staff and students, including instruction in library use and organization of library programme; supervision of processing of books and other materials for library use; supervision of maintenance of the library collection; chairing of meetings of the library committee; supervision of clerical staff and student assistants.

Clerical staff

There should be a minimum provision of one half-time clerical staff. The duties of the clerical staff are listed. Apart from routine clerical work this includes changing of books when student assistants are not available and supervising the library when the teacher-librarian is otherwise occupied.

Student assistants

Their duties are described: circulation (charging counter); processing of books and other materials for use; library housekeeping (dusting, cleaning, shelving and shelf-reading); mending and repair of books; maintenance of periodicals (filing paper clippings, etc.); publicity (posters, displays, exhibitions, etc.).

Library committee

A library committee consisting of the teacher-librarian as chairman with the principal as adviser and teacher representatives of subjects taught and languages used in the school. The committee should assist the teacher-librarian in the administration of the library by drawing up rules and regulations; promote the use of the library; promote co-operation with other teachers and students of the school; share responsibility for book selection with the principal and teacher-librarian.

LIBRARY PERIOD

There should be a minimum of one fortnightly library period for secondary 1 and 2 classes, to be used for library activities and not merely for the loan and return of books.

LOCATION, FURNITURE AND EQUIPMENT

Location

The school library must be centrally located for maximum accessibility to staff and students. If possible it should be adjacent to a classroom for future expansion.

Space requirements

The size of the library depends on the number and type of students. There must be adequate room for books and equipment as well as for students to use them. Essential areas to be provided are:

Reading space: an area for reading, circulating and shelving materials, including a minimum of 25–30 ft² (2.3–2.8 m²) seating per reader, with seating for 5 per cent of total student enrolment.

Reference space: an area for use of special reference materials.

Work and storage space: an area where materials are received, catalogued and processed for circulation, also serves as a storeroom for audio-visual equipment.

Glass panelling should be used if the three areas are separated as visible control is important.

Furniture and equipment

To ensure flexibility nothing should be fixed to the floor. Details of quantity, dimensions and arrangement of furniture will depend largely on amount of space allotted to the library and on other physical factors, e.g. wall space, location of windows, ventilation. Recommended items of furniture and specifications:

Shelving—open faced and height of shelves preferably adjustable—standard shelving for average sized books and special shelving for periodicals, newspapers and heavier and larger reference books; standard units of shelving suggested.

Periodicals and newspaper racks—special shelving for display and storage of at least 20–50 periodicals and 1 to 4 newspapers.

Tables and chairs—tables to accommodate not more than 4 readers, dimensions and table/chair heights recommended.

Study carrels—dimensions given.
Counter.
Card catalogue, etc.
Items of furniture and equipment and specifications are recommended for the workroom; also a book trolley and a typewriter.

Lighting

Good day lighting free from glare required; for artificial lighting a minimum of 20–25 lumens/ft^2 is recommended.

Air-conditioning

Should be provided wherever possible in order that books and other materials are protected from dust, humidity and insect pests, excessive noise avoided, and optimum conditions for study provided. When the library is not air-conditioned, ceiling fans should be provided at a minimum ratio of 4 fans for every 40 readers.

United Kingdom

There is no shortage of guidance of a qualitative nature about the place of libraries in schools and the principles on which they should be conducted. The most recent advice given by the central government has been the Department of Education and Science's *The School Library*.[1] Other qualitative advice has been given by the School Library Association, whose members are mostly teachers with some library training, working as school librarians, in such publications as *The Library in the Primary School*,[2] and *Libraries in Secondary Schools*.[3]

Some general statements about the importance of libraries in

1. Department of Education and Science, *The School Library*, London, HMSO, 1967 (Education Pamphlet No. 21).
2. School Library Association, *The Library in the Primary School*, London, 2nd ed. 1966 (a report of the Primary Schools Sub-committee of the SLA).
3. School Library Association, *Libraries in Secondary Schools*, London, 1972 (a report of the Secondary Schools Sub-committee of the SLA).

schools and about the minimum amounts of money considered
necessary for initial book stocks and annual maintenance grants for
secondary school libraries are issued periodically by the Association
of Education Committees (representing the local education authorities) and the National Book League in memoranda on *School
Library Allowances and Allowances for School Text Books, Stationery and
Materials*, last issued in 1971.[1]

For the fullest quantitative standards we have to look to two
items issued by the Library Association (whose members include
an increasing number of qualified librarians employed in school
libraries), the first in 1970, *School Library Resource Centres. Recommended Standards for Policy and Provision*,[2] followed in 1972 by *A
Supplement on Non-book Materials*,[3] an addendum produced because
it was felt that in the earlier document the field of non-book
materials had not been sufficiently explored.

These two publications contain a body of advice, qualitative and
quantitative, describing in detail both the minimum physical
requirements in terms of library provision—library materials, staff,
premises and equipment—and ways in which to organize and
administer this effectively.

What follows here is a brief commentary on selected aspects of
two complementary documents: (a) the School Library Association's *Libraries in Secondary Schools*, which discusses clearly and in a
most up to the minute manner the place of the library in the organization of the school and how it can best serve the school's educational objectives, and provides, at the same time, advice on
library provision and organization and the role of the school
librarian; and (b) the documents issued by the Library Association
which have to be read together. Considerations of space preclude
more. The documents themselves, which are readily available,
merit very detailed study by those concerned with school library
organization, seeking further guidance.

1. Association of Education Committees, *School Library Allowances and Allowances for
School Text Books, Stationery and Materials*, London, 1971.
2. The Library Association, *School Library Resource Centres: Recommended Standards for
Policy and Provision*, London, 1970.
3. The Library Association, *School Library Resource Centres: Recommended Standards for Policy
and Provision—A Supplement on Non-book Materials*, London, 1972.

LIBRARIES IN SECONDARY SCHOOLS, 1972

The library in education

The developing use of the library in all secondary schools was essential to the improvement of secondary education and the School Library Association desired to suggest ways in which this development might take place. The schools had not escaped the consequences of a recent 'explosion of examination taking', which had been one result of the needs of the nation for trained people, of increased social mobility and of the aspirations of parents for their children. As a reaction to this, the idea, starting in the primary school, of the pupil learning rather than the teacher teaching was gaining ground in secondary schools. New 'subjects' had emerged and inter-disciplinary studies. New media for learning favoured the practice of the pupil working individually at his own pace. The teacher's role would always be the same, but his ways of exercising it were undergoing changes. These changes in curricula and teaching methods would increasingly affect the library and the part that it would be called upon to play in the future. The school library was unique in its special context, its relationship with its users, and in the guiding influence that the whole teaching staff, including the librarian, could bring to bear upon its potential readers.

The school library served three main purposes, reference, study and recreative reading. These purposes could not be separated by clearly defined boundaries, and often more than one of them was present in an experience with a book. But for the purpose of discussion the division provided a serviceable framework.

In a primary school a child's library experience was, at best, a rewarding and joyous one. Often the whole school was the library. Books were to be found, and to be seen in use, everywhere and there might be a central collection resembling a conventional library. For many children the transition from primary to secondary school was bewildering and difficult. The easily accessible classroom collection of books, and the freedom to explore the corridors for more, usually disappeared. Secondary school librarians might feel that for the pupils of the first year, or even of the first two years, a pattern of library provision nearer to that of the primary school might be helpful.

The re-organization of secondary education was leading to diversity in the patterns of schooling in different areas, and in the ages of transfer from one school to another. It could no longer be taken for granted that sixth forms (normally age 16–18/19) would be found in secondary schools. Middle schools and sixth form colleges diversified the picture. Nevertheless the schools were basically for pupils from about the age of 11 to the time when they left school, at 16 for some and 18 or 19 for others. The range of age was wide, and the range of ability was the whole secondary school population.

The library in use: reference and enquiry

All other considerations—planning, administration and staffing—followed from use, and from the view of the library's function taken by the head of the school, its staff and its pupils. The active support of the head of the school was vital. He was responsible for ensuring that the school had a valid educational philosophy, which must include the full development of the library and its use. The active involvement of the teaching staff, especially of those influential in the framing of syllabuses and the development of teaching method, was crucial. A good library held a special place among the media that a teacher had at his disposal in the exercise of his craft. It provided a store of material, covering a very wide range, on which both teacher and pupil might freely draw. It was an extremely flexible medium, and its use could be adapted to the capacities and needs of individual pupils, amply justifying the claim that it added a new dimension to the process of learning.

There was no easily definable boundary between the use of a library for reference and its use for study. Study differed from reference in being more sustained, wider and deeper in scope. Reference might at any time lead into study. Successful teaching through the method of inquiry depended upon several factors. The pupils must discover exactly what they were being asked. They should have, in advance, some knowledge, however elementary, of the kinds of books that might be helpful and some familiarity with the arrangement of the books on the library shelves and of the catalogues.

New secondary school entrants needed an introduction to the library. In all but the smallest secondary schools, the librarian would need the help of other colleagues on the staff to cover even the introduction of the first-year pupils, if it was to be done in the first term. Some of the difficulties surrounding the running by the librarian of courses in library use, sometimes extending over several years, were pointed out. Introducing new pupils should ideally be a co-operative undertaking by the librarian and his subject colleagues. The allocation among them of responsibility for talking to the newcomers about books, for helping them to find the books and the references they needed, should be a matter for agreement and might vary from school to school. Reference work, and indeed any use of library resources, was not a 'subject' but a way of learning. Opinions varied as to how long, after the first term, an extended 'introduction' to the library should continue. Many agreed that a 'refresher' might be useful after a lapse of three to four years. The value of the 'library period' was discussed. It was suggested that better than a regular time-tabled period would be a system by which teachers could reserve a period in the library for their classes when they judged it would be useful.

The library in use: study

Learning by inquiry had its rightful place in education because it was the needs of teaching which called for it and were the basis for its use. Library study was one of a number of means of learning that the teacher had at his disposal. It did not supersede all or any of the other well-proved means. It supplemented them. Learning by inquiry was the particular contribution made by library study.

The implications for the library of a particular topic of study were obvious. It must have among its permanent book stock the books and periodicals needed, or the book stock must be supplemented by loans from other libraries or a school library service. This provision could not be made at short notice and called for co-operation between the librarian and his subject colleagues, and an informed understanding on the part of the librarian of what was involved.

The document discussed the dilemma of teachers, particularly those preparing candidates for external examinations, who had to choose between the duty to present to pupils as much of the corpus of subjects as they could take and the duty to enliven their minds, foster their interest and equip them to seek for understanding of their world after they had left school. It stated that, while there must be a basis of exact knowledge, the teacher might consider whether what was learned by personal involvement, by extensive reading and active inquiry, was not likely to be better remembered and more readily useful than that which was learnt in the other way. The association believed that it was profitable to maintain library reading and study through the examination years. The method of inquiry was an educational tool of fundamental importance and there was no substitute for it, though it was not the only way of learning. Time lost to formal instruction and practice was more than compensated for by greater maturity and self-reliance, themselves no small factors in examination success.

Reference was made to the syllabuses for the Certificate of Secondary Education examination, which increasingly included 'course work', pieces of individual study occupying a part of time allocated to a subject over a period of a year or more. The demands of 'course work' placed the library in a position of the greatest importance and, in view of the number of different assignments likely to be in train each year, called for a generous book allowance, spent with perceptive skill.

Space does not permit comment on the next three chapters on 'The Library in Use: Background and Recreational Reading', 'Premises' and 'Finance', but the final chapter, 'The School Librarian', raises general questions about the education, training and experience of the persons who have responsibility for administering the library.

The school librarian

Typically the secondary school library was run as a part-time duty by a member of the teaching staff with his own teaching timetable, reduced sometimes to allow for library administration. Teacher-librarians enlisted help from pupils and some had help and advice from a school library service. Some had clerical help, but they could rarely give sufficient attention to the library to enable it to play its proper part in the work of the school.

This normal pattern of school librarianship, the association considered, had one extremely valuable feature, the link between the library and the day to day work of the school through the teacher-librarian. This the association considered it desirable to retain. As schools became larger and more complex and the school library was used in a variety of new ways in teaching and learning, the existing form of organization was bound to break down.

Most teacher-librarians had acquired a minimum knowledge of library techniques and a Joint Certificate for Teacher-Librarians, instituted in 1956 by the School Library Association in conjunction with the Library Association, provided a basis for the study of school librarianship. Courses in preparation for the examination leading to this and other recognized qualifications in school librarianship had been organized by colleges of further education or of librarianship, as well as by one university institute of education and one university school of librarianship. Further courses were in contemplation. More general courses, national and local, had for many years been organized by the Department of Education and Science, the local education authorities, institutes of education or branches of the association.

The advent of large secondary schools, with complex library accommodation, larger book stocks, non-print material, and much increased use had led some local education authorities to appoint chartered librarians to run school libraries on a full-time basis. These professional librarians had shown that they could give service of a very high quality in school libraries. In a few large secondary schools teachers who were not chartered librarians had been appointed to take charge of such libraries, with no or few commitments to classroom teaching. This they had done with marked success. The significant new element in the situation had not necessarily been that of a different kind of training, but rather that the person in charge of the library had been able to devote most of his time to library work, even if, in order to keep in touch with the academic work of the school, he undertook a regular, though limited, part in subject teaching.

But the number of small secondary schools was diminishing. They were being replaced by much larger schools, rendering more and more out of date the existing pattern of school library administration. Also the pattern of teaching was changing, as had been described in earlier chapters. The school was becoming an environment designed to encourage pupils to learn through personal study, and subject teachers and school librarians were assuming an increasingly tutorial role. Teachers were demanding more efficient and more readily available support from their libraries and pupils were seeking more guidance, not only among books but among the other media that had brought a new dimension into the concept of a school library. The concept included not only the familiar library complex but also a diversified and integrated 'library resources centre'.

Such a 'library' should be open the whole of the school day, and for as much longer time as it was needed for reference and study. When open it could give its best service only if a librarian was present, able to assist teachers and pupils in finding books. The work of the librarian extended outside the library, to taking part in group learning and teaching and discussion with teachers. He therefore needed one or more assistants. The library, as a resource centre, would be concerned with audio-visual material and some such materials, at least, would form part of the library's stock. While the audio-visual materials might be dispersed throughout the school, there should be a union catalogue of them in the library, which should be equipped with apparatus for viewing and listening. Some school libraries would develop into full library resource centres and would have provision for making and distributing audio-visual materials. A knowledge of educational technology should therefore be found within the library's staff. There was need in any event for adequate clerical staff to enable the librarians to use their skill and experience where they were most needed.

School librarians must be aware of trends in educational thought and practice and understand the contribution that the library could make to the curriculum, to teaching method and to the personal development of the pupils. The librarians must be aware of sources of information about printed and other resource material and must be able to keep their colleagues informed about the services of the library. They must be equipped to organize the library and to control the pupils, having a practical knowledge of the psychology of children and skill in managing them.

A librarian in charge of a school library, assisted by one or more other school librarians, clerical assistants and, in a large school, perhaps an educational technician, should be fully conversant with developments in the curriculum and their implications for teaching and learning. He should be fitted by personality to work with subject teachers on equal terms. He should have the enthusiasm and ability to win the confidence of the head and senior members of the staff, inspire subject teachers to integrate the use of the library into their teaching and assist the heads of departments and others in the planning of courses.

The appointment of school librarians should be an educational appointment made in the same manner as appointments to the teaching staff and the persons appointed should be directly responsible to the head of the school. The librarian in charge of the school library should have qualifications comparable with those of the head of a major department and should join in discussion with heads of departments on equal terms.

The School Library Association did not accept as suitable in the long term for appointment to take charge of a school library, anyone who had not had both training and experience as a teacher and training and experience as a school librarian. A very few school librarians had dual qualification in teaching and librarianship but the association did not expect their number ever to meet the need. The association, therefore, considered that, besides those with double qualifications, school librarians should have training and qualifications that differed from the training and qualifications of either teachers or librarians taken separately, though partaking of elements of both. It desired to see the establishment of a specific initial training for a new profession of school librarian with its own courses and its own recognized professional qualification based on this specific training and appropriate practical experience. An important part of the course would be experience in libraries and observation and teaching in schools.

SCHOOL LIBRARY RESOURCE CENTRES: RECOMMENDED
STANDARDS FOR POLICY AND PROVISION 1970:
A SUPPLEMENT ON NON-BOOK MATERIALS 1972
INTRODUCTION

The absence of any published standards had handicapped progress and had led to extreme variations in the provision of school libraries. The situation needed urgent attention, since school libraries in the United Kingdom compared unfavourably with those in the United States, Canada, the Scandinavian countries and elsewhere.

Supplement
It was now commonly accepted that books and non-book materials,

complemented and supported each other and should be regarded as part of a unified collection. The appearance of non-book materials as sources of information and stimuli compelled the library to extend its range so as to continue to fulfil its natural role as a centre for learning, able to exploit all available methods of communication.

THE PURPOSE AND FUNCTION OF THE SCHOOL LIBRARY

The more important needs which a school library should meet were curricular requirements and background reading; cultural development and out-of-school interests; the provision of books for home reading; the provision of opportunities for learning how to use books and of training in the use of libraries.

Primary schools

The library should contain a collection of matter which would encourage and help the children to read with pleasure and help them in all the activities, discoveries and observations which they undertake under the guidance of their teacher.

Middle and secondary schools

In addition to the functions of a primary school library, the secondary school library needed to cater for development in the pupils' abilities and to encourage thinking as well as to provide information.

Supplement

The functions of the school library resource centre included the provision of all kinds of learning material for pupils and teaching materials for the staff. As a communication centre, it should give information on resources available in other parts of the school, from other service agencies (e.g. local authority school library services, other branches of the public library service, museums services), as well as in its own stock. It should also offer facilities for making such material, in a variety of media, by both pupils and staff. The range of materials would cover all which offered information and stimulus for learning experiences. (The activities of the school library resource centre were described in detail.)

The performance of these activities required co-operation, and the professional skills of the chartered librarian, the teacher, and producer/technician.

ADMINISTRATION, ORGANIZATION AND FINANCE

School libraries had developed unevenly and there was need for a reassessment of the place of the library in the school and a greater recognition of the part the public library should play in this.

The highest standards were more easily attainable where there was close co-operation between the local education authority and the library authority. No library could stock all the materials its users would need and few schools could provide all the services necessary for the efficient and economic running of their libraries. Co-operation between the public library and school library was essential if the library was to play an effective part in the life of the school.

The chartered librarian with his training in bibliography, his knowledge of books, his technical skills and his experience of library administration and organization had much to offer the schools. The professional skills of the teacher, his knowledge of children and his experience with children of all types of background made it possible for him to offer practical assistance in book selection and in the introduction and use of books with children.

All education authorities should have a defined policy on the provision of school libraries.

Facilities such as book purchasing and servicing, bibliographical and other advisory services, the circulation of loan collections, project/topic loan services, and the maintenance of collections of drama, music and audio-visual materials would usually be provided centrally.

The future development of school libraries would be towards resource centres, in which all types of communications media were used in addition to books. Already many schools collected films, records and tapes either as part of the library or in a separate audio-visual aids department. A professional librarian was well equipped to deal with them as they relied on library techniques of indexing and systematic arrangement for their successful exploitation, just as much as books.

Co-operation

Co-operation was necessary between chief officers, senior staff in education and library departments, between school library service staff, librarians, teachers and audio-visual aids advisers.

At national level, e.g. greater consultation between the Library Association and the various educational associations.

Between the education authority and library authority, e.g. over the application of standards of book provision, the planning of school libraries, the organizing of library courses for teachers.

At local level—concerned with selection of books and other materials, using panels of teachers, including subject specialists; public library visits; exhibitions; teachers' courses at which book exhibitions were provided; training of student teachers in the use of books and information about the services available from public libraries; meetings of school librarians; supplementary—centralized—services.

Supplement

The development from school library to resource centre was still in its formative stage in most schools, and it was unlikely that any one pattern of organization would be acceptable to all. The school library resource centre should be organized as a unit and be concerned with all relevant teaching and learning materials throughout the school.

There followed discussion under various headings. Under 'Finance', it was stated that such experience as there was suggested the following minimum levels for the successful operation of any school library resource centre: primary school: 350 pupils, capital expenditure £1,000 equipment, £500 materials; recurrent expenditure £2.50 per head. Secondary schools: (a) 500 pupils, capital £2,500, materials £1,500, recurrent expenditure £3 per head; (b) 1,000 pupils, capital £4,000, materials £2,200, recurrent expenditure £3 per head.

STAFF: DUTIES, STATUS AND QUALIFICATIONS

The document included a section on the role of a school library service as part of the education services of a local authority and the staffing of it by qualified librarians, suggesting the functions of the school library organizer and his team. For local authorities serving up to 100 schools, the staffing of the school library advisory service required a minimum of three full-time chartered librarians (with the experience and qualities stated), together with adequate clerical assistance. For authorities serving over 100 schools additional advisory help would be necessary, at least one full-time chartered librarian for every seventy-five schools. Additional services, such as the provision of loan collections, would require extra qualified staff. Rural areas with scattered school populations might warrant a higher staffing ratio in both advisory and supportive services. As the main pressure on the school library service was during term-time, a few posts for professional assistants might be considered suitable for chartered librarians working part-time.

Chartered librarians in schools

Professional help in the primary school would probably be provided by the advisory staff of the school library service, perhaps with the assistance of peripatetic librarians helping small groups of schools. It had been predicted that 'with the increase in the number of large comprehensive schools the need for full-time qualified librarians is likely to increase rapidly'.[1] It was considered essential that schools of 800 pupils and above should have the services of at least one full-time chartered librarian, and the basic scale of staffing given in Table 71 was recommended.

The functions of the chartered school librarian were discussed. They included the following duties: co-ordinating the selection of books and other materials, in consultation with the teaching staff; administering the library/resource centre; providing information, books and materials for pupils, organizing displays; providing bibliographical information on books and materials for staff for their own professional needs as well as for their teaching; in co-operation with the teaching staff, arranging for instruction in library skills, integrating this instruction as far as possible into the learning programme, and supervising the balanced use of the

1. Department of Education and Science, Library Advisory Council (England), Library Advisory Council (Wales), *A Report on the Supply and Training of Librarians*, London, HMSO, 1968.

TABLE 71

Number of pupils	Professional staff[1]	Clerical staff
800–1,000	1 librarian	1
1,000–1,500	1 librarian 1 assistant librarian	1
1,500 and above	1 librarian 2 assistant librarians	2

1. *Librarian*—a chartered librarian with experience and qualities outlined in the document. *Assistant librarian*—either an assistant in his qualifying year, having completed his examinations, or a chartered librarian working part-time. *Clerical staff*—where there was no central purchasing scheme, additional clerical staff would be required. Technical assistance would be required where there was a sizeable quantity of audio-visual material.

library by individuals, groups and classes; acting as a link between the school and all outside sources of information, and encouraging pupils to seek out their further information; maintaining contacts with local libraries and information centres; maintaining contacts with contributing primary schools and further education establishments, and with librarians in college (and institute) of education libraries; co-operating in the school library service with the in-service training of new colleagues, unqualified staff, students of librarianship and student teachers.

The document gave equal weight to two methods of appointment of professional librarians to secondary schools commonly used, that the librarian should be appointed directly to the staff of the school, and that he should be appointed to the school library service in the first place before being allocated to the school after an interview with the head of the school, and possibly the governors. The advantages of both methods were pointed out. Stress was laid on the need for sufficient clerical help and for adequate working conditions.

Many secondary schools would continue to have rolls below 800. Circumstances, particularly the development of the library as a multi-media centre, might warrant the appointment of full-time chartered librarians in smaller schools. Half-time posts for qualified librarians had been established in some smaller schools. Where two smaller schools were co-operating in curriculum matters it might be more satisfactory to appoint a full-time professional librarian to be responsible for the library provision in both schools, with an assistant librarian in each school.

The organization of smaller secondary school and most primary school libraries would continue to be the responsibility of teacher-librarians, some of whom would hold the teacher-librarian certificate sponsored jointly by the Library Association and the School Library Association.

Many teacher-librarians in primary, middle and secondary schools were not given adequate time in the school day to cope with the organization of the school library. This had not only placed an additional burden on busy teachers, but had fostered the view of the school library as an 'extra'. Local authorities should recognize that if the school library was to play an integral and positive role in the work of both primary and secondary schools, adequate staffing provision was a priority.

Supplement

This re-stated the staffing requirements with greater emphasis on the library as a library resource centre. It listed the skills required by the 'Organizer of the library resource centre', stating that the core of these skills was retrieval, organization and dissemination, which predisposed it towards the training of the level received by a chartered librarian. It was essential that such an appointee should have knowledge of, or rapidly make himself acquainted with, the fundamentals of the educational process.

It listed also the skills required for production/technical assistance and the clerical skills. The recommended levels of staffing referred to in the basic document were revised as given in Table 72.

TABLE 72

Number of pupils	Professional staff	Clerical staff
800–1,000	1 librarian 1 production/technical assistant	1
1,000–1,500	1 librarian 1 assistant librarian 1.5 production/technical assistants	1
1,500 and above	1 librarian 2 assistant librarians 2 production/technical assistants	2

STOCK: BOOKS AND OTHER MATERIALS

The school library must contain a well-balanced and carefully selected stock. There were some 30,000 books published annually in the United Kingdom, of which some 2,500 were intended for children, so the choosing of books was no easy task, though it became less difficult if all sources of help were used to the full.

Categories of book stock were discussed suitable for primary, and middle and secondary schools.

While emphasizing that the quality of the stock was as important as the number, the quantitative guidelines shown in Table 73 were laid down.

'Other materials' were referred to but this section has been superseded by the Supplement.

Supplement

An allocation of money had earlier been recommended for the purchase of non-book materials. As the demands of the curricula were variable and different subjects required a different range of material, it was considered inadvisable to stipulate quantities. It was suggested that each school library resource centre should contain a suitable amount of each of the following types of material (excluding books and periodicals dealt with in the main document) depending on the needs of the teaching staff. A list of twenty-three items followed, including pamphlets, maps and charts,

TABLE 73

School	Size of stock	Initial stock	Maintenance of stock
Primary	Not fewer than 8 books per child: total stock between 2,000 and 4,000	Not fewer than 1,000 volumes	One-third of stock replaced, one-twentieth rebound each year
Middle and secondary	Not fewer than 10 books per pupil below sixth-form level, and 15 per pupil at sixth form level	Not fewer than 3,500 volumes	One-sixth of stock replaced, one-tenth rebound each year

photographs, art prints, audio-tapes, gramophone records, globes, relief models, slides, film-strips, overhead projector transparencies, micro-forms and film.

Further sources of supply of these and other media should be available through the supporting services, administered by the local authority school library service.

Most non-book materials could be used in the normal learning spaces of the school library resource centre and required no extra room. Some would need sound-proofed carrels. Minimum quantities of various items of equipment, supplementary to those used outside the school library resource centre (e.g. mains/battery or natural light viewers for slides and film-strips: primary 1 : 40; secondary 1 : 50) were proposed.

Other advice concerning equipment and technical matters, e.g. reprographic, sound and photographic services, was given.

SCHOOL LIBRARY ACCOMMODATION

In the main document advice was given in regard to accommodation and as general guidance total areas were suggested as follows:

Primary schools: upper junior and central library area, 220 ft² (20.44 m²); infants library area, 160 ft² (14.87 m²); lower junior library area, 180 ft² (16.72 m²). This gives a total of 560 ft² (52.02 m²) for 7 class school, 280 children.

Middle and secondary schools: main library, 2,500 ft² (232.25 m²); librarian's workroom, 150 ft² (13.93 m²); visual aids storage and workroom, 200 ft² (18.58 m²); group room, with blackout facilities, 500 ft² (46.45 m²); room for small groups/seminars, 250 ft² (23.22 m²). This gives a total of 3,600 ft² (334.45 m²) for 8 form entry.

Supplement

This suggested that the minimum provision for a middle or secondary school library resource centre should be: main library, 2,500 ft² (232.25 m²); librarian's workroom, 150 ft² (13.93 m²); audio-visual workroom, 300 ft² (27.86 m²); planning and reprographic area, 500 ft² (46.44 m²); facilities for studying material, 750 ft² (69.66 m²). This gives a total of 4,200 ft² (390.1 m²).

United States of America

National standards for school libraries in the United States were first formulated in 1918 by the Library Committee of the Department of Secondary Education of the National Education Association. Such standards have continued to be developed by the American Library Association, regional accrediting associations,[1] state departments of education, and professional associations of school librarians. Regional and state school library standards have changed rapidly, particularly since 1960, when the American Library Association published *Standards for School Library Programs*[2] based on experience in schools which have very good school libraries.

The Office of Education of the United States Department of Health Education and Welfare, published in 1960 a study of state department of education responsibilities and services for school libraries.[3] This served as a basis for a policy statement by the Council of Chief State Officers in 1961.[4] This refers to the aspects of school library work for which the state departments of education should provide standards, recommends the American Association of School Librarians' standards as a guide for developing state standards and states certain basic principles for the development and implementation of them. A comprehensive report was issued by the Office of Education in 1964, *Survey of School Library Standards*,[5] analysing regional and state standards showing, *inter alia*, the relation of these standards to the national standards. It includes the official

1. Regional accrediting associations set standards, *inter alia*, for school libraries as part of their evaluation of schools to determine whether a school can be admitted to membership.
2. American Association of School Librarians, *Standards for School Library Programs*, Chicago, Ill., American Library Association, 1960.
3. Mary Helen Mahar, *State Department of Education Responsibilities for School Libraries*, Washington, D.C., United States Department of Health, Education and Welfare, Office of Education, 1960.
4. Council of Chief State Officers, *Responsibilities of State Departments of Education for School Library Services, A Policy Statement*, Washington, D.C., Council of Chief State Officers, 1961.
5. United States Department of Health, Education and Welfare, *Survey of School Library Standards*, Washington, D.C., 1964.

statements of school library standards by regional and state organizations and state departments of education, and discusses their characteristics and differences. (In general, national standards for media programmes are higher quantitatively than state and regional standards. Over the years, higher national standards have tended to improve state standards.)

Discussing trends in 1964, the report comments on the adoption increasingly of standards for elementary schools and the application of general school library standards to both elementary and secondary schools; the practice of administering the school library as an instructional materials centre; a tendency to rely more on certification of school librarians within the framework of teachers' qualifications and less on the system of basing the amount of professional education required on the varying enrolments of schools; the development of centralized school library services administered at the school system level and of centralized school library supervision; and the activity in school library standards revision and in the formation of new standards in states which have not had them.

In 1965, the Department of Health, Education and Welfare, Office of Education, issued a publication of its Bureau of Educational Research and Development entitled *Library Facilities for Elementary and Secondary Schools*.[1] This discusses trends in education and their significance for school libraries and sets out guidelines for planning school libraries. Quantitative recommendations contained in this publication are based on those given in the American Library Association's *Standards for School Library Programs, 1960*, and on standards for school libraries developed by state departments of education.

The development of school libraries in the United States has been greatly stimulated by the Elementary and Secondary Education Act, 1965, which authorized the United States Office of Education to make grants for five years for the acquisition of school library materials and to the Knapp School Libraries Project, financed by the Knapp Foundation and funding eight demonstration schools, each co-operating with a college of education, from which the general conclusion could be reached that wider and more effective

---

1. United States Department of Health Education and Welfare *Library Facilities for Elementary and Secondary Schools*, Washington, D.C., 1965.

use of the libraries resulted from better materials and more adequate staff.

In November 1967, the Knapp Foundation continued its interest and support in the school library field through a $1,163,718 grant to the American Library Association for the School Library Manpower Project, to be administered by the American Association of School Librarians. This project evolved from problems identified during the Knapp School Libraries Project. The School Library Manpower Project was designed to study and submit findings regarding the lack of sufficient professionally trained school library personnel. Phase I of the project focused on a task analysis study leading to new occupational definitions of school library personnel.[1] In Phase II, the project has implemented the development of six innovative experimental programmes in school library media education. The full evaluative report of these six programmes will be published in late 1973.

Current standards for school libraries in the United States were published in 1969 by the American Library Association and the National Education Association under the title of *Standards for School Media Programs*.[2] The standards were prepared by a widely representative joint committee of the American Association of School Librarians[3] and the Department of Audio-Visual Instruction of the National Education Association, in co-operation with a large number of important professional (mainly educational) and other associations. The joint document largely replaces the 1960 *Standards for School Library Programs* and the two documents issued by the Department of Audio-Visual Instruction of the National Education Association,[4] hitherto the current standards documents in this field.

1. American Library Association, *Occupational Definitions for School Library Media Personnel*, Chicago, Ill., 1971.
2. American Library Association and National Education Association, *Standards for School Media Programs*, Chicago, Ill., and Washington, D.C., 1969.
3. This is both a division of the American Library Association and a Department of the National Education Association.
4. The Department of Audio-Visual Instruction, National Education Association, *Quantitative Standards for Audio-visual Personnel, Equipment and Materials in Elementary, Secondary and Higher Education*, developed by Gene Faris and Mendal Sherman. Washington, D.C., Department of Audio-Visual Instruction, National Education Association, January 1966 (mimeo.); W. R. Fulton, *Criteria Relating to Educational Media Programs in School Systems*, Washington, D.C., Department of Audio-Visual Instruction, National Education Association (mimeo.). Both titles are part of a study conducted under the auspices of the United States Department of Health, Education and Welfare, Office of Education.

The 1969 *Standards for School Media Programs* were developed primarily for individual school building programmes. In 1972, revision of the building level standards for the district/system/regional level was begun. Both the revision and the new publication are jointly sponsored by the American Association of School Librarians and the Association for Educational Communication and Technology (formerly Department of Audio-Visual Instruction).

CURRENT STANDARDS

The two objectives stated for this new joint publication are to bring standards up to date and to co-ordinate standards for both school library and audio-visual purposes. The term media is used to refer to both printed and audio-visual forms of communication and their accompanying technologies; other terms commonly employed in this combined approach are media programme, media specialist and media centre.

The standards describe the service of the media programme in the school, and note the requirements for the staff needed to implement the programme. Standards are given for a unified programme, but they can be applied in schools having separate school libraries and audio-visual centres.

The standards apply to schools with 250 or more students but can serve as guidelines to certain schools with fewer than that number of students.

In setting out a number of qualitative standards, the document stresses the importance of schools having adequate library and visual aid resources, stating that:

Today, educators and other citizens realize that educational programmes of vitality, work and significance to students and to society depend upon excellent media services and resources in the schools.

The media programme is described as a resource for learning and a resource for teaching, and the resources and services of the media centre are seen as a fundamental part of the educational process, enabling students and teachers to make a multi-media or intermedia approach to and use of materials, selecting from among many resources the media best suited to answer their specific need.

It is recommended that, wherever possible, separate school libraries and audio-visual departments should be combined to form a unified media programme and that new schools should start with a unified media centre and programme of services. The new standards do not cover the specialized services and other needs of schools for handicapped children, for which standards have been recommended only for schools of the deaf.[1]

STAFF AND SERVICES

Discussing the elements of the media programme, standards are stated for professional and non-professional staff.

Professional staff

The professional staff provides teachers and students with a wide variety of services of which the following are significant examples: serving as instructional resource consultants and materials specialists to teachers and students; working with teachers in curriculum planning; teaching the effective use of media to members of the teaching staff; assisting children and young people to develop competency in listening, viewing and reading skills.

Where there are two or more professional staff members, one should be the head of the media centre. If the major preparation of the senior professional is in the library field, the second should have a speciality in the audio-visual field and vice versa. The head of the media centre should have the status at least equal to that of head of the subject department.

There should be one full-time media specialist for every 250 students or major fraction thereof.

All media specialists responsible for instructional decision should have, as part of their professional preparation, a knowledge of certain fundamentals—which are described—in the general field of education and in areas related to media resources and services. The

1. *Standards for Library—Media Centres in Schools for the Deaf. A Handbook for the Development of Library-media Programs,* Washington, D.C. Captioned films for the deaf, United States Office of Information, 1967; sponsored by the American Instructors of the Deaf.

need for specialization in the school media field and in the professional education of media specialists is stressed and recommendations are made about this specialization, which can focus on the level of school, the subject matter or the type of media. In-service training is stressed so that media specialists can update and expand their professional competence. All professionals with responsibility for making instructional decisions should be certified as qualified teachers.

Supporting staff

The supporting staff of the media centre should include media technicians and media aides, the latter for largely typing and other clerical duties. Such staff make it possible for the media specialists to concentrate their time on professional work. At least one technician and one aide should be employed for each professional media specialist in schools of 2,000 or fewer students. Additional technicians and aides should be appointed to support special activities such as television, broadcasting and language laboratories. In a school with more than 2,000 students, the number of technicians and aides might be adjusted; for the number of 2,000 the ratio of supporting staff to media specialists might be less than the recommended 2 : 1.

SELECTION, ACCESSIBILITY
AND ORGANIZATION OF MATERIAL

Before recommending quantitative standards for the material resources of the centre, the document sets out a further series of qualitative standards dealing with policies and procedures governing the selection, accessibility and organization of the material. A few examples are quoted here:

Selection policies

The collection meets the requirements of the various curricular areas and provides for the diverse skills of individuals representing all levels and types of ability.

Selection procedures

The co-operation of teachers and curriculum personnel in the selection of materials for the media centre is always enlisted, and their suggestions receive priority consideration . . . teachers and curriculum personnel welcome and must have the services of qualified media specialists in selecting resources for teaching and learning in the school.

Accessibility of materials

In the media centre:

The media centre is open at all times of the school day, and also before and after school. In order to expand services to students and teachers and to obtain greater returns from the school's investment in materials and equipment, these hours are being extended to include evenings, Saturdays and vacation periods. . . . Some co-operative arrangements may be made among a group of schools to rotate evening hours of service so that one media centre at a time is open to students.

In the classrooms and other teaching areas:

Resources of the centre are made easily accessible throughout the school. Materials from the media centre are sent to classrooms and other teaching areas, not served directly by a formally organized branch, on a short or long-term work basis. The use of such sources as film-strips and 8 mm films is important and each student should have access to materials and necessary equipment in the classroom and other teaching areas.

Organization of materials

Advice is given about the best organization and arrangement of materials. Cataloguing and processing of material should be undertaken centrally to ensure expert service and economy of effort, and to leave professional staff in the media centre free to work directly with students and teachers.

THE RESOURCES OF THE MEDIA CENTRE:
SIZE AND EXPENDITURE

The quantitative standards recommended for the nature and extent of the materials to be provided are derived from the principles and qualitative standards previously discussed.

Among the detailed standards recommended for schools of 250 students or over the principal are the following. Excluded are textbook collections and dictionaries, encyclopaedias, magazines and newspapers for classroom use.

Books. At least 6,000 to 10,000 titles, representing 10,000 volumes, or 20 volumes per student, whichever is greater.

Magazines. Elementary school (K-6) 40–50 titles; (K-8) 50–75 titles; junior high school 100–125 titles; secondary school 125–175 titles; all schools—in addition: necessary indexes and duplication of titles and indexes as required.

Newspapers. Elementary school, 3–6 titles; junior high school, 6–10 titles; secondary school, 6–10 titles; all schools—1 local, 1 state and 1 national newspaper.

Pamphlets, clippings and miscellaneous material. As appropriate for the curriculum and for other students' interests.

Film-strips. 500 to 1,000 titles, representing 1,500 prints or 3 prints per pupil, whichever is greater (the number of titles to be increased in larger collections).

8 mm films. Single concept—1.5 films per student with at least 500 titles supplemented by duplicates. Regular length—no precise standard; abundant number recommended.

16 mm films. Number acquired would depend on various factors. Recommendation: access to a minimum of 3,000 titles, supplemented by duplicates and rentals.

Tape and disc recordings. 1,000 to 2,000 titles representing 3,000 records or tapes or 6 per student, whichever is greater (the number of titles to be increased in larger collections).

Slides. 2,000 (including all sizes of slides).

Graphic materials (e.g. art prints; reproductions). 1,000 with duplicates as needed.

Transparencies. 2,000 plus a selection of subject matter masters.

Standards are also recommended for material for the use of administrative and teaching staff. A school of 250 or more students should provide: 200–1,000 book titles; 40–50 professional magazine titles, with duplicates, also an education index. Advice is given as to the types of material to be included in the professional collection.

EXPENDITURE

Discussing the desirable level of expenditure on the maintenance of an up-to-date collection of materials in the media centre, it is recommended that not less than 6 per cent of the national average operational cost per pupil should be spent per year per student (1968–69 estimated national average per pupil expenditure was $680; 6 per cent was approximately $41). Normally, half the expenditure should be on printed materials and half on audio-visual materials. The amount would be used to purchase basic material for both the individual school and system media centre, and does not include the cost of general textbooks, reference material housed permanently in classrooms, closed circuit or subscription television, electronic learning centres and other specified items. Where there are separate school libraries and audio-visual programmes, each should have its share of the funds, ordinarily not less than 3 per cent of the per pupil cost.

PREMISES AND EQUIPMENT

Standards are stated in general terms dealing with: (a) environment—functional design; inviting appearance; good lighting; sound proofing; (b) location and space—in quiet area; easily accessible to students and teachers; accessible without opening the entire school for extended hours of service; variations in the design and arrangement of media centres.

Detailed specifications are given for space required for different rooms or purposes. The figures are based on an enrolment of 1,000 students or less, and should be increased proportionately in larger schools. They should also be increased if there is more than one media centre or a media centre with resource or satellite centres. Examples of significant standards: areas for reading and browsing; areas for individual viewing and listening: space based on 15 per cent of student enrolment at 40 ft² (3.7 m²) per student, minimum space for 50 students, no more than 100 students should be seated in one area; for individual study and learning; for story telling (elementary schools); for information services—the instructional programme in some schools may require that from 33 per cent to 75 per cent of the student population be accommodated in the media centres, 30–40 per cent of seating capacity should be for individual study areas, including carrels; 3–6 conference rooms with 150 ft² (14 m²) each, movable walls to allow for combining areas; 200 ft² (18.6 m²) for small group viewing and listening in addition to space for conference rooms; 900 to 1,000 ft² (84 to 93 m²) for group projects and instruction in research, flexible space, equivalent to a classroom equipped for instructional purposes; 800–1,000 ft² (74 to 93 m²) for media production laboratory;

600 to 800 ft² (56 to 74 m²) for a centre for professional materials for teaching staff, should be designed as a teachers' conference room adjacent to media production laboratory.

Optional spaces include television and radio studios and computerized learning laboratories. Standards for all kinds of equipment, largely audio-visual, are described.

SUPPLEMENTARY SERVICES

Standards are also indicated in descriptive terms, showing how the media centres in individual schools depend on and should be supplemented by school systems media centres (serving one or more school systems), regional and state media centres.

Standards for library service
in developing countries

The writer has been asked by Unesco to prepare a set of standards for the different types of libraries which might be applied in the developing countries. In principle there should be no more difficulty in producing standards for these countries than for others, which, though more highly developed economically and in other ways, are without adequate library services. Library standards for the developing countries are, however, likely to have some marked differences from those in certain other countries, if only as a reflection of certain distinctive characteristics, such as relatively low levels of gross national product, literacy, amount of library material available in local languages and published in the country, as well as the lack of trained and educated staff.

It cannot be ignored that the level of library service at a given time and place depends not only on the desire but on the capacity of a country to provide the physical resources needed. Even in the more highly developed countries there are great differences in the levels of service, whether actual or recommended. Often standards which are based on good current practice represent for a country only the best that can be afforded at that time. No attempt is made to justify them on more rational grounds.

In some poorer countries it may not be possible, even in the foreseeable future, to provide a library service of a satisfactory standard over the whole country. This is no reason why a service of high standard should not be produced in particular areas of the country and subsequently extended to others, which is what has been happening in developing countries in Africa, of which Tanzania is a good example, and in other parts of the world. A more widespread provision of a sub-standard service is likely to be uneconomic and might prove of little value. It is therefore desirable to establish, as the new IFLA public library standards[1] set out to do, the minimum which it is worth while to provide, so that governments can appreciate what kind and level of library services they should be providing—and indeed must provide if the countries are to develop economically. The detailed requirements can only be worked out on the spot by persons with a knowledge of local conditions. These would have to have regard to the resources which could be made available. But the requirements can be worked out within a general framework, the outline of which can be derived from the statements of standards of library service which have been studied.

The framework could be on the general lines of the models following. The main headings, under which basic standards have been written and other subordinate standards can be easily drawn up, are applicable to all types of libraries. No attempts have been made to state quantitative standards as it is in those areas that local circumstances and local knowledge and experience must be applied. Much work would need to be done by librarians in respect of their own countries or regions in describing the minimum needs of the different types of libraries. The needs will vary with the extent to which the provision of library and information services is run as an integral part of economic, cultural and educational planning and the extent to which provision is made for integrating the planning of such services into other development plans.

The working party set up by the Public Libraries Section of IFLA to revise the earlier public library standards considered whether to formulate separate standards for developing countries, but, after consulting member associations, decided that this was not desirable as the general objectives in all countries were the same, the only modifying factors being the pace at which development could take place.

The 1973 IFLA public library standards paid particular attention to the application of the standards to developing countries. It may be useful to indicate some of the guidance given to developing countries or which is particularly applicable to them.

---

1. International Federation of Library Associations, Section of Public Libraries, *Standards for Public Libraries*, Pullach bei München, Verlag Documentation, 1973.

Paragraph *16*

In some countries library services have been provided on a national basis. This method may be especially appropriate in a developing country where a large administrative unit is particularly important, if limited resources are to be used to the greatest extent.

Paragraph *18*

The smallest administrative unit for public library purposes (defined as a unit of public library service which is independent in the sense that it has its own governing body, receives and manages its own funds and appoints its own staff) that can be contemplated in any circumstances would have a population of 3,000. Below this figure no useful standard can be defined. It should be made absolutely clear that such a figure is only acceptable if no other solution is possible—e.g. in areas with an extremely low density of population or extreme difficulty of communications. Wherever possible, the administrative unit should be a much larger one in terms of population. The smaller the unit, the more important it is that it should co-operate with other units.

Paragraph *21*

Very small communities and isolated homes need to be served by mobile libraries, deposit collections or postal services. . . . Deposit collections, sometimes the only practicable alternative to mobile libraries, are expensive in regard to bookstocks, and are often frustrating to users. They are acceptable only when difficulties of communication leave no alternative.

Paragraph *24*

In countries with developing library services, the recommended levels of provision cannot be attained immediately, but in small communities in particular the stock of books should be in sight of the standards laid down. A stock of less than 9,000 volumes cannot give a range of material nor be considered an adequate base for satisfactory service.

Paragraph *25*

Generally, the standards relate to literate population, but even so the stock of 9,000, appropriate to a unit of 3,000 population, is considered a minimum.

Paragraph *27*

Even in a small community, a basic collection of reference material is necessary, and this is particularly true in developing countries, where there may be few reliable sources of information outside the library. Provision may, however, be limited by the insufficient production of reference works relevant to the country in question, or in indigenous languages.

Paragraph 36

The standards for accessions may sometimes have to be modified to take account of the amount of national book production, which may be unbalanced in relation to public library requirements. This applies particularly in some developing countries. It will usually be necessary, however, to supplement the country's own output by acquiring books published in other countries and in other languages, particularly in technical subjects.

Paragraph 41

The provision in libraries of periodicals (including newspapers) may be particularly important in developing countries with low standards of literacy, since periodicals are often especially valuable for the newly literate. In such countries, moreover, the production of periodicals is usually in advance of book production.

Paragraph 43

In developing countries in particular, the cost of providing audio-visual materials, and the equipment needed for its use, must be weighed very carefully against the potential use of the material. . . . audio-visual materials may provide a more effective medium (than printed materials) for certain kinds of communication.

Paragraph 68

Population is regarded as the most satisfactory basis for the formulation of staffing standards, particularly as far as qualified staff are concerned, but the other factors mentioned (volume of use; the range of services required) may require the modification of any standard based on population alone; this will be particularly true in a developing service, where the value to be attached to all three factors needs to be regularly reviewed.

Paragraph 71

In the postulated minimum administrative unit of 3,000 population with 9,000 books, some periodicals and a service both to adults and children, a full-time qualified librarian will be justified. Some clerical assistance will also be necessary.

Paragraph 76

In developing countries, lack of training facilities may make the appointment of sufficient qualified librarians difficult in the early stages. Initially, these librarians may, in some cases, have to obtain their training in other countries. Where this is the case it is particularly important that the developing public library service should organise in-training facilities, until training within the educational system of the country becomes feasible.

Paragraph 80

In certain circumstances it may even be possible for a public library to serve simultaneously as the library of a school or other educational institution, especially when that institution aims to meet more comprehensively the cultural and social needs of the community. By such means as these the community will often be able to gain the maximum use and value of the related facilities.

Frank Gardner, who as chairman of the public libraries section of IFLA was responsible for the production of these new public library standards, commenting on a statement of public library aims and objectives recently published in the United Kingdom, has suggested that the definition of objectives, not for the application of management techniques but for the most useful distribution of scarce financial, material and human resources, is a necessity in a developing country.

Naturally the objectives would be different—co-ordination with adult literacy organisations, central direction of school library services, emphasis on lending rather than reference would be prominent. The provision of materials and methods would be more sparingly outlined.[1]

At the third of four regional conferences, in Kampala in 1970 (the other conferences being in Quito (1966), Colombo (1967) and Cairo (1973)), organized by Unesco, the meeting of librarians and documentalists from twelve African countries agreed that a single national body should be established in each country responsible for the development of a fully integrated national library service, and that among its functions should be the establishment of national standards for the efficient operation of library and information services.

A measure of what was considered as appropriate for developing countries in Africa was given in the report of the conference.[2]

---

1. Frank M. Gardner, 'Public Library Aims and Objectives', *Unesco Bulletin for Libraries*, Vol. XXVII, No. 4, July-August 1973.
2. Unesco, *Expert Meeting on National Planning of Documentation and Library Services in Africa. Final Report*, Kampala, Uganda, December 1970, Unesco (mimeo., COM/MD/18, Paris, March 1971). Also E. Max Broome, 'The Organization and Planning of Library Development in Africa: An Account of the Meeting of Experts on the National Planning of Documentation and Library Services in Africa, Kampala, Uganda, December 1970', *Unesco Bulletin for Libraries*, Vol. XXV, No. 5, September-October 1971.

Quoting actual figures for the African countries of book stocks available as a low target for the different types of library, the conference recommended moderate and high targets for total book stocks to be reached by 1980.

For national libraries, where the actual figure was estimated at 50 volumes per 1,000 literates, moderate and high targets of 75 and 100 volumes respectively were set. For university libraries the actual figure of 50 volumes per student was retained as a moderate target and the 1980 figure was set at 75 volumes. For school libraries a much greater rate of improvement was proposed, the figures expressed as volumes per student being actual 0.1; moderate 0.5; and high 1.0.

For public libraries the figures, like those for national libraries, expressed as volumes per 1,000 literates, were based on the total of literate population and were actual (low target) 100; moderate target 250; and high target 500. This gives only a broad measure of the extent and rate of the improvement proposed. Had the figures been calculated on the basis of the total literate population actually served within the catchment areas of libraries, as were the figures for universities and schools, they would have been very different and more useful as 'library standards'. For comparison, the new IFLA public library standards, which in general relate to literate population, require minimum book stocks of 2 volumes per inhabitant in all but the smallest communities. In these the requirements are greater.

Costs in 1980 were estimated on various assumptions in relation to the estimated cost at that date of total educational expenditure. This resulted in figures showing library services representing 4.9 per cent and 7.3 per cent of total educational expenditure for the moderate and high targets, compared with 2.9 for 1970.

Documents like this indicate how far such countries still have to go to reach generally acceptable minimum standards of library service and that this will take a considerable time to achieve.

One final point is made at the risk of repetition. There are different library needs and different types of libraries. Where the resources are available it is common, and may be most appropriate, to cater for different needs in separate libraries. This, as well as best suiting the convenience of the users, has the advantage of ensuring the supply of the same or similar material from several sources. But, where human and material resources are scarce, and are likely to remain so for reasons not solely connected with the availability of money but also connected with shortage of library materials and of suitable staff, it is necessary to co-ordinate library provision to ensure optimum public use.

The standards drawn up on the basis of the model may need to reflect decisions taken about the provision of libraries or library services fulfilling multiple roles. In some countries university libraries are fulfilling many of the functions of a national library and are likely to continue to do so. In at least one country, Singapore, the national library is providing the public library service. There are combined university and city libraries and combined public and technical college libraries in certain countries. Combined public and school library service is commonly found and, as the IFLA public library standards suggest, this may often prove to be the best way to proceed.

MODEL STANDARDS FOR LIBRARY SERVICE

National library	Libraries in universities and colleges

Role and function

Provides for the benefit of the nation generally, and scholars and research workers in particular, the following: Basic: (a) the outstanding and central collection of the nation's literature; (b) a major collection of literature in foreign languages of particular interest to the country; (c) a national bibliographical service.
According to circumstances: (a) co-ordination of the leadership in the organization of a national library service; (b) research in library techniques; (c) education in librarianship at an advanced level.

Provide, in co-operation with other libraries, library and information services for the benefit of the students and staff as an essential part of the university's or college's facilities for study and research. They should also make their facilities available, under suitable conditions, to other serious scholars and research workers.

Structure and government

This would vary according to circumstances, for example, it might be com-

The library should be administered by a librarian directly responsible to the

413

National library	Libraries in universities and colleges

bined with a major university. There might be more than one national library, divided by function or otherwise. The library should be under the executive control of a librarian of high qualifications and suitable experience.

head of the university or institution. A library committee with advisory functions only should be appointed consisting of representatives of the teaching staff and students. All library provision and staff in departmental and other libraries in the university or college should be under the control of the librarian, and principles under which separate collections are administered should be stated. The library should co-operate fully with other university or college libraries and with the national and other libraries so as to secure the maximum concentration of bibliographical and other resources.

Services

Standards should indicate that: The library should provide: (a) reference collection of the nation's literature complete for current publications through legal deposit and as complete as possible for earlier literature; (b) major reference collection of materials in foreign languages; (c) National Bibliographic Service, compiling and publishing a national bibliography and national union catalogue.

Lending (apart from specially created national lending libraries) should be controlled, no material provided under legal deposit being lent, except duplicate copies, but photocopying facilities should be available.

The library should issue publications relating to its work and library services generally.

Standards would be required indicating the nature of the library's services and how far the library should directly assist other libraries, with the supply of books and other material.

The library should provide accommodation for independent study by students and research workers, together with the printed and other material required for their work and cultural development. It should provide instruction in the use of the facilities offered by the library. It should provide for the library needs of academic staff and other appropriate persons, including industrial firms and organizations and members of professional groups. It should provide a central catalogue of library holdings and central acquisitions and processing, and library materials should be readily available, with as much open access as possible.

National library	Libraries in universities and colleges

Materials

The library should provide access to materials in all forms, books, manuscripts, pamphlets, periodicals, newspapers, music, maps, prints, engravings, as well as other means of communication, such as micro-film, gramophone records, tapes, computerized data, bibliographical aids, such as lists of current and older publications, catalogues, indexes, etc.

The library should provide all appropriate forms of material by which information and understanding can be acquired: books and other forms of printed material, maps, illustrations, pictures and various types of audio-visual material.

Standards should state how the quality of the material should be assured and recommend minimum holdings of the different material according to local bibliographical and other circumstances. Materials should be selected by the librarian and staff, in association with the teaching staff and others concerned as users.

Quantitative standards for book and other materials must be calculated by local librarians having regard to the extent of available local language material and the extent to which material in other languages will be useful. Accession standards must be worked out on a country basis, having regard to the state of publishing, the extent of use, the physical quality of books and other material produced in the country, and other factors.

Staffing

Standards should indicate the nature of academic and library specialisms required in the library, and the part staff should play in other work, e.g. research and education and training.

Standards should indicate the extent to which professional members of staff should be involved in the educational programmes of the institution, instructing the students and others in the use of the library and in access to bibliographical and other information, and in other ways.

Standards should:
Stress the vital importance of staff adequate in numbers and quality from the highest professional to the lowest clerical and manual worker, since without them the most comprehensive collection of library materials is almost useless.
Define the minimum personal, educational, professional and other qualifications necessary for work at various levels in the particular type of library, which consists basically of successful selection and organization of materials and promotion of their use.

State that professional staff should, except in the smallest service points, be available to provide professional services at all hours when libraries are open or when such services are required.

Define broadly the nature of professional duties within the library and state that sub-professional, clerical and other staff should be employed in sufficient numbers to enable professional staff to undertake the maximum amount of professional work.

Indicate numbers or proportions of professional staff and other staff, having regard to relevant factors such as population, student and staff numbers, readership, issues, accessions, and other circumstances.

State that conditions of appointment and employment should be such as would attract suitable persons to undertake the work and posts should be organized as part of a career service.

Standardization and statistics

Standards should provide that, since the quality of service is affected by the efficiency of the technical procedures adopted in the library and by the way human, material—and financial—resources are used, libraries should, as far as possible, employ standardized procedures, e.g. in cataloguing and classification. Standards should be such as to permit input to and access to the main international mechanized bibliographical information services.

Standards should prescribe the regular collection of selected statistics, on a common basis as recommended by Unesco, so that the extent to which the service measures up to recommended national or international standards can be ascertained, the use made of the library studied, and valid comparisons made with other libraries.

Premises

General

Standards should indicate:

That all libraries should be housed in premises suitable for the efficient performance of the library's various functions.

That new library premises should be planned on a functional basis (aesthetic and other considerations being secondary), should be flexible and, while being built to satisfy foreseeable needs, should be capable of extension.

The importance of a suitable location for both main and subordinate libraries, relative to the convenience of users and to facilitate the library's task of encouraging the use of its facilities.

The importance of making the library buildings and furnishings attractive to and comfortable for users, and of giving attention to such features as good lighting, temperature, ventilation and noise control.

Ways of measuring areas of accommodation required for different purposes, based on figures for: (a) books in open shelving and limited access or closed book stacks, and for storage of other material; (b) readers in reference libraries, reading rooms and other parts of the library, according to type of accommodation (seats only, large or small tables, carrels, etc.); (c) staff and work processes; (d) amenities (e.g. toilets, refreshment facilities) and services (e.g. air-conditioning); (e) other library purposes, such as exhibitions, lectures, meetings, classes, staff training; (f) provision for adequate movement of users and staff during periods of maximum use.

Each country—or group of countries—will need to work out building standards according to the particular local circumstances which are likely to affect the total amount of space and proportions required for each purpose. For very large libraries, special libraries and national libraries, there is less prospect of standardization, but for all libraries the advice given in authoritative publications, including *Unesco Manuals for Libraries*, Nos. 10 and 14, *The Small Public Library Building* and *University Libraries for Developing Countries* and the IFLA public library standards are likely to prove of value.

Special library	Public library	School library or resource centre

Role and function

Standards should indicate the general ways in which the libraries provide, in co-operation with other libraries, services for the benefit of:

The members, staff of the organization providing the library and to others concerned with the activities or subject field of the organization.	The whole community, to enrich life individually and collectively. Its scope should be broadly defined in relation to education, leisure and recreation, the library and information needs of local commerce, industry and government agencies, and the extent to which the library acts as a cultural centre.	The students and staff of the school, as an aid to teaching and learning and to the cultural improvement and recreation of the individuals concerned.

Structure and government

The library should be under the control of a competent administrator of suitable training and experience either as a	The library should normally be provided by an organ of local, regional, state or central government, singly or in	The library should be administered as part of the school and subject to its conditions. The library should also be associated with a larger

Special library	Public library	School library or resource centre
librarian, information scientist and subject specialist, responsible directly to top management in the organization concerned.	association. The library organization should be capable of establishing and maintaining a comprehensive and efficient service. While policy decisions should preferably be made by democratically elected persons, day to day management should be in the hands of a professional librarian.	school library organization, provided by the area administering the school or a larger unit, or the public library service, so that the maximum number and range of books and other materials and staff services can be made available.

Services

Standards should indicate that:

The library should provide materials for reference or lending, information and other services to further the objects of the organization served, bibliographical services such as literature searches, translations, abstracts and indexes, and other means for the efficient dissemination of information, and provision should be made for minority language groups.	The public library service should include lending books and other suitable material to all literate adults and children, and a reference and information service to all sections of the community. The library should co-operate, if necessary acting jointly with school and other educational institutions and other community institutions and groups. The service should be available to all without discrimination. The borrowing of printed and all (or most) other material, and the reference and information service,	The library, or resource centre, should provide a lending and reference service to students and staff and organize book and non-book material for their use throughout the school. It should also provide instruction to the students in the use of books and accommodation for independent work. It should play an active part in the preparation of instructional material involving the use of books and other media. It may be involved in the provision and administration of audio-visual services throughout the school.

Special library	Public library	School library or resource centre
	should be without special charge. 'Standards' should outline desirable levels of service, including as much open access as possible, and patterns of service points.	

Materials

| The library should provide a variety of forms and types of material appropriate to the particular library, such as books, pamphlets, reprints, translations, periodicals, technical reports, patents, specifications and standards, and audio-visual materials and special collections in printed or other forms. The range and depth should be determined by the objects of the organization. | The library should provide books and other printed material and also other forms of material such as films, records, tapes, slides, illustrations, through which information can be given and knowledge and understanding acquired. Categories of material should be defined. Facilities should be provided for access to contemporary programmes of radio and television. Other standards should indicate how the comprehensiveness, quality and objectivity of the material should be assured and recommend minimum quantitative standards, appropriate to local circumstances, for printed and other kinds of material. | The library should provide for pupils and staff access to books and other printed material, as well as other media, such as records, tapes and films, for both reference and lending purposes, together with suitable accommodation for reading and research. The provision should be in support of the school curriculum, and of the general cultural development of the pupils. |

Quantitative standards for book and other materials must be calculated by local librarians having regard to the extent of available local language material and the extent to which material in other languages will be useful. Accession

Special library	Public library	School library or resource centre

standards must be worked out on a country basis, having regard to the state of publishing, the extent of use, the physical quality of books and other material produced in the country and other factors.

Staffing

Special library	Public library	School library or resource centre
Standards should define the various posts required, library administrator, literature searchers, abstractors, translators, information systems specialists.	Standards should state that specialist staff should be used for certain work, e.g. with children and schools, reference, advice to readers, music and other subject specialists, and should be available to support the work of other members of staff.	Standards should define the respective roles of teachers, with some library responsibility and training and qualified librarians, and should state the point at which, and the duties for which, qualified librarians and media specialists are required.

General

Standards should:

Stress the vital importance of staff adequate in numbers and quality from the highest professional to the lowest clerical and manual worker, since without them the most comprehensive collection of library materials is almost useless.

Define the minimum personal, educational, professional and other qualifications necessary for work in the particular type of library, which consists basically of successful selection and organization of materials and promotion of their use.

State that professional staff should be available to provide professional services at all hours when libraries are open or when such services are required.

Define broadly the nature of professional duties within the library and state that sub-professional clerical and other staff should be employed in sufficient numbers to enable professional staff to undertake the maximum amount of professional work.

Indicate numbers or proportions of professional staff and other staff, having regard to relevant factors such as population, student and staff numbers, readership, issues, accessions, and other circumstances.

State that conditions of appointment and employment should be such as would attract suitable persons to undertake the work and posts should be organized as part of a career service.

Standardization and statistics

Standards should provide that, since the quality of service is affected by the efficiency of the technical procedures adopted in the library and by the way human, material—and financial—resources are used, libraries should, as far as possible, employ standardized procedures, e.g. in cataloguing and classification. Standards should be such as to permit input to and access to the main international mechanized bibliographical information services.

Standards should prescribe the regular collection of selected statistics, on a common basis as recommended by Unesco, so that the extent to which the service measures up to recommended national or international standards can be ascertained, the use made of the library studied, and valid comparisons made with other libraries.

Premises

General

Standards should indicate:

That all libraries should be housed in premises suitable for the efficient performance of the library's various functions.

That new library premises should be planned on a functional basis (aesthetic and other considerations being secondary), should be flexible and, while being built to satisfy foreseeable needs, should be capable of extension.

The importance of a suitable location for both main and subordinate libraries, relative to the convenience of users and to facilitate the library's task of encouraging the use of its facilities.

The importance of making the library buildings and furnishings attractive to and comfortable for users, and of giving attention to such features as good lighting, temperature, ventilation and noise control.

Ways of measuring areas of accommodation required for different purposes, based on figures for (a) books in open shelving and limited access or closed book stacks, and for storage of other material; (b) readers in reference libraries, reading rooms and other parts of the library, according to type of accommodation (seats only, large or small tables, carrels, etc.); (c) staff and work processes; (d) amenities (e.g. toilets, refreshment facilities) and services (e.g. air-conditioning); (e) other library purposes, such as exhibitions, lectures, meetings, classes, staff training; (f) provision for adequate movement of users and staff during periods of maximum use.

Each country—or group of countries—will need to work out building standards according to the particular local circumstances which are likely to affect the total amount of space and proportions required for each purpose. For very large libraries, special libraries and national libraries, there is less prospect of standardization, but for all libraries the advice given in authoritative publications, including *Unesco Manuals for Libraries*, Nos. 10 and 14, *The Small Public Library Building* and *University Libraries for Developing Countries* and the IFLA public library standards are likely to prove of value.